*IN SHORT THIS GENERATION HAS
CONCEIVED AN INTENSITY OF MOVEMENT
SO GREAT THAT IT HAS NOT TO BE SEEN
AGAINST SOMETHING ELSE TO BE KNOWN,
AND THEREFORE, THIS GENERATION
DOES NOT CONNECT ITSELF WITH
ANYTHING, THAT IS WHAT MAKES
THIS GENERATION WHAT IT IS AND
THAT IS WHY IT IS AMERICAN, AND THIS
IS VERY IMPORTANT IN CONNECTION
WITH PORTRAITS OF ANYTHING.*

GERTRUDE STEIN,
"PORTRAITS AND REPETITION"

MERCE CUNNINGHAM

FIFTY YEARS

Chronicle and Commentary by
DAVID VAUGHAN

Edited by
Melissa Harris

APERTURE

APERTURE GRATEFULLY ACKNOWLEDGES THE GENEROUS SUPPORT FOR
MERCE CUNNINGHAM: FIFTY YEARS FROM

PHILIP MORRIS
C O M P A N I E S   I N C.

ADDITIONAL SUPPORT HAS BEEN GENEROUSLY PROVIDED BY

THE ELGERBEAD FUND
THE LYNNE AND HAROLD HONICKMAN FOUNDATION
BARNABAS McHENRY
MARION STROUD SWINGLE
ROBERT A. YELLOWLEES
TOMMASO ZANZOTTO

CONTENTS

Unless otherwise noted, all dances in *Merce Cunningham: Fifty Years* are choreographed by Merce Cunningham (MC) and danced by the Merce Cunningham Dance Company.

MC in rehearsal for *Un Jour ou Deux*, Paris Opéra, 1973. Photograph: François Hers. Endpapers: MC and Dance Company, 1968. Photograph: James Klosty. Page 2: MC in *Fabrications*, 1987. Photograph: JoAnn Baker.

John Cage, 1972. Photograph: Dorothy Norman.

IN MEMORY OF JOHN CAGE
(1912–1992)

AND FOR ALL OF MERCE CUNNINGHAM'S DANCERS
PAST, PRESENT, AND FUTURE

This book records and celebrates a half century of choreography by Merce Cunningham. His first works were presented in August 1942, when he was a soloist in Martha Graham's company; that occasion also saw the beginning of his collaboration with John Cage. My original intention was that 1992 should be the cutoff date for this book, not only because of the anniversary it represents but also because it was clear that Cunningham was at that time going through an extraordinarily creative period that showed no sign of coming to an end. And if the book were to be completed, a cutoff point had to be declared.

The vagaries of book writing and publishing are such, however, that 1992 came and went and the book was still not finished, let alone published. In August of that year, Cage died. Cunningham has said that he "counts his beginning" from the joint concert he and Cage gave in New York in April 1944. In 1994 he was able to realize a project he and Cage had discussed before Cage's death, a major work to be called *Ocean*. Since this was in essence their final collaboration, it seemed logical to postpone the cutoff date by two years. Accordingly, the "fifty years" of this book's title represent the period from 1944 to 1994, when *Ocean* finally reached the stage.

As Cage would have wished, Cunningham went back to work on *Enter*, the dance he was choreographing at the time, the day following Cage's death. Three months later, in November of that year, the Merce Cunningham Dance Company played its first engagement at the Opéra de Paris Garnier, presenting the new, hour-long work. The *rideau de scène* for the performances at the Opéra was based on a drawing by Cage, which he had chosen for *Enter* before his death. Also at the Garnier, Cunningham's most recent film collaboration with Elliot Caplan, *Beach Birds For Camera* (with music by Cage), had its first public screening.

None of these events, separately or together, constituted the end of an era in the overall history of the Merce Cunningham Dance Company—not even the death of Cage. He was immediately succeeded as the company's musical advisor by David Tudor, whose association with Cunningham and Cage had begun in the late '40s. *Enter*, which had a score by Tudor, and *Beach Birds For Camera* both formed part of the creative continuum of Cunningham's career. Tudor died in August 1996, four years almost to the day after the death of Cage. Takehisa Kosugi, a company musician since 1976, had already been appointed musical director, thus ensuring continuity in that aspect of the company's operation.

Many people have said that it is impossible to write about Cunningham's work—or at any rate to convey in words what that work is like. Cunningham himself likes to speak of dancing in terms of "facts," and I have seen my own task in writing the text of this volume as the compilation of a sourcebook of information on his

work. I have attempted little in the way of description of the dances. Rather, I have tried to provide whatever facts I could assemble about each dance, especially concerning the process by which it was created, and whenever possible using Cunningham's own words. There is a great deal of misinformation and misunderstanding to be found in the writing about Cunningham. My modest hope is to provide some basic information that will help future writers to avoid some of the errors that have been made in the past. I have decided to keep quotations from reviews of Cunningham's work to a minimum, if only because such quotations would extend the length of an already voluminous text.

As is well known, Cunningham and Cage proposed a number of radical innovations in the course of their work together. The most famous, and controversial, of these concerned the relationship of dance and music, both of which are time arts. In the early dances they made together, dance and music shared an agreed time structure, coming together at certain key points but otherwise pursuing independent paths. As time went on, even those key points disappeared, and the relationship became freer still, eventually reaching a state in which the only thing dance and music had in common was coexistence in the same time and space.

Other conventional elements of dance structure were also abandoned: conflict and resolution, cause and effect, climax and anticlimax. It goes without saying that Cunningham has not been interested in telling stories or exploring psychological relationships: the subject matter of his dances is the dance itself. This does not mean that drama is absent, but it is not drama in the sense of narrative—rather, it arises from the intensity of the kinetic and theatrical experience, and the human situation on stage.

Both Cage and Cunningham made extensive use of chance procedures: Cage carried them through to the process of realizing a work in performance, but Cunningham has preferred to use chance not in the performance of his choreography but in its composition. Even so, there are those who believe that the dancers toss coins in the wings before going on stage, where they improvise. Nothing, of course, could be further from the truth. Quoting Coomeraswamy, Cage was fond of saying that what he and Cunningham aspired to was "the imitation of nature in the manner of her operation." Cunningham's dances are not lacking in structure, but the structure is organic, not preconceived.

Paradoxically, Cunningham's use of chance processes produces not chaos but order. The British music critic Desmond Shawe-Taylor once wrote about the equal importance, in formal construction, of the elements of surprise and of fulfilled expectation. Both of these can occur in a chance-generated piece, but our expectations may be fulfilled in unexpected ways. Even in a chance piece, limitations are imposed by the existence of a gamut of available movement material from which the phrases must be put together—and, further, by the choice of that material that is then given over to chance. And chance results in unforeseen ways of placing the phrases in space and time. Nevertheless, talent is clearly not excluded: as with any other way of composing, ultimately what counts is the quality of the imagination and craft that go into making the process work.

I have chosen to structure this book chronologically, in the form of a chronicle of Cunningham's work, dealing with the aesthetic developments described above as they occurred. The reader, of course, is free to read the book in a nonlinear fashion—using chance processes, perhaps. In an early exercise of what has come to be known as deconstruction, Frances Starr, the editor of the earlier book *Changes: Notes on Choreography* (1968), subjected Cunningham's texts to chance processes, with the object of making a book as much like the dances as possible. I have, so to speak, reconstructed them again for the convenience of the reader.

It may be helpful to let the reader know something about my own relationship with Merce Cunningham and with his company. I immigrated to the United States from England in 1950, to take up a scholarship at the School of American Ballet. At that time Cunningham was teaching a class once a week at the school, on Mondays at 1 P.M., for which Cage played the piano. I had studied with a remarkable teacher in London, Audrey de Vos, who taught not only ballet (in somewhat unorthodox ways) but also a form of modern dance that she had devised herself. I was therefore interested in modern dance, and I knew something about Cunningham because I used to read all the American dance publications I could get my hands on. So I took Cunningham's class within a week of my arrival in New York. After a few months Cunningham went away on tour with Cage, and never came back to the school. I have to admit that I do not remember very much about his classes. (If I had known that I would end up as his archivist, I would have kept notes.) Mostly I remember Cage thumping away on the piano, playing "Three Blind Mice," or what I still thought of as "God Save the King." For one reason and another, I did not see any of their work until April of 1953, when I saw *Sixteen Dances for Soloist and Company of Three* at a season of American dance at the Alvin Theater. It changed my life, and since then I have never missed a Cunningham performance if I could help it.

During the 1950s, avant-garde dance activity outside the Cunningham company was limited to a few choreographers, most of whom worked in isolation. The work of such soloists as Sybil Shearer, Katherine Litz, and Merle Marsicano was uniquely personal and belonged to no school. Like Cunningham, and at about the same time, Jean Erdman, Nina Fonaroff, Erick Hawkins, and Shirley Broughton had broken away from Martha Graham's company to choreograph independently. James Waring's highly theatrical pieces influenced not only younger dancers who worked with him (who included Lucinda Childs, David Gordon, and Yvonne Rainer) but also the composers and painters with whom he collaborated. Alwin Nikolais, who had worked with Hanya Holm, began making his multimedia abstract dances with his own company. Paul Taylor's early concerts were boldly experimental; like Cunningham, he collaborated with Robert Rauschenberg, who contributed ideas as well as designs.

In 1955 I went back to London for a year, and while I was there published a series of articles in *Dance and Dancers* about what I had seen in New York, in which I wrote about Cunningham for the first time. Remy Charlip, then still a member of Cunningham's company, showed him what I had written, and he invited me to take his classes again—at that time he taught in a studio he rented at Dance Players. I got to know him, and the members of his company—we often used to go and eat at the Automat after class. (This was before the days of the macrobiotic diet that Cage and Cunningham followed in later years.)

In December 1959, Cunningham opened his own studio on the top floor of the building on the corner of Sixth Avenue and 14th Street where the Living Theater had established its theater and workshops. He invited me to come and work as the studio secretary. By that time I had begun to pursue a career as an actor. All actors need part-time jobs, and this was better than waiting tables or temping. When necessary, I could take time off to be in a play—or, later, to go to London for six months to research my book on Frederick Ashton.

In the 1960s, avant-garde dance activity suddenly proliferated. Much of it originated from the Judson Dance Theater, which had grown out of a dance-composition course conducted at Cunningham's studio by the musician Robert Ellis Dunn, whose wife, Judith Dunn, was a member of the Cunningham company. Dunn's classes were based on ideas derived from experimental composition classes given by Cage at The New School for Social Research in New York during the late 1950s. Although the choreographers associated with the Judson Dance Theater and with the postmodern movement that stemmed from it rejected certain aspects of Cunningham's work—its technical finish, its theatricality, the fact that Cunningham himself remained firmly in control—they were undoubtedly deeply influenced by it.

During the winter of 1963–64, Cage told me that the company had received several invitations to perform abroad, notably in India (from the Sarabhai family) and Japan (from the Sogetsu Art Center in Tokyo). He and Cunningham wanted to build an overseas tour on the basis of these invitations, and Cage asked me if I would undertake the task of putting such a tour together. In return, I would go on the tour as an administrator. (Fortunately, Lewis Lloyd, who had more experience with such work than I did, and was at that time married to Barbara Dilley Lloyd, a dancer in the company, was also to be employed in that capacity.)

During that winter, I wrote letters to everyone Cage, Cunningham, Tudor, or any of their associates could think of who might help us to get an engagement. One day, for example, Cunningham received a letter from his mother, who had taken to globe-trotting after his father's death: visiting Bangkok, she had seen a dance performance, of which she enclosed the program. I wrote a letter to the presenter, asking if they could suggest an impresario or patron. Four months later I received a letter from the *Bangkok World Newspaper*, suggesting that I write to the chairman of the Bangkok Music Group. After a lengthy correspondence complicated by delays in the delivery of letters and cables, and by a reorganization of the Music Group, arrangements were finally made. The whole thing snowballed, and the single date in Bangkok, en route from India to Japan, eventually became a Royal Command Performance. "I feel like a Queen Bee," wrote the chairman of the programme committee, Countess Borice Radeski. "Whatever it is a Queen Bee does that makes the other bees swarm, that is what has happened in Bangkok. The whole place is swarming and the enthusiasm is running very high." The fee was only $500, but the sponsors moved the company to a better hotel and paid the difference. Other engagements were arranged almost as fortuitously: one day at the studio we received a visit from the London theater producer Michael White, who said he would book us into Sadler's Wells for a week in July, a very important engagement.

The tour that resulted lasted six months, and took us around the world. It was in some ways a wonderful experience and in others a terrible one, but I think I can truly say that it was a turning point in the company's history. Things were not necessarily easier afterward, but the company's international importance was firmly established.

I continued to work as the studio administrator and sometime company manager on tour, still with occasional leaves of absence for professional engagements. The Cunningham Studio moved from the Living Theater building to another studio at 498 Third Avenue, and, when that was no longer habitable, to the premises at Westbeth, in Greenwich Village, where the company has had its studios and offices since 1970. As part of my job I had, more or less informally, kept records of the company's performances and tours—programs, press clippings, photographs, and so on. In 1976 Jean Rigg, then the company's administrator, decided that this aspect of my work should be formalized. She secured a pilot grant from the National Endowment for the Arts that would pay my salary as archivist, a part-time position, for two years. When the two years were up, it was clear that the project was open-ended. Cunningham, the staff, and the board of directors decided to keep me on in the position I have occupied ever since. This book may be regarded as one of the major projects of the Cunningham Archives.

I must therefore thank the National Endowment for the Arts for the initial pilot grant, and the Cunningham Dance Foundation for continuing to employ me. I must also thank the John Simon Guggenheim Memorial Foundation for a fellowship that enabled me to conduct my research at an early stage of the project, the Ingram Merrill Foundation for a generous grant, and the Mac-Dowell Colony for a residency where I began the actual writing, several years ago. Thanks are due also to the Philip Morris Companies for their support of the book's publication.

Among many friends and colleagues who have helped me with advice, exchange of ideas, or simply with the wish to see this book completed I must mention two who, to my great sadness, have not lived to see the finished work: Lindsay Anderson and Dale Harris. I am grateful too to Joan Acocella, Richard Alston, Charles Atlas, Carolyn Brown, Elliot Caplan, Remy Charlip, Michael Cole, Robert Cornfield, William Gaskill, Alan Good, Mark Lancaster, Lewis L. Lloyd, Alastair Macaulay, Gordon Mumma, and Valda Setterfield for similar help and encouragement. Also to Jean Erdman, Mary Emma Harris, John Heliker, Joyce Wike Holder, Elizabeth Jennerjahn, Irwin Kremen, M. C. Richards, Dorothy Berea Silver, Marianne Preger-Simon, and Annie Suquet.

Past and present staff and board members of the Cunningham Dance Foundation whose help was invaluable include Skip Barnes, Art Becofsky, Michael Bloom, William Cook, Marc Farre, Suzanne Gallo, Marleine Hofmann, the late Chris Komar, Martha Lohmeyer, Bénédicte Pesle, Judith Pisar, Jean Rigg, Allan Sperling, Michael Stier, Robert Swinston, Patricia Tarr, and Suzanne Weil. To my editor, Melissa Harris, my grateful thanks are due; her initial approach to Merce Cunningham with a proposal for a book of photographs spurred me on to complete a manuscript that had remained too long in limbo. Also at Aperture, I'd like to thank the designer of this book, Wendy Byrne, as well as David Frankel, Ivan Vartanian, and the publisher, Michael Hoffman.

I must also acknowledge the assistance of the following: Sarah Taggart, Jasper Johns Studio; David White, archivist, Robert Rauschenberg Studio; Amy Hau, archivist, Isamu Noguchi Foundation; Madeleine Nichols, curator, Dance Collection, New York Public Library for the Performing Arts; the archives of Cornish College at the University of Washington, Seattle; the Office of Archives and History, Raleigh, North Carolina; Laura Kuhn, executive director, John Cage Trust; Erik Näslund, director, Dansmuseet, Stockholm; Jane Pritchard, archivist, Rambert Dance Company; Margarete Roeder; Ornella Volta, Archives de la Fondation Erik Satie, Paris; Susan D. Ralston, editor and international coordinator, Alfred A. Knopf, Inc.; Leslie Hansen Kopp, executive director, Preserve; Ellen Jacobs; Christina Sterner, Baryshnikov Productions, Inc.; and Mimi Johnson, Performing Artservices.

Above all, of course, I must thank Merce Cunningham himself, both for the work that is the book's subject and for the patience with which he has submitted to my questioning. I will always be grateful to Bonnie Bird and to John Cage, who wanted this book and gave me many hours of his valuable time. The book is dedicated to his memory and also to all of Merce Cunningham's dancers, past and present, whose names will be found listed in alphabetical order at the back of the book.

David Vaughan, New York, January 1997

you have to love dancing to stick to it.   it gives you
nothing back, no manuscripts to store away, no paintings
to show on walls and maybe hang in museums, no poems to
be printed and sold, nothing but that single fleeting
moment when you feel alive.   it is not for unsteady souls.

and though it appeals through the eye
to the mind, the mind instantly rejects
its meaning unless the meaning is
betrayed immediately by the action.
the mind is not convinced by kinetics
alone, the meaning must be clear, or
the language familiar and readily
accessible.

The kinesthetic sense is a separate and fortunate
behavior.   it allows the experience of dancing to
be part of all of us.

but clarity is the lowest form of
poetry, and language, like all else
in our lives, is always changing.
our emotions are constantly being propelled by some new
face in the sky, some new rocket to the moon, some new
sound in the ear, but they are the same emotions.

You do not
separate
the human being
from the
actions he
does, or
the actions
which sur-
round him,
but you can
see what it
is like to
break these
actions up
in differ-
ent ways, to
allow the
passion, and
it is pas-
sion, to ap-
pear for each
person in his
own way.

It is hard for many people to
accept that dancing has nothing
in common with music other than
the element of time and division
of time.   the mind can say how
beautiful as the music hints at,
or *strikes out* with color.

but the other extreme can be seen
& heard in the music accompanying the movements of the
wild animals in the Disney films.
it robs them of their instinctual
rhythms, and leaves them as car-
icatures.   true, it is a man-made
arrangement, but what isn't?

the sense of human emotion that a
dance can give is governed by fam-
iliarity with the language, and the
elements that act with the language;
here those would be music, costume,
together with space in which the dance happens.

Joy, love, fear, anger, humor, all can be "made clear" by
images familiar to our eyes.   and all are grand or meager
depending on the eye of the beholder.

What to some is splendid entertainment,
to others is merely tedium and fidgets;
what to some seems barren, to others
is the very essence of the heroic.

And the art is not the better nor the worse.

—MERCE CUNNINGHAM

THE EARLY YEARS

Prologue

CENTRALIA 1919–1937

Merce Cunningham—his original given names were Mercier Philip—was born on 16 April 1919, in the small town of Centralia, Washington State, where the family lived at the southwest corner of F and First streets. His father, Clifford D. Cunningham, of Irish descent, was a lawyer, and his mother, Mayme Joach, was from a family of Slavic origin (her grandfather came from Prague). Neither parent had any connection with the theater, though Cunningham has said that his father had a certain histrionic talent in the courtroom,[1] and liked to go to the vaudeville shows in town.

It's true, I think, that both my parents had an instinct for adventure. Both left the middle of the country to come west for their careers. My mother came from Minnesota, to teach school. My dad came from Kansas, to study law. I once asked him why he hadn't set up practice in a city, Seattle maybe. He said it was a conscious decision because he wanted to be able to do all kinds of law, from homesteading cases to defending murderers. He said he felt he'd be free in Centralia, and knowing his temperament, I can imagine also that [he] didn't want somebody else telling him what to do.[2]

Cunningham was the second of the family's three surviving sons (another son died in childhood). Both of his brothers, Dorwin (D. J.) and Jack, followed their father into the legal profession. The family was Roman Catholic; Cunningham has said that his mother described him dancing down the aisle of the church at the age of three.[3] The first school he attended was St. Mary's Academy in Centralia.[4] At the age of about ten, Cunningham asked to be allowed to go to a local dancing school, where he learned the sailor's hornpipe. The only dancing he had seen was in the vaudeville shows his parents took him to at the Liberty Theater in Centralia; he also remembers his mother taking him to see a touring company's performance of *Rio Rita*. (Later, he was deeply impressed by the films of Fred Astaire.) "More than dancing," he would remember, "it was the idea of being on stage, in a theater, that fascinated me."[5]

Some time later Cunningham attended a recital given by pupils of Mrs. Maude M. Barrett, who went to the same church as the Cunninghams and had

opened a dancing school ("The Barret School of the Dance"), first in the garage of her home, later in a studio at 608–10 North Tower Avenue. "What really got me hooked on theater," Cunningham has said, was Mrs. Barrett's own performance at this recital:

She came out in a yellow dress and started swinging Indian clubs, and all the time she was talking to the audience. Then she pulled something down over her dress—afterward I figured out it was an elastic—and walked on her hands all over the stage, still talking to the audience. *Rio Rita*, forget it!

This experience had a profound and electrifying effect on Cunningham. However, it was not until a year or two later that he actually began to study with Mrs. Barrett. With five or six other local children, Cunningham went for a weekly class at which she taught them tap-dance routines that she had done in vaudeville:

The fascinating thing about her was that she made every one different. I can hear her now, she made it *sound* different, the quality of the sound and the rhythm. . . . She showed me, too, I think only once, but when she did I never forgot it, the thing with the foot that I used later in *Antic Meet* [a kind of twisting and turning in and out of one foot along the floor]. She said, "This is a dance I used to do," and she did this amazing thing.

Her daughter, Marjorie, was a year or so older than I, and there were these little situations around Centralia, the Grange Halls, sometimes schools, various little things where they sometimes asked Mrs. Barrett if there were someone who could come and dance, so

Page 11: MC at Black Mountain College, summer 1948. Photograph: Hazel-Frieda Larsen. Above, left: MC's mother, Mayme Joach, at age 20, 1916. Above, center: MC's father, Clifford D. Cunningham, 1930s. Above: Mercier Philip Cunningham, at 18 months, 1920.

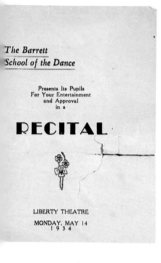

The Barrett
School of the Dance

Presents Its Pupils
For Your Entertainment
and Approval
in a

RECITAL

LIBERTY THEATRE
MONDAY, MAY 14
1934

PROGRAMME

OVERTURE

POET and PEASANT - - - - - By F. V. Suppe
Mrs. Nina B. Fale, Piano
Miss Elinor Holmes, Organ

1. **SCOTCH REVIEW** - - - - - Harry Lauder

Thalia Collias	Majel Fale
Betty Ellen Benedict	Barbara Bigbee
Donelda Foron	Margaret Dickeson
Patsy Ramsey	Kathleen Galvin
Ann Loofbourrow	Ann Bieker
Janet Mullen	Vera Sparber
Margaret Lucas	Marjorie Barrett

Mercier Cunningham

2. **THE BARR TWIN'S SPECIAL** - Arr. By Harding
Rosemary Barr   Jerry Barr

3. **WALTZ CLOG** - - - - - - - - Ball
Inez Roush

4. **TOE DANCE** - - - - - - - Harry Warren
Elizabeth Metzger

5. **GYPSY-SPANISH DANCE** - - - - - Hubay

Kathyrn Jones	Patricia Headington
Majel Fale	Isabel Heffner
Frances Ramsey	Adrienne Loveridge
Anna Marie Shiffelbine	Marie Rice

6. **BUCK and WING DANCE** - - Arr. By Harding
Mary Knowles

7. **WALTZ CLOG TRIO** - - - - - - Ball
Harriet Stark   Uceyle Barrett   Ruby Brown

8. **GRECIAN NAUTCH DANCE** - - - Zamecnick
Marjorie Barrett

9. **MILITARY and BUCK DANCE** - - - Garland
Thalia Collias

PROGRAMME

10. **FRENCH FOLK DANCE** - - - - Massanet

Mrs. Rucker	Mrs. Heinricher
Mrs. Bigbee	Janet Mullen
Ruby Brown	Mrs. Bigbee
Margaret Stark	Harriet Stark

11. **ACROBATIC SPECIALTY**
Ann Bieker

12. **SHANGHAI LIL** - - - - - Harry Warren
Geisha Girls
Mary Knowles   Thalia Collias   Majel Fale

13. **SHANGHAI LIL Song and Dance** - Harry Warren
By Marjorie Barrett and Chorus

Kathleen Galvin	Margaret Dickeson
Margaret Lucas	Patsy Ramsey
Ann Loofbourrow	Vera Sparber

14. **THE BOWERY ACT** - - - - - - Ball
Thalia Collias   Majel Fale

15. **SAILORS' HORNPIPE** - - Arr. By Harding

Leon Barrett	Vera Sparber
Patsy Ramsey	Mercier Cunningham
Margaret Dickeson	Kathleen Galvin
Jack Ramsey	Margaret Lucas

Marjorie Barrett

16. **THREE LITTLE RUBENS** - - Arr. By Harding
Barbara Bigbee   Betty Balch   Donelda Foron

17. **OVERTURE**

18. **RUSSIAN DANCE** - - - - - Moussargsky
Mercier Cunningham

29. **THE FARMERETTES** - - - - - - Brown

Harriet Stark	Marjorie Barrett
Ruby Brown	Uceyle Barrett

Janet Mullen

MC in *Russian Dance*, arranged by Mrs. Maude Barrett, ca. 1934.

Marjorie Barrett and MC in an exhibition ballroom dance arranged by Mrs. Maude Barrett, ca. 1935.

Marjorie often did a tap dance. And as I continued with Mrs. Barrett, Marjorie and I began to perform in these Grange Halls, little clubs, I think even sometimes in little theaters.

I remember she taught us a whole soft-shoe routine, and we did it one summer at the local fair. I had a derby and a salt-and-pepper suit—I don't know where she got that, and of course it didn't fit me, but it didn't matter—and spats and a cane. Marjorie probably had a big hat and a long dress—it was a very fancy dance.

We continued, and the next year, when I was probably in junior high, we began to perform more and more and we did exhibition ballroom things. We had two numbers, as I recall; one was probably Mrs. Barrett's version of a tango—it was to that music that was in an Astaire film, "The Continental," and I think we probably called it that—and the other dance I don't remember, but I know we had two. I had a borrowed dress suit, which also didn't fit, and she

had a long dress. We began to have an act, as time went on; we got more things, we did a tap thing together, and I did a solo, and then we would do a finale. I had a specialty act: Mrs. Barrett said, "I'm going to teach you a Russian dance"—I didn't know what this was at all—"I saw a Russian dancer in Seattle and I'm sure you can dance just as well as he can." So she made up this dance, she probably remembered the things she saw, and I did all those things on the floor, the cobbler step, and I had a Russian costume, black satin pants and a white satin shirt and a hat, and some kind of fake boots. So that was our act—we had like four numbers.

Cunningham performed this "Russian Dance" (to music of Mussorgsky) at a recital by pupils of the Barrett School of the Dance at Centralia's Liberty Theater on 14 May 1934. In the same program he is listed as having danced in "Scotch Review" (music by Harry Lauder), in "Sailors' Hornpipe," and in a "Soft Shoe Duet" with Marjorie Barrett.

In the summer of 1935, before Cunningham's senior year, he and Mrs. Barrett and Marjorie, together with her young son Leon and her pianist Mrs. Fale, set out on "a short and intoxicating vaudeville tour"[6] that took them down the West Coast as far as Los Angeles. They drove in Mrs. Barrett's old car, with their costumes in a trunk in the back, and played in amateur shows, theaters, even "quite a few nightclubs"—wherever they could pick up dates.

I remember one of those situations when we . . . stood huddled and cold in a sort of closet that was the lone dressing room, behind the tiny platform that was the stage this time, and our teacher was in the front of the hall making last-minute preparations. Finally she hurried back, took one look at . . . us, and smiled and said, "All right, kids, we haven't any makeup, so bite your lips and pinch your cheeks, and you're on." It was a kind of theater energy and devotion she radiated. This was a devotion to dancing as an instantaneous and agreeable act of life. All my subsequent involvements with dancers who were concerned with dance as a conveyor of social message or to be used as a testing ground for psychological types have not succeeded in destroying that feeling Mrs. Barrett gave me that dance is most deeply concerned with each single instant as it comes along, and its life and vigor and attraction lie in just that singleness. It is as accurate and impermanent as breathing.[7]

Cunningham graduated in 1936:

Six lines of activities follow Mercier Cunningham's name in the 1936 Centralia High School annual, the most of any of his senior classmates that year.

He was president of his junior class, assistant editor of Skookum Wa Wa [the high school annual], junior and senior plays, Columns staff, Music Club, Scholarship Club, Dramatic Club, Hi-Jinx, opera, Hi-Y and music meet.[8]

Some of his classmates would reminisce about him:

Beulah Craig says "His dancing stood out before anything else. If the Hi-Jinx Club was giving a performance, Merce was sure to give group and solo performances and showed his artistic ability by making up many of the dance routines. . . ."

Mertyl Ingraham remembers driving by the Cunningham home on summer evenings while they were growing up and hearing Merce play the piano. He was an excellent jazz player.[9]

After graduating from high school, Cunningham, "to get out of Centralia," joined his older brother at George Washington University in Washington, D.C. He took literature courses, theater history, and speech, but dropped out after a year and went back to Centralia.

SEATTLE 1937–1939

Cunningham still wanted to be in the theater, and his parents' view, remarkable for a small-town couple at the time, was that if that was what he wanted, he should go and learn about it. They went to Seattle to talk to Nellie C. Cornish, who had founded the Cornish School (now Cornish College of the Arts) there in 1914, "the first school in the Western United States to offer comprehensive training in the arts," including theater and dance. Mrs. Cunningham knew a lady who knew Miss Cornish and could vouch for her respectability and seriousness. Mr. Cunningham was impressed by her; his attitude, Cunningham says, was in any case that "people should do what they want to do, as long as they worked at it. He was quite open, and never put any pressure on me, nor any obstacle in the way of my going there. So I went, and it was wonderful."

Miss Cornish was the second of the extraordinary women who had a great influence on Cunningham in these early years. "She was like Mrs. Barrett, she had that kind of energy and interest in what you were doing—Miss Cornish had that on a big scale." He remembers Miss Cornish saying that there were no grades, no schedules, "and I thought, if there's a school like this in Seattle, imagine what there must be in New York. But I quickly found there was nothing like it there—in fact, the only other school I have found that offered the same kind of open experience was Black Mountain."

"I headed for the drama department," Cunningham told an interviewer years later. "I remember playing a witch in a tacky production of *Macbeth*—but it was Miss Cornish's idea that if you were going to work in one art, you should know about the others."[10] Theater students were required to take dance classes, which, as Cunningham says, "I wanted to do anyway." A dancer with Martha Graham's company, Bonnie Bird (like two other Graham dancers, Dorothy Bird—they were not related—and Nina Fonaroff), had studied at the school,[11] and Miss Cornish asked Graham to release her so that she could come and teach there, which she began doing at the same time Cunningham arrived. He soon switched his major from drama to dance.

We had a technique class at something like eight in the morning, and that lasted an hour and a half. Then in the first year several times a week there was a eurythmics class, taught by Doris Dennison. Then we had theater, say from eleven to twelve-thirty; one year it was with a man named [Alexander] Koriansky, who was a marvelous, extraordinary teacher; it was very straight Stanislavsky. He was a very interesting man—he took us one day to the Art Museum, for the theater class, and proceeded to instruct us in Chinese vases. I thought that was just amazing. . . . Then we had classes in theater and art history once a week; music classes, I had the piano for a while; in the early afternoon we had dance composition classes, then some kind of rehearsal, then some other kind of technique class later in the day, and rehearsals

in the evening, either for theater or dance, depending on what you were involved in—the first year it was primarily theater.[12]

Bonnie Bird would remember Cunningham as he first appeared in her class:

Very young-looking, about eighteen, with a broad-boned frame, very slim and tall, with the head of a satyr. Close-cropped, curly hair, and a kind of marvelously still face, until it [became] animated with a laugh which would be very sudden and bright. Also capable of great self-consciousness at this point, so that he literally blushed when he was given direct attention, or, as I remember, touched for correction. . . .

The technique was the Graham technique of that vintage. They also had ballet classes [taught by Irene Flyzik and Dorothy Fisher, the Martha Graham dancer Nelle Fisher's sister], choreography, music; the first year I was there Ralph Gilbert, who later went to New York and became an outstanding accompanist for Graham, was my accompanist. Merce was a very quiet student, very hard-working. . . .

Looking back now on the activity of that year, it's astonishing to me how much we used creatively every bit of material that came either out of the students or out of me or out of Ralph, because within that year, and these were certainly not finished young dancers by any means, they were thrust into performing, for

small audiences at schools and ladies' clubs. I remember even touring to what was then the Western State College of Washington, in Bellingham, where the president had invited us to perform.[13]

The programs sometimes began with a demonstration of Graham technique, and otherwise consisted chiefly of pieces choreographed by Bird, including a suite of preclassic dances she had developed in the composition classes, which were modeled on those taught by Louis Horst: preclassic forms in the first year, modern forms in the second. During her first year Bird also choreographed an ambitious work called *Dance for Spain*, in response to the Spanish Civil War, with music by Gilbert. Cunningham performed in this dance, which was first given at Cornish on 18 and 19 March 1938, then repeated on 6 May at the Moore Theatre in Seattle, in a program "to aid wounded Spanish fighters against Nazi-imported troops."[14] An item in the Centralia paper announced the March program with the headline "Local Boy in Cornish Dance".[15]

On 29 and 30 April 1938, Cunningham danced in a recital by pupils of Irene Flyzik, the ballet teacher at Cornish, in which he took the role of a sharpshooter in a suite called *Charivari*, to music from Smetana's opera *The Bartered Bride*.[16] (Cunningham has no recollection of this event, nor of studying with Flyzik.) On 19 December of the year before, as a

Left: Self-portrait by MC, ca. 1939. Below: On tour in Washington State, ca. 1938. Left to right: Fedor Stojak, Bonnie Bird, Ralph Gilbert, Dorothy Herrmann, MC, Mary Grant, and Syvilla Fort.

member of a chorale ensemble from Cornish, he had sung carols in the annual Christmas concert at the Washington Athletic Club. He also appeared in various of the school's dramatic productions, including two popular English plays, the farce *George and Margaret*[17] and the mystery *The Amazing Dr Clitterhouse*,[18] even though he was no longer a drama major. Cunningham also remembers acting in productions of *Le Bourgeois Gentilhomme*, in which Koriansky told the cast to imagine that they were members of Molière's company, and of *The Cherry Orchard*.

Bird spent the summer of 1938, the end of both her and Cunningham's first year at Cornish, teaching in a summer school at Mills College, in Oakland, California. Cunningham went as her assistant. Another workshop was being taught at the school by the California choreographer Lester Horton, who created a new work for his students, *Conquest*, about the struggle for economic and social justice as exemplified in the history of Mexico. The music was by Lou Harrison, who also collaborated with Horton on the set designs. Horton's assistant and co-choreographer was Bella Lewitzky; she and Cunningham danced the leading roles, with Dorothy Herrmann, another of Bird's pupils from Cornish, in the supporting cast.

Lewitzky remembers that Horton's rehearsals often went on until two o'clock in the morning. "Merce had the longest neck, other than Hans Züllig in the Ballets Jooss, that I've ever seen. He was very quiet; when things got difficult he tuned out, and withdrew into himself."[19] According to Horton's biographer, Larry Warren, Cunningham later "recalled choreographic sessions in which Horton, seated in a chair and smoking a cigar, would somehow design ingenious lifts, and how Lewitzky bounded off into space at the slightest suggestion from the choreographer."[20] *Conquest* was performed at Mills College on 5 August 1938.[21]

After the 1937–38 school year, Gilbert decided to go to New York, which meant that Bird had to look for a new accompanist for the Cornish dance department, a position that also involved composing music for her own and her students' choreography. She first asked Harrison, a dancer as well as a musician, who had worked with her at Mills, but he was reluctant to leave San Francisco. He suggested that she get in touch with John Cage, a young composer then living in Carmel, California, with his wife, Xenia Andreyevna Kashevaroff. Bird went to see them, and Cage agreed to take the job.

Cage, born in Los Angeles in 1912, had studied musical composition with Richard Buhlig, Adolph Weiss, Henry Cowell, and Arnold Schönberg; and he already had radical notions of his own. "John was marvelously stimulating," Bird said. "The creative work of the students took on a whole new dimension. . . . I remember his using the floor like a great blackboard, on which he drew; he got the students to recognize time in terms of divisions of time and space, and made visual analogies for them."[22]

During that second year Bird had to go to New York for two weeks, during which Cage took over the composition class, and that, Cunningham says, was "a revelation—suddenly there was something very precise and very strict to work with. He simply made us make things—you had to think about it, not just have some feeling about what you were going to do next, but *think* about it, and that was an extraordinary experience." Cage himself would say of these classes that he was trying to arrive at "a way in which the dance and the music could be composed at the same time rather than one waiting for the other to be finished before you fitted the music to the dance or fitted the dance to the music. So I was teaching the dancers to compose, using percussion instruments."

In 1939 an article by Cage, "Goal: New Music, New Dance," appeared as part of a series called "Percussion Music and Its Relation to the Modern Dance" in Horst's magazine *Dance Observer*. The text began, "Percussion music is revolution. Sound and rhythm have too long been submissive to the restrictions of nineteenth-century music. Today we are fighting for their emancipation." It continued, prophetically, "Tomorrow, with electronic music in our ears, we will hear freedom." Finally, Cage wrote of the idea with which he was then preoccupied, "the simultaneous composition of both dance and music," concluding, "The form of the music-dance composition should be a necessary working together of all materials used. The music will then be more than an accompaniment; it will be an integral part of the dance."[23]

It was at Cornish that Cage organized his first percussion orchestra. The players included Xenia Cage, Doris Dennison (the eurythmics teacher), Margaret Jensen (another member of the music faculty), and Cunningham. The group gave concerts on 9 December 1938 and 19 May 1939. Through one of these performances Cage and Cunningham met the painter Morris Graves, who attended apparently under the impression that the concert was to be a conventional one, and with the intention of disrupting it. "When this thing started, he was so overcome that he yelled, 'Jesus in the everywhere,' and had to be carried out."[24]

On 30 January 1939, the Seattle Symphony League sponsored a "History of Ballet" program as a prelude to a visit to the city by the Ballet Russe de Monte Carlo (16–19 February 1939), on its American tour. Bird and her group performed her French court dances in this program.[25] When the Ballet Russe arrived, a call went out for supers for *Petrouchka*, and Cunningham and some of the other students went down to be in it, though they had no idea what the ballet was about. Another time, Lincoln Kirstein's Ballet Caravan company came to Seattle, and Cunningham got in to see it by sneaking in backstage. (Kirstein has said that he met Cunningham at Cornish in 1938—perhaps on the occasion of the Ballet Caravan visit.[26]) He also saw the Humphrey-Weidman company ("I didn't like that at all").

Cage remembered that the first thing that impressed him about Cunningham was his extraordinary elevation, "and then the quality that he has had all his life is the appetite for dance—at that time his appetite was not to make his own dances, it was just, really, to dance." The programs that Bird's pupils gave, however, under the name of the "Cornish Dancers"—at the Seattle Elks'

MC in dances performed at the Cornish School, 1939. Clockwise from top left: *Skinny Structures*, choreographed and performed by Syvilla Fort, MC, and Dorothy Herrmann. Three performance views from *Imaginary Landscape*, choreographed by Bonnie Bird, music by John Cage. Two performance views from *The Marriage at the Eiffel Tower*, choreographed by Bonnie Bird. Two performance views from *Three Inventories of Casey Jones*, choreographed by Bonnie Bird (standing at left in upper image).

Club, for example, on 30 November 1938, and at the College of Puget Sound in Tacoma in early January 1939—began to include dances choreographed by Cunningham: *Unbalanced March*, a solo, and *Jazz Epigram*, a duet choreographed and danced with Dorothy Herrmann. These works originated in Bird's second-year composition class dealing with modern forms. In Cunningham's recollection, the music for these dances (by Paul Hindemith and Ernst Toch respectively) came from a collection of modern piano pieces that Cage would play for the class, from which the students would choose something to use for their studies.

At a "Hilarious Dance Concert" given by the Cornish Dance Group in the Cornish Theater itself on 24 March 1939, Cunningham, Herrmann, and Syvilla Fort performed *Skinny Structures*, in which each of them choreographed and danced a solo and then the three jointly choreographed a trio as a finale. (The solos grew out of an entertainment the dancers had devised for a party, at which Cunningham also did a soft-shoe solo.[27]) The rest of the program consisted of dances choreographed by Bird: *Three Inventories of Casey Jones* (music by Ray Green), *Imaginary Landscape* (music by Cage), and *The Marriage at the Eiffel Tower* (music by Cage, Henry Cowell, and George McKay; text by Jean Cocteau). Cunningham (whose first name was given as Merce for the first time in this concert) danced in all three of Bird's pieces; in the last he played the role of the General.

Imaginary Landscape was another dance that had originated in one of Bird's classes, during which "the question arose as to what would be the nature of an audience's response to seeing only isolated parts of dancers' bodies moving in a time-free spatial 'conversation.'"[28] Bird choreographed a dance based on this idea, for which Cage wrote the music—a piece, *Imaginary Landscape No. 1*, that "is in effect a piece of proto-*musique concrète*, though naturally, since at that date there was no tape, the instruments were records of constant and variable frequencies (then available chiefly for audio research), cymbal, and string piano (Henry Cowell's manually muted grand piano). The original performance took place in two separate studios, the sounds being picked up by two microphones and mixed in the control booth."[29] This original recording was made in the radio studio of the Cornish School by John and Xenia Cage, Doris Dennison, and Margaret Jensen.[30]

Cocteau's *Les Mariés de la Tour Eiffel* was originally written for Rolf de Maré's Ballets Suédois in 1921, when the music was composed by members of Les Six. Cage, wishing to continue this kind of collective composition, invited McKay, who taught at the University of Washington, and Cowell, who was in San Quentin at the time, to contribute to the score, which was written for a variety of instruments, "from toy whistles to two pianos."[31] Cage's contribution, "Rubbish Music," was taken from collections of nineteenth-century salon pieces. Bird and her husband, Ralph Gundlach, were the narrators.

Concerned to open up the students' experience of the arts in general, John and Xenia Cage and Bonnie Bird organized exhibitions, including one of work by the northwestern painter Mark Tobey and one of drawings by Paul Klee. Bird also introduced Cage to Nancy Wilson Ross, then living in Seattle with her husband, the architect Charles Ross, and just beginning her study of Eastern philosophies, on which she was to become an authority. Invited to lecture at Cornish shortly before the opening of the Klee exhibit, which ran from 26 January to 9 February 1939,[32] Ross chose as her subject "The Symbols of Modern Art." This is the lecture mentioned by Cage in his book *Silence* as being on the subject of "Zen Buddhism and Dada," which Ross specifically linked in the course of her talk.[33] Cunningham does not remember being present.

Ross would come to believe that artists living in the Northwest in these years were particularly receptive to the philosophy of Zen Buddhism. Tobey, for example, had recently returned from a trip to China and Japan, where he had studied philosophy and painting, and he was eager to share "his newly acquired knowledge of such things as haiku and Zen stories." Ross would later write,

> Why did these early encounters with Zen philosophy, aesthetics, and humor fall on such responsive eyes and ears? Was it simply that Zen's "time" had mysteriously come round that so many of us began to feel, think, and even act differently? Morris Graves began painting new objects in new ways. His titles caught the imagination: *Little Known Bird of the Inner Eye, Joyous Young Pine*. John Cage began experimenting with new approaches to music, to sound; Merce Cunningham started to explore a new space in dance. . . .
>
> Did the landscape in which we were then living contribute to our intense appreciation of early Chinese Song landscapes and Zen *sumi-e*, ways of seeing and of painting that were at once old and new to us and of which fortunately the Seattle Art Museum could show us superb examples? Several of us, to be sure, had grown up in a sort of "participation mystique" with nature in that incomparable Pacific Northwest landscape so very like old Song paintings. We had sensed in our deepest selves the relationship of immensity and intimacy as in snowcaps and lichens; we were accustomed to the magic of fog, concealing and revealing, and to waterfalls "forever different yet forever the same," like the encircling sea. We had had occasional glimpses of the profound mystery by which a seed pod, a single flower, a mossy stone can in itself suggest a totality as vast, yet as related, as the sunset stretching out behind an endless row of snow-crowned mountains.[34]

Bird would agree that they were all influenced by the climate and topography of the Northwest.

Bird also recalled their interest in the legends of the aboriginal inhabitants of the region. A great friend of Cunningham's, Joyce Wike, studied anthropology at the University of Washington (and was later on the faculty of the University of Nebraska, Lincoln). During Cunningham's second year at Cornish she attended dance classes there in the afternoons, and also took part in performances.

(Wike was a member of Cage's percussion orchestra and appeared as a Bridesmaid in *The Marriage at the Eiffel Tower*. She was also, according to Cunningham, "a marvelous ballroom dancer—we used to dance all night long." Cage for his part would recall that "Joyce Wike and Merce Cunningham used to save enough money by not eating for three days so that, on the fourth day, they could dine in Seattle's finest restaurant."[35]) According to Bird, Wike had a considerable influence on Cunningham: "Her interest was in the preservation and analysis of Northwest Indian dances, and her own training was in part to prepare her for this work." She auditioned at Cornish by doing an actual Indian trance dance. Wike now says that this dance was "a total fake," but she did live and work with American Indians for some months to witness their dances, most of which took place in winter, when they could not fish or hunt outdoors. Cunningham, together with Bird and her husband, once accompanied Wike to an American Indian reservation to see a ceremony.

Through Wike, Cunningham became "absorbed," said Bird, "in the ancient traditions of the potlatch and the Indian ceremonials. The Northwest Indian dance is spirit dancing, quite different from the group dancing of the Southwest—it's always solo dancing, one dances only when one has 'caught one's song' and is filled with the spirit that takes over, that invades

one." Wike was also a friend of Morris Graves's, and he too visited the reservation with her.

In the summer of 1939, the Bennington School of the Dance held its sixth session at Mills College, with the intention of opening itself up to the "influences belonging inherently to the West," and making itself more accessible to students in that part of the country. The results, it was thought, would be "permanently felt in a new enrichment and strong consolidation of the whole field of the dance."[36] Martha Graham, Hanya Holm, Doris Humphrey, and Charles Weidman were all to teach at Bennington that summer, and Bird arranged for Cunningham, Dorothy Herrmann, and Joyce Wike, among others of her students, to attend. (Cunningham says that he and Wike hitchhiked to California.) Herrmann was another of Cunningham's friends at Cornish, and his frequent partner, "a perfectly beautiful dancer," he says. (Later, having married another fellow student, Edward Weston's son Cole, she moved to California and gave up dancing.)

At Mills, Cunningham enrolled in a "Percussion Accompaniment" course taught by a Miss Boas, a "Rhythmic Basis of Dance" course taught by Norman Lloyd, and an "Experimental Production" course taught by Martha Hill, Arch Lauterer, and Ben Belitt.[37] Soon after their arrival at Mills, in the art gallery there, Cunningham and Herrmann performed a duet that Bird had recently choreographed for them. According to Bird, people were astonished to find such a high standard of training on the West Coast: "They'd had two years of very hard work, a lot of performance experience, and though they were still young and coltish in many ways, they had a demeanor and a concentration that were marvelous." John and Xenia Cage also made the journey to Oakland, and on 27 July presented a concert of percussion music there, in which Cunningham again performed.[38] The concert was favorably noticed by Louis Horst in *Dance Observer*.[39]

Martha Graham was not due to arrive at Mills until the summer school had been in progress for a couple of weeks. When Ethel Butler, who taught in her absence, saw Cunningham in her class, "the most magnificent creature of a man I'd ever seen," she called Graham, who was in Santa Barbara with her mother, to tell her to come right away to "grab this man before anybody else does. . . . He was spectacular."[40] During the summer a documentary film, *Young America Dances*, was made at the school; Cunningham is immediately recognizable in the opening shots of a class in progress.

Above: MC at the Cornish School, ca. 1938. Opposite: MC and Dorothy Herrmann in a duet choreographed by Bonnie Bird, Mills College, summer 1939. Photograph: Eleanor Lance.

On the last day of the session, 11 August 1939, in a "Final Demonstration of Techniques from the Major Course in Dance," Cunningham (billed as "Mercer" Cunningham) danced in the "Men's Dance" from Doris Humphrey's *New Dance*, choreographed by Charles Weidman. The other performers were Weidman himself, José Limón, and Gregory MacDougall. Cunningham also performed a solo of his own composition, *Courante, Contagion*, in a demonstration of work made for Louis Horst's class.

> The prevalent idea [in the Bennington period] about dance structure was taken from musical structure. The Horst idea dealt with what he called Pre-Classic Forms and another course entitled Modern Forms—which weren't really forms; they were styles more than anything else. You had to learn the Pre-Classic Forms because those were the forms on which dancing was made. But my experience with Cage led me to the idea that musical structure per se was not necessarily what was involved, but that time was involved, so that you could use a time structure between the dance and the music. Louis's ideas didn't seem to me to be necessary. I didn't find them pertinent, though I admired him.[41]

It appears that (as Ethel Butler predicted) Doris Humphrey wanted Cunningham to join the Humphrey-Weidman company, and he was also offered a scholarship to Bennington College itself, in Vermont. But then Martha Graham told him that if he came to New York he could dance in her company. This was the invitation he decided to accept. (Graham said the same thing to Dorothy Herrmann, but she was unable to accept because she was a Canadian citizen.)

When Cunningham went home to Centralia at the end of the summer he announced to his parents his intention of going to New York. His mother's mouth fell open in astonishment, he recalls, but his father said to her, "Let him go, he's going to go anyway." His father had been supportive throughout Cunningham's time at Cornish, giving him a small but sufficient living allowance; Cunningham had offered to get a part-time job, but when he had told his father what he did every day at school his father had said, "That's enough." In the second year, Miss Cornish had given him a part scholarship.

The course at Cornish was a three-year one, though the school gave no degree as such. Had Cunningham completed the course, he would have been required to present a graduation concert of his own choreography. (The students prepared these concerts without assistance from the faculty unless they requested it;[42] it was for Syvilla Fort's graduation concert in the spring of 1940 that Cage composed his first prepared-piano piece, *Bacchanale*, to simulate the sound of a gamelan orchestra.) But when Graham offered him the opportunity of going to New York, Cunningham knew he had to take it. Even so, the experience of Cornish was very important to him, especially of course the initial contact with

Cage. Cunningham never forgot Cornish; almost forty years later, when his company was in residence there, he was being given directions to the room where a press conference was to be held, and cut off his informant by saying, "Oh, you mean it's in Miss Cornish's apartment."

1939–1941

Cunningham arrived in New York in September 1939. When he went to see Martha Graham in her studio she said, "Oh, I didn't think you'd come." "I didn't say anything, but I thought, 'You don't know me very well, lady.'" Cunningham took class with her twice a day, until rehearsals began for the performances in which he was to make his debut. He was the second man to join Graham's company: Erick Hawkins, who had trained at the School of American Ballet, had danced in Ballet Caravan, and had even choreographed a ballet, *Show Piece*, for that company, had gone over to Graham in 1938. Graham at once began to choreograph roles for both men in her new pieces, starting with *Every Soul Is a Circus*, in which Hawkins was to be the Ring Master and Cunningham the Acrobat; in a trio called "Triangle," they would appear with Graham.

The performances took place in December, at the St. James Theater in New York, as part of a "Holiday Dance Festival" that also included performances by Ballet Caravan, plus single concerts on two evenings by the Korean dancer Sai Shoki and by Carmelita Maracci and her group. The first performance of *Every Soul Is a Circus* was on 27 December 1939. Cunningham, who again danced under the name of Mercier, wrote to Bonnie Bird,

> My debut was tremendously exciting, but the usual calm post-concerts didn't materialize as New York doesn't provide for such a thing. Action, time, living et al are so speeded up in this city that provision for such a relatively slow thing as "calm" is unprovided for. . . .
>
> [American] Document is undoubtedly the most exciting, breathtaking piece of dance one could hope to see in this era, I have seen it [in] performance and rehearsal maybe a dozen times and it still takes my breath away, and as for Martha, to see her is to wonder why other humans attempt to walk! . . . Carmi's [Carmelita Maracci's] concert was a knockout—choreography minus but what a dancer![1]

Nancy Wilson Ross was visiting New York that month, and also wrote to Bonnie Bird after seeing the Graham company:

> "Merce" was excellent in the *Circus*. He looked like that beautiful Picasso boy with the cropped head, in the pink and gray, of the Rose Period—and he moved beautifully.[2]

Speaking of this time many years later, Cunningham said: "She was such an amazing person, Martha, to watch—she was so very beautiful, and the lady could dance, no question about that." After Graham's death, in 1991, Cunningham told an interviewer,

Martha Graham was an extraordinary dancer. She was making a form of theater that was original and distinctly American. Thinking back on my first years in New York, I realize now, as I did then, how fortunate it was for me to be on the same stage with her.

She was small in stature but large in presence. Dancing with her, I had no impression of the difference between our heights. Those few years working with her and being in her company provided an experience of the dance that was not available elsewhere then. I have always been grateful for it.[3]

That was not the only kind of dancing that Cunningham went to see when he first went to New York:

I wanted to go to the Savoy Ballroom. You weren't supposed to go, but I went anyway and it was marvelous. And I couldn't *not* dance. So I went into a corner and I was dancing by myself, and after a while I realised that there was a circle of people around me, watching. I got embarrassed and I quit.

Cunningham sampled other kinds of night life:

I used to go sometimes to a nightclub called the Village Vanguard to listen to the jazz, Eddie Haywood and people like that. One night I was just about to leave, it was around midnight, when Max Gordon, the proprietor, said to me, "Stick around." So I stayed. And then these people came in, two black women and three black men, and one of the women got up and went and stood by a pillar and threw her head back and just sang. It was Billie Holiday. She sang for two hours. The rhythm was extraordinary, you never lost the words but the way she was sliding around the beat was astonishing.

During his first year in New York Cunningham also worked with a small theater group; he acted in e e cummings's *Him*, which was performed "a couple of times, not even in a theater, but in someone's apartment."

In the summer of 1940 the Graham company was in residence at Bennington College School of the Arts, Vermont, where, on 11 August in the College Theatre, Graham presented *Every Soul Is a Circus* together with two new pieces, *El Penitente* and the first version of *Letter to the World*.[4] Cunningham appeared as the Christ Figure in *El Penitente* and as March in *Letter*.

Of Graham's working methods, Cunningham says he remembers her asking him to work with her when she wanted to make a couples dance for the group. For his solo as March,

I sort of figured some things out and then I would show them to her and she would rearrange them, change them, accent them differently, or whatever, and then she added a

part when she came in in the middle of that solo—and the first performance in New York she forgot to come in, suddenly she wasn't there and I had to improvise. . . .

During that [second] year was when I started to go to the School of American Ballet. . . . It was actually Graham who suggested it; she said, "Go and see Lincoln [Kirstein]."

This was not something that Graham suggested to many of her dancers; in fact Nina Fonaroff thinks the only other one was Nelle Fisher, who was ballet-trained to begin with. As for Cunningham, she says, "One thought of him as coming from another source, he came as an entity, looked that way, thought that way. It was all right for her to do it, for some reason it was all right for Merce to do it, but it wasn't all right for us—nobody else would have thought of doing it." (Fonaroff also went to the School, but without telling Graham.[5])

Kirstein asked Cunningham why he wanted to study ballet, since he was a modern dancer. Cunningham replied that he liked *dancing*. Kirstein gave him a partial scholarship, and Cunningham took class as regularly as Graham's rehearsals and performances (infrequent at that time) allowed.

Graham revised *Letter to the World* substantially for its New York premiere, on 20 January 1941, at the Mansfield Theater, and made further revisions for later performances that season, the first of them at the Guild Theater on 7 April 1941.[6] Cunningham made a great impression as March; his leaping entrance ("Dear March, come in") is recorded in a famous photograph by Barbara Morgan. Reviewing this season in Minna Lederman's quarterly *Modern Music*, Edwin Denby wrote that Graham had "three fine dancers with her, Jane Dudley, Erick Hawkins, and Merce Cunningham, who by having dance characters of their own throw her personal quality into relief." He went on to discuss Cunningham in more detail:

Cunningham, the least finished dancer of the three, delighted me by his humor, his buoyancy, and his wholeness of movement, a singleness of impulse like that which makes Negro dancers so graceful. The empty lightness of his upheld arms when he leaps I have never seen elsewhere.[7]

The Graham company was again in residence at the second session of the Bennington College School of the Arts in the summer of 1941. There Graham choreographed another new work, *Punch and the Judy*, which received its first performance at the College Theatre on 10 August. Cunningham danced the role of Pegasus, described in a program note as "that force which enables us to imagine or to escape or to realize."[8]

Punch and the Judy was performed in New York for the first time on 28 December, at the Cort Theater. Denby again singled out Cunningham for his dancing in *Letter to the World* (which was performed in the same program), saying that "he is in his own way as noble and as touching a dancer as I know, one of the finest dancers in America."[9]

It was in the Fall of 1941. We were
assembled for the 4:30 class in the Martha
Graham Studio on lower Fifth Avenue.

There was a brief delay about the
class beginning. Three women arrived,
obviously expected by Graham who stood
waiting for them. They sat down and
class began.

I recognized one of the women,
Katherine Cornell, who was a friend of
Miss Graham's. And all of us realized as
the class began that the other two women
were Helen Keller and her companion.
They sat quietly watching the class
continue, Miss Keller's companion holding
her hand and via hand contact, describing
to her what was happening.

At the end of the class, Miss Keller
apparently asked if she could touch a
dancer. Miss Graham asked me to stand at
the barre. Miss Keller and her companion
came to my side. I was facing the barre,
could not see her, but felt the two hands
around my waist, like bird wings, so soft.
I began to do small jumps. Her fingers,
still around my waist, moved slightly as
though fluttering. I stopped, and was
able to understand what she said to her
companion.

"So light, like the mind."

—MERCE CUNNINGHAM, 1996

Martha Graham and MC in "Dear March,
come in," from *Letter to the World,* 1930. Photograph: Barbara Morgan.

1942

During his third year in New York, Cunningham moved into the loft at 12 East 17th Street, between Fifth Avenue and Union Square, that he would occupy for many years. Graham's studio was close by, on Fifth Avenue between 13th and 14th streets, and Cunningham began to go less often to the School of American Ballet and instead would work by himself before going to Graham's classes and rehearsals.

> I began to fear that the Graham work was not in lots of ways sufficient for me. I suppose it came about from looking at other dancing and being involved with the ballet—something about the air, and the way she thought about dancing. So I began to do this thing I do of giving myself a class every day, and trying to experiment and push further. I don't mean to say I knew everything, because I didn't, but I would do what I knew, and then push beyond that, and see what else I could find. . . .

On 14 March 1942, in Chicago, Graham presented a patriotic work, *Land Be Bright*, in which Cunningham appeared as Yankee, an orator.[1] The piece was dropped after one more performance. He also appeared as the Actor as Interlocutor in *American Document*, a speaking role originally taken by an actor, Houseley Stevens, Jr.

BENNINGTON CONCERT

On 1 August 1942, Cunningham and two fellow members of the Graham company, Jean Erdman and Nina Fonaroff, gave a joint concert of their own works in the College Theatre at Bennington College, Vermont, where the company was again in residence. Each of them performed solos, and Erdman and Cunningham did three duets that they choreographed together: *Seeds of Brightness*, *Credo in Us*, and *Ad Lib*. Cunningham's solo, *Renaissance Testimonials*, was divided into two parts, "Profession-Confession." Erdman recalls,

> It was John Cage's idea that we do a concert together. He and my husband [Joseph Campbell] were eager to have us get out from under

Above: Costume design sketch by Charlotte Trowbridge for *Credo in Us*, 1942, reproduced in *Dance Observer*. Left: *Credo in Us*, 1942, choreographed and performed by MC and Jean Erdman. Photograph: Barbara Morgan.

THE DANCE OBSERVER

presents

JEAN ERDMAN
NINA FONAROFF
MERCE CUNNINGHAM

TUESDAY, OCTOBER 20
WEDNESDAY, OCTOBER 21

Nine P. M.

in

A PROGRAM of DANCES

THE STUDIO THEATRE

108 WEST 16th STREET
Tel. CHelsea 2-9819

TICKETS NOW ON SALE BY MAIL

DANCE OBSERVER, 1 WEST 67th STREET
OR AT BOX OFFICE ON AND AFTER OCTOBER 16

ADMISSION: $1.10
ALL SEATS RESERVED

Photos by Bouchard

Page 28: MC in
Totem Ancestor, 1942.
Photograph: Barbara
Morgan.

Martha's thumb. . . . So at their prodding we started. *Seeds of Brightness* was an opening dance, a nice little number. I think Louis [Horst] thought it was too lyric.

Ad Lib was in the jazz idiom. We decided with John on the structure—that's the way you always proceeded with John. I was to have the blues theme and Merce was to have the fast theme. We each worked on our themes, and we agreed on where we'd be. . . . It was exactly as though we were jazz musicians, with definite themes, so we both knew what each other's movement themes were, and we knew how to relate.[2]

In fact, as the title indicates, *Ad Lib* was at least partly improvised. Some at Bennington were scandalized by this: Erdman recalled that Sophie Maslow came backstage and said, "You don't mean to say you actually improvised on stage, do you?"

The most ambitious of the duets was *Credo in Us*,

a satire on contemporary American mores, with a text of which a sample was given in the program:

They are happied husband and wifed.
They have harmonious postures. They
facade their frappant ways across a sacred spot.
Ah, but what! This breakage of pattern. And
he on-and-ons—is he only machine?—with her
unreality. But . . . soon breakage too.
So he searched for the Glory that was
Greeley's, and she wondered after. It killed time.
Ghoulish, however, digging back, this thing
in her broke through to ancestral gold; and he
was stampeded after. But that was no elixir.
Boiling both and retching, now finally with
fruitful efforts; a caraway! "Ah, such eyes."
But still a zombie.

According to Erdman, "We said the script was a translation from the French Surrealist magazine *Minotaur*. [This at the suggestion of Campbell.] However, it was truly written by Merce."[3] The music for the piece was by Cage, who, with his wife, Xenia, had just moved east from Chicago. (They had moved to Chicago in 1941; there Cage had taught a class in experimental music at the Chicago Institute of Design, at the invitation of László Moholy-Nagy.) During that summer the Cages lived first with Peggy Guggenheim and then (after she threw them out) in Erdman and Campbell's apartment in Greenwich Village. In exchange, Cage wrote the score for *Credo in Us*: "Merce and Jean gave me the time lengths and tempi and so forth, and I just wrote to fit with what they had done." (Cage did not attend the Bennington performance.) The score is "a suite of satirical character composed within the phraseology of the dance. . . . The instruments used are muted gongs, tin cans, tom-toms, an electric buzzer, piano and radio or phonograph."[4]

The program was repeated in New York on 20 and 21 October 1942, at the Humphrey-Weidman Studio Theatre on West 16th Street, with an important addition: *Totem Ancestor*, another solo by Cunningham, also with music by Cage, that was to remain in his repertory until the mid-1950s. The title suggests that in choreographing this piece Cunningham drew on his memories of the American Indian dancing he had seen in the Northwest. He does not deny the possibility, though he doubts there were specific references in the dance:

Some kind of primitive figure I suppose. I don't remember much of this dance. It was short, 2′

or 3′ [two minutes or three minutes] at most, perhaps less. The dance went on a diagonal line USL to DSR [upstage left to downstage right]. Cage wrote the music after the dance was completed. There were some jumps on the knees, and I remember a dancer, after a performance, backstage trying them and falling down. Secret delight! Originally I had wanted a design for the title so anyone talking about the dance would have to use something besides words to describe it.[5]

Totem Ancestor is one of the few Cunningham dances to have been recorded in Labanotation, by Lena Belloc.

1943

Cunningham and Jean Erdman were invited to repeat their part of the Bennington concert of the summer of 1942 at the Arts Club of Chicago on 14 February 1943. Here he dropped *Renaissance Testimonials* but added two new solos, *In the Name of the Holocaust* and *Shimmera*, both with music by Cage. Neither was ever performed again—at least not under those titles. (Cunningham thinks it entirely possible that he danced them again under different names—"that sometimes happened"—but there is no way to verify this.) *In the Name of the Holocaust* was the first of his dances to derive its title from James Joyce's *Finnegans Wake*, "a word play by Joyce . . . on 'In the name of the Holy Ghost.' [The dance was] religious in tone, very probably linked to my Catholic upbringing."[1] Cage's music for the dance was later rediscovered and often performed as a concert piece.

Cage's first concerts of percussion music, in Seattle, had been followed by others in Oakland, San Francisco, and Chicago. A week before the Cunningham-and-Erdman concert in Chicago, Cage made his New York debut with a concert at The Museum of Modern Art, on the evening of 7 February 1943, a Sunday. Cunningham performed in the orchestra, as he had in Seattle, together with some other dancers—Erdman, Mary Anthony, and David Campbell—as well as Xenia Cage, Graham's pianist Helen Lanfer, and others.[2]

Also at The Museum of Modern Art that spring a series of five "Serenades" was performed, consisting largely of new musical works. The third of these comprised three works relating to the Spanish poet Federico García Lorca, conducted by Leonard Bernstein: a ballet by the great Spanish dancer La Argentinita, *El Café de Chinitas*; "Homage to García Lorca," by Silvestre Revueltas; and a zarzuela, *The Wind Remains*, after García Lorca's *Asi que pasen cinco años*, with both music and adaptation by Paul Bowles. Cunningham was this work's dance director and appeared as a Clown. The piece was performed on the tiny stage of the museum's auditorium, the space still further restricted by Oliver Smith's set, which included a stage within a stage. Kermit Love had designed costumes, but these were not ready in time, and the

dancers had to supply their own. Cunningham made "two little dances" for himself.

That summer, Martha Graham and her company, having been inactive most of the previous season, were back at Bennington as artists-in-residence, although the summer school as such had been discontinued. On 18 July, a preview performance of *Deaths and Entrances* was given in the College Theatre, with improvised costumes. Cunningham appeared as the Poetic Beloved. The piece had its official premiere at the 46th Street Theater, New York, on 26 December 1943. The same evening saw the performance of *Salem Shore*, a solo for Graham with a text spoken offstage by Cunningham. Edwin Denby again singled out Cunningham for special praise: "Among the dancers in the company Merce Cunningham's long dance phrases, his lightness, and his constantly intelligent head are very fine."[3]

1944

John Cage was again encouraging Cunningham to strike out on his own. On 5 April 1944, the two men gave their first joint concert of solo dances and music, at the Humphrey-Weidman Studio Theatre on West 16th Street. Cunningham has written, "I date my beginning from this concert."[1] "The evening consisted of six solos by myself and three pieces of music by Cage, who had also composed the music for the dances."[2] One of these solos was *Totem Ancestor*; the remaining five, *Triple-Paced, Root of an Unfocus, Tossed as It Is Untroubled, The Unavailable Memory of . . .*, and *Spontaneous Earth*, were new. Cunningham designed his own costumes, and indeed the entire concert was self-produced. Cunningham and Cage paid to rent the theater, print flyers and programs (for which Cage designed the typography), and for the advertising.

The solos were two or three minutes. One was five or six minutes long. I changed costume between each one. I change very fast. It was a legacy from my vaudeville days with Mrs Barrett.[3]

TRIPLE-PACED

That was in three parts, each part was a different tempo, that's what the title was about: there was a medium part, and a very slow part, and the last part very fast.

ROOT OF AN UNFOCUS

The dance was concerned with fear. It began in conscious awareness of something outside the individual, and after its passage in time ended in the person crawling out of the light. The time structure allowed for this in a way that I felt more conventional structures, [e.g.] theme & variations, ABA, would not.

It was in three large sections, each section according to its tempo structured in lengths of 8-10-6 beats. The time structure was a square root one so Section I was 8 x 8 in length, Section II 10 x 10, Section III 6 x 6. The dance was five minutes long (1½′–2½′–1′).[4]

This use of a time structure allowed us to work separately, Cage not having to be with the dance except at structural points, and I was free to make the phrases and movements within the phrases vary their speeds and accents without reference to a musical beat, again only using the structural points as identification between us. Each of the five dances made this way had a different time structure and length which came out of my initial working with the movement for the particular dance.[5]

Though Cunningham also described *Root of an Unfocus* as "concerned with fear" in the series of interviews with Jacqueline Lesschaeve published as *The Dancer and the Dance*, he went to some pains to deemphasize this aspect of the work when talking with Calvin Tomkins:

A lot of modern-dance people in the audience liked [*Root*] because it seemed to them to be tied to an emotional meaning. . . . They thought it had to do with fear. It had nothing directly to do with fear as far as I was concerned. The main thing about it—and the thing everybody missed—was that its structure was based on time, in the same sense that a radio show is. It was divided into time units, and the dance and the music would come together at the beginning and the end of each unit, but in between they would be independent of each other. This was the beginning of the idea that music and dance could be dissociated, and from this point on the dissociation in our work just got wider and wider.[6]

Jean Erdman wrote a detailed description of the movement in this dance for the *Vassar Alumnae Magazine*:

The characteristic movement here is a circular kick from front to back which turns the dancer's body and face to a new direction. When the swinging foot touches the floor, a quick uneven shift of weight from one foot to the other is made; at the same time the head and eyes turn toward the opposite direction. Thus the dancer, though walking backward, seems to feel that he is progressing forward and appears to be searching. A sense of fear is con-

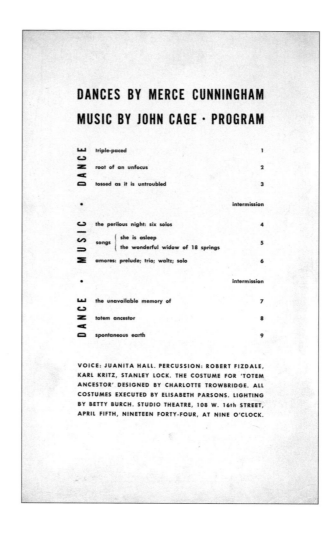

DANCES BY MERCE CUNNINGHAM
MUSIC BY JOHN CAGE · PROGRAM

DANCE		
	triple-paced	1
	root of an unfocus	2
	tossed as it is untroubled	3
•		intermission
MUSIC	the perilous night: six solos	4
	songs { she is asleep / the wonderful widow of 18 springs	5
	amores: prelude; trio; waltz; solo	6
•		intermission
DANCE	the unavailable memory of	7
	totem ancestor	8
	spontaneous earth	9

VOICE: JUANITA HALL. PERCUSSION: ROBERT FIZDALE, KARL KRITZ, STANLEY LOCK. THE COSTUME FOR 'TOTEM ANCESTOR' DESIGNED BY CHARLOTTE TROWBRIDGE. ALL COSTUMES EXECUTED BY ELISABETH PARSONS. LIGHTING BY BETTY BURCH. STUDIO THEATRE, 108 W. 16th STREET, APRIL FIFTH, NINETEEN FORTY-FOUR, AT NINE O'CLOCK.

Left: Program of 1944 concert, design and typography by John Cage. Opposite: MC in *Root of an Unfocus*, 1944. Photograph: Barbara Morgan.

veyed, not by facial expression so much as by the uneven, spasmodic rhythm, the strange ambiguous "walk," and the intensity with which the dancer rushes futilely to each new destination. The fear is conveyed through the space pattern too. The first part of the dance covers the stage vigorously; through the middle section the dancer seems to be turning in on himself in smaller areas and more frequently. Finally, he cannot move around at all, but only down to the floor in a circular back fall with a quick roll over to the knees and up; this is repeated many times in rapid succession. The end finds the dancer going off the stage on one knee, his body bent down over it, and nearly limp.[7]

The kind of relationship between music and dance proposed in this solo was a departure from a previously common practice in modern dance whereby the composer would be given the counts of a dance after it had been choreographed, and would then write music to fit them. "We were able to work independently," Cage said, "and we were getting free of this business of fitting one thing to another. I had long had that idea of letting the two arts collaborate without following one another, but it was with *Root of an Unfocus* that we really made some kind of progress."

Like *Totem Ancestor*, *Root of an Unfocus* remained in Cunningham's repertory until the mid-1950s.

TOSSED AS IT IS UNTROUBLED

An externalization of a laugh within the mind.[8]

The title is Joycean again, a paraphrase of the phrase "unhemmed as it is uneven" from *Finnegans Wake.* The music, for prepared piano, is "a lively dance in periodic rhythm written in the rhythmic structure of 7 times 7."[9]

It was like a clown. . . . It was a terribly difficult dance to do. . . . The costume was yellow tights, and there was something, not shoes, but something on my feet. And there was a headpiece, made of wire, which shook, like the outline of a clown's face. [Neither the footwear nor the headpiece have survived.] The dance was full of very rapid, tiny shaking movements, and it

involved a great deal of going up and down on to your heels, it was awful to do. . . .

THE UNAVAILABLE MEMORY OF . . .

That was a waltz, I think. That's all I remember. I had like a pair of pants and a coat. . . .

Yet another Joycean title: "We did a great deal of browsing," Cage said, "when we would look for titles—browsing in books—and I think this idea of finding titles in books came from Martha Graham. It's just that we were browsing in different books than she was—it was mostly *Finnegans Wake*, really. Then there was [Ezra] Pound, and [Gertrude] Stein of course, and e. e. cummings. . . . On top of the books that Merce was browsing in, he had always a very spontaneous feeling with respect to words, as he does with respect to movement. When he speaks of dance as steps, what he means is that he could stand up and immediately dance . . . and he could do the same thing with words." The influence of Joyce is discernible in Cunningham's own writing, such as the text for *Credo in Us* and other works.

SPONTANEOUS EARTH

The title is from a poem by e. e. cummings, "La Guerre II," from *Tulips and Chimneys*, 1923 ("O sweet spontaneous/earth . . . ").

That was a lyric dance—that's about the best I can remember about that.

In those dances, as I remember, I tried to find something, even then, that to me had some idea about movement that was different in each dance, not about a different subject. With the exception of *Totem*, these dances were all done within that rhythmic structure that John and I made.

Edwin Denby was in the audience for this program of dances, and reviewed it in the *New York Herald-Tribune*:

At the small Humphrey-Weidman Studio in the darkness of Sixteenth Street, Merce Cunningham and John Cage presented a program of solo dances and of percussionist music last night which was of the greatest aesthetic elegance. The audience, an intelligent one, enjoyed and applauded.

It was Mr. Cunningham's first solo recital, though he is well known to dance audiences as soloist in Martha Graham's company. His gifts as a lyric dancer are most remarkable. His build resembles that of the juvenile saltimbanques of the early Picasso canvases. As a dancer his instep and his knees are extraordinarily elastic and quick; his steps, runs, knee bends, and leaps are brilliant in lightness and speed. His torso can turn on its vertical axis with great sensitivity, his shoulders are held lightly free, and his head poises intelligently. The arms are light and long, they float, but do not often have an active look. These are all merits particularly suited to lyric expression.

As a dancer and as a choreographer of his own solos, Mr. Cunningham's sense of physical rhythm is subtle and clear. His dances are built on the rhythm of a body in movement, and on its irregular phrase lengths. And the perfection with which he can indicate the rise and fall of an impulse gives one an aesthetic pleasure of exceptional delicacy. His compositions too were in no way derivative in their formal aspect, or in their gesture; they looked free and definite at the same time.

The effect of them is one of an excessively elegant sensuality. On the other hand—partly because they are solo dances, partly because they lack the vigorous presence of the body's deportment characteristic of academic ballet style—their effect is one of remoteness and isolation. This tone may well be due to the fact that Mr. Cunningham is still a young dancer, who is only beginning to discover his own dramatic resources. But I have never seen a first recital that combined such taste, such technical finish, such originality of dance material, and so sure a manner of presentation.[10]

• • •

Below and opposite: Set designs by Arch Lauterer for *Four Walls*, 1944.

In the summer of 1944, Cunningham was engaged to teach for six weeks at the Perry-Mansfield Workshop, a kind of arts summer camp run by Charlotte Perry and Portia Mansfield in Steamboat Springs, Colorado, on the slopes of the Rocky Mountains. In his heavy schedule of classes, the most intensive teaching he had yet done, he still taught something close to Graham technique, with some modifications of his own. He also rehearsed his most ambitious work so far.

FOUR WALLS

I had written a dance-play lasting an hour that was to be presented in the Perry-Mansfield Summer Theatre. Cage wrote a piano score for it. I had asked if he could make the score fairly simple, not being certain of the pianist's capabilities in such a situation. We devised a rhythmic structure that included time-lengths for the script and the dancing, and then he composed the work for the white keys only. The rhythmic structure left me free to work with the dancers and actors in such a way as not to pin the words

or all the movements to specific notes, although the structural connections were observed.[11]

Cunningham asked Arch Lauterer, the designer of Graham's *Letter to the World* and *Deaths and Entrances*, who was also on the summer faculty at Perry-Mansfield, to collaborate on the direction and design of *Four Walls*. Lauterer sent him a rough sketch and floor plan in advance, with the scribbled note "So you can start." Cage had written the score, for solo piano, which would be played by Drusa Wilker, since he could not afford to travel to Colorado for the performance. According to Cage, this score, which includes two songs, has been seen as prefiguring the music of such composers as Philip Glass and Steve Reich: "It's full of passages that get repeated, and it's all white notes. It's in C, and it goes on and on. Both there and in *Credo in Us* I used the device of running the music up to the words, and leaving a space for the words, and then continuing the music." Cunningham has another memory of the score:

Cage was not present at the summer school, and at one point in the rehearsals, Arch Lauterer pointed out one part he thought too long, saying, "You must cut the music there." I agreed the section dragged, but did not feel that to cut the music was a solution, and would not have chosen to do so anyway. Searching about for another answer, I changed the dance movements and rephrased the timing of the scene; in other words, used the allotted structural time differently. The next rehearsal Lauterer said, "You see, it is much better with the music shortened."[12]

Cunningham's text, written in New York the previous year, is immature in some ways but is by no means the work of a novice. To a contemporary newspaper writer, it was a one-act play dealing with "a certain type of American family life,"[13] but the effect is closer to a kind of Greek tragedy in modern terms, oddly reminiscent, in fact, of certain plays written during the brief revival of poetic drama in Britain in the 1930s and '40s, such as T. S. Eliot's *Family Reunion*. Not unnaturally, *Four Walls* is also reminiscent of Martha Graham's expressionist style and turbid psychological content. The characters are indeed typical of "a certain type of American family": a weak but loving mother, a silent father, their rebellious son and daughter, and the daughter's ineffectual fiancé, plus a speaking chorus of "Six Nearpeople" (friends and relations, presumably) and a dancing chorus of "Six Mad-Ones." The opening stage directions say, "One should feel the rigid pattern of a family set by years of time, particularly in the parents, and the complete subservience to it. The Boy (Cunningham) is completely away from it inwardly, only observes it when convenient outwardly. The Girl (Julie Harris) fights it inwardly and outwardly."

The ensuing action is melodramatic: The Girl refuses to name the day when she will marry her undemonstrative fiancé; The Boy, her brother, suggests to him that he should behave more passionately toward her; but when he tries to do so, she kills him (offstage). Both the Boy and the Girl appear to retreat into madness, and in the end the members of the family are left alone, presumably locked forever in a prison of guilt and horror.

The play is written in thickly textured free verse, occasionally rhyming, and is full of vivid and complex, multilayered imagery. At times, the influence of Joyce is strong:

> Boy: Enter all the mad ones of my soul in silent svelted
>   cheap array—
>   enter zuerdon, beaded by a lead-fire.
>   enter magdoreed, beset by snares from oldenor—
>   enter gifts of porden-fire, ampheed-water, air of
>   bround, malkin line, brought by memories-in-skin.
>   the lady bountiful-of-sin,
>   the lady gatherer-of-poison-love,
>   the lady mad-by-blindman's touch,
>   the lady queen-in-sodden silk,
>   enter saggrined mellow eaten souls, turn my fury
>   into flames, take wing and lead me to the mad-view.[14]

A film compiled from material shot at Perry-Mansfield over several summers contains a few brief excerpts from *Four Walls*, filmed in the open air. In the first, a chorus of women (the Nearpeople), in long gray skirts with black gloves, their hands clasped and held tight against their waists, walk in straight lines, turning at right angles. Then another chorus (the Mad-Ones), in red, performs movement that is more free, though still in a conventional 1940s modern-dance style. The one compositional element that could be said to anticipate Cunningham's later work is that parts of a phrase are split up and passed from one group to another. In another excerpt the five principals are seen stepping forward and back, exchanging pregnant looks, sometimes kneeling, with gestures such as reaching out to one another or grasping the elbow of one arm with the other hand and slowly moving the hand down to the wrist. (Julie Harris does this.) They also move in simple walks. Finally Cunningham himself appears in a wild solo fragment: he does a series of leg-circles and fan-kicks coming from the back, taking him into spiral turns en dedans (perhaps similar to those Erdman described in *Root of an Unfocus*, above).[15]

The dance notator Els Grelinger was a scholarship student at Perry-Mansfield that summer, and attended rehearsals, which took place in the afternoon, to understudy Patricia Birsh (later Birch). She remembers finding the music difficult to count; there were long silences and isolated sounds, and sometimes the dancers had

to count up to 135 or so. Cunningham explained nothing about the meaning of the play, at least not to the chorus members. The roles for the two leading actresses consisted of fairly simple movements that alternated with the spoken lines.

> The set was quite beautiful. There were transparencies, you could see through everything; the walls, even the pillars, were arranged so that you could see through them. Those two women, Charlotte Perry and Portia Mansfield, were amazing—Portia Mansfield had run a whole vaudeville thing for years. They were amazing in the number of different kinds of things they offered, the number of people who came and got something from that situation.

Four Walls was performed once at Steamboat Springs, and never again in its entirety. Cunningham did take excerpts from his own role into his solo repertory, however, later giving them the title *Soliloquy*.

• • •

While at Perry-Mansfield, Cunningham somehow also found time to appear in a production of Ferenc Molnar's *The Swan*, with Julie Harris and Leora Dana.[16]

IDYLLIC SONG

On 20 November 1944, Cunningham and Cage gave their first out-of-town performance together, at the Woman's Club in Richmond, Virginia. Besides excerpts from *Four Walls*, the program also included *Idyllic Song*, Cunningham's first dance to music by Erik Satie—a Cage arrangement, for solo piano,[17] of the first movement of the *drame symphonique Socrate*, which Virgil Thomson had played (and sung) for Cage some time before. A program note read,

> The seeing of things hidden to everything but the personal, the individual imagination, "the sky's taste, the sea's tears, the suddenness of heavy branches, the wind around a leaf, the beauty around the inanimate totals of life," and the wooing of these to human touch.[18]

Cage was deeply impressed by this work, and wanted Cunningham to choreograph the rest of the score, but Cunningham did not feel he could do it as a solo.

> I thought about how to do it with other dancers, but never got any place because at that time I really didn't have any. I was still with Graham for one thing, and didn't have any people I was working with, so any ideas I had about it, I just shelved, and then it came up years later.[19] I wouldn't have wanted to use dancers trained in the Graham way, I probably might have been interested in using ballet dancers.
>
> I read the text [of *Socrate*, taken from the *Dialogues* of Plato], but the text is really about the Banquet, and I thought, well, I can't deal with that, but I thought maybe I could try a solo on the phraseology of the music, and I started to work. I remember trying something with my arms,

and I thought maybe I could do something in one place, and I examined the score. . . . Every once in a while John would come and play for me. I followed the phraseology of the music.

Idyllic Song was included in the program of Cunningham's second solo concert in New York, at the Playhouse at Hunter College on 9 January 1945.

Meanwhile, Cunningham had become increasingly dissatisfied with Graham's way of working.

> In that piece about the Brontës, *Deaths and Entrances*, she had one idea about me and one idea about Erick. . . . She would represent Erick as the dark side and me as the light side. It was like something she imagined, and we were never like a complete person.
>
> I must say that in *Penitente*, when we first did it, I had some sense of being an individual, but when *Appalachian Spring* came along—the summer before we worked on it I went to Perry-Mansfield to teach, and I wasn't around while she was doing some of it [at Bennington], but when I came back we started to work, to rehearse, and she said, "I don't know whether you're a preacher or a sailor or the devil," none of which was ever solidified, and she said, "Why don't you work on it?"
>
> So I and the pianist, Helen Lanfer, worked on it, and I made a dance, and when I had finished it I asked Martha to come and see it. I used a kind of gesture at the end—I thought, she'd talked about a preacher, and I would be a Baptist preacher, and I made a gesture of denouncing somebody, and she looked at all this and she said, "Oh, this is fine, now I know what to do with the rest of the piece." And I don't remember her changing that dance. When I saw it on the television I couldn't recognize it, but that's something else.
>
> But she was amazing—I was thinking of the experience of dancing with her, and there was for me anyway a marvelous rapport—if you were at ease with that kind of work and could act or think in that way, then she was a wonderful person to dance with. . . . I remember something in *Deaths and Entrances*, a duet, we had to walk off stage together, which was marvelous to do.

Appalachian Spring was presented at a concert of three new Graham works at the Library of Congress in Washington, D.C., on 30 October 1944. Each work had a score by a distinguished contemporary composer: *Appalachian Spring* by Aaron Copland, *Herodiade* by Paul Hindemith, and *Imagined Wing* by Darius Milhaud. According to Nina Fonaroff, Graham "loathed" the last of these:

> She didn't want to have much to do with it— she handed it over to us. She just gave us some idea of the subject matter, it was something to do with a woman alone in a castle or something, and I know Merce and I did a duet, and we made it together, and it was never done again. . . . But that was when she started letting go choreographically. She used to use people intuitively, and pull things out that were already there, but we didn't choreograph. I always felt with Martha that what she threw out was sometimes of more worth than what she kept in, she had Merce do some things [in *Letter to the World*] that were so extraordinary, that were never used—beautiful, kind of eerie, strange things, time-wise. I remember some kind of strange movement when she had him do cartwheels, that never got used, but was choreographically spellbinding.[20]

Cunningham's roles in *Appalachian Spring* and *Imagined Wing* were the last he created in the Graham repertory. As Graham herself put it, "He stayed as long as he validly could."[21]

1945

In his second concert with Cage, in January 1945, Cunningham performed *Soliloquy* for the first time in New York, as well as a new solo.

MYSTERIOUS ADVENTURE

Here Cunningham collaborated with a New York artist for the first time:

> We asked David Hare if he would do something, and he said yes, and he made something I had to wear on my head that was made out of plaster or something like that. I got it on, and it was so heavy—you'd start to move, and suddenly your head was on one side. And I couldn't get it off because it was stuck, and I was beginning to suffocate because there weren't any air-holes. Finally I said it was impossible.
>
> Jacqueline [Breton, Hare's wife] was very upset because she had this idea about David making a costume for the stage, and this didn't work, and I

MERCE CUNNINGHAM PROGRAM OF DANCES

triple paced	1
root of an unfocus	2
idyllic song (the seeing of things hidden to everything but the personal, the / individual imagination, and the wooing of these to human touch.	3
tossed as it is untroubled (externalization of a / laugh within the mind	4
	intermission
soliloquy	5
the unavailable memory of	6
mysterious adventure	7
	intermission
experiences	8
totem ancestor	9
spontaneous earth	10

MUSIC: JOHN CAGE. THE ACCOMPANIMENT FOR 'IDYLLIC SONG' AN ARRANGEMENT OF THE FIRST MOVEMENT OF ERIK SATIE'S 'SOCRATE' (PERMISSION GRANTED BY LA SIRENE MUSICALE, PARIS, AND ELKAN-VOGEL CO., INC., PHILADELPHIA, PA., COPYRIGHT OWNERS). THE MUSIC FOR THE SECOND PART OF 'EXPERIENCES' COMPOSED BY LIVINGSTON GEARHART. VOICE: VIVIAN BAUER. PIANISTS: JOHN CAGE AND RENATA GARVE. THE COSTUME AND OBJECT FOR 'MYSTERIOUS ADVENTURE' AFTER A DESIGN BY DAVID HARE. THE COSTUME FOR 'TOTEM ANCESTOR' BY CHARLOTTE TROWBRIDGE. COSTUMES EXECUTED BY ELISABETH PARSONS, AND BY IRVING EISENSTOT. HUNTER PLAYHOUSE, 68th STREET BETWEEN PARK AND LEXINGTON AVENUES. JANUARY 9, 1945 AT 9:00 P. M.

explained and I showed them, and they saw it didn't work, and they still felt it was my fault.

Then there was this object on the stage which was very odd-shaped. David made a design and John and I made it: two pieces of wood that were put together and stood not quite as tall as I am, V-shaped. It wasn't cut off straight, it had some kind of thing to make it stand, and then there were two arms made of wire at the back. We put some fringe on it, and then if you touched it, it simply quivered. It was at the back of the stage, on the side, and I had a kind of relationship with this thing, I would go away from it and down and then come back.

The dance was very quick, and had a lot of hopping about, like a mosquito, jumping about in the front; a lot of rapid movement back and forth, and going up and down. It was divided into sections, it was in some kind of structure, and two of the sections involved carousing with this odd-looking object.

The object was made of plywood and we rubbed paint on it, different greens and yellows and so on, so it looked like something out of a forest. The costume was black, with some things sticking out of it, and then there was this

headpiece which got modified. Later on it was redone, we remade the object and I had the costume made in a different way. It had a headpiece and mittens of some kind, one paw was different from the other paw.

The music, for prepared piano, "followed the rhythmic structure given by Merce Cunningham. The notation is conventional."[1] Writing in *Modern Music*, Elliott Carter described Cage's score as "an ingenious fancy . . . for prepared piano. This score, a maze of shivery strange and delicate noises, is a play of sound with neutral content and mood which allowed the dancer great latitude."[2]

Edwin Denby wrote of this program,

Merce Cunningham, a brilliant soloist in Martha Graham's company, and the most gifted of the young dancers who follow her, gave a solo recital last night at the Hunter College Playhouse. Though his first recital last year had been a distinct success with the audience, this second one was not. But Mr. Cunningham's quite exceptional merits as a dancer were as clear as ever and as interesting to a dance lover.

As a virtuoso in our modern-school technique he is second only to Miss Graham herself. His face is always expressive The elasticity, strength, and quickness in the legs and feet, the variety of bearing in the torso and neck, the clarity of motion in arms and hand allow him very striking effects. Better still is the variety of drive and speed which phrases his dances; and best is the improvisatory naturalness of emphasis which keeps his gestures from ever looking stylized or formalistic.

With his physical elegance and originality of gesture Mr. Cunningham combines a rare good sense in what a man dancing alone on the stage may with some dignity be seen to be occupied in doing. A man alone can suggest he is looking for something invisible, that he is trying out a trick, that he is having a bad time, or that he is just fooling. Cunningham's dances express these lyric possibilities with real imagination and subtlety. The unhappy numbers have dignity and the joking ones have humor. One funny one, *Mysterious Adventure*, with an absurd object on the stage (designed by David Hare), was long but alive all the time.

In short, Mr. Cunningham is an exceptionally gifted and exceptionally intelligent dancer. For dance enthusiasts whatever he does is a

Above: Program of 1945 concert, design and typography by John Cage.

pleasure to watch. But the variations of solo lyric dancing he shows are not sharp enough themselves to attract the intelligent audience he is equipped to interest. He does not create onstage different objective characters, but rather lyric variations of his own character. His genre, which hovers between lyric and character, is one that expresses itself best in comic numbers, in which the divided personality is a virtue.

A virtuoso like Mr. Cunningham is a rarity, and his ability is of the greatest value to modern-school dancing. For the moment, he shines best, however, in group compositions, where his character contrasts with that of other dancers. His solo recitals, impeccable as they are in taste, are not yet bold enough in expression to communicate to a general audience. But he has all the possibilities of becoming a great dancer, and we need as many of those as we can get.[3]

A few weeks later Denby wrote,

The young modern dancers . . . have been shifting their attention from social protest to lively dance action. They are taking ballet lessons, they are listening to the beat of dance music, learning a friendly stage manner and quick, neat footwork. They will leap up lightly whenever they get a chance. Probably they will soon dress as elegantly onstage as they already do off it. They go in more for professional finish and less for creative personality. . . .

. . . Mr. Cunningham reminds you that there are pure dance values in pure modern technique. He is a virtuoso, relaxed, lyrical, elastic like a playing animal. He has an instinct for a form that makes its point by repetition, each repetition being a little different, and the phrasing of each difference exceptionally limpid. He has a variety of drive and speed which phrases his dances, and better still an improvisatory naturalness of emphasis which keeps his gesture from looking stylized or formalized.

The kind of elastic physical rhythm he has strikes me as something peculiarly American, and it is delicately supported by the elastic phrases of John Cage's music. But Cunningham's stage character is still too cautious to carry a solo program. He appears either as a lonesome youth or as a happy hooligan; you would like him to show a franker character, too, or see him in contact with different people. So strong a body should also harden and strike, force one phrase and throw away another; it could risk a firm beat, or an attack open and generous. A serious solo program calls for more risk in expression. Amiable popularizers like the [Dudley-Maslow-Bales] trio don't lead you to expect much of a risk. Cunningham does, by his poetic style, by his brilliant gifts. There is no reason why he shouldn't develop into a great dancer.[4]

Mysterious Adventure was also performed during Martha Graham's season at the National Theater, on 17 and 19 May 1945—

Cunningham's last with her company. Denby found it "less effective" here than when shown in Cunningham's own program:

Mysterious Adventure presents him as a sort of playful animal creature of fancy, with long quivering feelers on his black cap and colored quivering clusters attached to his black tights. This creature hops, walks, and bounds with a constant feathery elasticity. It sees an odd object, investigates, retires, returns to it, and then goes lightly hopping on its way. It would be a foolish number but for the fact that it has the curious rhythm—placidly agitated—of a robin visiting a strange bird bath and the unhurried sense of time which such a creature lives by. There is no mimicry of animal motion in the number, but there is dance illusion of a nonhuman world. It is a difficult and delicate effect to try but an original and a serious one.

The secret of the effect, however, lies in the unexpected but complete stillness that now and then for a moment the figure has. This was far more visible with the simpler (less quivering) costume and the simpler, heavier object Hare had made for Cunningham originally.

The Cage score is a very beautiful one in its delicate strength.[5]

1946

"I wrote so much music for Merce," John Cage said, "that there was always a hankering on his part to have some music written by somebody else." Cunningham's third New York concert, at Hunter Playhouse on 12 May 1946, did in fact show a greater musical variety: one new solo, *The Encounter*, had music by Cage, but another was composed by Alan Hovhaness and a third was to a jazz drum improvisation by Baby Dodds. Another departure was the inclusion of a trio, *The Princess Zondilda and Her Entourage*, with music by Alexei Haieff.

INVOCATION TO VAHAKN

This dance, with music by Hovhaness, had a subtitle, "ancient armenian god-king." Hovhaness, of Armenian descent, may also have provided the idea, or at least the title, for the dance. Cunningham himself has no recollection of it.

FAST BLUES

Both choreography and music were improvised within a set structure.

I wanted to try the idea of not strict improvisation, but I had worked out ideas about jazz movement which would be free. The drummer would not follow me, but would also be free—in other words there was a separation—and I tried to make certain visual cues so that the drummer would know certain points in the dance, and would have some idea when to stop. I remember I tried to explain this to Baby Dodds [whom Cunningham had met through George Avakian], who was a marvelous drummer, a real extraordinary black jazz riff drummer, and I thought it was clear, but when we would rehearse he would always follow me. I kept trying to trick him, I remember, and I would just get exhausted, it was too complicated to do.

So that the idea of separation didn't work—I couldn't get him to be separate, because if I changed he would very quickly realize that and he would change with me, rather than, say, changing on his own and doing something different of his own, which he was unable to do. But I think as a piece it must have been very interesting, the two things together, though they weren't exactly what I had in my head. He was on stage, or else he was raised in the pit, I've forgotten which, but he was up, so he was seen. We only did it once.

Baby Dodds gave his own account:

In New York I also had a somewhat different job one time when I played drums for a dance recital given by Merce Cunningham. He had heard of my drumming and one day he came to the place where I was living and asked me to play something on the drums. I told him I didn't know what he wanted and he asked me to just start drumming. When I began he said, "That's what I want. I'll work out a routine to that." He asked me if I would be willing to play alone and I told him it made no difference to me. It was just like playing a show, when you've played one show you've played them all. We had only one rehearsal and that was for about an hour and a half the day before the show. I had never seen dancing just like that before and still don't know exactly what he was trying to represent.

At the Merce Cunningham recital we did that one number with only drums and the dance. It was something like my solo work but, of course, there was someone else I had to keep up with. Sometimes I'd have to hit the cymbal on the jumps and on the turns I would make a roll. Of course the dance was all his idea and I didn't know exactly what he would do next. That's like other shows, too, because you can never depend on what an actor will do. He may do something altogether different from what he rehearsed if he thinks it will make the act go over. That is, if he's versatile. And I had to be versatile enough to change with them. But I followed Merce Cunningham's routine quite easily. That came naturally to me. When you have drummed as long as I had you just sort of feel those things. You don't have to know exactly what you're going to do but it just works out that way. I got a big kick out of playing for that dance recital and the number went over very big, too.[1]

THE PRINCESS ZONDILDA AND HER ENTOURAGE: A THEATRICAL FANTASY BY MERCE CUNNINGHAM, IN THREE PARTS

As with *Credo in Us*, there was a text by Cunningham:

SWIFT PROLOGUE
Hail! We wish to greet you before the curtain rises!
　　What's the world in a grain of dust today?
Gathering sawdust to gain a time for any purpose.
　　Why breed a tongue today?
To prate of packing pilgrims on the palace porch.
　　Superb absurdity of the etiquette of the graven image.
Cast a web, count a web, weave a web fast—
　　Sink a web, sound a web, make a web last.
The Princess Zondilda and her entourage.
　　You've only to go on as you have started,
　　Mademoiselle, and you're bound to get
　　there.

ROYAL PROCESSION

SWIFT EPILOGUE
Pestilence Panacea, boxed in broadcloth. Post
　　yourself for the future.
　　Zondilda lost her protocol, the epaulets
her mother left her.
We've been hurled. But what's the world?
　　Why give it a thought? What a thought!
The Galley-West, my man, for all incurred.
　　Zondilda whipped out her sabers to cool
　　　the mob—
And lost her balance, eh?
　　Conceits of happy life![2]

Cunningham remembers,

It was like a little medieval play; we had a little entrance, then we did some words; the middle part was a dance, and we changed our costumes, what we wore we could change some way so it became something else, and then we changed back for the end, when the procession had to leave, and that made a little sequence. There was a set piece that we moved some way, it opened out for the middle part—it changed, so that the space was different, and the look was different, then we closed it up again for the end. It was like a little traveling group.

(This structure is somewhat reminiscent of Graham's *El Penitente*.)

The title role in *The Princess Zondilda* was played by Virginia Bosler, who remembers "preening and feeling very self-satisfied" while Cunningham and Katherine Litz, as her Courtiers, were "flirting behind my back, plotting to rob me blind and perhaps rub me out altogether." At one point she rode around the stage on Cunningham's back, with Litz holding her hand. The movement followed the music in some places, but in others had an "ad lib" feeling—her part was never absolutely set, "but we had to get in certain key things."[3]

The music, for chamber ensemble (flute, bassoon, trumpet, violin, cello, and piano), was by Alexei Haieff, a composer of a very different persuasion from Cage—his music was in a neoclassic, late-Stravinskyan style. (Balanchine later used his *Divertimento* for a ballet, and commissioned another ballet from him that was never produced.) Haieff himself conducted the performance. Cage said that he was trying to remove the feeling of aesthetic bias—to get as far away from his own music as possible.

• • •

Cunningham taught a June course at Genevieve Jones's studio in Pittsburgh, and he and Cage gave a concert, in which he danced as many as nine solos, at the Pittsburgh Playhouse.[4] His only other performance that year was a concert shared with Jean Erdman and Yuriko at the Central High School of Needle Trades in New York in October, when he danced three solos.

1947

THE SEASONS

The commission for Cunningham and Cage's most ambitious work so far came from a rather unlikely source. In 1946, Lincoln Kirstein had founded an association, the Ballet Society, for the primary purpose of providing George Balanchine with a situation in which he could make ballets without concern for commercial considerations. The first Ballet Society program, on 20 November 1946, had consisted of Balanchine's *Four Temperaments* and his new staging of Maurice Ravel's opera *L'enfant et les sortilèges*.

A secondary purpose of the Ballet Society was to give Kirstein himself an opportunity to promote collaborations among young choreographers, composers, and painters (as he had done previously with Ballet Caravan). Balanchine's absence in the spring of 1947, when he was guest *maître de ballet* at the Paris Opéra, afforded the occasion for an evening of such ballets: *Blackface*, with choreography by Lew Christensen, music by Carter Harman, and design by Robert Drew; *The Minotaur* (repeated, with some revision, from an earlier program), with music, choreography, and design respectively by John Taras, Elliott Carter, and Joan Junyer; and *The Seasons*, with choreography,

music, and design respectively by Cunningham, Cage, and Isamu Noguchi. The program was presented at the Ziegfeld Theater, New York, on 18 May 1947.

Meeting Cage in the apartment of Virgil Thomson in 1946, Kirstein had asked him if he would write a piece for the Ballet Society.[1] (Kirstein had of course met Cunningham earlier on, first back at Cornish and later when Cunningham took classes at the School of American Ballet.) At that point Kirstein was evidently less dismissive of modern dance than he later became (the Ballet Society had presented dances by the modern dancer Iris Mabry in its second program), and he presumably had seen some of the Cunningham-Cage concerts. But he did tell Cunningham that he wanted the ballet to have a beginning, a middle, and an end. Cunningham, for his part, "was more interested in the Joycean and Indian idea of life as being cyclical. Thus perhaps The Seasons as a subject."[2]

The title of *The Seasons* was first announced as *Northwestern Rite*,[3] and Cunningham initially wanted it to be designed by Morris Graves, whom he and Cage had met in Seattle several years before. It is clear from his notes that he was inspired by aspects of the Northwest—the climate, the topography, and the Indian art and legends—that profoundly influenced other artists who had lived and worked there. Among Cunningham's notes for the ballet is the catalogue of "Northwest Coast Indian Painting," which had been the opening exhibition at the Betty Parsons Gallery, at 15 West 57th Street, the year before (30 September–19 October 1946). In these notes, however, Cunningham also identifies the solo figure, his own role, as the Hindu god Vishnu, showing that it was not only *American* Indian mythology that he had in mind. Elsewhere in his notes he wrote, "Anybody is as their air and land is!"

During the summer of 1946 Cunningham had gone to visit his parents in Centralia, and also to Seattle to discuss *The Seasons* with Graves. But Graves ultimately decided that he could not work on the ballet, and sets and costumes were instead commissioned from the Japanese-American sculptor Isamu Noguchi, who had designed several of Graham's dances and would also design the Balanchine-Stravinsky *Orpheus* for the Ballet Society the following year. This change of designers naturally entailed a change in the nature of the imagery of the dance as finally presented on stage, but the structure that Cunningham and Cage evolved was still determined by their original ideas.

The Seasons is an attempt to express the traditional Indian view of the seasons as quiescence (winter), creation (spring), preservation (summer), and destruction (fall). It concludes with the Prelude to Winter with which it begins. The rhythmic structure is 2, 2; 1, 3; 2, 4, 1, 3, 1. . . . The sounds are a gamut (variously orchestrated) of single tones, intervals and aggregates.[4]

These numbers also refer to the time-lengths in minutes of the various sections, whose sequence was as follows:

Prelude I
Winter
Prelude II
Spring
Prelude III
Summer
Prelude IV
Fall
Finale (Prelude I).

Cunningham's notes suggest that he wanted to make a proper ballet, in the traditional sense, out of *The Seasons*—that is, a work with a theme as well as a choreographic structure (whether or not it had a beginning, a middle, and an end). His notes verbalize his ideas more fully than was his later practice, referring to various aspects of the work: dramatic action, poetic imagery, choreographic structure, movement qualities, staging, entrances and exits. They also prove that Cunningham was capable of dealing with serious, even profound subject matter if he wanted to.

As a general program note, Cunningham wrote,

> I have tried to used the materials of myth, that is, the wending of a span of nature's time, in my own terms. And if time and the seasons are inseparable, it seems to me that time and dancing are hardly less so. The preludes that announce each season attempt to catch moments that might exist in a life, or in any fraction of human time.[5]

The preludes, Cunningham said recently, "were like specific incidents: a love duet, a person alone. . . . Then the seasons themselves were more abstract, so to speak."

The Seasons was a comparatively short work (eighteen minutes at most), but it encompassed a theme of heroic dimensions, even if it did so, as Cage once put it, "in apple pie order." Cage and Cunningham were still working within a common rhythmic structure. Cage later wrote that the score was an "expression of [an East] Indian philosophical concept."[6] His score certainly gave added distinction to the musical side of the Ballet Society's programs, which included commissioned scores by Paul Hindemith, Igor Stravinsky, Elliott Carter, Vittorio Rieti, and others. Kirstein's later comment that the music "sounded rather like [Christian] Sinding's *Rustles* [sic] *of Spring*" belittles it unfairly.[7] *The Seasons* is in fact one of the most beautiful contemporary ballet scores. The orchestral writing is exquisite, limpid, and pointillistic; "the sounds are a gamut (variously orchestrated) of single tones, intervals and aggregates."[8] (The orchestration was done with the assistance of Lou Harrison, Alan Hovhaness, and even Thomson himself.)

Some of the dancers in the Ballet Society performing company were professionals, like Gisella Caccialanza, a pupil of Enrico Cecchetti who had danced in Balanchine's first American Ballet Company and in Kirstein's Ballet Caravan. Others, like Tanaquil LeClercq, were School of American Ballet students who had hardly danced in public before. (It was LeClercq who danced the "Summer" duet with Cunningham.) All were "classically trained, accustomed to the support of a metric phrase, unaccustomed to dancing or standing still without music to define or hold the movement."[9]

Although Cunningham says he did not work out all the movement in advance, it is evident from his

precise annotations in the piano score that he made careful preparations before his rehearsals, and the work went fast. He remembers that Christensen, who was responsible for scheduling rehearsals (these took place at the School of American Ballet), asked him how he was getting on, and when Cunningham told him he was nearly finished, Christensen said in that case some of his rehearsal time would be given to the other choreographers; but Cunningham refused to allow this. Parts of the movement were difficult for the ballet dancers, and Cunningham sometimes had to modify his first ideas. He talked to the dancers about the piece ("It's probably the only time I ever did it"), which Beatrice Tompkins said no one else who choreographed for them did. LeClercq would

later say of Cage and Cunningham, "They were extremely nice—and serious. So many choreographers are swamped by their music; not Cunningham. He really knew his business. He gave you the counts and they worked. It was a pleasure. . . . For Spring, the girls tied on little tails. This always got a terrific laugh, which made Merce angry."[10]

Noguchi's designs, naturally, brought to the piece an imagery that was Japanese rather than Indian, but this was not necessarily inappropriate to the original concept. Cunningham was aware of the close link between the Northwest and Japan. On the other hand, as Cunningham soon found, Noguchi had ideas of his own:

I saw *The Seasons* as a celebration of the passage of time. The time could be either a day, from dawn through the heat of midday to the cold of night, or a year, as the title suggests, or a life-time.

In the beginning there is darkness or nothingness (before consciousness). It is raining as the light grows to bare visibility, to die, and then to revive again, pulsating and growing ever stronger.

Suddenly in a flash (magnesium flash), it is dawn. (All this is done with light machines.) Birds (beaks for boys, tail feathers for girls) dance to the morning. The light becomes hotter, the throbbing heat becomes intense, until with violence it bursts into flames (light projections throughout).

Autumn follows, with strange, soft moon shapes, then the cold of winter. It is snowing; lines of freezing ice transfix the sky (ropes), and the man of doom walks into the dark.

Although *The Seasons* was presented only three times [there were actually five performances in all, on three different occasions], I have always felt it to be one of my best contributions. The costumes were comic and sad—like the human condition—somewhat like Mack Sennett bathing costumes, like birds with and without tail feathers. The beaks of red cellophane cones, mounted on white circular disks, were held in the dancers' teeth.[11]

Cunningham was prepared to adjust to Noguchi's ideas, though this was not always easy to do:

There were objects and masks: the masks were very difficult because you held them in your mouth, in the Japanese way; they were beautiful masks but it was very difficult because it was hard to do the dancing. There was a marvelous kind of wicker shape that I used in "Summer," when I had a duet for Tanny[LeClercq] and myself, a pas de deux, and at some point these three boys came out with this wicker thing and looked through it, as though you were on the bank of a river, with boys spying on you—it was a very beautiful shape.

In an interview, Noguchi spoke appreciatively of the freedom Cunningham gave him, as compared to the restrictions Martha Graham sometimes imposed. The interviewer (Frances Herridge) commented that "there were more props than dance," and asked about the "firecracker that went off for the bursting of spring":

That was supposed to be a tiny noise that no one would notice—part of the music. We had only one full rehearsal. You know the Sunday theater problem. Everything was confused. I intended to use moving pictures of real [snow] and rain on the backdrop. At the last minute we changed theaters, and the Ziegfeld had no camera equipment. I had to dash out for some stock snow and project it with a lantern slide.
Then Cunningham and I didn't get together on costuming. Some of the props I had meant for "Spring" symbols, he used for "Summer." But what a chance to experiment![12]

Earlier Ballet Society performances had taken place either at the Needle Trades High School Auditorium on West 24th Street, or at Hunter Playhouse, neither of them adequate for full-scale ballet performances. This program, however, originally scheduled for the Needle Trades High School, was presented at the elegant and spacious Ziegfeld Theater, on the Sunday evening of 18 May 1947, with a repeat performance the following day.

A description of *The Seasons* appeared in the Ballet Society yearbook:

The Seasons employed a number of theatrical devices in arresting combination to heighten the atmosphere of shifting moods in weather, time of day and night, and of the year's cycle. Designs of moving fire, snow-crystals, hail, water-drops and rain were projected against a transparent backdrop; a small, calculated explosion heralded the entrance of Spring; and the dancers added to their basic dress all manner of appropriate masks and properties. Birdlike hats, death-masks; sprigs of wild dogwood, butterfly-nets and a great kite, passed across the stage in their annual procession. Finally, the outlined symbol of a great crystallized geometrical form filled the entire scene.
The color came in sharp accents, and supplemented the exquisitely balanced sonorities of the music. The dancing was light, deliberately playful, gay but serious. The performance which concluded Ballet Society's first season was given a genuine ovation.[13]

Edwin Denby, always a champion of Cunningham's work, wrote in *Kenyon Review* that the production of *The Seasons* announced the appearance of "a remarkable choreographic talent":

His piece, though not in classic idiom, was danced cleanly by dancers classically trained. Its subject was phases of weather and subjective states induced thereby, a subject in the tradition of Thoreau. The phrases were brief but clear, the plastic instinct forceful and imaginative. Though the emotion was tremulous and delicate, the piece showed strength as a dance structure. Cunningham may prove to be a choreographer as soundly gifted as [Jerome] Robbins, though in a style as hermetic as Robbins's is plain-spoken.[14]

Years later, Kirstein wrote that "the ballet . . . was tender and pretty, but it had little virtuosic interest and was not particularly interesting for ballet-trained dancers to do."[15] Later still, he said in an interview that "*The Seasons* was the great-great-grandmother of *Watermill*"[16] (the Robbins theater piece that was presented by the New York City Ballet in 1972), but one would have to know what Kirstein thought of *Watermill* to say whether or not this comment was intended as praise. The anonymous author of the Ballet Society yearbook, however, wrote that "this work, perhaps the most extreme in terms of experiment of any offered during the Ballet Society's first season, was, in its own terms, the most successful collaboration,"[17] a judgment presumably sanctioned if not actually written by Kirstein himself.

In any case, when the Ballet Society was transformed into the New York City Ballet, *The Seasons* was in the repertory for its first, brief New York season at the City Center, in January 1949. Cunningham appeared as guest artist, with Pat McBride[18] in Gisella Caccialanza's role, which she had also danced in the Ballet Society revival the year before. It is also worth mentioning that Cunning-

Left to right: John Cage, Sonja Sekula, and MC, ca. 1947. Photograph: John Heliker.

took place on a regular schedule—the rehearsals on Mondays, Wednesdays, and Fridays at five o'clock, beginning three months before the concert. The piece was finished on time. "We didn't have extra rehearsals. . . . It was kind of respect for the person he was working with, and that kind of thing rubs off." *Dromenon*, according to Berea, was "some sort of a Greek ritual," its choreography including "a lot of air work." Cunningham was uncommunicative about the work's meaning.[20]

Cunningham's costume, by the painter Sonja Sekula, was a brown woollen unitard on which she painted designs directly while he was wearing it. (He wore this costume again for *Solo*, 1973.) Cunningham himself designed the women's costumes—long tunics in pleated gray crepe, with headdresses of pine branches, gathered by Cage. The dance was never performed again.

THE OPEN ROAD

The working title of this solo was *Western Dance*, "an evocation of the working landscape of the American West."[21] Harrison has written,

> "The Cunningham style" did not then exist—
> we were all trying out all sorts of things. We did
> talk together about the spirit of the piece and
> that spirit I tried to produce musically, in part
> through using a Coplandesque sound and
> rhythmic impulse—his style being then re-
> garded as very American and usably "Western."
> My memory does not bring to me a session in
> the studio in which I would have counted out
> his choreographed measures from an already
> choreographed work, so, unless Merce said
> otherwise, I probably composed my music first
> and he made the dance later. This was not my
> usual way of working for dancers, which was,
> indeed, the exact opposite.[22]

The music, written as was *Princess Zondilda* for a chamber ensemble, was conducted at the first performance by the composer, but was played in later performances on tour in his piano reduction.

According to Nik Krevitsky, the dance referred "to cow country almost as literally as did *Billy the Kid*. . . . An effort for spareness, perhaps, occasionally leads to picture rather than movement, but there is some good material, and this should be a pleasing number when it gains ease and can be itself."[23] Cunningham seems to have shared this opinion, for when he next performed the dance in New York, in May 1950, he had completely revised it.

ham was invited (probably, he thinks, at the behest of Muriel Stuart) to teach at the School of American Ballet from September to December 1948.

• • •

Presumably because he was occupied with the preparations for the ballet, Cunningham had not presented a concert of his own during the 1946–47 season, but in the fall of 1947 he began rehearsals for a program that was given at Hunter Playhouse on 14 December. He was clearly becoming increasingly interested in group pieces, and the program included not only a revival of *The Princess Zondilda and Her Entourage* but also a new work for himself and six women, *Dromenon*. Also included were a new solo, *The Open Road*, with music by Lou Harrison, and repeats of *Root of an Unfocus* and *Mysterious Adventure*.

DROMENON

> The dance concerns a number of women, their joining together for the purpose of evoking a spirit, its presence among them, and the consequent action.[19]

The cast's six women were mostly recruited from Cunningham's own classes (he had begun to teach independently). They included Dorothy Berea, a dancer in Graham's company who had seen Cunningham at the Graham studio when he came to teach his roles to John Butler and Mark Ryder. Unlike some she had worked with, Berea has said, Cunningham was very organized. His classes and rehearsals

1948

At the end of February 1948 both Cunningham and Cage were invited to take part in the National Inter-Collegiate Arts Conference, at Vassar College, Pough-keepsie, New York, its subject being "The Creative Arts in Contemporary Society." Cunningham, speaking on a Drama-Dance Panel, defined dance as "organized movement in a specified time and space." Explaining the difference between modern dance and ballet, he stressed that "dance need not, and indeed, should not have a literary meaning." "On the other hand," a Vassar publication continued, "Mr. Cunningham held that there is really no such thing as 'abstract' dancing, since the dance itself consists of the movements of the human body, which can never be abstract." He also spoke of a new relationship between choreographer and composer—"a cooperative interdependency." In the question period that followed, Cunningham was asked "whether or not it was necessary for the dancer to have a definite idea before he started to compose. Mr. Cunningham replied that a dance could be conceived in two ways: (1) the choreographer might have an idea which, in the process of composition, was shaped and translated by dance form, or, (2) he might start out with a simple step or pattern . . . which would acquire meaning as the basic pattern was developed."[1]

Another account said that Cunningham "feels that the meaning of dance is in the doing and that it should not try to put across an idea. Dancing for him is a reflection of human behavior in dance form, and because of this, it is [in] no way an abstract art."[2] This may be the first occasion on which these elements of Cunningham's developing dance aesthetic were stated in public and then in print.

In the four years in which Cunningham had been working independently, he and Cage had left New York to give single concerts on one or two occasions. Soon after the March 1948 revival of *The Seasons* by the Ballet Society, they set out on the first of the tours they were to make during the next few years.

> In the spring of 1948 Cage and I were touring, giving joint programs of music and dance. . . .
> At a college in Virginia [State Teachers College, Farmville, Virginia, April 1948], we were asked to give a lecture-demonstration. We chose not to do the conventional talking and demonstrating, but rather to make a short dance and piece of music in front of the largely student public. Explaining first about the rhythmic structure and

what this particular one would be, we proceeded to work separately, he at the side of the stage with a piano, and I in the stage space itself.

> As I remember, the structure was 8 x 8, divided 2-2-1-3. At the completion of any section, any 8, we would try it together, the dance and the music, the public applauding as each point was made. I explained we did not expect

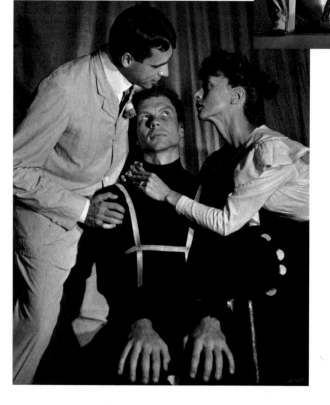

This page, top: *The Monkey Dances*, from *The Ruse of Medusa*, 1948. Photograph: Fred Fehl. Center: *The Ruse of Medusa*, 1948. Left to right: Buckminster Fuller and MC. Bottom: *The Ruse of Medusa*, 1948. Left to right: William Schrauger, MC, and Elaine de Kooning. Center and bottom photographs: Clemens Kalischer.

Opposite: MC teaching class at Black Mountain College, summer 1948, with Elizabeth Jennerjahn at right. Photograph: Clemens Kalischer.

to finish the work, that it was more of an act of process. But we did, to my amazement.[3]

Louis Horst was present at this lecture-demonstration, and said afterward, "Martha Graham could never have done that." The dance was never performed again.

Before heading west, the two men paid their first visit to Black Mountain College, the liberal arts college in North Carolina, from 3 to 8 April 1948[4]:

We had borrowed Sonja Sekula's car, and we had these few dates, they included the one in Virginia, and John said we should go—because we had days in between—to visit Black Mountain College. He had heard about this place, and always wanted to know more about it. So we drove there. It was in the spring, April, and we stayed a weekend. It rained the whole time. I remember that big dining-hall where all the activity took place, and the cantilevered building that Gropius built, the studio building. We stayed at the school. [Josef] Albers was there, and he asked us if we would do something for the students, so we must have done some kind of lecture. John played, and I danced, in a very informal way, and then we talked.

It was a lovely time, it was marvelous. . . . Two days later we were driving away—by that time I guess it had stopped raining—and we drove off, and we looked back, because they were waving, and there were lots of students there, and we saw all these presents they had put under the car for us. We had to stop and go back and get them—little pots and bits of food and everything that they had given us. And Albers invited us to come in the summer and teach. . . .

A report on the visit appeared in the *Black Mountain Bulletin*:

John Cage and Merce Cunningham visited Black Mountain College in April.

John Cage composes music. He is a young man and he writes music for the piano transformed into a combination of percussive sound and tone. . . . After the program, and after coffee in the community house, John Cage answered the questions of those who wondered what he meant to be doing and why he was doing it. He suggested that he was interested more in time than in harmonics. His music is structured according to duration in time, every smaller unit of a large composition reflecting as a microcosm the features of the whole. He said that he felt that the highest use of music was like that of anything a man "makes": to integrate a man's total faculties through the order of the composition. Primarily the work performs this function for its creator, but the nice thing about "art" (anything a man "makes") is that it may have the same power for another—a creative performer or audience. And, since integration may recognize itself in a stranger, a new society may one day

slowly take shape out of the present schizophrenia through our self-won coordination. It begins with music and ends with a common human nature.

Or, say, with the dance. Merce Cunningham is a dancer, composing, performing, teaching. Like Cage his interest is now mainly in time, movement in time, rather than poses. Cunningham and Cage work together, or perhaps one should say separately. Actually they work out the dance and music separately after having agreed upon a rhythmic structure. This permits freedom of invention equally, within known limits, and prevents the conventional synchronization of gesture and tone. Merce Cunningham gave for the community a program of dance exercises and dance compositions. It was a very beautiful and powerful expression of spiritual concentration manifested in movement. He also worked with students while he was here.

Consonant with their humility before the act of making something orderly and expressive of a total human being, these two artists made little of their biographies. . . . The current of creative energy since their visit has illuminated the college both in creation and in response.[5]

On their last date in the tour, Cunningham and Cage performed at Stephens College, Missouri, during a "New Arts Weekend" (7–9 May 1948) that also included a film presentation by Maya Deren. The poet and critic John Malcolm Brinnin, who was then on the Stephens faculty, was the programs' moderator.[6] Cunningham's concert included the first performance of *Dream*, a new solo.

DREAM

It was a lyric piece—it went on for quite a long time [five minutes], or what seemed to me then a long time. . . . All I remember is that there were a lot of terrible balances, having to stand up on one foot for a long time, and then relevé—after having stood there for a long time, then you had to go up and stay for a while.

Cage's music, for prepared piano, "was written in the rhythmic structure of the dance. . . . It employs a fixed gamut of tones and depends in its performance on the sustaining of resonances either manually or with the pedal."[7]

FIRST SUMMER AT BLACK MOUNTAIN

For the summer of 1948, Cunningham recalls,

Albers asked John if he knew of any painter who would be interesting, to also come and teach [at Black Mountain]—he was a marvelously open man that way—and John suggested Bill de Kooning, because he knew Bill and Elaine didn't have a dime, in fact they'd just been put out of their house. . . . So Bill and Elaine were there, we were all there for that summer, famous summer. I can't remember all the people there, except Bucky [Buckminster Fuller], and the Lippolds [Richard and his wife, the dancer Louise Lippold] came. . . . We met M. C. [Mary Caroline] Richards there. . . . They asked John if he would do something about having little music programs through the summer, and he thought about that and decided instead of having a pot-pourri, he would do all the works of Satie, like half an hour three times a week after dinner, either in the dining room or they would come to the rooms we stayed in which had windows that opened, and there was a piano there, and he'd play and people could sit outside. So he did everything, even the orchestral pieces or whatever, in some way or the other. . . . They did the *Socrate*.

The climax of this series was to be a production of Satie's play *Le Piège de Méduse*, which Cage had found in the rare-book collection of the New York Public Library, in an edition illustrated by Georges Braque. It had been performed by Mme. Darius Milhaud in Paris, and again at Mills College.

Bill de Kooning designed something for it, Elaine of course was in it. . . . We couldn't figure out what to do about the Baron—trying to think of people there and nothing seemed to work—and then finally, it might have been Elaine or John or somebody who suggested Bucky, and we asked him and he said yes. He was just marvelous, he did it very seriously. It was really a marvelous experience.

Cunningham appeared as Jonas, a mechanical monkey. Early rehearsals, under the direction of Helen Livingston, had not gone well. When she had to leave, it was decided to ask Arthur Penn, who had been a student at Black Mountain the year before and came back to teach an acting class, to take over the direction. Penn's improvisational approach to the text gave the cast greater freedom and confidence. He worked particularly with Fuller, who at first was inhibited in rehearsals, which were conducted in public. Under Penn's coaching, Fuller became much freer, and in the end gave what Cage called a "magnificent" performance.

Fuller himself would recall,

That group decided they wanted to put on a play and they wanted me to be in it. And I said, "I can't act; I never have. All I can do is talk

spontaneously, but I can't do anything where you have to rehearse."

And they said, "You must try. You're going to be the star of this thing, *The Ruse of Medusa* by Erik Satie—and you're going to be the Medusa."[8]

According to Elaine de Kooning, she accepted the role of Frisette because her "only words were 'yes, Papa.'"

The handsomest student on campus, William Schrauger, was chosen for an equally mute role as her suitor. The novelist Isaac Rosenfeld played the part of the Baron's surly butler. But it fell to Bucky to carry the play. His role was a kind of W.C. Fields aristocrat who talked constantly in non sequiturs. Bucky's marathon lectures made it clear that he had a prodigious memory, and we were not surprised at his great gift for comedy. It took many rehearsals before we could perform our parts without breaking up at his droll antics as the scatterbrained Baron. Arthur Penn, a student-instructor, was the director; and he was ingenious, indeed, at extracting characterizations from total amateurs. I was enchanted with the pert, mincing walk and fluttery gestures he devised for Frisette.[9]

As for the designs, Elaine de Kooning told it this way:

Since nobody else seemed interested, I designed the sets and costumes—if *design* is the word; *allocate* might be a better one. Bill transformed a huge stodgy desk and two nondescript columns into magnificent pink and grey marble with a technique he had learned at a decorator's shop in Holland when he was sixteen years old. The list of props—telephone, candelabrum, feather pen, inkwell, magnifying glass, thermometer, and Bucky's top hat—was turned over to students who were told they had a whole month to come up with things that were suitably oversized and flamboyant. Mary Outten, a pretty girl who was a wizard with a sewing machine, made a marvelous white Victorian dress for me out of gauze we bought in town for sixty cents a yard. And she sewed stripes of grey satin ribbon to Bucky's khaki work pants for a comical effect of elegance.

John Cage played the Satie score, and Merce created wonderful little entr'acte dances for his role. . . . [10]

According to Black Mountain historian Martin Duberman, "Penn found Cunningham's sense of the stage almost miraculous: he 'really existed up there—in a way that very few people I'd ever seen had.'"[11]

Cunningham: They made a post of some kind for me to sit on. I've forgotten what I wore; I had to sit still and then get up and dance, between scenes.

Elaine de Kooning: Everything went flawlessly the night of the performance. The participants all felt it was a sparkling event and that was that. There were no photographs to speak of and no recordings. [In fact there are a number of photographs, by Clemens Kalischer.] The sets and costumes were saved for a while and then vanished. I wore the lovely dress the following year in a movie called *The Dogwood Maiden* by Rudy Burckhardt (who also appeared at Black Mountain that summer to show his extraordinary city movies), and then the dress vanished too.[12]

Besides performing the music, Cage delivered a lecture that summer, "A Defense of Satie." Many people did not take Satie's music seriously at the time; exceptions were Cage and Virgil Thomson, who had introduced Cage to much of the music, including, as we have seen, *Socrate.* Cage's talk included a further definition of the kind of rhythmic structure with which he and Cunningham had been working for the last five or six years:

In the field of structure, the field of the definition of parts and their relation to a whole, there has been only one new idea since Beethoven. And that new idea can be perceived in the work of Anton Webern and Erik Satie. With Beethoven the parts of a composition were defined by means of harmony. With Satie and Webern they are defined by means of time lengths. The question of structure is so basic, and it is so important to be in agreement about it, that one must now ask: Was Beethoven right or are Webern and Satie right?

I answer immediately and unequivocally, Beethoven was in error, and his influence, which has been as extensive as it is lamentable, has been deadening to the art of music.[13]

The Ruse of Medusa was given its first and only performance on 14 August 1948. Duberman mentions talk of moving the production to New York, but it

came to nothing.[14] Cunningham's dances, however, immediately went into his solo repertory, under the title *Monkey Dances* (or sometimes *The Monkey Dances*), receiving their first independent performance at a concert he shared with Louise Lippold at Black Mountain a week after the production of *Ruse of Medusa*, on 20 August. That program also included another new solo, *Orestes*, and *A Diversion*, a trio for himself, Lippold, and Sara Hamill, who had also come to Black Mountain from New York for the summer.

ORESTES

Orestes remains Cunningham's only overt excursion into a realm that provided the subject matter for so many of Martha Graham's dances, Greek tragedy. According to the story, Orestes avenged his father, Agamemnon, by slaying his mother, Clytemnestra, and her lover, Aegisthus. An article on a later performance of the dance, at Vassar College on 9 March 1949, reports Cunningham and Cage announcing the work as "part of a suite of dance and music which will include many more scenes of the life of Orestes. This particular one showed Orestes torn with the decision of whether or not he should kill his mother."[15] Another article on the Vassar performance said that *Orestes* was "not the tragedy, as might be expected: Merce Cunningham's Orestes was pre-tragical; the disaster was not yet realized although already in the orbit of consciousness."[16] Cunningham's only comment when asked about this dance was, "My, so dramatic!" The larger project, evidently, was abandoned; *Orestes* was performed only seven times, and never in New York. The reason it was sometimes performed in silence, Cage says, is that his music was not suitable for "such dramatic subject matter."

A DIVERSION

This dance was performed to Cage's *Suite for Toy Piano*, which "employs a restricted gamut of tones, that of the nine 'white' keys from E below middle C to F above. These nine tones appear only in the third and fourth of the five pieces of this suite, the first and last of which employ only five tones, G to D." Again, the work was composed according to a rhythmic structure, 7, 7, 6, 6, 4.[17]

A Diversion was performed fairly frequently over the next two or three years, in different versions. At one point it acquired a program note:

A suite in five parts, which may be taken as referring to the legend of Krishna and the Gopis.[18]

Both Cunningham and Dorothy Berea expressed surprise when this note was quoted to them. (Cunningham has said, however, that the penultimate section of his 1953 dance *Septet* is based on the Indian legend of Krishna.). Berea remembers only that she enjoyed the piece because she had a pretty costume, in turquoise; "the hem had a facing of black velvet, which made it very heavy, so that it really got a lot of movement in it. . . . There was a lot of leggy stuff in that dance; it was a happy, joyful piece."[19] "There was," Cunningham says, "a little celebration at the end."

• • •

The work of Cunningham and Cage was often described as, or accused of, being Dadaist in nature; certainly both men increasingly rejected received ideas about music and dance, and expressed their own notions in their statements and in their works. They were, of course, much influenced by the ideas—not to mention the life and work—of Marcel Duchamp, whose art is often associated with Dada. As early as 1944, Cage had contributed a graphic design called *Chess Pieces*, made up of squares of musical notation, to an exhibition of works related to Duchamp's interest in chess, at the Julien Levy Gallery, New York.[20] Cage had also been aware of the analogy between Dada and another interest of his, Zen, at least since the occasion of Nancy Wilson Ross's lecture at Cornish early in 1939. "It is possible," Cage would write, "to make a connection between the two, but neither Dada nor Zen is a fixed tangible. They change; and in quite different ways in different places and times, they invigorate action."[21]

As for Cunningham, insofar as his dances had a Dadaist quality they may be said to relate to certain ballets presented by Diaghilev's Ballets Russes and by Rolf de Maré's Ballets Suédois, such as *Parade*, *Relâche*, *Mercure*, and *Jack-in-the-Box* (all of which, by no means coincidentally, had music by Satie), rather than to any previous works of the American modern dance.

1949

1949 was an eventful year for Cunningham and Cage. It began with two performances of *The Seasons* in the inaugural season of the New York City Ballet, on 14 and 22 January 1949, in which Cunningham appeared as guest artist. Early in February the two men left on their second tour of the United States, again driving Sonja Sekula's car. Their first stop was Winnetka, Illinois, where they had been invited by the dancer Sybil Shearer and her lighting designer, Helen Morrison, who lived nearby, in Northbrook. Shearer had offered to choreograph a solo for Cunningham, which they rehearsed on his arrival and which was included in his program at the North Shore County Day Theater on 3 February 1949—the first and only time he performed a work by another choreographer in one of his own concerts. The performance was reviewed in *Dance News* by Shearer herself, who gave the dance's title as *A Woman's Version of a Man's World*, though this was in fact its subtitle, the actual title being *Scribble Scrabble*.[1] The dance was never done again.

Cunningham and Cage traveled west through terrible weather. The car kept skidding on the icy roads, sometimes going off them altogether:

[When we left Chicago] we got up very early because our next step was Portland, Oregon, and we drove outside the city and we stopped to get some coffee in a truck-drivers' place, and we were sitting there looking at the map. And a truck-driver next to John said, "What are you doing?" and we said, "Well, we're planning a trip to Portland," and he said, "Are you crazy?" We said, "Well, no, we're touring, that's our next stop." He said, "Well, my advice to you is to go by way of Arizona."

So we drove south. That's when we went off the road again. And we began eventually way down some place to get out of the snow, finally. And we got to Flagstaff in Arizona, and there were huge snowbanks on the side, fourteen or fifteen feet high, and we just got through and went down far enough on the other side and it started to snow again, and the pass was closed. . . .

When they got into California, they heard that the weather in the north was still bad, so they decided to leave the car in Sacramento and take the train to Oregon, for performances at Oregon State College in Corvallis and at Reed College in Portland:

After a solo recital which I accompanied at a university in Oregon, Merce went to the office of the Women's Physical Education Department to pick up the check. The Head of the Department had not been pleased with the program. She asked whether Merce actually insisted on receiving payment. A discussion followed: we needed the money to get to the next engagement . . . , where the stage was small and the proscenium was low. Each time Merce jumped, his head disappeared from view.[2]

• • •

Until then, Cunningham and Cage had traveled, in their tours, back toward the West, where both of them had originated. At the end of the '40s the time seemed ripe for them to go in the opposite direction. In his late teens, Cage had dropped out of college and gone to Europe—to Paris, Madrid, and Berlin, among other places.[3] Now he received the assignment of covering music festivals in France and Sicily for the *New York Sun.* Armed with introductions from Virgil Thomson to French musicians, among them Pierre Boulez,[4] he and Cunningham set sail on the *Nieuw Amsterdam* on 24 March 1949, ten days after the last concert of their tour. They arrived in Amsterdam on 1 April 1949.[5] After a brief visit to Paris, where Cage learned that he had been awarded a Guggenheim Fellowship, they went to Sicily, where Cage was to cover the Spring Festival of the International Society for Contemporary Music in Palermo.

> At the Palermo opera house there was some unbelievable scarf dancing, and at Taormina some equally unbelievable vine dancing in a production of Euripides' *The Cyclops* in the Greek Theatre. Actually, the most exciting has been some folk dancing by boys in Italy in a little mountain village [Ravello]. Called *Maroquina,* it was Arabic in flavor, extremely wild and contained at the same time. The accompaniment was a barbaric beating on an enormous home-made tambourine and chanting. *That* was exciting.[6]

Cage and Cunningham returned to Paris via Rome, where the painter John Heliker, then at the American Academy, arranged a concert for Cage there. (It was Cage who had suggested the title *Perilous Night,* also the title of a composition of his own, for one of Heliker's surrealistic paintings of 1947.[7]) From Paris, Cage went south to another festival, at Aix-en-Provence. Cunningham, meanwhile, found a room in the Hôtel de Bourgogne, on the Île St. Louis, where he lived as frugally as possible. Renting a studio in the Salle Wacker, he worked by himself, as was his habit, and watched classes given by Olga Preobrazhenskaya and Madame Nora.

A young American drama student, Marianne Preger, in Paris that summer to attend the school of Jean-Louis Barrault and Roger Blin, had seen Cunningham in the Graham company. When she heard

Jean Hélion's studio, avenue de l'Observatoire, Paris, which served as the venue for MC's concert of 10 June 1949.

from the painter Ellsworth Kelly that he and Cunningham were living in the same hotel, and that Cunningham was looking for a studio, she introduced herself. Preger told Cunningham that Jacqueline Levant, who taught "*la danse moderne*" at Barrault's school, had a studio in the Salle Pleyel, and would be willing to let him use it, in return for teaching classes. Cunningham readily agreed, and taught class three times a week during the rest of his stay. In addition to Preger and Levant, his students included Rachel Rosenthal, later a noted California performance artist, and François Canton.

> The French attack on time is very peculiar. If a class runs from 6:30 to 7:30 they feel it's possible to arrive at any point within that hour and start the class. At least it keeps bringing in new faces.[8]

Cunningham was not impressed by the dancing he saw in Paris:

> Les Ballets de Paris of Roland Petit is comparable to our musical comedies, not as slickly done,

and on the whole our musicals have better dancers. Their ballets are more entertaining than our musicals, because the ballets don't pretend to be serious, but Agnes de Mille and Jerry Robbins are much better choreographers than Petit.[9]

He also remembers seeing a performance by a modern dancer named Janine Solane, at the Palais de Chaillot: "There seemed to be hundreds of girls in gold lamé dancing to Bach. . . . I couldn't believe it, hordes of people running from one side of the stage to the other."[10]

In June, Cunningham and Cage were invited to give a performance in the studio of the painter Jean Hélion in the avenue de l'Observatoire. They had met Hélion, who was married to Peggy Guggenheim's niece Pegeen, in New York. One day Cunningham and Heliker, who had joined them in Paris, were walking near Notre Dame and ran into Tanaquil LeClercq and Betty Nichols, another member of Balanchine's Ballet Society company, who had just arrived in Paris on vacation. Cunningham asked them to be in his concert, and they soon began rehearsing.

(LeClercq told Nichols, "We came for three months' cultural vacation, and after one week we're back in our tights again."[11])

The performance took place on 10 June 1949, at five in the afternoon.[12]

I invited a lot of people, they came and stood up, and I presented a few dances, they liked them, and this is all in preparation for a program later on. The marvelous thing about the theatre situation here is the rapidity and ease with which one can present something, and the low cost relatively. I gave two solos, a duet and a trio, and got a press notice; a good one.[13]

This notice may be the one referred to in an article by Maurice Pourchet in the 1950 issue of *Ballet Annual*:

One of my colleagues has written in *Arts* that their dances, to atonal music and a piano "préparé," would convert us to a belief in the mystic by their suppleness and rare beauty of physique.[14]

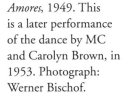

Amores, 1949. This is a later performance of the dance by MC and Carolyn Brown, in 1953. Photograph: Werner Bischof.

Both the duet and the trio were new dances to existing music by Cage.

AMORES

A duet with LeClercq to music, dating from 1943, of the same title (the outer movements, for prepared piano, of a suite of four pieces of which the inner movements are for percussion instruments).

EFFUSIONS AVANT L'HEURE

A trio whose title is a rough translation, or paraphrase, of the title of the music, *A Valentine Out of Season*, 1944 (also for prepared piano).

Among the audience were Alice B. Toklas, Alberto Giacometti, Roberto Matta, Martha Graham's benefactress Bethsabee de Rothschild, the American pianist duo of Arthur Gold and Robert Fizdale, Baron Moley (who had been Guillaume Apollinaire's secretary), and another of Balanchine's American ballerinas, Mary Ellen Moylan. Toklas told Cunningham she liked the dancing "because it was so pagan."

A second performance was arranged on 11 July at the tiny Théâtre du Vieux Colombier, in a program presented by the Club d'Essai of Radiodiffusion Française, under the title "*Soirée de l'imprévu*." This very mixed program of music, songs, and short scenes included a play by Max Jacob, whose actors invited Cunningham to repeat three dances from his program.

The painter Pavel Tchelitchew had crossed the Atlantic on the same boat as LeClercq and Nichols, and had shown them around Paris. He also took them to tea with Léonor Fini, who had designed *Le Palais de cristal* (Symphony in C) for Balanchine at the Paris Opéra, and was now designing costumes for a garden fête in honor of Lady Diana Cooper. Fini asked Nichols to dance at the party with Milorad Miskovitch, and as there was no choreographer Nichols suggested Cunningham, who arranged a pas de deux to open the fête. (The dancers were warned not to begin until the Duke and Duchess of Windsor were seated.) Women invited to the party were told that they should not wear white unless they were virgins; LeClercq, unaware of this, wore a red dress. As Nichols observed, "We were probably the only virgins there."[15]

This page: *Trio,* 1953 (a later version of *Effusions avant l'heure,* 1949). Two casts pictured, left to right: Marianne Preger, Remy Charlip, Jo Anne Melsher, Anita Dencks, Paul Taylor, and Carolyn Brown (replacing injured Viola Farber). Photograph: Louis A. Stevenson, Jr. Opposite: MC in *Two Step,* 1949. Photograph: Walter Strate.

Before that January 1950 concert, however, Cunningham would take part in a series of December 1949 performances at the City Center Theater, under the rubric of the New York City Dance Theater. This was one of many short-lived attempts to make a modern-dance "repertory company" out of an ad hoc aggregate of individuals and groups who actually remained stubbornly autonomous: Cunningham, Valerie Bettis, Nina Fonaroff, Eve Gentry, Katherine Litz, Iris Mabry, the José Limón company, the Charles Weidman company, the Dudley-Maslow-Bales Trio, and the Hanya Holm group. Cunningham performed on the evening of 18 December, giving the first New York performance of *The Monkey Dances* and the premiere of a new solo:

TWO STEP

The music, an instrumental version of Satie's music-hall song *La Diva de "l'Empire,"* was played at the premiere (as was *The Monkey Dances*) by a chamber orchestra conducted by Cage. (In later performances Cage performed this music as a piano solo.) Cunningham had presumably made *Two Step* in Paris, and may have worn the costume that he designed for it in an earlier dance—certainly he had been photographed in it (by Arnold Eagle).

When asked if any of the material in this music-hall-related solo came from Mrs. Barrett, back in Centralia, Cunningham said that "the middle part was a kind of soft-shoe, only more elaborate, turning around, and I put a break at the end of the phrase that probably came from her—I just made it bigger." Remy Charlip remembers Cunningham bounding out from the wings and seeming to cover most of the diagonal width of the stage in one leap.

Cunningham came to the conclusion after his trip that

Europe is fascinating, but not essential. Paris is a wonderful city, pleasant to see, to live in, and to enjoy. The food is superb, the parks are like being in the country, the museums, all that is superb. But I've seen no dancing that even touches what takes place in the United States. Dancing here is divertissement, a spectacle to be looked at and if it's accompanied by enough sets and costumes maybe it will cause a furore. . . . I saw the Opera Ballet here. It's almost as much of a farce here as it is in the United States. I'm beginning to wonder if there's any dancing left but folkdance, and the American. Am anxious to be back and working with dancers again. I've a date at Hunter Playhouse for a concert, January 15th. Been working all summer on it. [16]

1950s

1950

Both of the new dances that Cunningham had shown in Paris were included in his January concert. Tanaquil LeClercq appeared again in *Effusions avant l'heure*, now retitled *Games*, and in *Amores*; Betty Nichols had remained in Europe, and her part in *Effusions* . . . was danced by Pat McBride. With Dorothy Berea, Mili Churchill, and Anneliese Widman, Cunningham also performed two quartets—a third reworking of *A Diversion* and a new piece, *Pool of Darkness*. There were also four solos—repeats of *Two Step* and *The Monkey Dances*, the first New York performance of *Dream*, and a new solo, *Before Dawn*.

POOL OF DARKNESS

Pool of Darkness was a serious piece—probably psychological. The music [by Ben Weber] was very serious—it was a long piece. It was written before [the dance was]. . . . I gave [Weber] some kind of an idea about the way it was divided into parts. The choreography followed the phraseology—not so much the beat because it wasn't in that sense rhythmic, it was more "expressive." . . .

There was lots of rushing about. There was a phrase where they were running about, probably something to do with the psychology, and I thought they didn't always have to run, so I devised a turn, some kind of spinning where they used their backs. Well, I thought, that's much better, it's harder to do, anyway. It was very hard for them to learn to do it, because they would do it the way they had been taught, and that isn't what I was interested in getting. I think there were also some fast things, which were also very difficult for them to do because they weren't accustomed to doing fast things, complicated footwork of any kind.

On the subject of Weber's score, Cage said,

The music had all been music that I could play; then through the effort to have other music we developed the need for another musician because the music was beyond my technical ability, and that was first the case with the Ben Weber piece, and we had to find someone who could play it for the rehearsals, because at that time they rehearsed to the music, of which we had made a piano reduction. We had come back from Paris and I had brought the Boulez second piano sonata with me. I had met [the composer] Morton Feldman, and he said, there's only one person in America who could play that, and that's David Tudor. After that, Morty and David and I were often together.

Tudor, born in Philadelphia in 1926, was a virtuoso organist and pianist who had become identified with the music of contemporary composers, many of whom wrote pieces especially for him. At that time he was part of the circle of the composer Stefan Wolpe, with whom he had studied composition. Cage asked

Tudor to play the Weber piece. When he also remarked that Tudor must like it, he received the reply that Tudor couldn't stand it—"It was too romantic, romantic and chromatic, chromatic twelve-tone music." From then on Tudor was closely identified with Cunningham and Cage.

Pool of Darkness pleased those critics who would have been happy to see Cunningham work in a more orthodox way:

Mr. Cunningham is the protagonist of the conscious world, and a trio of three women . . . represent the forces that impinge upon his consciousness and then recede into the dream world. As the dance opens, he is alone. He comes out of a trancelike state, and builds to a climax of almost hysterical apprehension. The back curtain opens, as he freezes into immobility, and three women loom out of a pool of darkness. With vicious aggressiveness they fight their way into the orbit of his consciousness and finally leave him spent and inert. As the curtain conceals them from view, he spins in blind bewilderment, in a pattern of mechanical movement. *Pool of Darkness*, like so many modern dances, is an expression of frustration, but it is honest, powerful, and full of meaning. . . .[1]

In fact Cunningham abandoned the piece. Berea remembers having the distinct impression that he was not happy with it—that Widman kept asking questions about the psychological motivation of the movements that he was unable or unwilling to answer. (The description quoted makes the dance sound strikingly similar to a later piece, *Crises*.)

In his comments on the two solos, *Dream* and *Before Dawn*, Nik Krevitsky expressed a general dissatisfaction with the concert, and with Cunningham's work at that time:

Mr. Cunningham is one of the truly great dancers of our day, and watching him, no matter what the movement, is always a wonderful kinesthetic experience. Yet we cannot overlook, nor resist stating, the fact that he is in a creative phase which makes an entire program less than it might have been. Merce Cunningham is a dancer possessed with an electric physique capable of meeting any demands. His technique, his choreographic wisps of movement, make many demands, and he does meet them, but there is seldom any climax to the works themselves, and the form (except for the element of repetition) is swallowed up somewhere along the way, or disappears, or just never became a concrete structure. There are fleeting images, ideas of dances, tantalizing in their provocative sequences, but they never build to what we are sure Merce Cunningham is capable of. This does not mean to imply that he is a dancer who is incapable of meeting the challenges of choreographing. He has demonstrated his ability in the past with solos and with the large ballet, *The Seasons*.[2]

We may question whether Cunningham in fact had any interest in "building to a climax." During the late 1940s, Cage had studied Indian music and philosophy with Gita Sarabhai (in exchange for lessons from Cage in contemporary music and counterpoint),[3] and had attended lectures on Zen Buddhism given at Columbia University by Dr. Daisetz T. Suzuki; these studies would profoundly influence his ideas about musical composition. Cunningham also went to a few of the lectures ("when rehearsals allowed"), and his ideas about structure, like Cage's, were increasingly influenced by these Eastern philosophies. As has been noted, *The Seasons* embodied a view of the life cycle derived from East Indian as well as from American Indian sources.

Cage and Cunningham at this time used to frequent the Cedar Bar on University Place, a favorite haunt of New York painters, and to attend meetings of The Club, an artists' meeting point on Eighth Street that was started by Robert Motherwell in 1949, and of its successor, centered around de Kooning. There Cage delivered his "Lecture on Nothing," written in the same kind of rhythmic structure as his musical compositions. During the question period that followed, Cage, in a Zen spirit, "gave one of six previously prepared answers regardless of the question asked":[4]

> Everybody has a song
> which is no song at all:
> it is a process of singing,
> and when you sing,
> you are where you are.[5]

Cunningham's dances and Cage's music had more in common with the art of this period than with other dance and music. The Abstract Expressionist school that emerged during the 1940s gave first importance to the actual process of painting, the "action" or "gesture" of the painter in applying the paint—as in Jackson Pollock's method of allowing paint to drip over the canvas, as Meyer Schapiro wrote, in "endless tangles and irregular curves, self-involved lines which impress us as possessing the qualities not so much of things as of impulses, of excited movements emerging and changing before our eyes."[6] (Film footage of Pollock painting shows him almost dancing alongside the canvas as he hovers over it, dripping the paint onto its surface.) Such paintings, instead of constituting a finite and schematic design consciously determined by the artist, had the appearance of an arbitrary segment of something that could seem capable of extending beyond the canvas into infinity.

The audiences for Cunningham's concerts seemed to include more painters and poets than dancers or musicians. Yet there was an essential difference between what Cunningham and Cage were doing and the work of the Abstract Expressionist painters, whose subject was still, in the words of Calvin Tomkins, "the suffering self"[7] or, as Mark Rothko and Adolph Gottlieb insisted, "only that subject-matter is valid which is tragic and timeless."[8] Such content, of course, was precisely what Cunningham wished to eliminate from his choreography and Cage from his music. (Rothko and Gottlieb might seem to have more in common with choreographers of a previous generation such as Martha Graham and José Limón.) Like Marcel Duchamp, Cunningham and Cage wished to make works that were not "reflections of their own personal feelings."[9]

In the spring of 1950 Cunningham returned to Black Mountain College. Elizabeth Jennerjahn, one of his pupils there in 1948, had become the college's dance instructor, and invited him to teach there for a week during the summer.[10] Cunningham was also invited to teach during the summer at Louisiana State University in Baton Rouge, and to choreograph two works for the LSU Dance Group to perform at the Summer Festival of Art there. Both were to music by Satie.

WALTZ AND RAG-TIME PARADE

I went down there, and I remember going into this room, this place they worked in, and there was this motley group of people. And Blanche Duffy, the director, said, "Now, here's the LSU Dance Group . . . as you see, they're mixed . . . now you take that fellow over there, he's only come once before, but he's very eager." So I taught class—I was there two weeks—and at the end of this period they were to have some kind of program. I did solos and something with these people. The place was so hot, after about forty-five minutes they couldn't work any more, because the heat was so heavy. I thought, what in god's name can I do with this group? So I began to work—we had class late in the day and then rehearsed in the evenings, it was slightly cooler. And I made this *Waltz* for [a dozen] people, a huge, odd-shaped group. It was to Satie. . . .

I managed to make this piece and I got them moving around. Blanche was very pleased, because I don't think she'd ever managed to get all of them moving at one time. It didn't last very long; it was only two minutes or some

Pages 54–55: *Nocturnes*, 1956. MC and Viola Farber. Photograph: John Lindquist. Below: *Rag-Time Parade*, 1950. François Canton and Rachel Rosenthal.

thing. So I thought I should make another piece, and I looked this group over and I picked out six, two men and four women, who I thought were a little more energetic, and I made the *Rag-Time Parade*—that also only lasts about two or three minutes. I don't know what we did for costumes for the *Waltz*, we probably dug up some old costumes out of the wardrobe, Southern belle costumes probably, and for *Rag-Time Parade* I just made them wear old things—pants, coats—that I found, they had a huge wardrobe of costumes and I just plucked things out, and said, "you wear this," it was all mixed up. And I did solos—that was the program.

• • •

Cunningham's loft on East 17th Street was not large enough to hold classes in, and he was therefore obliged to rent studios. Marianne Preger had returned from Paris and for a while was his only beginning student, to be joined shortly afterward by Remy Charlip, Sudie Bond, Rachel Rosenthal, François Canton, and Julie Walter. Cunningham taught them *Rag-Time Parade*, which they performed in a couple of programs.

Charlip had been an art student at Cooper Union. A fellow student, a German painter called Marianne Benjamin, had taken him to a concert by the German modern dancer Harald Kreutzberg:

> He was the first dancer I had ever seen, and I was totally bowled over by him, and that was when I decided I wanted to be a dancer. She told me about Merce, and said if I wanted to be a dancer I should study with the best dancer there is, and we went together to New York City Ballet to see *The Seasons*, and that was the first piece I had ever seen of his. I remember sitting up in the balcony and not quite understanding what was going on—I remember snow, a projection of white dots on the Noguchi set—and it was all very strange to me. I also read a book by Carlo Blasis, and one of the things he said was, If you're going to study, study with a master, so I thought I should study with Merce, but I was too shy, even after I later met him socially through Lou Harrison. . . [11]

During the 1950–51 season, Cunningham was again on the faculty of the School of American Ballet, until he and Cage left to go on tour in the spring of 1951. (His last class there was on 26 March 1951.)

1951

At the beginning of the 1950s, Cage began to use chance operations in his musical composition. He and Cunningham were working on a big new piece, *Sixteen Dances for Soloist and Company of Three*.

> To facilitate the composition, . . . Cage drew up a series of large charts on which he could plot rhythmic structures. In working with these charts, he caught his first glimpse of a whole new approach to musical composition—an approach that led him very quickly to the use of chance. "Somehow," he said, "I reached the conclusion that I could compose according to moves on these charts instead of according to my own taste."[1]

The composer Christian Wolff introduced Cage to the *I Ching*, or *Book of Changes*, which had just been published by his parents' company, Pantheon Books.[2] As soon as Cage saw the charts used for identifying the names of the hexagrams, he made the connection with his own charts, and saw that he could use the book as the basis for the chance operations toward which he had been moving. His first composition involving chance was *Music of Changes* (for piano), followed by *Imaginary Landscape No. 4* (for twelve radios, each with two "players," one operating the wavelength and the other the volume control). Both these works continued to follow the square-root rhythmic structure that Cage had been using. He drew up charts for such elements as tempo, duration, kind of sound, and dynamics, then made choices among them by tossing coins, as when obtaining oracles from the *I Ching*.

> Value judgments are not in the nature of this work as either composition, performance, or listening. The idea of relation . . . being absent, anything . . . may happen. A "mistake" is beside the point, for once anything happens it automatically is.[3]

Cunningham began to think about ways in which he could apply similar methods to choreography, which he used for the first time in *Sixteen Dances*.

SIXTEEN DANCES FOR SOLOIST AND COMPANY OF THREE

> The *16 Dances for Soloist and Company of Three* was special for me in my work. It was a long piece [53 minutes] intended to fill an evening. It was also the first time the use of chance operations entered into the compositional technique.
>
> The choreography was concerned with expressive behavior, in this case the nine permanent emotions of Indian classical aesthetics, four light and four dark with tranquillity the ninth and pervading one. The structure for the piece was to have each of the dances involved with a specific emotion followed by an interlude. Although the order was to alternate light and dark, it didn't seem to matter whether Sorrow or Fear came first, so I tossed a coin. And also in the interlude after Fear, number 14, I used charts of separate movements for material for each of the four dancers, and let chance operations decide the continuity.
>
> The work had an overall rhythmic structure to which Cage wrote the score, generally after the dances were finished. He composed it for both piano and small orchestra, distinguished by a number of unusual percussion sounds. Although each dance was a separate entity, we were begin-

This page: MC in *Six-teen Dances for Soloist and Company of Three*, 1951. Photograph: Gerda Peterich. Pages 60–61: MC teaching class in the 14th Street Studio, New York, ca. 1960. John Cage (at piano, at rear) and David Gordon (seated). Photograph: Seymour Linden.

ning to use "poetic license" in disregarding connecting points within the dances.[4]

The order became: anger, the humorous, sorrow, the heroic, the odious, the wondrous, fear, the erotic, and finally tranquillity. These were all solos with the exception of the erotic, which was a duet, and tranquillity, which was a dance for the four of us. The solos were concerned with specific emotional qualities, but they were in image form and not personal—a yelling warrior for the odious, a man in a chair for the humorous, a bird-masked figure for the wondrous.

There were postludes to a number of the solos. Following fear was a quartet with a small gamut of movements, which was different for each dancer, and this was choreographed by chance means. That is, the individual sequences, and the length of time, and the directions in space of each were discovered by

tossing coins. It was the first such experience for me and felt like "chaos has come again" when I worked on it.[5]

We spent a long time rehearsing it [about a year, according to Dorothy Berea]. It was so astonishing and strange, really strange to do that. I remember that when Joan Skinner came in [to replace Mili Churchill], she liked it, and she danced it with such a marvelous attack . . . it was as though it worked for her. It was the first time where you encountered a coordination, going from one thing to another, that I had not encountered before, physically—so how do you do it, if you're going to accept this idea at all, how do you manage to do it? You have to just fight with it, and struggle, and try to find the most direct way to go from one of these things to the other. There was a jig at the end of the first part, very quick; I remember there was some

THE FUNCTION OF A TECHNIQUE FOR DANCE (1951)

Since he works with the body—the strongest and, at the same instant, the most fragile of instruments—the necessity to organize and understand its way of moving is of great urgency for the dancer.

Technique is the disciplining of one's energies through physical action in order to free that energy at any desired instant in its highest possible physical and spiritual form. For the disciplined energy of a dancer is the life-energy magnified and focused for whatever brief fraction of time it lasts.

In other words, the technical equipment of a dancer is only a means, a way to the spirit. The muscles used in exercises every day are validly used only if it is understood that they lead the way, sustain the action. But it is upon the length and breadth and span of a body sustained in muscular action (and *sustaining* immobility is an action), that dance evokes its image.

The most essential thing in dance discipline is devotion, the steadfast and willing devotion to the labor that makes the classwork not a gymnastic hour and a half, or at the lowest level, a daily drudgery, but a devotion that allows the classroom discipline to be moments of dancing too. And not in any sense the feeling that each class gives an eager opportunity for willful and rhapsodic self-expression, but that each class allows in itself, and furthers the dancer towards, the synthesis of the physical and spiritual energies.

The final and wished-for transparency of the body as an instrument and as a channel to the source of energy becomes possible under the discipline the dancer sets for himself—the rigid limitations he works within, in order to arrive at freedom.

An art process is not essentially a natural process; it is an invented one. It can take actions of organization from the way nature functions, but essentially man invents the process. And from or for that process he derives a discipline to make and keep the process functioning. That discipline too is not a natural process. The daily discipline, the continued keeping of the elasticity of the muscles, the continued control of the mind over the body's actions, the constant hoped-for flow of the spirit into physical movement, both new and renewed, is not a natural way. It is unnatural in its demands on all the sources of energy. But the final synthesis can be a natural result, natural in the sense that the mind, body and spirit function as one. The technical aim is not to do a few or many things spectacularly, but to do whatever is done well, whether a smaller or greater amount of actual physical skill is required, and approaching as a goal, the flawless. To walk magnificently and thereby evoke the spirit of a god seems surpassingly more marvelous than to leap and squirm in the air in some incredible fashion, and leave only the image of oneself. And for that very reason, the dancer strives for complete and tempered body-skill, for complete identification with the movement in as devastatingly impersonal a fashion as possible. Not to show off, but to show; not to exhibit, but to transmit the tenderness of the human spirit through the disciplined action of a human body.

The dancer spends his life learning, because he finds the process of dance to be, like life, continually in process. That is, the effort of controlling the body is not learned and then ignored as something safely learned, but must and does go on, as breathing does, renewing daily the old experiences, and daily finding new ones. Each new movement experience, engendered by a previous one, or an initial impress of the action of the body upon time, must be discovered, felt and made meaningful to its fullest in order to enrich the dance memory.

The possibilities of movement are enormous and limitless, obviously, but the understanding of organization of movement is the high point of the dancer's craft. If the spine is taken as the center of radius, much as the animal makes it his physical conscience, then the action proceeds from that center outwards, and also can reverse the process and proceed from outward back to the center. The legs and arms are only a revelation of the back, the spine's extensions. Sitting, standing, extending a leg or arm, or leaping through air, one is conscious that it is to and from the spine that the appendages relate and that they manifest themselves only so far as the spine manifests itself. Speed, for instance, is not a case of the feet or arms twiddling at some fantastic tempo, but speed comes from the diligence with which the spine allows the legs and arms to go. At the same time, the spine can allow rapid action in the legs and feet, and by the control centered in it, allow serenity in the arms—seemingly still and suspended in the air. The reverse too is possible.

The spine, moreover, acts not just as a source for the arms and legs, but itself can coil and explode like a spring, can grow taut or loose, can turn on its own axis or project into space directions. It is interesting, and even extraordinary, to see the improvised physical reaction to most of the music of the nineteenth century, and then that to the folk form we know as jazz. The first is usually immediately apparent in the arms and legs, the second happens in the torso, or there is a definite visual indication that the movement impetus, however small or large in circumference, starts from an action in the torso. It is not really extraordinary, because of what lies at the root, but it is interesting to see.

Certainly everybody including dancers can leap, sit down and get up again, but the dancer makes it apparent that the going into the air is what establishes the relationship to the air, the process of sitting down, not the position upon being down, is what gives the iridescent and life-quality to dancing.

The technical equipment for a dancer involves many things. There must be an understanding of the correct vertical position of the body, and how it is obtained and held. This involves the problem of balance of the body, and the sustaining of one part against another part. If one uses the torso as the center of balance and as the vertical axis at all times, then the question of balance is always related to that central part, the arms and legs balancing each other on either side and in various ways, and moving against each other. If one uses the torso as the moving force itself, allowing the spine to be the motivating force in a visual shift of balance, the problem is to sense how far the shift of balance can go in any direction and in any time arrangement, and then move instantaneously towards any other direction and in other time arrangements, without having to break the flow of movement by a catching of the weight whether by an actual shift of weight, or a break in time, or other means. The dynamics of the torso are thus sustained, and distilled and not lost in moving from one direction to another.

Paul Weiss says in *Nature and Man*,

"the will is employed to discipline the body by making it the locus of techniques—means for acting well habitually so as to reach objectives mentally envisaged. There is little pleasure in setting about to master a technique. One must first concentrate on its different component movements and steps. Then one must firmly relate them by going over them in sequence again and again. But there are compensations. While the technique is being willingly mastered, the body and the mind are in accord, for a willing mastery of a technique requires that one keep in mind what one is doing and keep one's body from disturbing the intent of the mind. And so far as nothing arises which provokes the mind or body to work in opposition to the acquired technique, the technique promises a fairly enduring resolution of the conflict of mind and body. Though techniques enable a mind and body to work together for a considerable time, they tend to force the one or the other into a groove. The more a technique is mastered, the greater the risk that one will be too inflexible to overcome those oppositions between the mind and the body which are inevitable when the differently structured mind and body confront a novel situation."

One of the things that Western dance, and principally here in America, has not explored in any formal or technical sense, is the disciplined use of the face. The place we know of primarily that has made a continuous disciplined use of the face for definite expressive purpose—that is, a particular facial image for wrath, another for the hero, etc.—is the Hindu classical dance. But here in the United States where there has been an extraordinary amount of technical exploration into kinds of expressive movement, there has been little or no formal cognizance taken of the face. Every other part of the body has been subjected to many kinds of motion, the face left to its own devices.

The element that underlies both music and dance is time, which, when present in component parts, is rhythm. As an element coordinating the two arts, it is more useful when the phrase and parts longer than the phrase are considered, rather than the small particularities of accent and even of individual quantity. The concentration on the minutiae of rhythm in the music-dance relationship leads to the "boom-with-boom" device, giving nothing to either and robbing both of freedom. Working, however, from the phrase leads to a related independence, or to an interdependence of the two time arts. Accents, even and uneven beats, then appear, if they do, where the music continuity or the dance continuity allows them to. (That is, an accent in the music is an incident in the music continuity which does not necessarily appear in the dance, and vice versa.)

In coordinating dance and music the one should not be submerged into the other, as that would tend to make one dependent upon the other, and not independent as they naturally are. The dance and music can be brought together by time, by a particular rhythmic structure of time involving phrases, which indicate the meeting points convenient for use, thereby giving to each a freedom to expressively play with and against a common structural idea.

Plato, in the *Timaeus*, says, "Time is the moving image of eternity." Time, the very essence of our daily lives, can give to dancing one of the qualities that make it, at its most beautiful, a moving image of life at its highest.

—MERCE CUNNINGHAM

place where they got to sit down for four counts, and Dorothy Berea said, "You sure have to rest fast in this dance."

In each of those pieces I tried to get a different idea about the use of space. In the jig, for example, that was the four of us, it would fan out and come back. . . . For anger, there was some kind of large, strident gesture; the warrior [ended up] shooting himself or hitting himself and crawling off the stage, making these terrible sounds. . . . It was a big, complicated work, interesting to do because of what seemed enormous complexities at the time, and the structure was not rigid, but very clear in each one, so that you had to deal with that as well as any ideas about the expressive thing. . . .

The formal ideas in the choreography, music, and costume design have been described by Cunningham's other principal collaborator in the piece, Remy Charlip:

The music and the costumes have a formal arrangement, which allows for a single change for each dance. In the music, John Cage started with a specific set of sixty-four sounds for the first dance, and for each pair of dances replaced eight sounds with eight others, until at the end there was a completely new set of sounds. The first piece started with harsh and sharp sounds, and in the last piece there were long and resounding sounds. The costumes were treated in a similar manner, with dark and warm colors in the beginning, and with one costume change for each dance, ending in cool, light colors in order to contribute to the final, serene effect.

Mr. Cunningham's arrangement of the sequence of dances was based on the conviction that it is possible for anything to follow anything else, and that the actual order of events can be chanced rather than chosen, the resultant experience being free and discovered, rather than bound and remembered.[6]

There were various "additions and props," some of them made by Cage and Cunningham themselves. In the twelfth dance, Cunningham remembers, a trio, "two of the girls dragged another one in a basket, and they wore white, transparent dresses, like little kids." Charlip made the mask Cunningham wore in the "wondrous" solo, from a drawing by John Heliker; he built the mask on a plaster cast of Cunningham's face. (Heliker remembers going to look at Northwest

MC as "Odious Warrior," from *Sixteen Dances for Soloist and Company of Three,* 1951. Photograph: Gerda Peterich.

Indian masks at New York's Museum of the American Indian before making this drawing.[7])

In the "ballad of the odious warrior," Cunningham wore a fantastic patchwork coat made by two bibulous friends of his, Antoinette Larrabee and Constance Smith, decorated with bits of fringe and lace, bells, metal ornaments, and beads. In this solo Cunningham made "use of vocal sounds, shouts, groans and grunts. . . . Some see this dance as a hunter frightened by his hunt, others as an exuberant drunk on a binge."[8] After this came a "blues" duet of "two girls in a night-club," wearing "some kind of draped garment."

• • •

Once again Cage and Cunningham went west in the spring. In Seattle, Cunningham performed a new solo:

VARIATION

This was another chance dance, in which Cunningham set himself what proved to be a virtually insoluble problem:

They were classic ballet steps, arranged in a chance order, and it was impossible, *I* couldn't do it. You're supposed to do without preparation four pirouettes, suddenly. . . . There was one day when I was working in the studio when I found a way to do it, but I could never do it again, I just couldn't hold it. It was in three parts, an andante, an adagio, and an allegro; the first two were separate, and the second went from the adagio directly into the allegro. It wasn't terribly long, two or three minutes at the most, but it was just impossible to do. I had made a gamut of ballet steps, and I took each step and figured out the way I thought it was done, and then I made a chance order of these, and not all of them came up. I did it some place . . . and I told the man backstage he could turn the lights on and off, and in the performance I remember being in the air trying to do these steps which involved beats and all this stuff, and the lights went out. . . . He really did his job, that fellow. . . . So I realized that there had to be certain limitations about that—those steps were hard enough to do anyway.

The ballet steps Cunningham used included "inversions of the entrechat, the cabriole, the rond de jambe, preparations for a turn without making the turn."[9] Notwithstanding the solo's "impossibility," one reviewer said that it "squelched any suspicion that he has not mastered the traditional dance technique."[10] Louis Horst, however, felt that this "balletic solo," even though the movements had metamorphosed through their subjection to chance procedures, "seemed to have no place on a modern dance program."[11]

David Tudor remembers rehearsing this solo with Cunningham: "He didn't take cues from the music, but he had to know where he was in terms of time. I think this helped toward forming Merce's discipline in later works. The thing that I was learning was not just to hear the rhythm of the music but to see it in terms of time passing."[12]

• • •

At one point in the summer of 1951 Cunningham gave a performance on Martha's Vineyard, which included another new solo:

BOY WHO WANTED TO BE A BIRD

Years ago, I gave two or three dances one evening in some small place on Martha's Vineyard. There was no music at all. Afterward, a lady in the audience came up and asked how could I possibly do this dancing without music, because there was no rhythm. At that particular moment, in this funny, dark little place, a gorgeous moth flew in and began moving in the most spectacular way around the one light. And I just pointed.[13]

The solo, about which Cunningham remembers nothing, was never performed again.

1952

There was no spring tour as such in 1952, but Cunningham paid a brief return visit to Black Mountain College, where he taught classes and performed a *Suite of Six Short Dances*, to recorder music. Made for the occasion, the suite was never performed again.

The summer was busy. In June there was to be a Festival of Creative Arts at Brandeis University, in Waltham, Massachusetts. Leonard Bernstein, the festival's musical director, commissioned Cunningham to choreograph two works for a concert on 14 June in the university's new open-air theater, where "they had lots of geraniums but no toilets."

EXCERPTS FROM SYMPHONIE POUR UN HOMME SEUL[1]

Leonard Bernstein asked me to do choreography for what he said was music concrete [by Pierre Schaeffer with the collaboration of Pierre Henry], and which was programmed as *musique concrète*, and whatever else it may have meant to the spectators, did mean it had been composed directly on magnetic tape, and was played over the loudspeakers via the tape. Bernstein decided that the music should be played twice, one immediately following the first, because of its novelty. I, not feeling that visual repetition is thus equally engaging, made two separate dances, the first a solo for myself, the second a dance for a company of [eleven], decidedly mixed, containing a few excellent dancers I had brought from New York, and the rest students who were unskilled as dancers and inept as stage performers. I couldn't pretend that the majority of the company could dance well and did not like the idea of pretense. It occurred to me that they could do the gestures they did ordinarily. These were accepted as movements in daily life, why not on stage? To these movements I applied chance procedures.

The costumes too were from daily life, Filene's Basement. We had $30 to get all . . . of them. . . .

Since the music was not countable the way dancers had ordinarily counted up till then, this freed the immature performers from any dependence upon it for support. Then time became a mutual field in which both the sound and movement progressed. This and the found movement also freed them from embarrassment or fright, and the event was realistic rather than forced, and they could enjoy it.

How do you start? Well you go through the thing of these mixed up people. . . .

Chance procedures applied completely here.
I—Solo: movement simple to complex/repeated to phrases
II—for company, for the most part untrained: movement in charts included simple steps: e g running, walking, skipping, hopping; and pantomime gestures: e g sleeping, filing nails, combing hair, various popular dance steps, washing hands.

The group did on occasion do one of these at the same time but not in unison, i.e. 10 persons washing hands, each in own momentum. The length of time any event or group of events took was gained by applying chance procedures to seconds & minutes. A given sequence might have a duration of 15″, i.e.

5 persons filing nails	}
5 persons combing hair	} duration 15″
4 persons skipping	}[2]

For this dance, given the amateur standing of the greater number of dancers, I kept the timing strict. [In fact, Cunningham used only two or three students from Brandeis in this dance—more were in the other work he made for the Festival (see below).] e g 15″ in length—but allowed freedom as to [how long] each filed his nails, or skipped. As to where in the space they ran, that again was precise, obtained by chance means, the given direction was kept strict.

e g 2 persons running	}
4 persons sleeping	} 12 seconds
8 persons doing the Bunny-hug	}[3]

This was rehearsed for several weeks—the first rehearsals were strictly each-on-his-own regulated by where he had to get and my calling the time-shots. But after a week or two, the dancers began to be aware of where each other was in the space. It adds a visual cue.[4]

Historically, *Excerpts from Symphonie pour un homme seul* marked the first time everyday gestures were used in performance simply as movement—that is to say, without mimetic significance. Just as Duchamp's "readymades" "put forward the new dictum that any object could be art if an artist said it was,"[5] Cunningham here was stating that any movement could be dance if he said it was. The relation of dance to music in this piece—that of simultaneity of occurrence—represented the logical conclusion of the way in which Cunningham and Cage had been working together for the last ten years.

I thought, with that music, which didn't interest me that much as music, that the only way to deal with it was certainly not by count, that was impossible, or by some idea about the sound, being affected by the sound. I didn't like that idea to begin with—you'd always be late, because the electronic sound happened so quick, you'd never hit it on the nose, you couldn't possibly, unless it were counted out, which this was not. . . . So that's why I thought, well, I'll just make the dance in terms of lengths of time, so I set up this procedure with both the solo and the company piece, with different gamuts for each, but figuring out how long in time any given part of the dance took, and I knew the length of each part of the piece, of the

sound, and then of course because the sound remains the same all the time, there gradually got to be cues.

The working situation was terrible, the people who ran the festival didn't know anything, and they all didn't think this was ever going to work—not Lenny, he wasn't there, but the people there, because they had no experience with theater, and they always think you don't know what you're doing. I was working in a very difficult space in relation to what the stage was like. . . .

LES NOCES

The other work that Bernstein commissioned from Cunningham was of a very different nature—a new version of Stravinsky's choral ballet *Les Noces*, originally presented by Diaghilev's Ballets Russes in Paris in 1923, with choreography by Bronislava Nijinska. Cunningham used four or five Brandeis students in the chorus, though it was led by his own dancers; the principal roles were also filled by experienced performers. *Les Noces* was performed only once.

Cunningham asked a student in his class, Donald McKayle, to be in the Brandeis performance. The New York dancers rehearsed in the city at first, then later at Brandeis. McKayle remembers that in *Les Noces* Cunningham followed the music and the dramatic idea, with some dances that had no narrative content, including his own athletic solo. They rehearsed to a recording of the music, whose constantly changing meters were followed in the choreography, though McKayle does not remember that the dancers counted very much—rather, they kept together through a kind of rapport.

McKayle's duet with Anneliese Widman captured the feeling of the parents' loss; elsewhere their dances contained "big, spatial, leaping movement." There was no particular attempt at a Russian peasant style. There was, however, "a raw quality, not sophisticated."

McKayle believes that the movement was worked out in advance, as was the quite different movement for the *Symphonie pour un homme seul*, in which "nothing followed anything else, there would be a difficult technical combination then you had to look at your watch or wash your hands, and it was one problem to figure out how to accomplish those different tasks." There were no counts at all. The dancers were given no freedom of choice—the dance was set (though Cunningham's solo changed every time he did it, as his interest in it grew). Even in rehearsal the sequence of ideas in the group version remained the

Above and right: Howard Bay's costume designs for *Les Noces*, 1952. Opposite: *Les Noces*, 1952. MC at center. Photograph: Morris Beck. Pages 66–67: MC in *Changeling*, 1956. Photographs: Edward Meneeley.

same; the dancers' only freedom was in the way they performed the mimetic gestures.

For *Symphonie*, "Remy did the costumes by chance—he made a chart, then went to Filene's Basement to find things." The lighting designer, however, John Ransford Watts, refused to have anything to do with the chance idea. When McKayle saw the piece later, under the title *Collage*, it looked very different to him—some of the sequences were the same, but they occurred at different times.[6]

• • •

Immediately following the Brandeis performance, Cunningham taught a six-week summer course at the Dancers Studio in New York (16 June–25 July).[7] Then he and Cage went back to Black Mountain, at the invitation of Lou Harrison, who had become head of the music department.[8] They were also to teach at a Summer School of Fine Arts in nearby Burnsville, organized by what was then the Woman's College of the University of North Carolina at Greensboro, with a dance program from 30 July to 19 August.[9] Cage taught composition and also worked with the dance students. Here Cunningham's assistant was Jo Anne Melsher, a former student at Manhattan's High School of Performing Arts who had begun studying with Cunningham when she was only fifteen. The three commuted between Black Mountain and Burnsville in a Model A Ford that Cage and Cunningham had found. An added complication was that Cunningham was suffering from appendicitis, but was unwilling to take time out for

an operation and convalescence. His doctor, Shailer Upton Lawton, had told him to try to dance as little as possible and to keep an ice pack on his stomach whenever he could. Somehow Cunningham got through the summer without an emergency.

The Burnsville Summer School was associated with the town's Parkway Playhouse, which that season presented five plays, ending with the musical comedy *Brigadoon*, in which "the dance, music and drama programs combined."[10] Cunningham did the choreography, and also performed the role of Harry Beaton. Meanwhile, those in residence at Black Mountain—including Cunningham, Katherine Litz, M. C. Richards, Charles Olson, Franz Kline, Hilda Morley (Stefan Wolpe's wife), Nick Cernovitch, and Remy Charlip—wrote, produced, and performed another musical comedy, of a rather more ribald character, called *Occupe-toi de Brunhilde*.[11] The title paraphrases that of a Feydeau farce, *Occupe-toi d'Amélie*.

That summer also saw a performance of greater significance:

> At the Black Mountain Summer School in 1952 Cage organized a theater event, the first of its kind. David Tudor played the piano, M. C. Richards and Charles Olson read poetry, Robert Rauschenberg's white paintings were on the ceiling, Rauschenberg himself played records, and Cage talked. I danced. The piece was forty-five minutes long and, as I remember, each of us had two segments of time within the forty-five to perform our activity. The audience was seated in the middle of the playing area, facing each other, the chairs were arranged on diagonals, and the spectators unable to see directly everything that was happening. There was a dog which chased me around the space as I danced. Nothing was intended to be other than it was, a complexity of events that the spectators could deal with as each chose.[12]

The time brackets were arrived at by chance methods. Coffee cups were placed on the seats, and when coffee was served to the audience, the performance was over.[13] According to Cage, the event also "involved . . . films, slides, [and] radios." Richards and Olson "recited from the tops of ladders." Cage's own reading was of "my Juilliard lecture, which ends: 'A piece of string, a sunset, each acts.'"[14]

Accounts of the event, whether by participants and spectators or by people who were not actually present, differ on many points, no doubt because of the sub-

SPACE, TIME AND DANCE (1952)

THE DANCE IS AN ART IN SPACE AND TIME.

The classical ballet, by maintaining the image of the Renaissance perspective in stage thought, kept a linear form of space. The modern American dance, stemming from German expressionism and the personal feelings of the various American pioneers, made space into a series of lumps, or often just static hills on the stage with actually no relation to the larger space of the stage area, but simply forms that by their connection in time made a shape. Some of the space-thought coming from the German dance opened the space out, and left a momentary feeling of connection with it, but too often the space was not visible enough because the physical action was all of a lightness, like sky without earth, or heaven without hell.

The fortunate thing in dancing is that space and time cannot be disconnected, and everyone can see and understand that. A body still is taking up just as much space and time as a body moving. The result is that neither the one nor the other—moving or being still—is more or less important, except it's nice to see a dancer moving. But the moving becomes more clear if the space and time around the moving are one of its opposite—stillness. Aside from the personal skill and clarity of the individual dancer, there are certain things that make clear to a spectator what the dancer is doing. In the ballet the various steps that lead to the larger movements or poses have, by usage and by their momentum, become common ground upon which the spectator can lead his eyes and his feelings into the resulting action. This also helps define the rhythm, in fact more often than not does define it. In the modern dance, the tendency or the wish has been to get rid of these "unnecessary and balletic" movements, at the same time wanting the same result in the size and vigor of the movement as the balletic action, and this has often left the dancer and the spectator slightly short.

To quibble with that on the other side: one of the best discoveries the modern dance has made use of is the gravity of the body in weight, that is, as opposite from denying (and thus affirming) gravity by ascent into the air, the weight of the body in going with gravity, down. The word "heavy" connotes something incorrect, since what is meant is not the heaviness of a bag of cement falling, although we've all been spectators of that too, but the heaviness of a living body falling with full intent of eventual rise. This is not a fetish or a use of heaviness as an accent against a predominantly light quality, but a thing in itself. By its nature this kind of moving would make the space seem a series of unconnected spots, along with the lack of clear-connecting movements in the modern dance.

A prevalent feeling among many painters that lets them make a space in which anything can happen is a feeling dancers may have too. Imitating the way nature makes a space and puts lots of things in it, heavy and light, little and big, all unrelated, yet each affecting all the others.

About the formal methods of choreography—some due to the conviction that a communication of one order or another is necessary; others to the feeling that mind follows heart, that is, form follows content; some due to the feeling that the musical form is the most logical to follow—the most curious to me is the general feeling in the modern dance that nineteenth-century forms stemming from earlier pre-classical forms are the only formal actions advisable, or even possible to take. This seems a flat contradiction of the modern dance—agreeing with the thought of discovering new or allegedly new movement for contemporary reasons, the using of psychology as a tremendous elastic

THE OBJECT OF THE DANCER IS TO OBLITERATE THAT.

basis for content, and wishing to be expressive of the "times" (although how can one be expressive of anything else)—but not feeling the need for a different basis upon which to put this expression, in fact being mainly content to indicate that either the old forms are good enough, or further that the old forms are the only possible forms. These consist mainly of theme and variation, and associated devices—repetition, inversion, development and manipulation. There is also a tendency to imply a crisis to which one goes and then in some way retreats from. Now I can't see that crisis any longer means a climax, unless we are willing to grant that every breath of wind has a climax (which I am), but then that obliterates climax, being a surfeit of such. And since our lives, both by nature by the newspapers, are so full of crisis that one is no longer aware of it, then it is clear that life goes on regardless, and further that each thing can be and is separate from each and every other, viz: the continuity of the newspaper headlines. Climax is for those who are swept by New Year's Eve.

More freeing into *space* than the theme and manipulation 'holdup' would be a formal structure based on *time*. Now time can be an awful lot of bother with the ordinary pinch-penny counting that has to go on with it, but if one can think of the structure as a space of time in which anything can happen in any sequence of movement event, and any length of stillness can take place, then the counting is an aid towards freedom, rather than a discipline towards mechanization. A use of time-structure also frees the music into space, making the connection between the dance and the music one of individual autonomy connected at structural points. The result is the dance is free to act as it chooses, as is the music. The music doesn't have to work itself to death to underline the dance, or the dance create havoc in trying to be as flashy as the music.

For me, it seems enough that dancing is a spiritual exercise in physical form, and that what is seen, is what it is. And I do not believe it is possible to be "too simple." What the dancer does is the most realistic of all possible things, and to pretend that a man standing on a hill could be doing everything except just standing is simply divorce—divorce from life, from the sun coming up and going down, from clouds in front of the sun, from the rain that comes from the clouds and sends you into the drugstore for a cup of coffee, from each thing that succeeds each thing. Dancing is a visible action of life.

—MERCE CUNNINGHAM

jective nature of each person's response. That evening, for example, Francine du Plessix Gray wrote a journal note:

At eight thirty tonight John Cage mounted a step-ladder and until 10:30 [sic] he talked about the relation of music to Zen Buddhism while a movie was shown, dogs ran across the stage barking, 12 persons danced without any previous rehearsal, a prepared piano was played, whistles blew, babies screamed, coffee was served by four men dressed in white, Edith Piaf records were played double-speed on a turn-of-the-century machine. . . . [15]

No other account mentions twelve dancers; du Plessix Gray also seems to remember the event as rather longer than it actually was.

Calvin Tomkins, in his *New Yorker* profile of Cage, adds the detail that still photographs were projected on the walls.[16] Michael Kirby, in the introduction to his anthology *Happenings*, adds further information: he and others state that what Cage read was "a lecture on Meister Eckhart." By Kirby's account, only Richards was on a ladder, while "Charles Olson and other performers [were] 'planted' in the audience [and] each stood up when their time came and said a line or two." Kirby says that movies were projected "on the ceiling," and he describes them: "at first they showed the school cook, then the sun, and, as the image moved from the ceiling down the wall, the sun sank."[17]

Barbara Haskell, in the catalogue to the Whitney Museum of American Art's 1984 exhibition "Blam! The Explosion of Pop, Minimalism, and Performance 1958–1964," amplifies further, stating that Cage read "excerpts from the medieval German mystic Meister Eckhart, after which he performed a composition with radio. . . . Later, Tudor poured water from one bucket to another while Rauschenberg projected abstract slides and film clips onto the ceiling."[18] If this account is accurate, it would suggest that Tudor performed Cage's "Water Music," a composition of that year.[19] According to Mary Emma Harris, a black-and-white painting that Franz Kline had made at the college that summer was also displayed, along with four of Rauschenberg's all-white paintings. As Harris says, the "considerable disagreement about just what did happen in the performance . . . is as much a measure of its success as of the faulty memories" of those who were present.[20]

In devising this event, Cage was influenced both by his involvement in Zen and by his reading of Antonin Artaud's book *The Theater and Its Double*, which M. C. Richards was translating that summer, reading each chapter aloud to her friends as it was completed.

We got the idea from Artaud that theater could take place free of a text, that if a text were in it, that it needn't determine the other actions, that sounds, that activities, and so forth, could all be free rather than tied together; so that rather than the dance expressing the music or the music expressing the dance, that the two could go together independently, neither one controlling the other. And this was

extended on this occasion not only to music and dance, but to poetry and painting, . . . and to the audience. So that the audience was not focused in one particular direction.[21]

This event and Cunningham's choreography for *Symphonie pour un homme seul* could be said to have crystallized the Cage-Cunningham aesthetic—the denial of the center, the structure in terms of time, the creation of what Cage called "a purposeless, anarchic situation which nevertheless is made practical and functions."[22] These performances decisively established Cage and Cunningham as leaders of the avant-garde in the United States, whose influence was felt not only in dance and music but in painting and theater.

Rauschenberg had been a student at Black Mountain in the fall of 1948, having enrolled in the semester following the summer of Cage's Satie festival; he left at the end of the 1949 spring semester. He had met Cage and Cunningham in New York in the spring of 1951, at the time of his first show at the Betty Parsons Gallery. Cage said: "There was from the beginning a sense of absolute identification, or utter agreement, between us."[23] Rauschenberg had returned to Black Mountain in the fall of 1951, and the three men were there together the following summer. It was at Black Mountain that Cage and Cunningham saw for the first time Rauschenberg's all-white paintings, which gave Cage the courage to compose his "silent" piece, 4′33″. During that summer Rauschenberg switched from all-white to all-black paintings, made from strips of newspaper dipped into black paint and glued to the canvas. In October, he left for Rome with Cy Twombly, who had also spent the summer at Black Mountain.[24]

During their tour west in the spring of 1951, Cunningham and Cage had stopped in Denver, where Carolyn Brown and her husband, the composer Earle Brown, saw Cunningham dance. During her childhood, in Fitchburg, Massachusetts, Brown had studied dance with her mother, Marion Rice, a devoted teacher of the Denishawn system. She had later studied philosophy at Wheaton College in Norton, Massachusetts, but had continued to dance there, among other things choreographing a ballet based on Dostoyevsky's *The Brothers Karamazov*, with an all-female cast. In Denver, Carolyn Brown attended classes Cunningham taught at Jane McLean's studio, where she was studying. "Merce gave two master classes. I took both of them. I'd never seen anyone move like that—from such a quiet center, with such animal authority and human passion."[25] Cage told her that Cunningham was looking for a partner, preferably not from one of the New York dance studios—one whom he could form according to his own dance style and aesthetic. At the time, it did not occur to her that she might be that dancer—she was not even thinking of dancing as a career.

In the summer of 1951 the Browns had visited New York. Renewing their acquaintance with Cage, through him they met people like Morton Feldman and the artists Richard Lippold and Ray Johnson, who all lived in the same tenement building, at 134

Monroe Street in Manhattan.[26] Cage was "amazingly generous and encouraging to Earle," according to Carolyn Brown, urging him to write more music. Tudor played a piece by Earle at a concert at the Cherry Lane Theater. The Browns returned to Denver for the winter; when Tudor passed through on a concert tour, he stayed with them.

In August 1952, the Browns left Denver for good and moved to New York. Carolyn Brown wanted to take classes with Cunningham again, but she still wasn't thinking seriously of becoming a dancer—her intention was to continue studying philosophy, at Columbia. Earle Brown finally talked her out of this, however, and she instead entered the dance department of the Juilliard School of Music, so that she could get a degree and become a teacher.[27] In the fall, after Cunningham returned from Black Mountain, Brown also began taking his classes at Stuart Hodes's Dancers' Studio on East 8th Street, between Broadway and University Place. Cunningham remembers noticing her there and thinking, "She can dance."

During the fall and winter Cunningham began working on *Suite by Chance* with his regular students; at some point in the winter there was a studio showing of part of the piece, danced by Sudie Bond, Jo Anne Melsher, Marianne Preger, Remy Charlip, and Cunningham himself. Cunningham remembers that "some of the Abstract Expressionist painters" attended this showing, Philip Guston and Bradley Walker Tomlin among them.

1953

In its first public performance, at the Festival of Contemporary Arts, Urbana, Illinois, in March 1953, *Suite by Chance* shared the program with a revival of *Sixteen Dances*, in which Jo Anne Melsher replaced Anneliese Widman.

SUITE BY CHANCE

Carolyn Brown had learned some of the part that Sudie Bond had danced at the preview: "Natanya Neumann did most of it," she has said, "and Merce gave me a tiny little section—I think that was my audition." This was the first time the dancers were called "Merce Cunningham and Company" on the program, though this performance was actually transitional between Cunningham's performances with an ad hoc group and the establishment of a company on what would prove to be a permanent basis.

In a lecture-demonstration at the Brooklyn Institute of Arts and Sciences on 15 April 1953, at which *Suite by Chance* was rehearsed, performed, and discussed, Cunningham "explained the 'hows' and 'whys' of both the dance and the music. . . . By tossing coins he decided what movements went where and in how many counts. Mr Cunningham got the idea while watching the chance relationships of people in the street, through a high window." In the question period after the performance, "the most provocative questioner asked if the *Suite* was an abstract dance.

Mr. Cunningham answered that he did not see how humans could be abstract, as 'the meaning of the dance exists in the activity of the dance. A jump means nothing more than a jump.' Mr Cunningham concluded, 'Dancing is expression of life; if this is not valid, life is not valid.'"[1]

Some years later, Cunningham wrote, "*Suite by Chance* is exactly what the title says."[2] The structure, he has said, was "very classic": "The first movement was andante; the second movement was very slow; the third a little faster; the last movement was very fast."[3] According to Carolyn Brown, the last movement "had a lot of unison, hard, turning, fast movement, which for us at that time was very hard to do it well and keep together. It was the kind of work he did later [in the 1980s], only not so much of it, not so continuous."[4]

> About the music, a commissioned score for electronic sounds by Christian Wolff. It is composed directly on magnetic tape by aid of cutting and splicing the tape itself and then recorded on tape or on a record. This actually makes the tape recorder the instrument. The relationship between the dance and music is one of co-existence, that is, being related simply because they exist at the same time.
>
> The dance was constructed in and originally in rehearsals worked against a metric beat. Mr. Wolff's score was constructed in inches per second. So, during the course of rehearsing and performing the dance we changed our time relationship to seconds and minutes.[5]

A cue sheet reproduced in Cunningham's 1968 book *Changes: Notes on Choreography* clearly shows, however, that the dancers took cues from easily recognizable places in the music. In a larger sense, the piece followed a time structure, as in earlier dances; one page of notes reads, "Curtain opens on empty stage/Music alone for 1st 4½ [minutes]/I enter on 6½/Girls enter together at structural point." (There follows the comment, "*c'est ça*.")

There were charts for "every single element"—the gamut of movements, durations, directions in space:

> These charts had taken several months of several hours daily to complete, and the movements in them were purposefully as unadorned and flat as I could make them.
>
> It was almost impossible to see a movement in the modern dance during that period not stiffened by literary or personal connection, and the simple, direct and unconnected look of this dance (which some thought abstract and dehumanized) disturbed. My own experience while working with the dancers was how strongly it let the individual quality of each of them appear, naked, powerful and unashamed. I feel this dance was classical—precise and severe—however unfamiliar the continuity, however unclassical the movements, in terms of tradition, and the stillnesses, that is, held positions by the dancers, may have been. It was unprompted by references other than to its own life.[6]

The chance process used in *Suite by Chance* was described in detail by Remy Charlip in *Dance Magazine*:

For this dance, a large series of charts was made: a chart numbering body movements of various kinds (phrases and positions, in movement and in stillness); a chart numbering lengths of time (so that a phrase or position could be done in a long or short duration, or, in the case of the impossibility of lengthening the time of a movement, as for instance, a single step, it could be repeated for the length of time given); a chart numbering directions in space (floor plans).

These charts, which defined the physical limits within which the continuity would take place, were not made by chance. But from them, with a method similar to one used in a lottery, the actual continuity was found. That is, a sequence of movements for a single dancer was determined by means of chance from the numbered movements in the chart; space, direction and lengths of time were found in the other charts. At important structural points in the music, the number of dancers on stage, exits and entrances, unison or individual movements of dancers were all decided by tossing coins. In this way, a dancer may be standing still one moment, leaping or spinning the next. There are familiar and unfamiliar movements, but what is continuously unfamiliar is the continuity, freed as it is from usual cause and effect relations. Due to the chance method, some of the movements listed in the charts were used more than once in different space and directions and for different lengths of time, and, on the other hand, many movements, to be found in the charts, do not appear at all in the final choreography.[7]

Suite by Chance also exemplified Cunningham's concept of space. "Originally," he has said, "it was made to have the audience on four sides, and when we went to Black Mountain, it worked, because there the audience could be on four sides."

In applying chance to space I saw the possibility of multidirection. Rather than thinking in one direction i e to the audience in a proscenium frame, direction could be four-sided and up and down. When performed as such, exits and entrances were arranged to suit existing aisles,

or if arranged by us, the aisles were placed at the four corners. . . .

The dancer is at a given point in the dancing area. That point in space and/or that particular moment in time concurrently is the center for him and he stays or moves to the next point to the next center. Each dancer had this possibility. So, from moment to moment and from point to point, the dancers moved separately.[8]

At what proved to be the last performance of the dance, in San Francisco on 15 November 1955, a program note was added:

All the elements of this dance were arrived at by chance manipulation of selected materials. This method was employed to encourage maximum play of possibilities, beyond the ordinary range of the choreographer's [word omitted] and memory. The work presents itself starkly, lyrically, without narrative or descriptive image. The dance begins with an extended solo and ends in a virtuoso acceleration by the whole company.[9]

(Earle Brown has said, "There was always a whirligig near the end [of Cunningham's dances]. Chasing tails."[10])

• • •

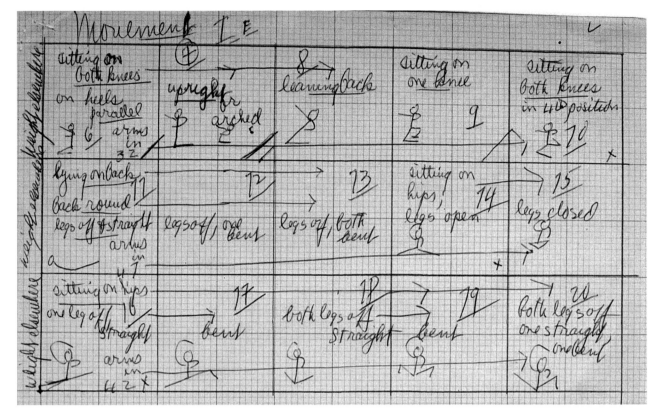

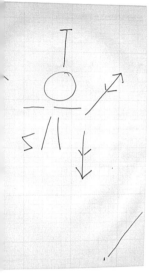

Opposite: MC in rehearsal with David Tudor (seated), ca. 1952. Photograph: Robert Rauschenberg. Above and right: MC's charts for *Suite by Chance*, 1952.

Looking back at this period in which she was first working with Cunningham, Carolyn Brown says,

When Earle and I moved to New York, our friends were Merce and John [Cage] and David Tudor, and Remy Charlip and Nick Cernovitch, so we saw each other and talked about the ideas that were going on—over supper and between going to movies on 42nd Street. Viola [Farber] was sometimes a part of that, so was Marianne [Preger]. But because Earle was working with John and David on [Cage's] tape project, we saw a lot of them, and the ideas were being discussed. And we were meeting the painters—Bob [Rauschenberg], though I don't remember Jap [the painter Jasper Johns] at that time.

The excitement then—because I was living with a composer—was in the ideas about indeterminacy and chance that Earle and Morton Feldman and John were involved in, and each of them contributed something of his own. I think Merce listened a lot; as I recall he didn't join very much in the aesthetic discussions, but I think he was very influenced by them.

During that year John taught a kind of composition workshop for dancers at the studio Merce used. We met once a week, in the evening. He used a lot of the ideas that he was involved in, like using the imperfections on a piece of paper—Merce was beginning to use that procedure, also. We also did pieces—I made a trio, it was called *Trio for Five Dancers*, because there were never more than three dancers on at a time, using those techniques of John's. I think it was always through John that I knew about the ideas that Merce was working with.

Later on, a year or two later, John did another workshop at the Sheridan Square studio. Merce was never around—well, he was hovering, he would be in the back, and he listened. Remy did a wonderful piece, using a kind of crossword puzzle format, with colors—a chance piece. Each one of us was a color, a wonderful scheme that developed from John's course. John at that time was the go-between—if you had a problem, you had to talk to John.[11]

In April 1953 there was another of the periodic attempts to bring together modern-dance companies of various persuasions, in a season of American dance at the Alvin Theater on 52nd Street. Advertised as "Two Weeks of the Greatest in Contemporary Dance," this venture was sponsored by the Bethsabee de Rothschild Foundation. Sharing a program with the Martha Graham Company on Saturday 18 April, and with the Graham and José Limón companies on Tuesday 23 April, Cunningham was asked to repeat *Sixteen Dances*, with the same cast as at his January

71

1952 revival. (Natanya Neumann, who was in *Sixteen Dances,* also appeared as the Pioneering Woman in Graham's *Appalachian Spring.*) The first performance occasioned a *scandale* reminiscent of the Diaghilev company's first performance of *Parade* in 1917: most of the audience consisted of adherents of one or the other orthodox groups, united, if in nothing else, in their detestation of everything Cunningham and Cage did and stood for. The program's presenters complained that Cunningham's piece, performed without an intermission, was too long.

> I had a terrible time. But Anna Sokolow was so marvelous—she'd come with Dorothy Bird, and was sitting in front of a man who didn't like the music, or didn't like any of it, and he kept talking and she kept turning around and telling him to be quiet, and he just talked once too often and she turned around and hit him. . . . We've been friends ever since.

On 23 June, when Cunningham was again in residence at Louisiana State University in Baton Rouge, he shared a program with the student dance group in the university's Summer Festival of Art, performing his *Variation,* the solo version of *Symphonie pour un homme seul,* and a new dance:

SOLO SUITE IN SPACE AND TIME

In *Music for Piano,* the accompaniment for *Solo Suite,* Cage used a chance process in which the notes or tones corresponded to "imperfections in the paper upon which the piece was written."[12] Cunningham adapted this procedure for his choreography:

> The spacial [*sic*] plan for the dance, which was the beginning procedure, was found by numbering the imperfections on a piece of paper (one for each of the dances) and by random action the order of the numbers. The time was found by taking lined paper, each line representing five-second intervals. Imperfections were again marked on the paper and the time lengths of phrases obtained from random numbering of the imperfections in relation to the number of seconds.[13]

> I made gamuts of movement, and then the order was all done by chance. There's one dance that repeats, that's the way it happened. The whole thing lasted about fifteen minutes, it was terrifying, the last one was awful, full of leaping, I didn't do the whole thing, it was too hard. And each leap was different, one with straight

legs, one with both knees bent, and on and on, and then you had to do it all over again, all of which I faithfully tried to do. It was marvelous to work at but exhausting to do. I didn't do it many times, the whole piece was too hard.

As so often in Cunningham's work, it was not difficult to detect the presence of nature imagery in these solos. More than thirty years later, in 1985, Cunningham taught one of them to Rob Remley, and told him he should be like a cat hiding in long grass and stalking its prey. This solo ended with Cunningham kneeling downstage right and slowly turning his head. It was an unforgettable image— Cunningham turned his head so slowly that it was almost imperceptible, like Nijinsky in *L'Après-midi d'un faune.* (The solo was danced again later by Thomas Caley.)

At the same time, the piece clearly indicated the direction in which Cunningham's work was heading. As Carolyn Brown has written,

> *Solo Suite in Space and Time* . . . is what might be considered "Cunningham classical." It is not without dramatic intensity. But the form, the movement in space and time, is like pure water: clear, transparent and reflective. Merce begins his deep involvement with time and space with this solo. . . . [14]

• • •

Cunningham had been invited to Black Mountain again later in the summer, and this residency was to be of momentous importance.

> I thought about it, and I thought I'd rather go than not go, but I'd rather not go alone. So I said I'd like to bring some dancers with me, and that I wouldn't take any salary, in order to pay for their being there—I would have to get them down there, which we did some way, on buses. We managed—there were seven of them. The

Above: MC in *Solo Suite in Space and Time,* 1953. Photographs: Dora Cargille Sanders. Opposite: Rehearsal break, ca. 1952. Left to right: Remy Charlip, Marianne Preger, Viola Farber, Carolyn Brown, Jo Anne Melsher, Anita Dencks, and MC.

school put them up and fed them, and in return I gave classes for the company and students, we had class in the morning and then we rehearsed.

During the preceding couple of years, the dancers Cunningham was training had been joined first by Jo Anne Melsher, then by Carolyn Brown, Viola Farber, Anita Dencks, and Paul Taylor. Farber, Dencks, and Taylor were at Black Mountain for the whole six weeks of the summer session, to be joined by Brown, Melsher, Marianne Preger, and Charlip for the last three weeks, during which they rehearsed a whole repertory including three old dances—*Symphonie pour un homme seul* (now renamed *Collage*), *Rag-Time Parade*, and *Suite by Chance*—and three new ones: *Banjo*, *Dime a Dance* (which used material Cunningham had developed in his classes in New York), and *Septet* (which Cunningham had started in New York). Cunningham also made a new solo for himself.

These dances were performed in two concerts in the college dining hall, on Friday and Saturday 21 and 22 August, with Cunningham and his dancers being joined by three students in the summer session, Ethel Brodsky, Deborah Moscowitz, and Timothy La Farge. While rehearsing the Tarantella from *Dime a Dance*, Preger sprained her ankle, and was unable to perform in the concerts; her role in *Septet* was divided between Dencks and Farber.

On the first evening the first part of the program consisted of student work, solos by Dencks and Moscowitz, and *Mother-Son Duet* from Paul Taylor's *Jack and the Beanstalk*, danced by Taylor and Farber to music written and performed on the guitar by Preger. (The whole ballet was given at a Dance Associates concert in New York in 1955.) The second half was danced by Merce Cunningham and Company, billed thus, and included *Collage*, *Variation*, *Banjo*, and *Dime a Dance*. Charlip was billed as "Entrepreneur and in charge of spectacle," which, he says, meant that he went to a cotton mill, bought blue fabric for something like ten cents a yard, and made a huge cyclorama from it. The programs, designed by Cage and Earle Brown and printed by them on the college printing press, were white-on-white, with embossed lettering. (According to Carolyn Brown, Cage and her husband were not in Black Mountain for the whole summer, coming only in time for the concerts.)

BANJO

Banjo was a lighthearted piece of Americana, choreographed in more or less orthodox fashion to music by Louis Moreau Gottschalk.

> We had a rehearsal pianist who played for classes, and he tried to play this *Banjo* music, and I remember Viola [herself an accomplished pianist] making a face. So I went to David Tudor and I said, I know you're busy—because he was getting ready to give a music program—but could you just come and play the piece once so the dancers could hear it? So he came over one day and sat there and played this thing, it sounded like fifty banjos going on, and they said, now we understand.

DIME A DANCE

This is a grab-bag of dance. All the dance company is on the stage ready to dance 7 of 13 solos, duets, trios and the like. Which seven these are is not known by any one of them beforehand, but is determined by chance means in the course of seven pantomimes.

At Black Mountain College, August 1953, one of the audience, after paying a dime, picked a card from a deck of cards which designated the dance to be performed. The title refers to that situation.

The music, performed by David Tudor, pianist, has been selected by him from the vast literature bequeathed to us by the 19th century.[15]

At later performances, the method of determining which dances would be done, and in what order, was changed:

Left: *Banjo*, 1953. Left to right: Timothy La Farge, Jo Anne Melsher, Remy Charlip, Marianne Preger, Carolyn Brown, MC, and Anita Dencks. Photograph: Arnold Eagle. Inset top and bottom: *Banjo*, Jacob's Pillow, 1955. Left to right, top: Anita Dencks, MC, and Viola Farber. Left to right, bottom: Carolyn Brown, MC, Marianne Preger, and Remy Charlip. Photographs: John Lindquist.

There were short pantomimes between each dance which ended with one of the dancers selecting an object, e.g. a scarf, some caps, a veil, from a basket. This object cued the next dance to be presented. Thereby indeterminacy in a small way entered into performance. The great hang-up was to remember what the object referred to quickly enough to continue. The object too cued the music, 19th century piano pieces selected by David Tudor [from the series "Music the Whole World Loves to Play"] on no grounds other than their own quality. If the dance was longer than the piece Tudor was playing he started in at the beginning again and stopped again. Equally so the other way.[16]

The opening pantomime was performed by Preger, who remembers "going on stage and winding up an imaginary old gramophone, and putting on a record." (This part was given to her because she had studied with Marcel Marceau in Paris.) This pantomime determined not only which dance would be done but also, in some cases, who would do it: all the dancers learned some of the numbers and had to be ready to perform them. "The Tango," however, was a duet for Melsher (with a rose between her teeth) and Cunningham; "The Insect" was a solo for Farber;[17] and "The Eclectic" was a solo for Cunningham, which he usually performed as an encore if it had not come up in the course of the performance. (The title referred to the fact that the dance was made up of "bits of things out of different people, Martha, Jean Erdman, Katy Litz, and Sybil [Shearer].") Although *Dime a Dance* was not performed after the company's first year, as late as 1957 Cunningham performed a solo from it that he called "Beethoven" in a lecture-demonstration at Ann (later Anna) Halprin's Dance Deck in Marin County, California, on 13 July.[18] In 1971, he began to include "The Run" from *Dime a Dance* in Events, full-evening performances made up of excerpts from various pieces, which the dance company began to present in 1964. In 1972 he taught Chris Komar a solo ("Oriental Dance") originally composed for *Dime a Dance* but not used; Komar performed this dance in Events.

• • •

The Saturday 22 August program at Black Mountain was wholly devoted to the Cunningham company, opening with *Solo Suite in Space and Time*. Next came another new work, *Septet*, followed after an intermission by the new *Solo* (later called *Untitled Solo*). The program was completed by *Rag-Time Parade* and the

first two movements of *Suite by Chance*. During the intermission before the last of these pieces, the chairs in the dining room were rearranged so that the audience would be seated on four sides, as Cunningham originally intended for *Suite by Chance*.

SEPTET

The title of *Septet* refers not to the number of dancers in the piece but to the fact that Satie's music, its title *Trois morceaux en forme de poire* notwithstanding, is in seven parts. "Working titles" for the seven parts appeared in a later program note (Satie's own titles for the parts are given here in brackets):

> In the Garden [*Manière de commencement: Allez modérément*]
> In the Music Hall [*Prolongation du même: Au pas*]
> In the Tea House [*I: Lentement*]
> In the Playground [*II: Enlevé*]
> In the Morgue [*III: Brutal, Modéré (Comme une bête)*]
> In the Distance [*En plus: Calme*]
> In the End [*Redite: Dans le lent*]

The poetic ambiguity of the music and dance titles express[es] the character of this ballet, whose subject is Eros, and whose occurrence is at the intersection of joy and sorrow.[19]

When asked where the subtitles originated, Cunningham answered, "They're from me." They were, in other words, invented by him to identify the various sections for rehearsal purposes, and did not necessarily reflect their content.

Satie's piece *Trois morceaux en forme de poire* tempted me as so much of his music had. It has 7 sections. I made a piece for 6 dancers, 3 couples, but out of respect for Satie called it *Septet*.

This is one of the last times I used a wholly intuitive procedure. I had the ideas ahead of time and figured out which piece of music would be used for which dance although the dance didn't necessarily fit the music. I wanted a lively dance.

It is a theater dance. It turned out to be continuously practical—no scenery, the simplest of costumes, would accommodate to any size stage. If only Cage & Tudor were around to play the music of course. As Viola Farber said, you not only need a pianist who is capable but also willing! Other musicians were shocked originally because they didn't think it was the way music should go with dance. For instance in the music there would be several loud chords and we'd stand perfectly still.[20]

Cage would write,

The continuity of *Septet* is not logical from movement to movement. At times it seems profoundly sad and noble, at other times playful and surprising. It provides an experience that one is unable to resolve, leaving one, as a dream often does, uncertain of its meaning. . . .

The movements [of the music] vary from the orientalism of the first to the popular French folk and music hall styles of some of the others. While Satie was working on the composition, he took what he was doing to Debussy who said that the music lacked form. Satie then gave it the title, "Three Pieces in the Form of a Pear."[21]

The choreography is similarly varied in style: at the rise of the curtain the three women are discovered posed like statuary, in a diagonal line. Cunningham enters and paces about among them.[22] The second movement is a "music hall" solo for himself, "with faces," as he wrote in manuscript notes on the piece:

holding his hands flat in front of his face, he opens them to reveal a comic or tragic expression. There follows the first of two interludes in which a little social encounter takes place among some of the dancers, two couples who meet and change partners after Cunningham has approached and shaken hands with one of the women. The third movement is a slow, gravely lyrical duet for Cunningham and Carolyn Brown. The fourth movement begins with an allegro duet for the other two couples; Brown enters and joins the other two women in a tender trio, as their partners go off. Then Brown is joined by Cunningham and Charlip in a version of the quartet that opened this movement.

After another changing-places interlude, the three couples line up in a diagonal for the fifth movement. First the women drop toward the floor in a dead fall; the men, holding their hands, prevent them from hitting it. Then the dancers move into two lines facing one another, stepping into a kind of Virginia-reel for-

Below: *Septet*, 1953. Left to right: Viola Farber, Bruce King, MC, Carolyn Brown, Marianne Preger, and Remy Charlip. Photograph: W. H. Stephan. Inset: MC rehearsing penultimate section of *Septet*. Left to right: Jo Anne Melsher, Carolyn Brown, and Marianne Preger. Photograph: Ara Ignatius.

mation, changing places, doing a do-si-do, the men swinging their partners. They move into concentric circles, spinning around the stage, and end up in a line across the front, where the men support the women in different poses. In the sixth movement, Cunningham and the three women assume a series of *poses plastiques*, a sequence that inevitably recalls passages in Balanchine's *Apollo*. (Cunningham rejects this comparison, saying that the quartet in fact refers to the legend of Krishna and the Gopis.) The last movement is a slow, processional finale in which the dancers line up across the stage in a friezelike formation. Brown detaches herself from this line and circles the stage, returning to take an arabesque penchée, supported by Charlip. The line re-forms and slowly moves offstage, with Cunningham and Melsher at the end. She takes his hand and leads him off the stage, walking backward and going into a backbend as she does so.[23]

The music undoubtedly helps make *Septet* accessible, and the choreography, like the music, is alternately grave and gay; that is the essence of its poetry. Audiences were not always sure how to take *Septet*, however: because Cunningham's "solo of a desperate clown"[24] was so obviously funny, they would often continue to laugh during his "sadly amorous duet with Carolyn Brown."[25] Cunningham himself seems to have been aware of this problem; in his notes on the ballet, he writes, "What makes a movement at one moment grave, and the same at the next, humorous?"[26]

UNTITLED SOLO

(Called *Solo* at the first performance.)

The first in a trilogy of solos with music by Wolff, all concerned with the possibility of containment and explosion being instantaneous. A large gamut of movements was devised for this solo, movements for the arms, the legs, the head and the torso, which were separate and essentially tensile in character, and off the normal or tranquil body-balance. These separate movements were arranged in continuity by random means, allowing for the superimposition of one or more, each having its own rhythm and time-length. . . . [27]

It was a terribly difficult dance. David Tudor used to come to rehearse with me at Black Mountain, not every day, of course, because it was done in a sense to the music, although it was not strict, I didn't follow it note by note, because Christian's music was so complex, and

so difficult for me to hear—I mean even without dancing, and with dancing it was incredible, I just had to have some kind of cueing, so David would come and play it.

The physical things were ghastly, I had to struggle to get them—that's when I sat down in despair and David said, "Well, it's clearly impossible but we're going right ahead and do it anyway." But he came every day for the last two weeks: I would do it, then he would very nicely play it again. It was inch by inch—I just couldn't hear it, and do it. When he played it, I could hear it—but then while you're doing it, doing two or three rhythms at once, and then the music is doing something totally different—you felt as if you were going to sail right off into space at any moment.

Carolyn Brown has written,

In *Untitled Solo* . . . , though it is choreographed by chance procedures, the atmosphere is clearly and intensely dramatic. An earlier solo, *Root of an Unfocus*, seemed to tell a story, to be *about* something. . . . But at this time both Cage and Cunningham were dealing in more specific dramatic terms with regard to content. *Root of an Unfocus*, structure aside, appeared almost narrative in its dramatic character. In contrast, *Untitled Solo*, to my mind, is not *about* something, but *is* that thing. It tells no story, but is dynamically the raw, direct, immediate essence—a reality.[28]

Cunningham, for his part, has written,

The dance as performed seems to have an unmistakable dramatic intensity in its bones, so to speak. It seems to me it was simply a question of allowing this quality to happen rather than of forcing it.[29]

• • •

Above: White Oak Dance Project revival of *Septet*, 1953, 1996. Left to right: Ruthlyn Solomons, Raquel Aedo, Mikhail Baryshnikov, and Patricia Lent. Photograph: Steven Caras. Opposite: MC in *Untitled Solo*, 1953. Photograph: Arnold Eagle.

As winter approached, Cage and Cunningham decided that the success of the inaugural performances of what would come to be known as Merce Cunningham and Dance Company justified the gamble of a New York season. At a cost of $725, they booked the Off-Broadway Theater de Lys (now called the Lucille Lortel), on Christopher Street in Greenwich Village, for a series of eight performances in holiday week, 29 December 1953 through 3 January 1954. To the repertory performed at Black Mountain in the summer, Cunningham added three earlier solos, *Root of an Unfocus*, *Totem Ancestor*, and *Two Step*, as well as the duet and trio he had made in Paris in 1949, *Amores* and *Effusions avant l'heure*, the latter now retitled *Trio*, and one entirely new group dance, *Fragments*. *Suite by Chance* was to be done in its entirety.

That fall Cunningham had a studio of his own for the first time, at 224 West 4th Street, on Sheridan Square. Here his dancers took class and rehearsed. The season at the de Lys was staged with the help of a $4,500 gift from the architect Paul Williams. As before, Cage and Cunningham did practically everything themselves. Cage had asked Robert Rauschenberg to design the program, but his design, according to Calvin Tomkins, "turned out to be so complex, with words superimposed on images and other words, that Cage decided it was unusable; he paid him a hundred dollars and designed another program himself."[30] Charlip designed the flyer, which was printed in several different colors.

Cage kept meticulous figures on accountant's worksheets, in calligraphy as exquisite as that of his scores, carefully noting small sums lent by himself,

Left: MC rehearsing *Untitled Solo*, 1953. Photograph: Robert Rauschenberg. Opposite: Robert Rauschenberg's first decor project, a collage for *Minutiae*, 1954.

Cunningham, Tudor, Carolyn Brown, Charlip, and others to pay incidental expenses. Some of these loans were repaid. Other friends helped by advertising in the program. Cunningham himself received no fee; the other dancers were paid $47 for a week's rehearsal (having, of course, rehearsed all through the fall without pay) and $87.50 for the week of performances. The net income from ticket sales was under $3,000.

A well-known press agent, Isadora Bennett, was engaged as publicist, and put out a lengthy and informative press release. There was an advertisement in the *New York Times* the Sunday before Christmas, and the programs were listed in the Sunday dance pages of both the *Times* and the *Herald-Tribune*. No reviews appeared in either paper, however. Margaret Lloyd reviewed the season in the *Christian Science Monitor* for Saturday 9 January 1954, a week after it had closed, and it was mentioned in an article on Cage in the issue of *Newsweek* for 11 January 1954. The only New York daily to review the season was the German-language paper *Aufbau*, on 15 January 1954, under the headline "*Tanz auf Abwegen*" (Dance led astray). The three dance publications paid more attention. In *Dance Observer* the performances were covered by Robert Sabin, Nik Krevitsky, and Louis Horst;[31] in *Dance News*, by Anatole Chujoy;[32] and in *Dance Magazine*, by Doris Hering.[33] Both Chujoy and Hering found the nonchance pieces preferable to those composed by chance processes.

FRAGMENTS

The sounds and sights of this dance occur in the contemporary world of magnetic tape, fables of science, and atomic research. The silence of the middle part marks the extremity of the dance's contrasts.[34]

Cunningham has little recollection of *Fragments* (there is no reference to it in either his own *Changes* or Jacqueline Lesschaeve's book of interviews with him, *The Dancer and the Dance*). According to Carolyn Brown, it took chance methods to an extreme; each part seemed to have been made separately, so that there was no relation between them—"it was as if we were out in space." The present writer remembers it as being extremely dry, though Lloyd found it "piquant . . . a whirligig of unrelated sound and movement, nonrepresentational and of course noncommunicative."[35]

The dance's outer sections were performed to music for magnetic tape by Pierre Boulez, the middle part in silence. For the dancers, *Fragments* was technically demanding. Marianne Simon remembers that there was "a lot of jumping," and that "we learned a lot of new falls," to which Carolyn Brown adds, "yes, and they hurt."[36] Neither *Fragments* nor *Suite by Chance* lasted long in the repertory; *Fragments* was performed only six times after the de Lys season, *Suite by Chance* only twice. Cunningham attributes this to their complexity; keeping them in repertory would have required an excessive amount of rehearsal time that he preferred to use for the creation of new works.

On 20 January 1954, less than three weeks after closing at the Theater de Lys, the company appeared in the small theater (then called the Music Hall) at the Brooklyn Academy of Music, with a program consisting of *Suite by Chance*, *Fragments*, *Septet*, *Banjo*, and *Dime a Dance*. But it was almost a year before they performed again, on 8 December 1954, in the same theater. In that later performance they gave *Fragments* again, as well as *Amores*, *Banjo*, and *Collage*; two solos by Cunningham, *Solo Suite in Space and Time*, and *Untitled Solo*, and the first performance of an important new piece, *Minutiae*, which they had rehearsed during the year.

For the second Brooklyn Academy of Music concert there was an important change in the company's personnel: Paul Taylor had left to devote himself to his own choreography, and was replaced by Timothy La Farge, who had been a student at Black Mountain in the summer of 1953.

MINUTIAE

Minutiae marked the beginning of Robert Rauschenberg's regular collaboration with Cunningham, a collaboration that was to last ten years.

I had always been interested in working with artists: Isamu Noguchi with . . . *The Seasons* . . . ; David Hare with a handsome but unfunctional costume for [*Mysterious Adventure*], unfunctional in the sense that it was too heavy to wear to do anything; Howard Bay with mediocre costumes and set for the Brandeis production of *Les Noces*. These were not collaborations so much as designs after the fact of the dance.

But with *Minutiae*, a different idea about the addition of decor came in. I asked Robert Rauschenberg to make something for it. The dance was not finished. I did not tell him what to make, only that it could be something that was in

Minutiae, 1954. Left to right: Karen Kanner, Carolyn Brown, and Viola Farber. Inset, top: *Minutiae*, 1954. Left to right: Viola Farber, Marianne Preger, and Karen Kanner. Inset, center: *Minutiae*, 1954. Left to right: Carolyn Brown, Viola Farber, Karen Kanner, and Marianne Preger. Inset, bottom: *Minutiae*, 1954. Left to right: Carolyn Brown and Marianne Preger. Photographs: John G. Ross.

the dance area, that we could move through it, around it, and with it if he so liked.

He made an object and beautiful as it was, I knew it wouldn't work, because it needed a pipe to hang on. [Cunningham felt there was no guarantee that the theaters in which the company danced would even have fly-space.] He made a second one through which we walked, huddled, and climbed. It was like an object in nature.[1]

The three-dimensional freestanding open construction that Rauschenberg finally produced relates both to the "Red Paintings" that he exhibited at the Charles Egan Gallery, New York, in the same month as the first performance of *Minutiae* and to the "Combines" he was beginning to make, such as *Charlene* (also 1954, now in the Stedelijk Museum in Amsterdam). For *Minutiae* he used paint, fabric, and paper (mostly from comic strips), as well as a mirror hanging on a string, revolving in a hole in the front panel.

As for the choreography, the title *Minutiae* "was explicit. The movements were small in scale, details only. They were found by watching people out the window of the studio in the street. At least that's what I replied when asked. But it wasn't entirely true."[2] (A program note for a later performance read, "The dance . . . uses small, short, abrupt movements arising from an observation over a period of time of people walking in the streets."[3]) It will be remembered that Cunningham had cited a similar source for the movements in *Suite by Chance*. In further explanation of the movements in *Minutiae*, Cunningham wrote,

They were, mostly, movements anyone does when getting set to do a larger movement. They were (and are) the movements before the effort. The procedure was by chance, with each dancer, there were six [*sic*], being given a separate line, like a separate life, occasionally coming together. The object made by Rauschenberg was added to the scene with no visible derangement other than that of any object being where it is. The music by John Cage was added too. So there were now three elements, the movement, the sound, and a visual action—the action in this case being a small mirror in the object, hung in such a fashion that it moved as we came close to it and the wind carried it. It was during a rehearsal of *Minutiae* that I saw my first light run-through without dancers.[4]

Cunningham characterized the kinds of movement used in the piece as follows:

Fragments/repetitions: hobbling, crawling, walking, hops. Added to those were fragmented hand, arm, shoulder and/or head movements—added to those could be hip and body movements all short.[5]

These general categories were further broken down into lists of "Movement Areas" with multiple choices under each heading, from which selection was made by tossing coins. Under "Head," for example, were "Normal," "sides turning," "up & down," "tilted," "circling," and "Indian" (the last presumably referring to the lateral movement of the head used in Hindu dance); under "Shoulders": "forward & back," "up & down," "circling"; under "Hands": "clasping opp. arm: (a) wrist (b) forearm (c) elbow joint (d) upper arm (e) shoulder (f) shoulder blade." The movement possibilities were given in suitably minute detail: under "Crossing Fingers" Cunningham listed "(a) crossing & crissing (b) twirling thumbs (c) gesticulating with forefinger (pointing) (d) gesticulating with whole hand (throwing—side of hand out) (e) Indian clasp (f) crooking fingers." Under "Feet" a number of locomotive possibilities were listed: "shuffling/stamping/shifting weight/sliding/brushing/jumping/extending/turning/running/walking/hopping/skipping."[6]

Cunningham's instructions to himself for his chance procedures are similarly detailed. Chance determined every element of the choreography—the number of people performing a given passage, time, space, and the movements to be performed. The set became another element the dancers had to deal with: "It's like having something in the landscape."

The dance began with a solo for Cunningham, which Carolyn Brown watched from downstage, sitting and hugging her knees. Later Marianne Preger and Remy Charlip slithered out under Rauschenberg's set piece, behind which they had been waiting. Most of the movement consisted of fragmentary phrases, and Marianne Simon remembers that there was also a lot of stillness in the piece.

• • •

It was during 1954 that Cunningham received his first Guggenheim Fellowship, for "creative activity and choreography."[7]

When the information was released that Merce Cunningham had been awarded a Guggenheim Fellowship, someone asked him what he was going to do with all that money. His reply was one word: Eat.[8]

In fact, when applying to the John Simon Guggenheim Memorial Foundation, Cunningham had listed among his projects "Completion of Work involving Solo and Duets to music of Erik Satie (*Socrate*)," a project that did not come to fruition until 1970, when he made *Second Hand*, and "Work for company involving elements of pantomime and american folk forms, folk here implying not only western and new england dance forms, but also the jazz idiom." (I have followed the capitalization, or lack of it, as in Cunningham's typewritten application.)

An item in *Dance Observer* quoted the "two general ideas" involved in Cunningham's plans:

The first is concerned with the exploration of dance movement in time that is free of pulse, that is, where the idea of tempo based upon a fixed metric beat no longer exists; the second is the use of chance as a method of finding continuity, that is, continuity thought of as being the continuum of one thing after another, rather than being related by psychological or thematic or other cause-and-effect devices.[9]

1955

The company had its first touring dates in the spring and summer of 1955. In May there was a single appearance at Bard College, Annandale-on-Hudson, New York, at which a new dance was performed. A few days later this dance was seen in New York City at a performance for the Japan Society at the Henry Street Playhouse.

SPRINGWEATHER AND PEOPLE

Springweather and People was presumably the dance referred to in Cunningham's Guggenheim application of 1954, though it differed from his description there. According to Cunningham, "*Springweather* was a very long piece, we worked a long time at it, we had some kind of a showing of it in the studio once, I remember Richard Lippold came." Marianne Simon remembers that there were again long stillnesses in the piece. Carolyn Brown says that "compared to the other pieces of his that I'd done, except for *Septet*, it seemed to me the most lyrical and dancey, and even conventional, in a way, though certainly the music wasn't conventional."

That music's composer, Earle Brown, has said,

Springweather and People, 1955 (first version). MC and Carolyn Brown. Pages 86–87: MC's choreographic notes for *Suite by Chance*, 1956.

Merce gave me his time structure, which I meditated upon and then ignored. I composed the piece in my own way, just making a relationship to his time, the time of his dancing. I remember the worry that the dancers, or Merce . . . had about using the music, getting to know the music too well, and keying off it too often. The score of *Springweather* is full of tremendously dense, chaotic things and also places where there's a long, long held note or two. The density of the music fluctuates widely. Merce did not know my music for the work when he choreographed the piece; and when I first experienced the music and dance together, I was astonished at how effective the lack of synchronization was, dramatically—if you let yourself be taken by the drama that wasn't put into it but was there anyway, intrinsically.

An extraordinary moment in it was Merce coming out of the wings in a leap at a point in the music when there was only one note being played on a violin. Merce flew on the one held note. A dancer other than Merce—a composer other than myself—would have supported that leap with a dramatic musical flourish. . . . Merce's leap was stunning dramatically the way it joined that one violin note, much more astonishing than it would have been to anything else I could have written in order to support it.[1]

The music, composed especially for the dance, was played in a piano transcription at the first performances. At the performance of a revised version at Brooklyn on 30 November 1957 (in fact the last performance of the dance in its complete form), the music was played in its orchestral version.

As to the "artistic collaboration" on the costumes, Remy Charlip believes that he did most of them: "I was very interested in accordion pleating, and most of the women's costumes were of silk that was accordion pleated, it was very beautiful. I'm not sure now what the other people did—maybe we worked out some things together."[2]

• • •

In July the company danced at Jacob's Pillow Dance Festival in Lee, Massachusetts, sharing a program with Alicia Alonso and Erik Bruhn and the Spanish dancer La Mariquita, a mixture of ballet, modern, and ethnic dance typical of the program's promoter, Ted Shawn. In the fall, after a couple of dates in New York State (one in New City on a night when it

THE IMPERMANENT ART (1952)

There has been a shift of emphasis in the practice of the arts of painting, music and dancing during the last few years. There are no labels yet but there are ideas. These ideas seem primarily concerned with something being exactly what it is in its time and place, and not in its having actual or symbolic reference to other things. A thing is just that thing. It is good that each thing be accorded this recognition and this love. Of course, the world being what it is—or the way we are coming to understand it now—we know that each thing is also every other thing, either actually or potentially. So we don't, it seems to me, have to worry ourselves about providing relationships and continuities and orders and structures—they cannot be avoided. They are the nature of things. They are ourselves and our materials and our environment. If a dancer dances—which is not the same as having theories about dancing or wishing to dance or trying to dance or remembering in his body someone else's dance—but if the dancer *dances*, everything is there. The meaning is there, if that's what you want. It's like this apartment where I live—I look around in the morning and ask myself, what does it all mean? It means: this is where I live. When I dance, it means: this is what I am doing. A thing is just that thing. In painting, now, we are beginning to see the painting, and not the painter nor the painted. We are beginning to see how a painted space is. In music, we are beginning to hear free of our well-tempered ears.

In dance, it is the simple fact of a jump being a jump, and the further fact of what shape the jump takes. This attention given the jump eliminates the necessity to feel that the meaning of dancing lies in everything but the dancing, and further eliminates cause-and-effect worry as to what movement should follow what movement, frees one's feelings about continuity, and makes it clear that each act of life can be its own history: past, present and future, and can be so regarded, which helps to break the chains that too often follow dancers' feet around.

There doesn't seem to me the need to expound any longer on the idea that dance is as much a part of life as anything else. Since it takes place in one form or another almost constantly, that is evidence enough. The play of bodies in space—and time. When I choreograph a piece by tossing pennies—by chance, that is—I am finding my resources in that play, which is not the product of *my* will, but which is an energy and a law which I too obey. Some people seem to think that it is inhuman and mechanistic to toss pennies in creating a dance instead of chewing the nails or beating the head against a wall or thumbing through old notebooks for ideas. But the feeling I have when I compose in this way is that I am in touch with a natural resource far greater than my own personal inventiveness could ever be, much more universally human than the particular habits of my own practice, and organically rising out of common pools of motor impulses.

Since dance as a part of life seems self-evident enough—a few words about what dance is not. "Not this, not that." Dance is not social relationships. Though it may influence them. Dance is not emoting, passion for her, anger against him. I think dance is more primal than that. In its essence, in the nakedness of its energy it is a source from which passion or anger may issue in a particular form, the source of energy out of which may be channeled the energy that goes into the various emotional behaviors. It is that blatant exhibiting of this energy, i.e., of energy geared to an intensity high enough to melt steel in some dancers, that gives the great excitement. This is not feeling about something, this is a whipping of the mind and body into an action that is so intense, that for the brief moment involved, the mind and body are one. The dancer knows how solidly he must be aware of this centering when he dances. And it is just this very fusion at a white heat that gives the look of objectivity and serenity that a fine dancer has.

Our ecstasy in dance comes from the possible gift of freedom, the exhilarating moment that this exposing of the bare energy can give us. What is meant is not license, but freedom, that is, a complete awareness of the world and at the same time a detachment from it.

In thinking about contemporary dance, I am concerned here with the concert dance, I find that it is the connection with the immediacy of the action, the single instant, that gives the feeling of man's freedom. The body shooting into space is not an idea of man's freedom, but is the body shooting into space. And that very action is all other actions, and is man's freedom, and at the same instant his non-freedom. You see how it is no trouble at all to get profound about dance. It seems to be a natural double for metaphysical paradox.

In reference to the current idea that dance must be expressive of something and that it must be involved with the images deep within our conscious and unconscious, it is my impression that there is no need to push for them. If these primordial, pagan or otherwise archetypical images lie deep within us, they will appear, regardless of our likes and dislikes, once the way is open. It is simply a matter of allowing it to happen. The dancer's discipline, his daily rite, can be looked at in this way: to make it possible for the spirit to move through his limbs and to extend its manifestations into space, with all its freedom and necessity. I am no more philosophical than my legs, but from them I sense this fact: that they are infused with energy that can be released in movement (to appear to be motionless is its own kind of intoxicating movement)—that the shape the movement takes is beyond the fathoming of my mind's analysis but clear to my eyes and rich to my imagination. In other words, a man is a two-legged creature—more basically and more intimately than he is anything else. And his legs speak more than they "know"—and so does all nature. So if you really dance —your body, that is, and not your mind's enforcement—the manifestations of the spirit through your torso and your limbs will inevitably take on the shape of life. We give ourselves away at every moment. We do not, therefore, have to *try* to do it. Our racial memory, our ids and egos, whatever it is, is there. If it is there, it is there; we do not need to pretend that we have to put it there. In one of my most recent solo works, called "Untitled Solo," I choreographed the piece with the use of "chance" methods. However, the dance as performed seems to have an unmistakable dramatic intensity in its bones, so to speak. It seems to me that it was simply a question of "allowing" this quality to happen rather than of "forcing" it. It is this "tranquillity" of the actor or dancer which seems to me essential. A tranquillity which allows him to detach himself and thereby *to present* freely and liberally. Making of himself such a kind of nature puppet that he is as if dancing on a string which is like an umbilical cord: mother-nature and father-spirit moving his limbs, without thought.

My use of chance methods in finding continuity for dances is not a position which I wish to establish and die defending. It is a present mode of freeing my imagination from its own clichés and it is a marvelous adventure in attention. Our attention is, normally, highly selective and highly editorial. But try looking at events another way and the whole world of gesture, the whole physical world in fact, is as if jabbed by an electric current.

It has been a growing interest in "each thing-ness" that has led me to the use of chance methods in finding dance continuity.* In my case, and for one particular work, this involved an elaborate use of charts from which came the particular movements, the rhythm (that is, the division and the duration of the time they were done in), and the space they appear in and how they divide it. There were separate charts for each of the three elements—movement, time, and space. Then I tossed pennies to select a movement from the movement chart, and this was followed by tossing pennies to find the duration of that particular movement, and following that the space and direction of the movement were tossed for. This method might lead one to suspect the result as being possibly geometric and "abstract," unreal and non-human. On the contrary, it is no more geometric than the lines of a mountain are, seen from an airplane; it is no more abstract than any human being is, and as for reality, it is just that, it is not abstracted from something else, but is the thing itself, and moreover allows each dancer to be just as human as he is.

One of the things that has interested me for a long time, is how our balance works, not the fact that we can balance in many different ways and so find out how many ways, but just that we do balance at all, and how. On two legs or one. Dancing has two things in it: balance of the weight, and shift of that weight in space and time, that is, in greater or smaller areas, and over longer or shorter lengths of time. It depends upon the flexibility of the architecture of the body. The variety of that flexibility is limited only by the imagination of the dancer and you can see where that has brought us already. I suppose there are actually relatively few movements that we do, and it's probably most pleasant for the dancer in his searching for movement if he lights upon one of these in a straightforward simple way. Lack of fullness in a particular movement, or exaggeration of a movement outside the particular limits of its own shape and rhythm produces mannerism, I should think. And, equally so, the fullest possible doing of a particular movement with the minimum necessity of visible energy and the clearest precision in each element of that movement might possibly produce style. But when this is allowed to go out the window for further effect, prolongation of pose for bravura or other such delights of the performer's ego, then the first thing lost is serenity, and in the rush to catch up, the dancer stumbles, expressively if not physically.

Buckminster Fuller, the architect, once spoke of his feeling that man had migrated around the globe via two means: with the wind, that is under sail and perhaps eastward generally; and against the wind, that is across the land. This image of movement and resistance somehow makes me think of how an idea of mobile and static could be witnessed in the ways a dancer can be trained. The prime motivation can either be made a static one, that is by letting the position of the torso come first within the possibilities of its flexibility, and then to that adding the activity of the legs, or the prime motivation can be put in the legs, making a mobile situation upon which the back and upper limbs rest. This all presumes that a relationship runs up and down the spine into the arms and legs, to begin with, and that the base of the torso where the legs join the back both stops the action of the limbs and allows it to continue. And the wondrousness of being free and clear with both of these bodily components at the same time!

But the pleasure of dance does not lie in its analysis, though one might sometimes be led to think otherwise. Dancing is a lively human activity which by its very nature is part of all of us, spectators and performers alike. It's not the discussion, it's the doing and seeing—of whatever kind. As an adolescent I took lessons in various forms of American popular stage dancing including tap and a kind of exhibition ballroom. But my teacher insisted there was not such a thing as just "tap," there was "the waltz clog," "the southern soft shoe," "the buck and wing," and all were different, and she would proceed to show us how they were different. The rhythm in each case was the inflecting force that gave each particular dance its style and color. The tempo for a slower dance, for instance, allowed for a certain weight and swing and stopping of the arms that wasn't indicated in a faster dance. These lessons eventually led to performances in various halls as the entertainers for local events and finally a short and intoxicating "vaudeville tour." I remember one of these situations when we (there were four of us) stood huddled and cold in a sort of closet that was the lone dressing room, behind the tiny platform that was the stage this time, and our teacher was in the front of the hall making last minute preparations. Finally she hurried back, took one look at the four of us, and smiled and said, "All right, kids, we haven't any make-up, so bite your lips and pinch your cheeks, and you're on." It was a kind of theatre energy and devotion she radiated. This was a devotion to dancing as an instantaneous and agreeable act of life. All my subsequent involvements with dancers who were concerned with dance as a conveyor of social message or to be used as a testing ground for psychological types have not succeeded in destroying that feeling Mrs. Barrett gave me that dance is most deeply concerned with each single instant as it comes along, and its life and vigor and attraction lie in just that singleness. It is as accurate and impermanent as breathing.

—MERCE CUNNINGHAM

* The actual technique of "choreography by chance" is the subject of an article by Remy Charlip in the January 1954 issue of *Dance Magazine*.

rained so torrentially that the audience was unable to leave the theater after the performance, and one at Sarah Lawrence College), the company flew to the West Coast to perform in Santa Barbara, Los Angeles (at the University of California), San Francisco, Portland, Tacoma, and finally Seattle, traveling between cities in borrowed cars.

It was on this tour that Nicola Cernovich (Nicholas Cernovitch) joined the company as lighting designer. Cernovich, a friend of Charlip's, had been a student at Black Mountain, where he worked in photography and graphic arts as well as dance, and had participated in Cage's 1952 theater piece. In New York, he had been working at the Orientalia bookstore on Fourth Avenue. He learned about stage lighting from a book Charlip gave him, and in later years became celebrated in the profession.

In the fall, Cunningham staged some dances for the production by the Living Theater of a play by Paul Goodman, *The Young Disciple*, subtitled "a martyrology in three acts," directed and designed by Julian Beck. Music for a song in the play, "The Midnight Sun," was composed by Ned Rorem, but Cunningham used music from Pierre Schaeffer's *Symphonie pour un homme seul* (the music for *Collage*) for his dances.

1956

In May 1956 the company had a single out-of-town date, at the University of Notre Dame in South Bend, Indiana, where three new dances received their first performance. Unfortunately the concert's date proved to coincide with that of the university's commencement exercises, so the show had hardly any audience.

GALAXY

Galaxy, as its subtitle ("a quartet of solos") indicated, consisted of four solos performed simultaneously. A program note enlarged on this idea:

> The complexity of this dance and its music is in imitation of complex situations in nature, where, for instance, air, earth, fire, and water act at one and the same time.[1]

I tried in the making of each solo to keep it separate space-wise, there were possibly some things I had to arrange when they did it, but that was the principle and each solo I tried to make as different as possible, I made it on the dancer, for the particular dancer, and it was really a solo which didn't relate to the others at all. So there were four separate things going on at the same time, but they were long, rather than fragments, whatever it was, a three- or four-minute dance. It was very fast.

I don't remember whether I wrote out things or simply made the dance. But I would do one and then, in a sense, try to forget it, so when I made another one I wouldn't relate it to the one that had gone before, except to remember some way where it went in the space. The random element was the disconnection between the four people—it wasn't made with chance procedures, it was made on the four dancers. I just made a dance for each one in that length of time, each one had not only different movements but different structure. They were made so that they could be done together or separately.

Earle Brown's score is composed according to his "open form" idea, and he has written that *Galaxy* was Cunningham's "first truly 'open form' [spontaneous performance] dance. . . . It was a very severe and 'classic' dance and very difficult to do, and perhaps to watch." Cunningham, he says, was afraid that the dancers would collide.[2]

Charlip's costumes were notable for their exuberant fantasy: Brown's was decorated with feathers, Farber's with many-colored buttons sewn to the leotard over her abdomen, Preger's had a gold satin cape with lamé lining, and Charlip's incorporated Indian embroidery with small pieces of mirror.

LAVISH ESCAPADE

Subtitled "An adventure into an uncharted territory,"[3] this was the second in Cunningham's trilogy of solos to music by Christian Wolff.

> The trilogy used chance procedures in the choreography, sometimes in the smallest of fragments and at others in large ways only. David Tudor would present a program of piano music and there would be one of these works in it. I would hear the piece, and immediately afterwards ask Xian if he would allow me to make a dance with it. He was always generous.[4]

Lavish Escapade was made with the same principle as *Untitled Solo*, with an enormous number of gamuts of movement which were then put together, which was frightfully difficult.

These gamuts included movements not only for various parts of the body (e.g., "sitting on derrière and moving by haunches") but for the head and face as well—the eyes, eyebrows, and mouth (Cunningham's notes to himself list the sources of these as Noh masks, eye exercises, and Indian books).

Very often, you did something slow with your arm, for example, and something rapid with your feet—but the arm had to do something large against this—and this set up a kind of opposition. It was physically very difficult for me to do—I tried very hard to keep the rhythms, not to let them slip. And also the juxtapositions, because of the chance thing, of getting from one thing to another, just the getting to it, and I didn't do anything about that other than go there as directly as I could—that in itself was part of the drama, because just to do that was so intense. It wasn't a question of

John Cage with prepared piano, 1950s.

result, *Lavish Escapade*, in performance, had the terrifying and inescapable intensity of a nightmare.

SUITE FOR FIVE

Suite for Five in Space and Time (the last four words were soon dropped from the title) was made by adding a trio, a duet, and a quintet to Cunningham's earlier *Solo Suite in Space and Time*. (Cunningham originally also planned a sextet, with Bruce King as the third male dancer, but King was unavailable during part of the rehearsal period and the cast was reduced to five.) The piece underwent various modifications during the next two years, reaching its definitive version in Muncie, Indiana, on 1 July 1958, where Cunningham's solos were reduced from five to three, and a solo ("A Meander") for Carolyn Brown was added.

A program note read,

> The events and sounds of this ballet revolve around a quiet center, which, though silent and unmoving, is the source from which they happen.[6]

The music was Cage's *Music for Piano (4–84)*, of which the composer wrote,

> The sounds of this music correspond to imperfections in the paper upon which the music was written. The number of sounds on a given page and other aspects of the composition were determined by chance operations. The dynamics, tempo, and the nature of the noises are determined by the pianists.[7]

Cunningham accordingly

> decided to do the same thing to ascertain the space points for a dance called *Suite for Five in Time and Space* [*sic*]. The Suite eventually came to comprise seven dances. The spacial [*sic*] plan for each dance was the starting point. Using transparent paper as a grid, a bird's-eye view of the playing space, I marked and numbered the imperfections, a page for each dancer in each of the dances. In the *Duet*, the *Trio* and the *Quintet* I superimposed the pages for each dancer to find if there were points where they came together and would allow for partnering or held poses, some form of liaison between them. The time was found by taking lined paper, each line representing five-second intervals. Imperfections were again noted on the paper and the time lengths of phrases obtained from chance

technical problems, jumping, or multiple spins, or things like that, but the positions were so awkward, to do fully and then get to the next one, and do it fully, to do them so that they made some kind of dance sense.

Cunningham himself knitted the costume, a kind of union suit in multicolored stripes with one very long leg. The chance possibilities even included changes in the costume.

Although Cunningham insists that the dramatic quality in this and the other two dances in the Wolff "trilogy" is inherent in the movement, it seems possible that the experience of working on *Untitled Solo* made him anticipate a similar intensity in *Lavish Escapade*, and that he allowed for it. At all events, his notes divide the dance into four sections whose titles adumbrate a dramatic progression:

#I Hatch scheme
#II Reset stage
#III The Trial[5]
#IV Dénouement

Elsewhere in his notes the phrase "under duress" appears, and the word "necromancer," which would seem to indicate that the combinations of movement arrived at by chance suggested certain images to him.

The choreography followed the structure of the music, and the fact that, as Cunningham puts it, "you have a certain amount of activity to do within a certain amount of time creates a kind of urgency." As a

numbering of the imperfections in relation to the number of seconds.

This was one of the first dances where meter was completely abandoned, and we, the dancers, had to rely on our own dance timing to guard the length of any phrase, and the timing of a complete dance.

Cage's *Music for Piano*, which was played with the dance, is variable in time. Although the dancers came to know the sequences of sounds, the sounds do not necessarily happen at the same points from performance to performance. And, as sometimes occurred, with the addition of pianists and pianos, the sound was augmented and the original piece had other layers with it.

The total length of a given dance, however, remained identical each time. Through many performances, the duration of the pieces varied little. After a period of, say, three months of not rehearsing, the dancers (assuming they were the same ones, of course) would come within five to ten seconds of a two-minute and forty-five-second dance.[8]

The action of the dances is deliberate, that is, the movements are short or long, often surrounded by stillness and allowed to take place without strict regard for musical cues. The movements may strike or not with the sounds. . . .

The dances . . . were all designed to be presented with the audience on four sides and are so given when situations allow for this. The space and directions were accepted as they happened rather than adjusting the dancers to make lines or face each other.[9]

Exits and entrances were arranged to suit existing aisles, or if arranged by us, the aisles were placed at the four corners.[10]

Paradoxically, perhaps, one of the most notable attributes of *Suite for Five* was its classic purity and serenity. When asked about this, Cunningham said,

I always thought it had that quality when we first did it, not only the shapes and all that but the way it's so clearly what it is, it doesn't pretend to be anything else. You have to be able to do large movement clearly in that piece, and not do any excess. In the beginning we always did it on these terribly tiny stages, but as we began to get on bigger stages, it worked; we began to go out—we knew where we were supposed to be in the space, so that without adding anything to the movement, you make it take you where you need to be in a new space, and that makes the movement get bigger. That's how you do that kind of thing—you don't add things, you make the thing itself bigger.

I think it's that kind of thing, and also the fact that we were able to continue the class work, that kept us going. There wasn't anything else, I mean in the dancing part—there were ideas, but things happen only when you dance, you can go on talking forever.

The classic element was especially notable in the duet, "Suspended Moment," which was even constructed, by coincidence or not, like a classic ballet pas de deux in miniature. Following Cunningham's second solo, "Stillness," there was a blackout. When the lights came up Cunningham was kneeling center stage, facing stage right, holding Brown balanced horizontally across his shoulder, arms outstretched. In this position he slowly rotated on his knees. When the rotation was complete, Brown stepped down. There followed a series of supported poses, after which Cunningham moved away from Brown on a backward diagonal, very close to the floor, first with one leg then the other stretched out behind him, his arms to the side with the hands pressed against the floor. Before each shift of weight from one leg to the other, he sharply struck the floor with the tips of his fingers. After a brief solo by Brown, the duet ended with a fast coda full of sissonne-like jumps.

The trio and quintet were more unconventional, even arbitrary. "The dancers," Cage wrote, "are often alone or independent, even when several are on the stage at the same time. Out of this solitude, meetings take place between them, brief or extended."[11] The separate paths traced by the dancers and the clusters they formed when they came together typified Cunningham's spatial concept:

one dancer might be jumping up and down in one place while another moved swiftly in a diagonal and a third and fourth briefly held a supported pose. (As a kind of equivalent to the silences in Cage's music, Cunningham's choreography at this time was punctuated by long moments of immobility.)

As always, there was a sculptural quality in the groupings formed when dancers came together, however fortuitously—for example, the moment in the trio when the two women stood facing each other with arms outstretched, their hands joined together with palms flat, and the man hung from their shoulders. An indelible image is the final one of the trio, when Marianne Preger, left alone on the stage, held her arms straight in front of her, moved them up and down several times from the elbow, then slowly straightened them again as she arched her torso backward.

Even when reduced in number from five to three, Cunningham's solos testified to his virtuosity, in terms not only of elevation and speed but of slow, sustained movement. The first solo, "At Random," began with him standing with feet together and slowly bending his knees until he was squatting on his heels, from which position he stretched out first one leg, then the other, in front of him, after which he rose to the standing position again. His innate sense of drama informed even the simple deep plié in second position with which this solo ended. The isolated sounds of Cage's score—struck on the keyboard or the woodwork of the piano, or plucked on its strings—made for a calm, pellucid atmosphere in which the movements were seen with perfect clarity.

NOCTURNES
in five parts, "from dusk to the witching hour"

As a result of the company's performances at Jacob's Pillow in the summer of 1955, Ted Shawn commissioned a new work from Cunningham:

A new work? A light one? *Nocturnes*. . . . But I asked for a light work! [Cunningham is summarizing Ted Shawn's com-

plaint.] Well, it's all in white. It has been described as "a sequence of rendezvous." I like that description. It was for six dancers and the movement was complex. I made separate lines for each dancer. Occasionally a line for a dancer crosses one nocturne to the next (e g Viola Farber, No 2 and No 3). I was interested in finding a chance procedure that would function in terms of the music and the atmosphere of the music, composing to a written piano score, the five Nocturnes of Satie.[12] Movement phrases were kept somewhat free of musical phrases perhaps beginning with the sound but taking [their] own time, now and then ending with the phrase. The random operations gave the separateness of the dancers—where they might come together. Also much of the time-length. The rest was done on the dancers and with the music.[13]

Nocturnes was a white ballet. . . . There were 6 dancers who would divide into couples momentarily, and then fragment into 6 individuals who appeared in the space and disappeared from it, or remained only partially seen. . . . I have only a few scattered notations and some photos. One note reads: Categories—passing steps, adagios, physical feats, stances (stillness). The 4th dance was a duet for Viola Farber and myself. What an extraordinary supple quality she had![14]

Some of the movements were developed in Cunningham's classes:

I set up not only fragments of steps but semi-sequences, which might be used in the chance

gamut, and might come up in such a different order that the arrangement would not be one that you could predict. I kept trying to find things that would move through space.

The music was given: I divided each Nocturne into large sections, and there was silence in between the pieces in which we did something, and I tried to allow for that in the chance procedure. The detail had to be related more or less to the music, to its rhythm. I also divided each person's part up—not in every piece, but in some of them. I made a gamut of movement for each of the dancers, and allowed for the fact that they might come together, and when they came together I would do it on the music. And also I tried to set up a different movement gamut for each piece. For example, it opened up with three or four people, Viola and Carolyn, and maybe the two men—I didn't come in right away, and Marianne came in later, that was part of the chance thing. And then when Marianne entered, although that came on a musical structural point, still it was a chance thing that she would come in then—the structure was made that way.

All through the pieces there are joinings, when two people join and separate; at one point when it came out to two people I decided to make a duet out of it. . . . I allowed the music structure to take care of the length.

As with *Septet*, Cunningham gave the five sections of the piece working titles:

#1 Children at dusk
#2 Bits and pieces of night

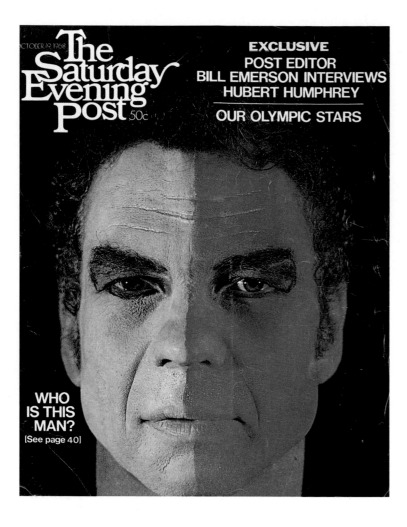

#3 Metamorphoses (trees to humans to clouds
to leaves to arms to water to bodies to mist)
#4 L'Amour
#5 Black and sorrow (witching hour).

In this case the titles were never printed in the program, but simply reduced to the subtitle, "from dusk to the witching hour."

I'm sure that the music itself, the quality of the music, had a lot to do with the quality of
the movement—since I was using the music,
I would listen to it, I had records. John came sometimes and played for rehearsals.

Nocturnes possessed an unusual consistency, and indeed potency, of atmosphere, tranquil and mysterious as a landscape seen in bright moonlight. (P. W. Manchester described it as a "moonstruck masquerade."[15]) The piece was almost a collaboration in the Diaghilev sense, with choreographer and artist working to realize the same conception.

Rauschenberg's designs for *Nocturnes* were among the most beautiful he made for Cunningham. The stage was divided into two areas, each with its own atmosphere. To stage left at the rear there was a scrim through which the dancers could be dimly seen. The rest of the stage was open and bathed in white light. "When

the image of night was presented to Robert Rauschenberg," Cage would write, "he thought of moonlight."[16]

It was the first performance of *Nocturnes* in New York. It was also the small stage in the Brooklyn Academy of Music. Rauschenberg had put up the set, the scrim was a transparent white net, and the opaque structure at the side was a wooden frame covered with white oilcloth. We had just finished our rehearsal and the firemen arrived. "You can't use that, you will have to change it." "But the performance is tonight." "So, change it, or we will close your show." They left and a great silence. Rauschenberg said, don't worry, I'll figure out something. Bleakly, we dressed and went off to eat and rest, leaving Rauschenberg (and [Jasper] Johns?) in the middle of the stage looking at the oilcloth.

We returned several hours later, to find the two of them covering the frame with green boughs of what looked like a rubber plant. It had become a garden, fresh and slightly wet. Rauschenberg was on a ladder, smiling at us.[17]

The hastily improvised set was used at this performance only; as Cunningham has said, "They would have had to go into the woods every time." At subsequent performances the flat was replaced by an ingenious collapsible arrangement made of white satin that could be expanded or contracted to fit any height of stage.

According to Cunningham, the scrim that extended from the flat to the wings came about as a result of chance procedures:

When I came to the place where I decided to make a duet for Viola and myself, there was something in the chance procedure about other people, but separate from the two people, so then I thought of the possibility of having that thing in the back, because that could be some kind of separate arrangement, and that went on all the way through. . . . There were places in the duet where we held, where the possibility of silence came up, or being still, and I put that on the musical structure—that we would be still at this point, I think there were two or three points like that. But the people in the back weren't still—they weren't there all through the piece, they entered and were there for a while, then they went away.

The duet was one of Cunningham's most lyrical and tender, with beautiful lifts. The piece also contained some of his characteristic sculptural groupings, such as the "star" configuration. Cunningham's own role exploited his elevation. The final image was unforgettable: Cunningham behind the scrim, jumping up and down, his hands fluttering, like a moth at a window screen.

The dancers' basic costume was white tights, with white leotards for the women and white shirts for the men. (When Rauschenberg told Cunningham this, he said, "Then I won't put any falls in it.") Rauschenberg designed the men's makeup, with one side of the face painted white and the other a color (red, yellow, or blue). The women wore fantastic headdresses—Rauschenberg "had in mind 'inhabited seashells' and the water-colors of Holbein."[18] Carolyn Brown wore a small round mirror on top of her head, and at certain points a white shoulder-length veil; when the mirror caught the light it shone like the evening star. For her duet with Cunningham, Viola Farber wore an arch-shaped structure of white net stretched on a wire frame that fitted over her arms. Marianne Preger wore a square white headdress like an oversized mortar-board with tassels at each corner. Preger wore bracelets and Farber garters made of pink stones.

1957

The year began with a performance at the Brooklyn Academy of Music (again in the Music Hall) on 12 January, at which *Minutiae* was given for the last time.

On 27 April, at Cunningham's suggestion, four choreographers—Shirley Broughton, Katherine Litz, Merle Marsicano, and himself—took part in a symposium at the Henry Street Playhouse, with the present writer as moderator. Following this, works by each of the choreographers were performed, with the Cunningham company dancing *Suite for Five*. Cunningham's statement was precise and poetic:

The nature of dancing is stillness in movement and movement in stillness, as a plant waits to grow, or as the flash of lightning hangs in the air. No stillness exists without movement, and no movement is fully expressed without stillness.

But stillness acts of itself, not hampered before or after. It is not a pause or a premonition.

If one thinks of dance as an errand to accomplish, as a message to be sent, then one misses the *spring* along the way. If one's concern is self-expression, then the proper area is psychoanalysis.

You are standing on a street corner waiting for a friend. He is late, or you think he is late; your impatience grows because he does not come. You see everyone and everything in a *not*-relation; everything and everyone is not the person you await. Finally he arrives, and you find he's not late at all. But your anxiety has kept

you from seeing and has created only more nervousness.

Stand on the same street corner waiting again, but without anxiety about when the errand will be accomplished. Now this is theater. Visually aware, you see that each individual passing, walking, or standing still, is different, that he moves differently, that the store fronts are different as different people stand looking into the windows; that, without any intention of being self-expressive, each person is extraordinarily so. Each action as it happens, and as you are aware of it, is absorbing. It doesn't make much difference whether your friend arrives on time or late. You have been a spectator in the audience, using your faculties as you watch the players in action.

Dancing is of divine origin, and to try to express that divinity is like pinning jelly to a wall. It only escapes you. It expresses itself if one gives one's life to dancing out of love for it, out of reverence for the nature of its action, and the discipline necessary to allow for that action.

The source of life in any dancer is his inactivity in a gesture or movement. It is equally so for the spectator who wants to share that life. That is, the liveliness that dancing can have is not in what the movement comes from, but in what it actually is as the dancer does it, and how it is surrounded and inhabited by stillness. When stillness also lives in a spectator's mind, he will perceive the movement as though he himself had done it.

The most revealing and absorbing moments of life are the ones that have no past or future— that happen, as it were, without relevance— when the action, the actor, and the spectator are unidentified—when the mind, also, is caught in mid-air.[1]

Cunningham spent much of the summer teaching on the West Coast: in July, at the Idyllwild Arts Foundation and the Welland-Lathrop Studio in San Francisco; on 13 July he gave a lecture-demonstration at Ann[a] Halprin's Dance Deck in Marin County, where he remembers turning his head in a solo from *Suite for Five* and seeing a full moon; and in August he taught at Gloria Newman Schoenberg and Nik Krevitsky's Sark Studio in Los Angeles, and at the Dance Drama School in Long Beach. In the fall he resumed teaching at the Dance Players Studio in New

Opposite: MC in the makeup designed by Robert Rauschenberg for *Nocturnes*, 1956. Photograph: John Launois.

York, and, once a week, for the Dance Circle of Boston.[2]

He also began rehearsals for another performance in the Music Hall at the Brooklyn Academy of Music on 30 November, at which the company would give three new works and the revised and redesigned version of *Springweather and People*, which had not been seen in New York; this was, however, also its last performance in its entirety.

LABYRINTHIAN DANCES

in four parts, "area without exit"

This was first performed at the Brooklyn Academy Music Hall, the small lecture-hall that had been converted into a stage, a fair width, but no depth. The dance was designed for a square box-like space with all sides equal. Of course, there is give-and-take on this, as few stages arrange themselves that way, but can a postcard be a cube? When we toured the dance immediately following this first performance, it was presented several times on stages with an adequate playing space. The dance turned out to be a different work. It was not just the opportunity to finally have room enough to do the steps, but that the separation of the dancers in degree could be made visible, and one of the probabilities in the choreography could be made actual.[3]

Josef Matthias Hauer was a composer of the Viennese school who had invented a twelve-tone system of his own.[4] David Tudor brought his music to Cun-

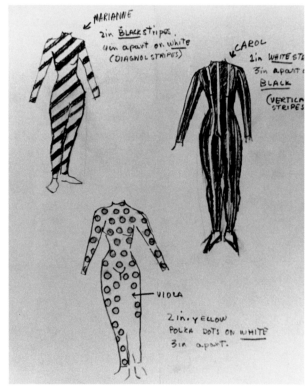

This page: Robert Rauschenberg's decor and costume designs for *Labyrinthian Dances*, 1957. Opposite: *Merce Cunningham, Dancer 6*, 1957. Photograph: Imogen Cunningham.

ningham with the proposal that it be used for a dance. The dance's title is taken from that of one of Hauer's four-handed piano pieces.

That was a very geometrical kind of dance, the same way the music was so ordered . . . the dance had an architecture. The dancers never left the stage, it was as though they were inside some kind of square. The reason we didn't do it many times was that I didn't want to do it [on inadequate stages], so I just made something else. But I liked the idea of an area that you can't get out of, but it's full of passage-ways, like

98

a maze—there's no escape, but you really don't know that.

Cunningham's notes for the piece have been lost, and he has no clear recollection of the compositional process:

> I was using the musical structure, and, given the idea of an "area without exit" in which everybody would stay, I used a chance procedure for the space, but what it was I don't remember. And I think it also allowed for those times when people were there, in any particular spot.

Margaret Lloyd wrote that "the dancers moved in orbits of their own, for the most part ignoring each other, but not for a moment allowing us to ignore them."[5] This may indicate that Cunningham's chance process involved a different movement gamut for each dancer. Although Cunningham naturally made no overt reference to the legend of the Minotaur, the title of Hauer's music, *Labyrinthischer Tanz*, may have prompted the use of the kind of movement often described as "archaic": two-dimensional, angular, with the dancers seen in profile.

The music was "troublesome" for the dancers, difficult to count, according to Carolyn Brown. She remembers that Marianne Preger (who had changed her name to Simon on her marriage) had an adagio section with slow extensions, while the others did "strange turning things" around her.[6]

Rauschenberg's set consisted of a large white cube, six feet square, with black circles, four feet in diameter, painted on it. (As can be seen from the design,

EXCERPTS FROM LECTURE-DEMONSTRATION GIVEN AT ANN HALPRIN'S DANCE DECK (13 JULY 1957)

. . . . Dancing is an act of concentration taking visible form in a way that cannot be done otherwise. It is its own necessity. It is an old art, and it is a manifestation of man's activity. It has changed as man has inhabited the world, and as man's habits have changed. Yet of course it remains the same. And dance from one corner of the globe to its opposite has a similarity. Watching some folk dancers in Mexico last summer, I saw they were using the sides of their feet for moving, including large jumps into the air, and it immediately brought to mind the wild leaping in the same fashion of the Kathakali dancers of India.

. . . . The dancer starts with two legs, and the two basic things this reveals as applied to movement are: first, the balance of any given position; and second, how to shift from that balance to any other balance. How in other words to maintain balance in a flexible fashion so as to be able to move in a variety of ways, and in different intensities.

But how to find out about this balance, and these changes of balance and how to make them work in our own bodies? To begin with, the human body has clear and defined limitations. We cannot move as the serpents do, and what is more we cannot quite understand how they move, and this is one of the causes of our fear of them—as Emily Dickinson said, it was one of nature's creatures that brought "zero to the bone," but even closer to us, we cannot move as the antelopes, or the elephants, or even the dogs that inhabit our world so familiarly. The structure of the human body permits of certain circumscribed actions. They are limited in species, but, within the species, infinite in variety. . . .

(Dance demonstration #1: at random, from *Suite for Five*)

Dance is movement of the human body in time and space. With the two, time and space, I find the first to be more flexible.

We can divide time in a freer way, in a more varied and complex way, and still make clear what is being done, while with space we can certainly be complex within the prescribed area, but it can look, not so much complex, as confusing.

Ordinarily, the dancer deals with a fixed space set by outside convention, the dimension a box with a view from one side.

But here on the dance deck there is a totally different situation. Aside from the obvious openness in the architectural arrangement, there is another freedom for the dancer. There is no necessity to face "front," to limit the focus to one side.

There are two points to deal with in space and one leads to the other:

1 the point you effect from, and
2 the direction affected.

That is, the dancer can be in a particular point in space and then, direct the body to any other point in the space. It is as though you are continually going from where you are, and not that you are relating to a downstage and an upstage or center stage. You are always the center, and so with each dancer if there is more than one. Perhaps there seems the danger of bumping, but as John Cage pointed out, one of the definitions of choreography is how not to bump, except when so desired.

One learns primarily by imitation in dance. Certainly for a long time the daily class is simply trying to imitate what is given by the teacher. But not only the exercises are to be "imitated," but the manners surrounding them, the way to begin and end an exercise for example. This is important for later on, as it is the exact knowing of each single instant that makes the dance alive, and if you do not know where you are before you begin, you will not know where you are when you begin.

(Dance demonstration #2: Beethoven [from *Dime a Dance*?])

This daily class or repetition that the dancer does each day can become boring or exhilarating, depending upon the attitude the dancer brings to it, that is, it is done as though it were an act of dance and thus can become meaningful to the dancer, or it is done as a necessary exercise. It is useless to bring the body to it, and that sluggishly, and leave the mind and spirit around the corner.

It is just this bringing into focus of everything, even if out of an hour-and-a-half class it happens for only a moment, it is just this pulling together that will give you a chance to let your instincts work for you. Involuntarily, people are forced to let their instincts work for them every day, walking, getting off a bus, holding bundles, crossing streets, turning corners. Our instincts help us in all of this. And in a dance class, a situation may be made in which these instincts work, in the fullest possible way, where the dancer learns to trust, not his mind, but the instinct that got us standing on two feet, and that with every child born in the world, gets it to doing the same thing. . . .

In this sense I do not understand how a human can do something that is abstract. Everything a human does is expressive in some way of that human. It may be a perverted action but that still implies human even if from rather than to or of.

For me there is an ecstasy in dance beyond the idea of movement being expressive of a particular emotion or meaning. There can be an exaltaton in the aura that the freedom of a disciplined dancer provides that is far beyond any literal rendition of meaning.

(Dance demonstration #3: *Untitled Solo*)

. . . . Continuity is what comes after what. Like when one says, this morning I will get up and have a cup of coffee, and then walk downstairs to see if the mail has arrived, and then shave, and then go to take a technique class, and then have lunch. Or I remember when I was ten being chided by the Sister for not setting the altar properly, and then the next time I served Mass I tried to do it so properly that I caught my surplice on fire, escaped to the sacristy hastily to remove it, and then had great trouble explaining to my mother that she would have to provide a new one. That is a continuity in memory. And history is one big continuity by being history.

So in composing a dance, in making a dance continuity, the procedure has been to discover how you feel or think one movement should follow another. What movement means in relation one to another.

But now there is a different way of looking at continuity. In contemporary art and music, one of the major interests has been the separation of each element, one left distinct from the other and having no connection, other than that they exist in the same time and space.

In my own work, wanting to find the utmost in freedom from my own feelings, directly, or my memory of continuities and ideas about how movement ought to follow one from another, I have used a chance procedure to obtain the continuity. That is, in the choreography, chance is used to dictate what movement followed any given movement, and correspondingly so, the time and space, that is, the duration and division of the given movement, and what place it happened in.

My feeling about dance continuity came from the view that life is constanty changing and shifting, that we live in a democratic society, and that people and things in nature are mutually independent of, and related to each other.

(Dance demonstration #4: "Stillness" from *Suite for Five*)

Dance is an independent art, but there is more variety when other elements are added; music, decor, costumes, lights. It becomes theatre.

With the music, in the same sense that the dance elements are separate from each other, that the individual dancers can be separated from each other, so with music, the relationship is one of time, of taking place in the same time and in so doing, allow for greater variety. In this way of working, time becomes the structure, the thin

web of steel on which the movement is hung, rather than the brick-by-brick masonry of themes of music, or sequences of movement.

Time is not meant as pulse or metronomic speed, but as span or length, and not evenly segmented like a ruler, but with the possibility of even and uneven, like a tree or a bush, the weather or the year.

. . . . Music for magnetic tape opens to the composer a world of sound that was not possible before. Both as to the kind of sound made available to compose with, and the actual process of composing.

For the dancer working with magnetic tape music, the principal concern is one of time. With it, time is no longer measured by meter or by a particular pulse.

It is measured by so many inches per second. This way of measuring time is also used by contemporary composers for music played on conventional instruments. David Tudor, the American pianist, has made a number of programs of contemporary American and European piano music both here and in Europe. Ordinarily he used a small regular stopwatch on the side of the piano to keep track of the tempo. But while in Cologne he was to play at the radio station, and there was a large stopwatch on the wall that he could use. While rehearsing, he noticed he could play more notes in the same time that it took the large clock to cover a second, than when he used his small watch.

. . . . This way of working is an extreme feeling about the nature of dance and choreography. By extreme I mean removed from the literal or the abstracted. It is a realistic approach to the materials of the art, fully open to the sensations and feelings that man brings to his actions.

It is done with the belief and full conviction that man is part of nature and society and that he inhabits his art actions with himself.

(Dance demonstration #5: *Collage*)

—MERCE CUNNINGHAM
(Revised by MC, February 1997)

101

Rauschenberg originally planned three cubes, but, presumably through lack of space, only one was used.) The only touches of color were the yellow polka dots on Viola Farber's costume. (According to Brown, the other women hated their costumes.)

CHANGELING

This dance completed Cunningham's trilogy of solos to piano music by Christian Wolff, of which the first two were *Untitled Solo*, 1953, and *Lavish Escapade*, 1956. All three represented the stranger, more disturbing side of Cunningham's imagination. According to Brown, Cunningham himself sometimes used to say that he was convinced that he was a changeling.

The dance, which involved chance procedures similar to those of the other two Wolff solos, was characterized by contorted body positions. Brown has commented, "The problems in dance lie in the limitations of the human body; though Cunningham did devise the movement for three solos for himself . . .

On 15 May 1958, there was "a retrospective concert of twenty-five years of the music of John Cage" at Town Hall in New York, with a distinguished company of musicians. The concert ended with the first performance of *Concert for Piano and Orchestra*, with David Tudor as solo pianist and an orchestra of thirteen players, conducted by Cunningham. According to a program note, this is

> a work without a score. The conductor, like the players, has his own part. He represents a chronometer of variable speed. . . . The orchestral accompaniment may involve any number of players on whatever instruments, and a given performance may be of any length.[1]

Cunningham, impeccably attired for the occasion in white tie and tails, stood before the orchestra and solemnly rotated his arms, each rotation representing a minute (in the score's terms, rather than in real time).[2]

A few days later, on 21 May, Cunningham and Carolyn Brown gave a concert at the University of Pittsburgh. The program included *Suite for Two* (the duet version of *Suite for Five*), with the addition of Brown's solo "A Meander," *Amores*, and a suite from *Springweather and People*. Cunningham also danced yet another version of his solo from *Collage* (still called *Collage I*, though in the future this solo would be called *Collage III*).

That summer, Cunningham and his company were invited for the first time to be in residence at the Connecticut College School of the Dance, in New London (7 July to 17 August). There Cunningham both taught classes and rehearsed two new works to be performed in the Eleventh American Dance Festival at the end of the session. Although he found the teaching and rehearsing schedule grueling, and certain faculty members were clearly not in sympathy with his aesthetic, the residency afforded six weeks in which he and his dancers were housed and fed and could rehearse without having to run off to jobs elsewhere, and this was a real luxury.

ANTIC MEET

Let me tell you that the absurd is only too necessary on earth.   —Ivan Karamazov[3]

"Meet" is used in the sense of an athletic meet; "clichés of vaudeville and various styles of dancing take the place of contests."[4]

Opposite: MC rehearsing *Changeling*, 1957. Photograph: Vytas Valaitis. Above: MC conducting John Cage's *Concert for Piano and Orchestra*, 1958.

by dividing the body into parts, listing the possibilities of those parts, and then superimposing one action on to the other by tossing coins to determine the final movement, he discovered that the execution of the resulting choreography was nearly impossible, and it took months of rehearsal to accomplish it."[7] Cunningham for his part has said that "all three succeeded in becoming continuous if I could wear them long enough, like a suit of clothes."[8] But Brown says that "in *Lavish Escapade*, some of the final movement superimpositions were so difficult he was never able to realize them completely."[9]

PICNIC POLKA

Picnic Polka was a companion piece to *Banjo* (1953), with which it was always performed. (*Banjo* was very short and the additional number made a more useful program item.) Again it was Tudor who suggested the music, *Ses yeux*, by Gottschalk. *Banjo* was a piano solo, but the music for *Picnic Polka* was a duet, which Tudor played with Cage. Both pieces were dropped from the repertory after half a dozen performances.

Robert Rauschenberg had asked Cunningham about his ideas for the pieces he would be working on during the summer. "That seemed reasonable," Cunningham says, so on 12 July 1958, he wrote Rauschenberg a letter. His notes on the dance for which Cage was to provide the music, "which I've barely begun and that should be unbegun," are unusually extensive:

momentary title and hoped-for actual:

Antic Meet

it's like a series of vaudeville scenes which overlap.

tentative outline:

approx-
imate
times:
3½′

1st scene with everyone. and maybe with a large stop-watch on the stage, which can be turned on by someone or turn of itself or not turn atall [sic]. also the whole thing might be slightly like an entrance parade.

2½′

2nd scene, duet with carol [Carolyn Brown] and me, i have chair strapped on back, which is like a large mosquito that won't go away. (I had thought of this as another person, but too difficult to do and also make dance) maybe chair is like a leech, like chairs are. this can be actual chair or made-up one, in any event it should be light weight, indeed! (also thought of using crutch here)

1½–2′

3rd scene, sport et divertissement, #1, viola, crossing with great trouble a huge square, tiniest possible movements of feet continuing for long, long time, she might be loaded down with bundles,

but some movement of arms and head, and torso, but not so headlong.

3′

4th scene, a kind of mock battle, whatever that means, maybe somebody gets stabbed in the back and hauled off or on, this has everyone in it, who can still stand up.

2–3′

5th scene, a tumbling act with one tumbler missing, but no one knows that but you and me. in the middle of act one goes off and comes back in overcoat, or large apron, or ? and continues. (sport et divertissement #2)

kind of half-way mark

4′

6th scene, street scene, comments of crowd, maybe balloons in costumes that can be shifted from back to front. a good deal of running in to each other. this is all sort of half-assed yet, but I have a few visions about it.

2½′

7th scene, this is the sweater act with four sleeves, and 4 girls like bacchantes and lamenting in long dresses, maybe transparent with the tights embroidered in large leaves.

2′

8th scene, shoot the chutes, everybody falling as though they didn't mean it. I've been working on this one, and the trouble is they do look as though they didn't mean it.

3′

9th scene, vaudeville number, a solo with a few interruptions, slightly like a rubber-leg dance.

Opposite: MC in "room for two," from *Antic Meet*, 1958. Photograph: Richard Rutledge. Opposite, inset: "room for two," from *Antic Meet*, 1958. Carolyn Brown and MC. Photograph: Marvin Silver. This page, left: "bacchus and cohorts," from *Antic Meet*, 1958. Left to right: Viola Farber, Carolyn Brown, Shareen Blair, Barbara Lloyd, and MC. Photograph: Marvin Silver. This page, right: "sports and diversions #2," from *Antic Meet*, 1958. Left to right: Remy Charlip, and MC. Photograph: Matthew Wysocki.

3½′ **10th scene**, exodus with banners, several varieties of [illegible—"hopping"?] movements, perhaps a game of hop-scotch, some jazz movements, and a little delsarte.

there are also many interruptions here and there: entrance in bathing suit, get under a large piece of cloth and emerge fully clothed including cloth.

I have one in mind that is like a very formal preparation for something that ends in disaster, I hope it will look like I've melted into the floor.

there are a few more undescribable as yet, in fact nothing is really, I must try it out.

I left one scene out, with cynthia and carol a short ballet number, in which one throws stones at the other, and the other dumps

water in retaliation, a few other things then they have a fight and leave.

this all comes from dostoevsky.[5]

I was in Connecticut and Bob was in New York, so I wrote him, and tried to make it clear what I was doing although it was changing, as you can tell from the letter—and also not to tell him necessarily what to do. And then he asked me to come down, later that summer, and see what he'd done. And I went down with John—Jap [Jasper Johns] and Bob were living way down-town on Warren Street, and he brought out all these things, and it was just wonderful. . . . He put one of those parachute dresses on, it was just incredible-looking. . . . I think it was then that he asked me, if I had a chair, could he have a door. I said, of course. And he asked me if I could use a fur-coat—he'd seen this fur-coat, when he was out shopping, and I said, oh, absolutely, I'll find some way to use it. It was all marvelous—and then the dark glasses, one thing after another he brought out. He'd seen this bunch of paper flowers in a magic shop, and he asked me if I could use it, and I said again, absolutely. So then I thought about it, and I was working on the first dance, I hadn't finished, and I thought, oh, maybe that would work there, so I tried it out. . . . And he made those marvelous undershirts with the tattoo. . . .

For the musical accompaniment, Cage decided to use a version of the new *Concert for Piano and Orchestra*. Cunningham has written,

This was one of the first times I gave him only the length of the total dance (twenty-six min-utes), but no time points in between. His score is indeterminate in length, and also in the pro-portions within the piece, so even though the dance was set, we could not count on the sounds as cues, as they never fell in the same place twice. The dancers' unsupported time-span was expanding.[6]

The order of events, and their content, were, as anticipated, somewhat different in the finished work from Cunningham's tentative description in his letter to Rauschenberg. Each of the numbers (or "vaude-ville scenes") was given a subtitle:

"opener"
This was, as Cunningham had indicated, a kind of "entrance parade." The idea of the large stopwatch on

MC in "a single," from *Antic Meet*, 1958. Pho-tograph: Marvin Silver.

stage was abandoned. Cunningham moved among the other dancers rather as he had in the first section of *Septet*, a clownlike figure "who falls in love with a society whose rules he doesn't know."[7] Finally he produced the conjuror's paper flowers from his sleeve, buried his face in them, and went off.

"room for two"
In this duet with Brown, Cunningham wore a chair strapped to his back, as he had described. The door Rauschenberg had asked for was on wheels, enabling it to be moved out from the wings, apparently of its own volition, but actually by Brown, who was behind it, and then stepped through a funny yet disturbing, Magritte-like image. Cunningham says that Rauschenberg thought he would find a door backstage in New London, saying "every theater has a door." Cunningham was not so sure, but Rauschenberg was convinced, so he said no more. "So we got to Connecticut, and of course there wasn't any door, and then I didn't see him for a day—he went off and bought a door." Brown wore a beautiful white Victorian nightgown that Rauschenberg had found. When she stepped through the door, Cunningham took her hand and led her around the stage, like a cavalier with a classical ballerina. His original idea had been to carry her sitting on the chair, but this proved physically impossible. Instead he knelt so that the chair touched the floor, and Brown sat on it, demurely pointing her toes. At another point, Brown took an arabesque, leaning on Cunningham's shoulder as he lunged forward, opening his mouth in a silent yell. Cunningham has said that he thought of the chair as the kind of "burden" people carry through life. At the end, Brown went off the way she had come—through the door, while Cunningham left with a kind of large skipping step, brushing the palms of his hands in an "I wash my hands of this" gesture.

"mockgame"
This was probably the eighth scene in Cunningham's original scheme, the "shoot the chutes." It began with three women—Viola Farber, Cynthia Stone, and Marilyn Wood—marching on and performing a series of arm movements, ending with a fall. Brown ran on as if late after making the change from the previous number, and joined in with a speeded-up version of the same sequence, catching up with the others by the end.

Later the dancers put on black cotton tank-top undershirts with hoops sewn into their bottoms, so that they stood away from the body. The stage became a sort of circus ring with everyone leaping and falling. There was one sequence in which the dancers leaped into the air, arching their bodies and landing in a fall on their back with one leg in the air. One couple slid to the floor, landing nose to nose. In this circus Cunningham was again the clown, vainly trying to keep up with everyone and not succeeding.

The number ended with the passage mentioned in the letter, the "formal preparation for something that ends in disaster." Cunningham made an elaborate preparation for a grande pirouette but ended up crouching on the floor with one leg twisted around the other, in which position he somehow managed to crawl offstage.

"sports and diversions #1"
This was the "short ballet number," danced not by Brown and Stone but by Brown and Farber, wearing lace camisoles over their leotards and performing conventional ballet combinations (both women studied with Margaret Craske, the famous teacher of the Cecchetti method) such as chassé, pas de bourrée, sissonne. In an interlude, they mimed the actions Cunningham had described: as Brown performed a short adagio, Farber stealthily picked up imaginary stones and flicked them at her, knocking her off balance; Brown retaliated by filling an imaginary bucket with water and emptying it over Farber, who was doing her own adagio. Farber shook the water out of her eyes and the dancing resumed, but the quarrel erupted again, and the two went off grappling with each other.

"sports and diversions #2"
This was the "tumbling act," for which Cunningham and Charlip wore burlap tank-tops on which Rauschenberg had painted tattoolike designs. The two fell to the floor, rolled along, and jumped over one another. Again Cunningham appeared to be incompetent, missing beats and fumbling. At the end, Charlip collapsed, and Cunningham went off, to return wearing a long and mangy raccoon coat (something else Rauschenberg had found). He took hold of Charlip's hands and dragged him offstage, as Cunningham has said, "like a Rotarian hauling off a fellow-drunk."

"social"
This section was perhaps the "mock battle" of the original scheme, though different in its final form—the nearest Cunningham has come to social satire. The subject seemed to be the lack of communication among people in a social situation like a cocktail party. The dancers wore dark glasses (again found by Rauschenberg) with mirrorlike lenses. At the beginning a large cardboard refrigerator box moved across the back of the stage, apparently of its own volition, like the door in "room for two." When it passed the halfway point it deposited Wood, who was revealed sitting on the floor. (Later the box had to be replaced by a piece of black velvet, because it could not be taken on tour: "we so often played in theaters where the box itself took up most of the stage space—we couldn't get it in or out of the wings.")

Gradually the other dancers (except Cunningham, who was not in this scene) came onstage, slowly opening first one arm, then the other, in front of them, turning their heads from side to side, and continuing these movements as they walked around the stage or paused on half-toe, like people in a trance. Finally Wood locked one arm around Charlip's throat and seemed to be strangling him as they moved offstage together.

"bacchus and cohorts"
"The sweater act with four sleeves, and 4 girls like bacchantes and lamenting in long dresses." The dresses were parachutes Rauschenberg had found in an army-supply store; the sweater

with four sleeves, and no neck-hole, was designed by Cunningham himself, and knitted by him with Valda Setterfield's help. Although Cunningham downplays this aspect of the scene, "bacchus and cohorts" is clearly a parody of a Martha Graham dance. Cunningham had watched one of Graham's classes earlier in the summer, but when asked if it had suggested this idea, he said,

No, I think probably that was always in my mind, except that it started with the idea of that sweater—not a sweater necessarily, but something where somebody's caught. Then I began to think about it, and then the idea occurred to me of the sweater with no head and all those arms. That's what it started from—everybody thinks it's all about Graham, but they miss the point that it's about both those things. I thought, what would the dance be, and then I thought of all those Graham gestures, but if it had been only that I wouldn't have been very interested in it. Chaplin says someplace, you mustn't do one thing which might be funny, you've got to have a lot going on at any time, so that it keeps mounting up.

Be that as it may, the dance certainly looked like a wickedly funny parody of Graham. Cunningham tried to put on the sweater, but was defeated by the absence of a hole for his head. Meanwhile the four women entered like the chorus in Graham's *Night Journey*, with a Graham-style triplet changing to a kind of slow march, kicking each leg up in a grand battement and then going into a low arabesque with flexed foot, one cupped hand held against the forehead. They advanced toward Cunningham, who jumped up and down stage center. He moved his hips from side to side, then rolled his head in a circle. The women leaned backward, bending at the knees, then surrounded Cunningham and brought their arms over in a cross formation with him at its center. He collapsed to the floor. The women slowly marched off. Cunningham, left alone, rose and walked to the back of the stage, where he slowly and deliberately tied the two spare sleeves of his sweater in a knot above his head, the way Graham used to make some adjustment to her headgear. He walked forward with his hands held together in front of him. Arriving at stage center, he pulled the sweater off his head, walked to the wings, and brought out a small table on which he proceeded to lay knife, fork, spoon, and glass. He dusted off the table with the ends of the sweater sleeves, and left the stage.

"sports and diversions #3"
A solo for Farber, no. 3 in the original scheme. Instead of providing the "bundles" that Cunningham had envisaged, Rauschenberg gave her an open umbrella with Christmas tree lights inside it—a fantastic, beautiful object. The dance was much as Cunningham described it, a gradual crossing of the space with sudden changes of direction and many small movements of the feet—something Farber was superbly equipped to perform.

"a single"
Cunningham's vaudeville number, though without the "interruptions" he originally planned. For this dance he wore white workman's overalls, white shirt, red necktie, and white lace-up dancing shoes. The dance was a kind of quintessential soft-shoe, without any actual tap steps—just little slipping, sliding movements of the feet. There was the step he remembered from his days with Mrs. Barrett—the foot turning in and out, while he gave a little wave with one hand. "She once did that, she only did it one time that I remember, she did two or three steps that way, and she did it very beautifully, she had a wonderful sense of that kind of dancing. She said, Oh, this is something I did, and then she just did it. She never did it again, but I remembered it all those years."

"exodus"
The finale was again different from Cunningham's original description, though the things he mentioned—"hopscotch, some jazz movements, and a little delsarte"—may well have been submerged in it. The dance was a typical Cunningham "whirligig" finale, in Earle Brown's phrase;[8] as Jill Johnston suggested, it "could be a spoof by Mr. Cunningham on himself."[9] Cunningham again does not deny this, but also says "it was like one of those old films where everything goes so fast, like the Keystone Kops, where they start chasing each other, rushing about, and then it all falls apart." Each dancer had his or her own movements, moving diagonally across the stage in a clump that kept flying apart and then re-forming, with Cunningham himself still trying to keep up with everybody. The curtain came down while all this was still going on.

Like all good comedy, *Antic Meet* had a serious undercurrent, as is suggested by the epigraph from *The Brothers Karamazov* ("this all comes from dostoyevsky").

That summer when I was at Connecticut, I hadn't seen Martha Graham in all those years, and she was there, and so I went and said hello, and I very politely said, could I watch a class? So I sat there watching this class and at one point Martha made one of those grand statements, then said "and" and they all started, and she had to scurry away like a frightened rabbit or she would have been knocked down. That's what I mean—all of a sudden this inadvertence takes place, the whole thing falls to pieces in front of you. And I thought, that's exactly what I'm involved in, making that piece. It happens so constantly in life, you make some grand adjustment and then it just crumbles. Or you step on a banana peel.

Cunningham has remarked that at its first performance at the American Dance Festival, *Antic Meet* was well received because it was funny. As if in confirmation of this observation, *Antic Meet* usually got the best reviews in a mixed bill. Sometimes, though, critics' guesses at the humor's targets were startling: most surprising, perhaps, was the description of the Graham-style chorus in "bacchus and cohorts" as "four feathered maidens out of *Swan Lake*."[10]

SUMMERSPACE
subtitled "a lyric dance"

First planned in the round, with the numbers (1–6) for exits and entrances being placed equidistant around the circle. The lines through the space would take on a global feeling, wouldn't they?[11]

With *Summerspace* (the summer part of the title came after the dance was finished, but the notion of space was always present), the principal momentum was a concern for steps that carry one through a space, and not only into it.

Like the passing of birds, stopping for moments on the ground and then going on, or automobiles more relentlessly throbbing along turnpikes and under and over cloverleaves.

It entailed an enormous amount of paperwork. But a good deal of it was done before the summer teaching began . . . and also part of the actual dance.

Perhaps this space-play was enhanced by the rehearsal area we used. It was a large room, roughly 100 feet long by 50 feet deep.

The movement gamut for the piece was simple. From each number in space [upstage right was no. 1, upstage left no. 2, center right no. 3, center left no. 4, downstage right no. 5, downstage left no. 6] to each other number went a line, each presuming the reverse so there were 21 in all. Each one had a sequence of movement relating to it, ranging from simple to complex.

To this gamut of movement in given space-directions was applied a chance procedure. It was done in this order:
1. Direction, i.e., from where to where. This gave the movement its basic form.
2. Whether the movement was done fast, medium, or slow.
3. Whether the movement happened in the air, across the surface, or on the ground.
4. Length of time in seconds, assuming 5″ as a minimum.
5. Shape of space, i.e. in what way the space was covered (straight lines, diagonal lines, circular, and so on).
6. Number of dancers involved in this particular action.
7. Did they perform this action together or separately.
8. Did they end the action on or off stage.

Below: MC's notations of floor patterns for *Summerspace*, 1958, reproduced from his book, *Changes*. Right: *Summerspace*, 1958. Left to right: Viola Farber and Carolyn Brown. Photograph: Richard Rutledge.

109

In this dance, the lengths of time were enlarged. Previous to this, the lengths of the dances had been fixed in short time periods, one minute, 2½, up to 5 minutes, or according to the musical phrase. Here I decided to have a dance roughly 15 to 17 minutes long. The time has never been fixed closer than that. Different size stages make the lengths different, and extend or diminish the time. [Morton] Feldman's score allows for this. If we did fix it to a length as being "what it should be," in trying to reproduce this exact length on the next stage, we would be imitating and approximating something. I decided to let it be what it was each time.

As much as possible I worked with a single dancer all the way through his actions except where movement came directly in contact with another dancer. Perhaps this is what gives the dance its sense of beings in isolation in their motion along with the sense of continuous appearance and vanishing.[12]

In his letter to Rauschenberg, Cunningham did not go into detail about *Summerspace*. He simply described it as a dance "with new work, a new inter-section for orchestra by Morty. About 15 minutes long, seems to be doing with people and velocities, at least a hell of a lot of it is on the fast side, four girls and Remy and myself, I have the feeling it's like looking at part of an enormous landscape and you can only see the action in this particular portion of it. I hope it's dazzling rather than willy-nilly."[13] (It appears that *Velocities* was Cunningham's original title for the dance.) Rauschenberg's response was to paint an abstract, pointillist backcloth (executed with the help of Johns, using Day-Glo spray paints and a stencil) that, like a Jackson Pollock painting, might be taken as an arbitrary segment of something that could in theory be extended into infinity. For Cage, the effect was "as though one were looking out the window of a moving train [at] a landscape of dance, knowing that the dance never stops and that one always sees only a small part of it."[14]

This notion about the stage space was inherent in the compositional process that Cunningham outlines in his notes; it may, indeed, have been the initial concept from which the process arose. One may guess that Cunningham's image of birds flying and alighting also came into his mind early, since his sources of movement ideas are so often in the observation of nature. (He also had plenty of opportunity to observe the movement of automobiles on highways during the company's tours.)

It was while Cunningham was working on the piece that he decided to use the word "summer" in the title. Certainly Rauschenberg's decor suggested that season: although the backcloth was abstract, its pointillist character recalled those Impressionist landscapes in which the eye is dazzled by myriad shifting fragments of color. The costumes were similarly dotted with color, spray paint actually being applied to leotards and tights as the dancers wore them. This suggested the camouflage that conceals animals or insects in their environments—though the dancers did not in fact quite "blend" with the backcloth when at rest, as was the intention. The backcloth was originally small, about nine feet high; Rauschenberg's idea was that it would be like a landscape seen in the distance. As Cunningham has said, however, "I knew that in the theater it looks different, and by the next performance he had doubled its height."

Cunningham has spoken of a certain "lazy" quality in Brown's performance of the movement—"not technically lazy," but, he says, the deliberate way she moved was "evocative—and yet the shapes were so vivid."

Summerspace is one of the most striking examples of Cunningham's collaborative method, in which the artists work independently rather than in close consultation, yet each creative element makes a potent contribution to the whole. "Feldman was once asked how we could do this, how we could work without knowing what the others are doing," Cunningham said. "'It's like this,' he said. 'Say you're getting married and I tell you the dress won't be made until the morning of the wedding. But I also tell you it's by Dior.'"[15]

In combination, Cunningham's choreography, Rauschenberg's decor, and Feldman's limpid score produce the effect of a hot, still summer afternoon. The dancers' sudden bursts of speed and equally sudden suspensions make them look like dragonflies skimming and hovering over the surface of a pond and then zigzagging away, and the delicate clusters of notes in the music are like bubbles rising to that surface. At one point there is a muffled rumble in the bass, like distant thunder. (The music was originally composed for orchestra and was performed with one at the premiere, and occasionally later; other performances were accompanied by a two-piano version.) That these effects were the fortuitous results of the combination of the various elements was made evident at an Event performance at the Merce Cunningham Studio in

Opposite: MC in a 1965 performance of *Summerspace*, 1958. Photograph: Farrell Grehan.

1977, when parts of *Summerspace* were danced, in brown costumes, to Joan La Barbara's "Thunder" music, with a completely different effect—the piece looked more like a stormy day in the fall.

An analysis of the choreography would show that it is indeed composed of the elements that Cunningham put into his movement gamut: the trajectories followed by the dancers, from one entrance to another; passages of swift, intricate footwork and others in which a movement was performed adagio—Farber's slow diagonal, for example, in which she several times sank down until she was sitting on one heel, with the other leg stretched in front of her, and slowly opened first one arm then the other. (As in the "social" section of *Antic Meet*, Cunningham too performed a similar movement in *Summerspace*, in first position plié, and with the head turning from side to side in a different rhythm from that of the arms.) Cunningham interpreted "in the air" as meaning that the dancers either jumped or went on relevé (the jumping sequences included a passage in which two men circled the stage, passing in midair as they passed the upstage center point); "on the ground" could mean either a fall, such as Brown's swift descent from a relevé to a kind of arabesque à terre, or a movement like Farber's, described above. The dancers' paths were straight lines, diagonals, and circles.

Such an analysis is not, of course, necessary for the appreciation of *Summerspace*, which might in fact seem one of the most immediately accessible of Cunningham's dances, and has been frequently revived by other companies. Yet Cunningham has remarked that at the first performance most of the audience simply did not see the work, let alone comprehend it—"it all passed in front of them, but they didn't see it." Indeed Louis Horst reviewed the piece dismissively, saying that the piece "did not, to this observer, realize any of the high standards so patently evident in [Cunningham's] three works presented earlier in the week [*Antic Meet, Nocturnes,* and *Changeling*]."[16] And P. W. Manchester complained that the piece "straggle[s] all over the stage with no beginning, no middle and no end"—precisely the effect Cunningham wished to achieve.[17]

Considering that *Summerspace* has acquired the status of a "signature" work, it has had an oddly erratic history in the Cunningham company's repertory. It was not performed on the 1959 tour, then was performed only a few times early in 1960 and once early in 1963. It was given frequently in 1964 and 1965, however, especially during the 1964 world tour. Cunningham then gave it a ten-year hiatus with

his own company, during which it was revived elsewhere—by New York City Ballet, the Cullbergbaletten in Stockholm, and the Boston Ballet. It was also revived in 1976 by the French company Théâtre du Silence. Its last performance by the Cunningham company, at present writing, was in the fall of 1979.

Early in 1966, Cunningham let it be known that he had a piece in his repertory that he thought could be adapted for ballet dancers—namely *Summerspace*—and Lincoln Kirstein, the company's general director, invited him to stage it for New York City Ballet. The basic choreography was unaltered, but Cunningham put the women on pointe, which inevitably changed the weight and attack of certain steps. Cunningham was surprised to find that not only the very slow movements but even the allegro ones were difficult for the ballet dancers. Especially difficult, though, were the rapid and sudden transitions from one to the other. Cunningham asked Brown to demonstrate some of the movement for the ballet dancers, who were astonished at her facility.

• • •

In October 1958, Cunningham, Cage, Brown, Tudor, and Nicholas Cernovitch briefly visited Europe to perform in Stockholm and Hamburg. In their first program, at the Royal Theater, Stockholm, on 5 October, Cunningham danced the solo version of *Collage, Changeling,* and "a single" from *Antic Meet*. Brown did her role from *Galaxy* under the title *Nebulosa*. Together, Brown and Cunningham performed *Suite for Two, Amores* (the last performance of this dance), the duet version of *Springweather and People,* and a new piece made for the occasion:

Night Wandering

The visit to Stockholm came at the invitation of Bengt Häger, director of the Dance Museum, then in the opera house itself, who had asked if it would be possible to make a dance to contemporary Swedish music. Tudor had played piano pieces by Bo Nilsson, and suggested that three of these would be suitable—one of them was in fact dedicated to him. "The music," Cage wrote, "is characterized by bursts of activity preceded and followed by long holds or pauses. Following the composer's direction, the music is heard through loudspeakers, high amplification being given to the piano."[18]

Cunningham made the dance very quickly:

If you have three days to make a duet (this happened in Stockholm with Carolyn Brown), do you worry about ideas, or do you make a dance

Night Wandering, 1958. Carolyn Brown and MC. Photograph: James Klosty.

various ways to carry his partner, at one point, for instance, holding her in front of him in an inert, crouching position. At another, she stood on his feet as he walked forward. In the dance's final moments Brown lay horizontally along his body as he rocked back and forth in a "bridge" position. Although Walter Sorell saw in this "a tender lullaby of love,"[21] Richard Buckle found *Night Wandering* "cold [and] menacing, the courtship of the Macbeths."[22]

The original costumes, by Cernovitch, consisted of tunics that Cunningham wore over trousers, Brown over tights. In 1963 Rauschenberg made new costumes in keeping with the Nordic character of the dance: overgarments of fur, worn with tights, that reminded one of Thoreau's quotation from Samuel Lang about "the Laplander in his skin dress."[23]

• • •

The tour ended in Belgium, where, in connection with the Brussels World's Fair, there was to be a performance of Earle Brown's *Indices*—the music for *Springweather and People*, in its orchestral version. This performance did not take place, partly because the necessary musicians were not available and partly because of a period of national mourning following the death of the Pope. Instead, Cunningham and Brown performed the duet version of *Springweather* on a local television station, to the piano reduction. Cage remained in Europe to take up a four-week residency in Milan at the invitation of Luciano Berio, during which time he worked on a major tape composition, *Fontana Mix*, and also appeared on an Italian-television quiz show, *Lascia o raddoppio* (an equivalent of *Double or Nothing*), as an expert on mushrooms. He won first prize and became a national celebrity. With the proceeds he bought a new Volks wagen Microbus for the dance company to travel in on tour.

Meanwhile Cunningham, back from Europe, resumed teaching classes in New York. In mid-December he went out to the University of Illinois in Champaign-Urbana to become dancer-in-residence in the College of Physical Education there. The first to take up this appointment, he had been chosen "for his eminence as a choreographer, performer and teacher, his artistic integrity and dedication, and his greatness as a person."[24] Cunningham first went out alone, "to work with dance students and faculty on choreographic problems. He will analyze his approach to dance, advise students on their dance and choreography, and will be available for lectures and lecture-demonstrations."[25] In addition, he was commissioned

involving two people, a man and a woman, together?[19]

After a couple of days he still had not finished the dance, so he said he would not be able to do the third piece, but Cage said he had to because Nilsson had already been paid for all three, so Cunningham went ahead and finished it.

Night Wandering began with a slow diagonal progression by the two dancers from upstage right to downstage left. Despite Cunningham's disavowal of any concern with "ideas," the dance almost inevitably called to mind images of immense snowbound landscapes. Cage, in fact, described it as follows: "Spacious and stark, it suggests slow motion through an endless Northern night."[20] Cunningham explored

to choreograph two dances to new scores, with his own company, which would join him in Urbana early in the new year for a concert to be given as part of a Festival of Contemporary Arts. (He commuted to New York to rehearse them there.)

1959

On 26 February at the University of Illinois, Cunningham gave a lecture-demonstration on the subject of music and dance. Eight students participated. The music consisted of excerpts from Satie's *Morceaux en forme de poire*, pieces by Cage for prepared piano, and a selection of nineteenth-century salon pieces. The pianist was Ben Johnston, composer of one of the scores Cunningham was to choreograph in Illinois, with Charles Schbrenner as second pianist for the Satie.[1]

A few days later, on 3 March, Cunningham gave another lecture, "Talk by a Dancer" (a title he has used frequently), in which he touched on the same subject. This time the danced illustrations, performed by Cunningham himself, were accompanied by music for prepared piano by Cage and excerpts from Pierre Schaeffer's *Symphonie pour un homme seul*, the music for Cunningham's *Collage*. A report on the talk in a university paper summarized some of Cunningham's remarks:

> "The dancer begins with physical awareness and balance," he said. In the daily class, "which he soon begins to love and hate," he learns the eight basic movements, with variations: bending, rising, extending, turning, sliding, skimming and brushing, jumping, and falling.[2]

For the last three weeks of Cunningham's residency at the University of Illinois, his company joined him for the final rehearsals of the concert that was to conclude it.

> During the dress rehearsal, I jumped and came down in a hole in the stage. I sat and checked my foot to see if it was broken. It wasn't, so I got up and asked the orchestra to begin again. The next evening [*sic*—it was a matinée] for the performance my foot looked like a meat loaf. I did manage both performances, and spent the next month in a whirlpool bath.[3]

The performances began with a revival of *Collage*, with Cunningham dancing his solo and thirteen members of the University of Illinois Dance Group

in the second part. In both the new pieces, "the musicians were on the stage in back of the dancers; the stage was extended over the orchestra pit."[4]

FROM THE POEMS OF WHITE STONE

How to give an atmosphere which was Chinese in character without treading the clichés of oriental gesture. As usual it was rhythm that gave the clue. When this is found gesture takes care of itself in the way it naturally does and no personal inflection becomes necessary. The way Americans look and walk [is] different from the Italians, say.[5]

From the Poems of White Stone was set to "a choral and orchestral composition" by Chou Wen-Chung, visiting research associate in music at the University. A setting of poems by Chiang Kuei, Chou's score introduced a more literary note than had been present in Cunningham's dances since *The Princess Zondilda*, thirteen years earlier, but this was minimized by the fact that they were sung in Chinese (the chorus, like the orchestra, was on stage, behind a scrim). Cunningham was probably relieved not to have to deal too literally with questions like "life/what does it mean?"[6] Cage commented to the present writer at the time that there was more unison movement in the choreography than had been customary. Cunningham agreed, but said that this unison would also break up at times, a device suggested by rhythmic shifts in the music:

> I thought that was the only way to get at the Chinese flavor of the music without pretending you were Chinese. So I did it through the rhythm; the movements would flow, they would go together, there was something that was held in the body, and the arm would continue it, so the eye was arrested in some way.

The women wore long dresses, designed by Rauschenberg, with headdresses in "a marvelous flower shape. . . . Remy [Charlip] and I had some kind of smocks." In a letter to a friend, Cunningham commented that "some [in the audience] wondered why there were medieval costumes in a Chinese piece, and the answer is of course, it was Chinese medieval."[7] The lighting, Cunningham says, was "murky."

GAMBIT FOR DANCERS AND ORCHESTRA

Originally announced as *Two for One*, this piece had a score by Johnston. Rauschenberg designed costumes with tights split into two colors. The dancers

Left to right: Bill Giles, Anna Morerka, Robert Rauschenberg, MC, John Cage, and Jasper Johns in Dillons Bar, University Place, New York, 1959. Photograph: Fred W. McDarrah.

had to wear shoes "because the stage was so appalling, so little and so rough."

Both of the new dances were performed only twice, on 15 and 16 March. They did not go into the regular repertory, partly because it would have been prohibitively expensive to perform the music. As far as he can remember, Cunningham did not use material from them in later dances.

• • •

When possible, the company traveled in the Volkswagen Microbus that Cage had bought, which accommodated the dancers, the two musicians (Cage and David Tudor), and the lighting designer/technical director (Nicholas Cernovitch or, later, Robert Rauschenberg). Cunningham and Cage took turns driving. Cunningham had now acquired a "personal manager," Isabelle Fisher, but still took charge of financial arrangements on the road. When he could afford it, he paid the dancers $15 per performance ($25 for two), besides paying all bills. Needless to say, he often operated at a loss, which he tried to make up by teaching master classes during the tours.

The company at this time was a closely knit group, spending most of its time together. Cage took charge of meals, either picking restaurants (for which he had an infallible instinct) or buying or gathering food for roadside picnics.[8] Once, on a free evening in a small town, several of them were trying to decide whether or not to go to the only local movie. Cage decided

Gambit for Dancers and Orchestra, 1959. Left to right: MC and Remy Charlip, with orchestra.

against it, saying, "I think I'll go and pull the wool over my eyes." Tudor remembered a motel in an Ohio town called Melody, or possibly Harmony, in which he, Charlip, and Cernovitch shared a room decorated with illuminated paintings—paintings with lights inside that kept them awake.

Early in the summer, Cunningham again arranged dances for a Living Theater production of a biblical play by Paul Goodman, *The Cave at Machpelah*, for which Ned Rorem wrote music and songs. (This time Cunningham used Rorem's music.) The play was produced at the theater company's new space, in a building on the northeast corner of Sixth Avenue and 14th Street in New York. The tiny but handsome theater was designed by the architect Paul Williams, a benefactor of the Cunningham company on several earlier occasions.

From 6 July to 16 August, Cunningham and his company were again in residence at the Connecticut College School of Dance, in New London, with performances in the Twelfth American Dance Festival during the last few days. On the first evening they repeated *Antic Meet* from the previous year, and on the second (14 August 1959) they gave the first performance of a new work commissioned by the Festival and rehearsed during the residency:

RUNE

Earlier working titles: *Autumn Rune, Sound of Autumn.*

A program note read, "The continuity of this dance is so arranged that it can change from performance to performance."

I had become interested in not having a fixed order to a piece. *Rune . . .* reflected this for the first time. It was a dance that interested me enormously, and I almost gave it up during the earlier rehearsals, as the complexity of getting it to function dance-wise with the dancers seemed too great. One of them [Judith Dunn] encouraged me, one low day, though, and I continued. Prior to a performance I would rearrange the order, and we would rehearse it as such, the complexity and difficulty demanding it. This became impractical with touring, and we gave it up. The demands it made on rehearsal time under such circumstances as against the amount of time available didn't coincide. We did however give it in three different orders over its history.[9]

The dance was made in a series of chunks of movement, some chunks involving the whole company (6), and others as little as one or two. These chunks varied in length, but as first arranged added up to five-minute sections, five in all, the whole being twenty-five minutes. All the sections were to be done at any performance, but the order they were in could be shifted. These changes produced certain problems of arrangement.

"In the first order I finish here and then triplet off stage. But with this new order I am supposed to begin the next phrase over there. How do I get there?"

"You use the triplets that previously got you offstage to now get you over there."

Or, more complex, a borrowing scheme came into the order:

"You use the sliding movement used in the first section of the first order to exit with, and here you use it to enter with for this new section."

This is explained cumbersomely, but what became clear in reordering is that I didn't have to make new movement, we could live off the interest of the first order, using motions in different places, where something was not necessary for exiting or entering or changing place it could be used later. The dance is technically difficult to do, as it is full of complicated steps, and sudden changes of tempo, done abruptly, and without premeditation, but in full arc if possible.[10]

Rune was perhaps the most rigorously classic of Cunningham's dances to date, and the most uncompromising. There was a deliberate use of stillness as an element of equal value to that of movement (analogous to Cage's use of silence). As usually performed, the piece began with Cunningham standing motionless in the upstage right corner of the stage for quite a long time, facing away from the audience, before turning and beginning his opening solo. This went on a diagonal trajectory to the downstage left corner: he leapt into the air with his left leg extended in front of him and his right leg bent under him, making wide, sweeping gestures. The fifth section (again, in the usual order) began similarly, with a solo that was a variation of the opening one; for instance, he slid to a sitting position with the left leg again extended in front of him as he went to the floor. Paradoxically, perhaps, the use of chance procedures produced a tight construction, with movement motifs being repeated and varied, such as the women's sidewise kneeling "walk," which was repeated later in a standing position.

Rune was one of Cunningham's first dances to use space in a layered way—the eye simultaneously takes in events in the foreground, middle, and rear of the stage, and these, while not necessarily related, do interact. Cunningham and the dancers had descriptive names for the phrases, more for quick identification in rehearsal than to indicate specific content. Thus "sunshine" identified a section in which Viola Farber stood in the upstage right corner, her arms outstretched, slowly rotating her upper body. (Farber's role made use of her extraordinary qualities as a performer, not only her beautiful line but also her strik-

ing presence.) Other phrases were called the "Yogi" and the "Cluster."

A title like *Rune* is not, of course, to be taken literally. Nevertheless, it is true that in Cunningham's notes the phrase "enter magicly [*sic*]" occurs several times, contrasted with "enter simple." Moreover, the piece contained several gestures that were distinctly mysterious. Two of these were associated with Farber: one was that of touching the palms of her hands before her face, another a "pulling" motion of the hands away from one another, both horizontally and vertically. At the end, everyone repeated the horizontal version of this, at various speeds, as they went off, following another whirligig finale in which everyone repeated his or her own fragmented phrase, in a bunch at stage center. Another gesture, performed by all of the women, was that of patting the floor beside them as they descended in a plié, rising and descending again to pat the floor on the other side.

Rune was the only one of Cunningham's dances of this period that he notated fully (in his own notation, consisting of written phrases and stick figures), and he has been able to revive it at times, a task made difficult, however, by its technical complexity. This may also explain why, although there have been several revivals, none was performed more than a few times.

Christian Wolff's music exists in two versions: "Music for Merce Cunningham" is for six or seven instruments; "Duo II for Pianists" is for two pianos. At the first performance the instrumental version was played (flute, piccolo, trumpet, trombone, strings, and piano, the latter played by David Tudor; Cage was the conductor). The score, Cage wrote, "sometimes restricts the performers to particular notes, and at other times allows them freedom of choice in terms of all the aspects of sound."[11]

Rauschenberg's costumes consisted of leotards and tights dyed in various shades of brown, perhaps reflecting the piece's working title; the second man's costume had a fur collar. (In 1982 Mark Lancaster designed new costumes in dark earthy colors; he designed yet another new production in 1995.)

• • •

The most important event in the remaining months of the year was the opening of the Merce Cunningham Studio—on the northeast corner of Sixth Avenue and 14th Street. The new studio opened with a two-week Christmas course; classes then continued on a regular schedule, except when the company was on tour. Isabelle Fisher, Cunningham's personal manager,

Rune, 1959. Left to right: Judith Dunn, MC, Remy Charlip, and Marilyn Wood. Photograph: Matthew Wysocki.

gave the secretary instructions on how to enroll students, which began: "1. Greet the student."

In October the company had performed in a brief dance festival at Douglass College, Rutgers University, New Brunswick, New Jersey, sharing a program with the companies of Anna Sokolow and Alwin Nikolais. The Cunningham company's performance, of *Suite for Five*, was prefaced by some comments by the choreographer. After describing the way the piece was made, Cunningham went on,

All this talking about dancing leads the audience to expect something.

The weather bureau prepares you to "expect snow," and up comes a sunny day.

I suppose I could say the dance *is* about silence; but just is silent, or has many moments in it that are *still*.

Now I've led you to expect something, and after seeing the dance, you might say it isn't silent at all; that it is full of activity.

An art, if it communicates anything, must have its communication in that place where the rational and the irrational do their intriguing and giddy duet; that area of response to nature where the action of nature, in all her twists and turns, is the evoking hand.

I think that dance at its very best, and as in all the arts, that *very* best is very rare, produces an indefinable and unforgettable abyss in the individual spectator—it is only an instant, and immediately following that instant the mind is busy—questioning, deciding; the feelings are busy, agitating, confirming or denying.

But there is that instant—and it does renew us.[12]

119

1960

The Cunningham company had not given a full program in New York since its last performance at the Brooklyn Academy of Music, in 1957. On 16 February, the company gave a single performance at the Phoenix Theater, on Second Avenue between 11th and 12th streets (now a cinema). The event was sponsored by Impresarios Inc. (Robert Rauschenberg, Jasper Johns, and Emile de Antonio). The top-priced ticket cost $8.33, at that time a record for a modern dance performance.

The year had begun with a short tour, on which the company performed the program planned for the Phoenix: *Summerspace*, *Rune*, *Changeling*, and *Antic Meet*. Only the solo *Changeling* had been seen in the city. The music was to be played by a small chamber orchestra. The concert was considered sufficiently newsworthy to be covered in both *Time* and *Newsweek*, though it was, of course, ignored by the critic of the *New York Times*. (Walter Terry reviewed it in both a weekday and the Sunday *Herald-Tribune*.[1])

The following month, Cunningham and Brown took part in a Composers' Showcase concert in New York, performing a program of compositions by Henry Cowell and Cage:

THEATER PIECE

This was a little more circumscribed than Cage's untitled event at Black Mountain in 1952 (often referred to as "Theater Piece").

This is a composition indeterminate of [*sic*] its performance. Time-brackets are given within which an action may be made. These actions are from a gamut of twenty nouns and/or verbs chosen by the performer. This gamut changes at given points, so that each part involves a performer in a maximum of 50 or 100 different actions. Means are supplied for the answering of four questions with regard to the activities within any one time bracket. The composing means were the materials of *Fontana Mix*.[2]

The *New York Herald-Tribune* music critic William Flanagan, though summing up the concert as "a dull evening" and admitting that he had left before the end, described the action:

The stage contained two dancers, a contralto, a trombone, a tuba, a pianist, a junk-littered table, a tub that caught water from a plastic-bag fountain that was suspended from the ceiling, several toys, and lots and lots of other things. The singer, a Miss Arlene Carmen, walked about and serenaded in French, English; she sang the "St Louis Blues." Assorted hands rubbed balloons, exploded paper bags, and sent toy objects into the audience. The tuba player, after playing solo fragments from . . . "the standard repertory," stripped to the waist, changed his shirt and jacket, poured and did away with a drink; he struck a small cymbal that he directly suspended into the tub of water. Mr. Merce Cunningham danced some and then took a scissors to his hair and snipped at it petulantly. Mr. Cage, meanwhile, stood solemnly off to the sidelines and, at arbitrarily divided points, counted in Arabic numerals.[3]

Flanagan omitted to mention that Brown skipped rope, then "read a newspaper while marking time to the wail of a trombone by flipping a garbage can lid with her foot." He also missed the finale, in which "a black-cloaked figure stalked across the stage bearing an American flag."[4]

After teaching (with Brown) a summer course at the 14th Street studio from 30 May to 8 July, Cunningham and his company were once again in residence at Connecticut College, from 11 July to 21 August, and at the end of the summer they performed in four programs of the Thirteenth American Dance Festival there. *Night Wandering* had its first American performance on 18 August. *Rune* was repeated on 19 August, together with a new work, *Crises*, which Cunningham had rehearsed during the summer.

CRISES

An adventure in togetherness. . . . I decided to allow for the dancers (there were five, four girls and one man) contacting each other, not only through holding or being held, but also by outside means. I used elastic bands around a wrist, an arm, a waist or a leg. By one dancer inserting a hand under the band on another they were attached but also at the same instant free. Where these contacts came in the continuity, or where they were broken, was left to chance in the composition and not to personal psychology or physical pressure. That is given, by random selection, the possibility of two dancers bending and turning together, then again, by random selection, whether they are attached, if so how, by holding each other, or by elastic, then if elastic, where it might go. From this I made the action. The gamuts of movement for each dancer were individualized to a great degree. The music (*Rhythm Studies* #1, #2, #4, #5, #7, #6 for player piano) by Conlon Nancarrow was added after the dance was choreographed.

One of the special characteristics of this dance was due to Viola Farber. Her body often had the look of one part being in balance, and the rest extremely off. Now and again it was like two persons, another just ahead or behind the first. This was coupled with an acute rhythmic sense. The dance is full of violence. How that came about through the above proceedings I don't remember, except if you have to bend and turn, attached or not to someone, and they are turning differently from you and at a greater or lesser speed, some kind of violence might occur.

Facts like these, attaching people together by outward means, always look as though they mean something. Well they do. Or rather they are. Here two persons are held together not only by the invisible bonds that can tie them

Pages 120–21: *Walka-round Time*, 1968. Photograph: James Klosty. Above: *Crises*, 1960. Carolyn Brown and MC. Photograph: John Wulp.

The moments at which an elastic band was slipped around a dancer's arm or waist were chance-determined. "It's about being attached—like a duet, a physical connection. I didn't want it to be done by grabbing, so it seemed to me that that was another way, and I tried those things out. But it was a random procedure."

The women's roles reflected not only the different dancers' ways of moving but their personalities. *Crises* began with a duet for Cunningham and Farber, who performed a series of violent dislocations of various parts of her body. "She was like someone you always knew would get there, but one part got there ahead of another." This gave a *farouche* quality to her stage presence in this role. At one point she and Cunningham half-crawled, half-slid along the floor side by side, with Cunningham propelling her by pushing her arm, to which his hand was attached by one of the elastics.

Brown too had a duet with Cunningham, in which she was like a wild creature being tamed by him. The entrance was memorable: Cunningham supported her by the waist and she leaned back, walking backward with high développés. Another extraordinary passage was Dunn's slow, deliberate cross, in which she paused every few steps on half-toe and slowly turned her gaze from one side to the other, creating an almost unbearable suspense. The piece ended, as so often, with a flurry of movement, the women approaching and withdrawing from Cunningham, who was in the middle, his mobility severely restricted by an elastic band around his knees.

but visibly, and without being the instrument of the holding.[5]

Cage commented on the dance:

This is a dramatic, though not a narrative, dance concerned with decisive moments in the relationship between a man and four women. The atmosphere is harsh and erotic. When two people are together, they are bound not only by invisible ties, but by actual elastic bands. In spite of such explicit relationships, Cunningham has made the situation mysterious, so that such questions as "What happened?" and "What does it mean?" are left to be answered differently by each observer.[6]

I had some idea in making up the gamut of movements that might be used that there would be rapid things, but there would also be very large things—if you did something very quick, then at the end of that to make something big, so that the whole thing had this almost spastic behavior, an abrupt way of going from one thing to another, but without some idea of transitions. How to make the movement stay big— often you can get into a certain position and you can see something to do, and you can do it small, but how to take that movement and make it large, so that it has a big edge to it. [This has been a constant concern of Cunningham's, both in his choreography and in his teaching.]

There were things about space, about getting to points where the movement phrase was taking you to; the nature of the movement you

had to do in that space would make the movement come out very abrupt and big and jagged. The same movement sometimes you might do in a smaller area, not having to go so far, and it could have a less abrupt feeling, because you didn't have to get such a distance in such a small time.

Nancarrow's music contributed greatly to the agitated atmosphere. These *Rhythm Studies* were composed in the early 1940s; Nancarrow himself laboriously punched holes in player piano rolls, creating an amazing multiplicity of jangling rhythms, which were then recorded. (In recent years Nancarrow's music has acquired new popularity because it has been perceived as prefiguring the minimalist music of the 1980s. Perhaps for this reason, many choreographers have used it.)

The costumes were simply leotards and tights dyed various shades of red; there was no set.

Responding traditionally to the disquieting quality of the dance movement, Rauschenberg decided to make it a "red" dance. However, the reds he uses range from pink through a deep red to one yellow, the color chosen for Viola Farber. Yellow functions here as the exaggerated extreme of red.[7]

• • •

As soon as the company finished its stint at Connecticut College, Cunningham set off for Europe again with Brown, Cage, and David Tudor. They were to perform at the XXIII Festival Internazionale di Musica Contemporanea, in Venice, at the time of the Biennale; at the 10th Berliner Festwochen, in

Opposite: *Crises*, 1960. MC and Viola Farber. Photograph: James Klosty. Above: *Music Walk with Dancers*, 1960. Left to right, foreground to background: Carolyn Brown, MC, John Cage, and David Tudor. Photograph: Manfred Leve.

Berlin; and in Munich and Cologne. Cunningham put together a program of solos and duets including *Suite for Two* (the duet version of *Suite for Five*) and *Night Wandering*. For the first and only time he was to perform all three of his solos to music by Christian Wolff—*Untitled Solo, Lavish Escapade,* and *Changeling*—on the same program. (*Lavish Escapade,* in fact, was never given again.) Between these three, Brown performed two solos that Cunningham had made especially for these engagements, *Hands Birds* and *Waka*. (A program note for *Hands Birds* reads, "The title is that of a poem by M. C. Richards," but in fact the title *was* the poem.) The program ended with another new piece, a duet named *Music Walk with Dancers*. None of these new dances was ever given again. Virgil Thomson, in a report from Venice to the *New York Times,* wrote, "Everybody, absolutely everybody, loved the dancing."[8]

On returning from Europe Cunningham resumed teaching at his 14th Street studio. It was about this time that the musician Robert Ellis Dunn began to conduct a series of composition classes there, assisted by Judith Dunn, then his wife. The participants included such dancers as Yvonne Rainer, David Gordon, Lucinda Childs, and Steve Paxton, and also some painters who were interested in making performance pieces. These classes led to the concerts of experimental dance at the Judson Memorial Church in Washington Square, out of which grew the "postmodern" phase of contemporary dance.

Cunningham was not directly involved in Dunn's classes, though he probably observed them from time to time, but clearly his influence was strongly felt, even in a negative sense. Cage was more important

still. Dunn had taken Cage's course in experimental music composition at The New School the previous year, and applied Cage's ideas in his own composition workshop. Following Cage's example, Dunn did not set himself up as an instructor, but rather encouraged the students to invent new dance structures, many of them game- or task-oriented.

There was a feeling among some of these younger dancers and choreographers, not excluding those who were members of Cunningham's company, that Cunningham wanted to retain too much control of his dances and their performance, and demanded too great a degree of theatricality and technical polish. This was the context in which Rainer later issued her famous manifesto beginning "NO to spectacle no to virtuosity. . . . "[9] Cage had abandoned such authority in the performance of his music, but Cunningham was too much of a choreographer to be willing to relinquish that control. He was not unaffected, however, by the experiments in Dunn's classes and later in the Judson Dance Theater concerts.

1961

In the summer of 1961 Cunningham made his first dance specifically for television, a *Suite de danses* to a jazz score by the Canadian composer Serge Garrant. The piece, which was "ten minutes long at the most," was commissioned by the Canadian television company Société Radio-Canada, rehearsed in New York, taped in Montreal on 12 June, and broadcast from there on 9 July. The costumes—leotards and tights—were dyed by Jasper Johns, and were the first this artist designed for Cunningham (although the two had known each other for several years, and Johns had on occasion assisted Robert Rauschenberg in his work for the company). Cunningham quickly realized that the space seen by the camera was different from that of the stage:

> I remember trying to figure out things for the camera, but I knew so little, and we had so little time, that I had no way of knowing whether it worked or not.

Cunningham was at Connecticut College again that summer, after a summer course at his own studio. To dance his most ambitious work so far, he took an augmented company: Shareen Blair and Steve Paxton joined the group, and Valda Setterfield—who had been an understudy in the previous three summers at Connecticut, and had replaced an injured

Viola Farber in some of her roles on the spring 1961 tour—also danced in the new piece:

ÆON

Though performed in Connecticut, *Æon* was commissioned by the Montreal Festival, and was first given there. Cunningham had earlier considered the titles *Stanzas and Actions* and *Combine* (Rauschenberg's word for his "assemblage" paintings, which included actual objects). The final title was appropriate to the work's scale. A program note read,

> This is a dance of actions, a celebration of unfixity, in which the seasons pass, atmospheres dissolve, people come together and part. Its meaning is the instant in the eye and ear, and its continuity is change.[1]

Cage later wrote the following description:

> This dance is epic in character, for, as its title indicates, a long time is involved [about forty-five minutes]. One event is followed, often overlapped, by another. At one point, as though it were the end of a period in history, the dancers come prostrate on the floor to a complete stop. The events, varied in character, generally elevated but not excluding fantasy and humor, form a history that can be told in many ways. That is, the dance is so made that it can be presented for a longer or shorter time, with more or less events and more or fewer performers, and the order that the events take can change from evening to evening.[2]

Events devised by Rauschenberg punctuated the piece. At the curtain's rise, three small magnesium explosions took place at the footlights, their smoke ascending and gradually clearing during the first few minutes. (This was somewhat reminiscent of one of Isamu Noguchi's effects in *The Seasons* of 1947.) During one leaping phrase the dancers were supposed to trigger small photo-flash bulbs attached to their wrists as they jumped; in another sequence, they unwound and passed among themselves a length of fire-hose. During the pause mentioned by Cage above, when the dancers lay prone, a "machine" passed above the stage, attached to a rope with a pulley. It was made of scrap metal—the skeleton of an umbrella, a dented aluminum water pitcher, and other odds and ends. A hurricane lamp hung below it, and the pitcher contained dry ice, which poured smoke. Cage described the machine as "an animated, slightly nonsensical object that occupies a space the dancers can't reach."[3]

Originally, it was intended that "crossovers [be] made behind a transparent curtain at the back of the stage, heightening the impression of people passing through their lives."[4]

As in *Antic Meet*, the dancers wore a basic costume of leotards and tights, to which various garments were added. Cage wrote,

> The dyeing of the tights and leotards, noticeably bluish, is in relation to the contours of the body. Rauschenberg attempted to give the impression that the bodies were colored but not covered.[5]

The added garments included pants, or chaps, made of feathers, worn by the men. In a slow duet, Carolyn Brown and Judith Dunn wore long veil-like sleeves that accentuated their broad arm movements. Brown also had a belt made of a rope to which various objects—a tin can, a sneaker—were attached.

The score used both Cage's *Atlas Eclipticalis* and his *Winter Music* (electronic version):

> All of the instruments make use of contact microphones and the amplification is such that sounds are distorted and transformed. The orchestral music (*Atlas Eclipticalis*) is a transcription from a book of maps of those stars in the great circle around the sun.[6]

Left: Robert Rauschenberg assembling the *Æon* "machine," Japan, 1964. Opposite, left: *Æon*, 1961. Left to right: Carolyn Brown, Steve Paxton, and MC. Opposite, right: *Æon*, 1961. Left to right: Carolyn Brown and Judith Dunn. Photographs: Richard Rutledge.

The composition means involved chance operations together with the placing of transparent templates on the pages of an astronomical atlas and inscribing the positions of stars.[7]

Æon in fact marks the introduction of "live electronic music" in the company's repertory. Before, live music had usually been played on the piano, by Cage and/or David Tudor (though sometimes with electronic amplification or distortion); occasionally, works like *Summerspace* and *Springweather and People* had been played in their orchestral versions. The music for *Crises* and *Suite by Chance* had been on tape. But Tudor was to devote himself more and more to the performance and, later, the composition of live electronic music, often using instruments that he himself had devised, and eventually he gave up playing the piano altogether.

A later member of the company described *Æon*:

It was vast and expansive; . . . it was like the history of the race somehow, [with] events of all kinds: little ones, big ones, cataclysmic ones, things that looked like war and pestilence, some lyric things. . . . It had scope, and it was really wonderful and difficult to do.[8]

Cunningham has written,

There were various trial orders of this dance, to see how one part could connect to the next. In the various ways we gave it (long version,

short version and tour version), I would leave out or add sections, I don't think they were transposed.

These trials were in my head and the notebook, not actually rehearsed this way.

The dance was 45 minutes long, after all it was called *Æon*. It eventually grouped itself into sections, I don't remember if this happened before the first performance in Montreal, perhaps it did. But I think the order had changed by the time we presented it the second time at the New London dance school later that month.

The machine could appear or not, [depending on] circumstances, the dancers went from one part to another: in the long version, everything; in the short version, everyone was in it, but one section was left out; in the tour version, several sections and dancers were not available.

As I read these notes over, I realize that one of our basic ideas was flexibility, that is, to take the circumstance for what it was, and present what we did in that, not as something which only represented or hinted at or was part of a whole, but what we gave in that place and time was the whole. Allowing each element in the spectacle to be separate, we could, under touring circumstances, rehearse more freely, without the need of a final "dress" rehearsal altogether. When the curtain time came, we all began, the

dancers, the sound, the machine if it was available, the flash powder if it could be set up, camera flash-lights on the dancers' wrists, if they were available, if they weren't the situation went on. It is a kind of anarchy where people may work freely together.[9]

This last comment well defines the nature of Cunningham's collaboration with his colleagues.

Æon was another Cunningham dance in which the various sections were named, in this case by Rauschenberg when he saw the dance in rehearsal: for example, "horse-tango," "moon-flower," and "gentlemencaller."

> In that piece—I wasn't playing a trick—I decided to try out something. I put a perfectly clear and concise theme and variations near the end—absolutely clear, with six variations, it's what the dancers called the "horror phrase." Nobody saw this. I knew they wouldn't, because you have to be told that there's a theme and variations, then you look for it. But it's an absolutely clear theme which is stated, and then the variations come along.

• • •

At the end of the summer, Remy Charlip left the company. The previous year he had been a founder of the innovative children's-theater company the Paper Bag Players, which occupied more and more of his time. His place was taken by Paxton. Rauschenberg did the lighting for the first performances of *Æon*, and now began to tour with the company as lighting designer and technical director, replacing Nick Cernovitch and Cernovitch's occasional substitute Richard Nelson.

Like Cernovitch before him, Rauschenberg knew little of stage-lighting technique, but by the same token he was free of preconceived ideas. In Cage's view he treated the stage not as a dark area but as one "illuminated, with white or near-white light, which can of course become dark momentarily. The lights are so set up that they can be acted upon spontaneously during an actual performance without pre-set cues. Rauschenberg's lighting is not an independent activity in this theater, but is provided in order to make the dancing visible and not censored or imposed upon by 'colored air' and its psychological implications."[10] As might be expected, professional theater technicians often considered Rauschenberg's approach crazy. On the other hand, according to Calvin Tomkins, Rauschenberg "found that other

people's lighting tended to alter the look of his costumes and sets. Having mastered the technical details on the job, he lit Cunningham's dances in the clear and undramatic style that Cunningham had always wanted. Cunningham felt that stage lighting should be like daylight, something dancers moved through. 'Bob agreed with that completely,' he said. 'He thought of lighting in flexible terms, a layer here and a layer there, like brushstrokes. Mostly white light. . . .'"[11]

Cunningham himself has said of Rauschenberg's contribution,

> [His] designing has ranged from a color scheme for basic leotards and tights to a complexity involving costumes and set. He has shown in all of this three things that the theater can absorb like water. One, the quality of the mysterious, or a poetic ambiguity set up as to what the object was. Two, a practicality—the gift to change something, by reduction or addition, or completely, depending on the immediate circumstances that the theater keeps providing. And three, a humaneness in respect to the individual dancer as to what he feels the dancer looks like, what makes that person and body interesting to his eye, and how to treat it visually.

Æon, 1961. Left to right: Steve Paxton, Carolyn Brown, Judith Dunn, Marilyn Wood, Viola Farber, and Shareen Blair (at rear). Photograph: Robert Rauschenberg.

And a dance whether only simply clothed, or involved with set, props, and costumes with headpieces and elaborate make-up, is not "eaten up" by these, but exists with them.

For a dancer he does the maximum thing a designer can do—he allows the dancer to be seen.[12]

1962

The year 1962 was the only one in Cunningham's entire career in which he did not present a new work. This was the period when artists were becoming interested in performance, whether by creating their own works ("happenings"), collaborating with choreographers like James Waring and Paul Taylor, or performing in pieces by the choreographers associated with the Judson Dance Theater (where the first "Concert of Dance" took place in July 1962). None of these works was easy to classify in conventional terms.

The Construction of Boston, performed just once, at the off-Broadway Maidman Theater, in May 1962, had a text by the poet Kenneth Koch and a mise-en-scène created collaboratively by Robert Rauschenberg and the European artists Niki de Saint-Phalle and Jean Tinguely. Cunningham reluctantly agreed to handle the overall direction, though in the end he could do little to control the participants, and on the night he asked John Wulp, the theater's manager, not to mention his name in the introductory announcement. Viola Farber and Steve Paxton appeared, but did not dance—instead they silently performed a number of everyday activities in an apartment setting built by Rauschenberg. The end result was less a collaboration than a free-for-all. Tinguely built a wall across the front of the stage, the completion of which brought the show to an end.[1]

1963

While touring in the winter, and preparing for a week of performances that he planned to give in a Broadway theater in the spring of 1963, Cunningham added Shareen Blair and William Davis to the company. Jasper Johns, together with Cage, Elaine de Kooning, the designer David Hayes, and theater producer Lewis L. Lloyd, had formed a foundation, the Foundation for Contemporary Performance Arts, to sponsor and fund-raise in the performance field; its first project was an exhibition and sale of artist-donated works to help finance this projected season, which was announced for mid-April in the March issue of *Dance Magazine*. Two new works and three New York premieres were advertised, the latter presumably being *Night Wandering*, *Crises*, and *Æon*.

The exhibition took place, at the Allan Stone Gallery, but the season did not. A newspaper strike that would have seriously reduced the amount of publicity the company could hope for made a postponement seem advisable. A news item in the July *Dance Magazine* stated that the season would take place at the Winter Garden, from 23 to 30 September 1963, but the theater proved unavailable, and the season was canceled.

From 17 June to 26 July the company was in residence at the University of California, Los Angeles. There had been further changes in personnel: Judith Dunn and Marilyn Wood had left in May, and the dancers who went to California were Carolyn Brown, Viola Farber, Shareen Blair, Barbara (Dilley) Lloyd (then married to Lewis Lloyd), William Davis, and Steve Paxton. (Later in the year, Cunningham also took in Sandra Neels.) Cunningham and Cage rented a beach house in Malibu for this group.

Besides teaching, Cunningham rehearsed two new works that were given at UCLA on 17 and 24 July, and that represented a new departure in his work. Two pages of his notebook describe "3 dances to make": the first is identified by the initials "DFE," standing for the title *Dances for Everybody*, but later came to be called *Field Dances*; the second is called *Variations*, later changed to *Story*. The third dance, *Winterbranch*, was not done until the following year.

> Both [*Story* and *Field Dances*] are concerned with variable factors during the performance. *Story* was the more complex of the two. But each dealt in fragments which could be freely changed in the order and place and time. . . . The fragments and sections for both dances were choreographed. . . . The variable factors were in the change of continuity, the length of fragments and sections and the changes in space.[1]

This implied a greater degree of indeterminacy than had previously existed in Cunningham's work, and was the closest he ever came to permitting improvisation.

FIELD DANCES

The original directions indicate "to be done anywhere." The original premise is a dance for X number of people—as the name suggests, a "field" of activity.[2] They have a number, about seven I think, of things or small events they can do together, and each dancer has one, two or three short dances he can deal with as he chooses. They can leave and enter at any point. Rehearsals consisted of each dancer doing all the various movements available to him. The movements given them are purposely simple. An aisle, a street, a field, a theater, a basketball court. The movements had been given to the dancers. The dancers are free to find the movement and speed within their own range, to do it as often as they want and complete it or not. Composed at UCLA, it was originally done with four dancers and [later] with nine. Space-wise, this could be an irregular area. The dance begins when the curtain goes up and ends when the time allotted for the particular performance, say 12′, is over.

The dancers made their own choices of movements, and their own decisions as to how many times they would do a given movement or phrase, at what tempo, and where in the space. They were also affected by the others' choices: certain movements called for a response. When the man sat on the floor, for instance, one or more of the women had to go to him, put her hands on his shoulders, and do a small jump.

To an interviewer in London, Cunningham gave a rather familiar account of the genesis of *Field Dances*:

> I watched some kids out of the window once—I was teaching at Boulder, Colorado—and I was sitting drinking my coffee—they were little children, five and six years old. They were running and skipping, and suddenly I thought, "They're dancing." There wasn't any music. They were having such a beautiful time. *Field Dances* came from that because I could see that they were running and skipping and to me it was dancing; but for them it wasn't different.[3]

Cage's account in a letter to a friend varies somewhat from this, but is on similar lines:

> Merce had made the dance thinking of my story in *Die Reihe* about traveling up to Boston and hearing the juke box while seeing the swimmers and noticing they went well together. So I made the music so that most of the sounds would come from 'other' places.[4]

Field Dances, Cage said, "begins, continues, and comes to an end only for existential reasons." His music for the piece was called *Variations IV*.

> The sounds of this piece are not determined. Means are provided for determining only the points in space, mostly outside the theater, from which the sounds originate. It can be performed by any number of players and could consist solely of opening and shutting the doors that lead out to the streets.[5]

Robert Rauschenberg's costumes were leotards with chiffon panels attached to the back for the women, and a sweatshirt for the man, over tights; all the garments were decorated with blotches of color. Cage wrote that they were "designed in Southern California, [and] the colors . . . are like the many flowers of the Southwest."[6]

STORY

Story, Cunningham wrote, was rather more complex:

> It is a dance for X-number of people and had seven dancers in it at its first performance. Since that time it has been given nineteen times in the United States, with the number of performers ranging from five to eight. [It was also given twenty-nine times during the 1964 world tour. *Story* was never performed in New York, though in 1994, Cunningham reconstructed some sections for inclusion in Events there.] The structure is indeterminate, and the length is

made to be varied. It has been as short as fifteen minutes and as long as forty.

> We played [*Story*] a great many times as it could involve one or all of the dancers, and be given under any kind of extreme circumstance. We have presented it, among other places, on a huge stage in Augusta, Georgia—actually a double stage that was situated between two auditoriums. In this case both halls were open and visible to each other with all curtains lifted, and one hall being populated, the other empty. We have presented it on the thrust stage of the Tyrone Guthrie Theater in Minneapolis, Minnesota, with exits through the tunnels under the seats; and on a minuscule stage in Duluth, Minnesota, where—to have more flexibility and space—we employed the floor of the auditorium in front of the stage, and the stairs and doors leading to it.[7]

> The dance was made up of a series of sections, solos, duets, trios, and larger units, that could freely go from one to the other, so their order was changeable. Within a section the movements given to a particular dancer could change in space and time and the order the dancer chose to do them in could come from the instant of doing them. Also the length of each section varied each time. The sections were given names for reasons of identification—"Object," "Triangle," "Floor," "Tag," "Space," "Entrance," and others. "Object," for example, refers to an actual object constructed fresh for each performance, which is moved or carried around the stage by the dancers. "Floor" indicates a duet for two of the women, Carolyn Brown and Viola Farber, which starts at any point in the space, on or off the stage. The two dancers move in a pronounced, slow tempo across the area, possibly separated, but more often together. In "Space," the dancers had possibility for improvisation within a space scale. There is a "Five-Part Trio," which is as it says, three people who have five phrases each to contend with, the movement in this section being swift. The entire number of possibilities consists of eighteen parts, all or any group of which may be done in a given performance.[8] Rehearsals consisted of each dancer doing all the parts of a given section.

> The music by [Toshi] Ichiyanagi is a composition, in the composer's words, for "sustained sounds, without attack and continuous." Into this atmosphere may come sharp, vibrant sounds. The composer has left the players free as to choice of instruments.[9]

> My original idea for the costumes was that they be picked up or found in the particular playing situation we were in, and that the set, or the way the stage looked, would also be devised from the existing circumstances and environment at the time of the performance.

> The variables in the structure, which are changed at each performance, are: the length of the whole, and the length of the separate sections, and the placement of the sections in the continuity. The relationship of the sound is constantly

varied, as the only agreement between the dance and the music is the length decided upon for that performance. Although the dancers listen to the sounds and are sometimes engaged by them, this is not a support and certainly cannot be counted upon to happen again.

The title does not refer to any implicit or explicit narrative, but to the fact that each spectator may interpret the events in his own way.[10]

Indeed a flyer advertising the first performance at UCLA said, "The title . . . is meant to indicate the possibility to each spectator of making (or not) his own narrative from it."[11]

The decor for *Story* was arrived at more or less in the way Cunningham wished: Rauschenberg usually constructed a set from material he found in and around the theater on the day of any given performance. When *Story* was given on four consecutive evenings in London during the 1964 world tour, Rauschenberg worked on a painting onstage during the performances; at the end of the last one, the painting was finished. (Called *Story*, it is now in the collection of the Art Gallery of Ontario in Toronto.) Earlier, at Dartington Hall in Devon, Rauschenberg and his assistant, Alex Hay, "brought in two ironing

Robert Rauschenberg and Viola Farber on set of *Story*, 1963, Paris, 1964. Photograph: Harry Shunk.

boards and proceeded to iron their shirts at the rear of the stage." In both these situations, Calvin Tomkins remarked, "the dancers felt somewhat upstaged."[12]

As for the costumes, the dancers wore a basic outfit of gold leotard and tights for the women and black tights and blue leotards for the men, to which they added garments gathered by Rauschenberg. This collection was carried in a large duffel bag and dumped on the floor backstage; the dancers were free to wear whatever they chose from it, and to change as often as they wished. "My favorite memory," Brown has written, "is of Barbara Lloyd putting on all the costumes she could manage, leaving the rest of us with next to nothing, and making herself so large and encumbered she could barely move."[13] This was in Japan, where, on another occasion (which proved to be the last performance of the dance), she took everything off, including her leotard and tights, then dressed again.

It is probably true that *Field Dances* and *Story* reflected Cunningham's reaction to the kind of experiments that were going on at the Judson Dance Theater, where choreographers tried not to exercise complete control over their performers. A running order, with timings for the various sections, was posted in the wings at each performance of *Story*. This order was to some extent chance determined, "except that there were certain practical limits" as to what could follow what, "but within those I would change it as much as I could." In *Field Dances* the dancers were even free to choose the sequence of the phrases (which were fewer and simpler than those of *Story*) and the length of time they spent on each one.

There was a feeling among the dancers that Cunningham disliked *Story*, precisely because he had relinquished a degree of control over it, which was against his instincts. The truth seems to be that it was the dancers who disliked the piece, feeling that the freedom it gave them was limited—that so many restrictions were built into the choreography, they felt just as constrained as when their roles were set. Cunningham had solos, duets with Brown and Farber, and trios with both of them, while the other dancers were relegated to being, as one of them put it, like a corps de ballet. This, it may be said, is not the impression one receives from the television film of a performance in Helsinki in 1964.

Anyone who saw some of Cunningham's own riveting performances in *Story* would find it hard to believe he disliked the piece, even though he may not always have enjoyed the way some of the dancers, and

This page: *Story*, 1963,
Connecticut College,
New London, 1963.
Left to right: MC,
William Davis, Viola
Farber, and Barbara
Dilley Lloyd. Photo-
graph: Fannie Helen
Melcer. Opposite, top:
Story, 1963, Ostiava,
1964. Left to right:
Sandra Neels, Albert
Reid, and Barbara
Dilley Lloyd. Photo-
graph: Jaroslav
Kokstain. Opposite,
bottom: *Story*, 1963,
Tokyo, 1964. Left to
right: Carolyn Brown,
John Cage, and MC.
Photograph: *Japan
Times*.

Rauschenberg, performed in it.[14] He himself has said that he very much liked a couple of performances of the work ("a couple of them I didn't like"). In Ostrava, Czechoslovakia, the curtain went up on a stage stripped to the walls. The performance began with Cunningham performing a solo in a small passageway at stage rear; the kafkaesque quality of this beginning was not lost on the spectators.

Story was in the repertory for two years, during which it was probably performed more than any other dance. As Cunningham has said, it could be done anywhere. It was dropped after the 1964 world tour, however. Several reasons for this have been given: it has been said that Brown wrote a letter to Cunningham, on behalf of the company, asking him to do so.[15] It is certainly true that Rauschenberg's contribution was so important, even if he did go too far sometimes, that once he left the company, at the end of the 1964 tour, there was almost no point in doing the piece. Cunningham's own explanation is that indeterminacy is simply not practical in a touring situation:

> As we toured more it got harder and harder on everybody, because by the time you get some place you're so tired, you can bring yourself physically together, but if in performance, while you're trying to keep your energy together, you also have your head jumping around, it's just very very hard, and there's a great tendency toward accidents, because you can't quite judge anything, your physical strength is not at its peak, and your coordination and so on.
>
> It's all right if you know exactly what you're to do, to bring it together and do it. One of the reasons we did *Story* everywhere was that it could be done in different spaces. One of the best performances, I remember, was in Osaka, with that wonderful bunch of musicians, they were in back of us, it was like a Kabuki stage. That was one of the performances where I thought, that's what the piece is about. All these things went on, and they all seemed to enter into this atmosphere. We did these silly things, or grave things, or whatever, and it all seemed to work. But so often it had to be done in truncated circumstances, it was just hopeless.

• • •

During the fall tour that year, Cunningham began to include a general note in the company's programs:

> Dancing has a continuity of its own that need not be dependent upon either the rise and fall of sound (music) or the pitch and cry of words (literary ideas). Its force of feeling lies in the physical image, fleeting or static. It can and does evoke all sorts of individual responses in the single spectator. These dances may be seen in this light.
>
> The music and dance co-exist as individual but interpenetrating happenings, jointly experienced in the length of time they take up and divide.[16]

1964

For two or three years, Cunningham and Cage had been receiving invitations to visit India, from the Sarabhai family, and Japan, from the Sogetsu Art Center, Tokyo. Cage had known Gita Sarabhai for some twenty years; he had taught her about contemporary Western music in exchange for lessons on Indian music. The invitation from the Sogetsu Art Center came about through Toshi Ichiyanagi, whose music Cunningham had used for *Story* and who sometimes played for classes at the Cunningham Studio. (He was at that time married to Yoko Ono.)

It was decided that the funds intended for the canceled 1963 Broadway season should go toward the cost of a tour in India and Japan. If enough dates could be found, the tour would also be extended to Europe. It would start in the spring of 1964.

The financing of a world tour was obviously a formidable problem. Available proceeds from the art sale staged by the Foundation for Contemporary Performance Arts—a little over $20,000—would not nearly cover it; and no help was forthcoming from the United States Department of State. Thanks to Porter McCray, the JDR 3rd Fund gave a generous grant for travel expenses to the Far East. (The sponsors in India and Japan had undertaken to cover the company only within those countries.) The company did not then command the kind of fees in foreign countries that it would later receive, and the income from performances would cover only about a third of the tour's cost.

Clearly the old system, whereby Cunningham himself pocketed the fee check and then paid everyone's expenses, would not work in an undertaking of this magnitude. His accountant, Rubin Gorewitz, accordingly advised him to incorporate himself. The Cunningham Dance Foundation was formed early in 1964, the first such corporation, I believe, in the modern dance field, though it has since become the practice for nearly every choreographer who forms a company of any size to do so within such a structure.

The tour was finally scheduled to begin early in June. Meanwhile there were further tour dates in the United States in February and March, culminating in a series of performances at the Wadsworth Atheneum in Hartford, Connecticut, during which almost the whole of the repertory for the world tour was performed, including two new dances:

PAIRED

This was a duet for Viola Farber and myself consisting of nine events to be done together, the sequence to be determined during performance. The events were color-cued, and offstage was a cue sheet.[1] There were preparatory running steps in between events during which either of us could go off stage, dip paint, [re-enter] and smear it on one another as a cue to the next movement. We tried doing it without the cue sheet but couldn't remember what color referred to what movement and what had been done and what was left to do. It was a violent dance. Once she kicked me in the forehead,

Rehearsal at the Cunningham Studio prior to the world tour, 1964. Left to right, seated: Barbara Dilley Lloyd, John Cage, Sandra Neels, Shareen Blair, and Robert Rauschenberg. Left to right, standing: MC, Carolyn Brown, Steve Paxton, William Davis, and Viola Farber. Photograph: Robert Rauschenberg.

another time I dropped her head on the floor, and again we cracked heads. Also one audience threw eggs and tomatoes (Paris).[2]

Hazardous as it was, *Paired* was tailor-made for Farber's personality, like her roles in *Crises* and other dances. Partnering Farber, Cunningham has said, was like partnering two people at once. "Once she said to me, don't worry, I'll get there, and I said, I *never* worry!"

WINTERBRANCH

Cunningham's notes from the previous year on "dances to make" describe the concept of the piece succinctly:

Falls—& Silence
everything is flexible
20′ length is permanent
divisions of space & time are flexible.[3]

Although there have been many interpretations of *Winterbranch*, the choreographic content was just what Cunningham said it would be:

I have a tendency to deal with what I call facts in dancing. In *Winterbranch*, what was involved was the fact of falling . . . that is going off the balance of two feet onto the ground. Falling—unless one wants to stay there—presumes the act of rising; that is getting up onto the two feet again. So that *Winterbranch* began with the physical fact of a human being falling and ris-

ing. Other factors, visual and sound factors, entered later . . . not to change the original fact, but to add to it.[4]

Nevertheless, Cunningham's further notes on the piece implicitly acknowledge the effect that it inevitably had on the spectator:

There is a streak of violence in me. . . . I was interested in the possibility of having a person dragged out of the area while lying or sitting down. This brought up a practical problem about stage splinters, bad floors, so I experimented with a piece of material on which the dancer would sit. Later Bob Rauschenberg turned this into pieces of canvas which we sometimes had difficulty keeping track of while abroad. The stagehands would see these lumps of canvas lying on the sides of the stage where we had carefully placed them and would remove them cleaning up.

The structure is simple. People—one, two or more—walk into an area, the performing space, they take positions, usually upright standing ones, adjacent to each other, and from that they engage in a movement configuration, usually falling. At the end of this activity they break off and walk out of the playing area, or perhaps the movement takes them off.

Winterbranch has caused some sort of furor wherever it has been presented, some places more, some places less. The most was in New

135

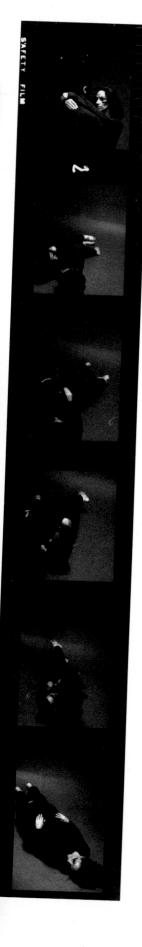

York City. It was made to change its order from performance to performance, but we do it the same way each time now. This is partially due to habit, but also to the spaces we are given to perform in and the shortness of time available for rehearsal when touring.

The sound element, *2 sounds* by La Monte Young, is an electronic extension of two different sounds, one low and one high, which goes continuously for most of the piece, 15 minutes.

The lighting is done freely each time, differently, so that the rhythms of the movements are differently accented and the shapes differently seen, partially or not at all. I asked Robert Rauschenberg to think of the light as though it were night instead of day. I don't mean night as referred to in romantic pieces, but night as it is in our time with automobiles on highways, and flashlights in faces, and the eyes being deceived about shapes the way light hits them.[5]

As additional protection, Rauschenberg dressed the dancers in sweatsuits and sneakers. He also had them paint black smudges under their eyes, as footballers do to counteract glare. (It seems that at one point Cunningham wanted them to wear "day-glo bibs of orange" or possibly "costumes from bandages."[6])

The dance began with Cunningham crawling slowly across the stage carrying a flashlight, his body encased in a tube of black fabric. Then began the series of falls of which the piece is constructed, in both fast and slow motion. The men hunched over and the women fell backward across their backs. Farber did a very slow spiral fall, landing on a tarpaulin that was dragged off by two men. Carolyn Brown fell back across Cunningham's body and he rolled across the floor, carrying her with him. Toward the end, five dancers moved across the stage in a cluster, falling and rising. Then Farber entered and threw a canvas sheet over them as they lay in a heap, and they crawled off under it. The last section was a reprise of several of the previous events. At a certain point an object made by Rauschenberg from materials he found in the theater (like the set for *Story*) was pulled slowly across the empty stage on a rope. Usually there was a lamp of some kind whose red light would blink on and off.

We called it the monster. And on one tour [after Rauschenberg had left the company, the composer] Pauline Oliveros was the monster. It was in La Jolla, where she was teaching. I met her on the street and she did a little dance, and I rushed over to say hello and she said, can you use me? And I said certainly, come to rehearsal tomorrow at noon. . . . . She was wonderful, she had sparklers, and she came in on a big kind of dolly, in a great huge dress, she looked like Gertrude Stein with fireworks.

In many places *Winterbranch* provoked a scandal.

In Sweden they said it was about race riots; in Germany they thought of concentration camps, in London they spoke of bombed cities; in Tokyo they said it was the atom bomb. A lady with us took care of the child [Benjamin Lloyd] who was on the trip. She was the wife of a sea captain and said it looked like a shipwreck to her. . . . . Everybody was drawing on his own experience, whereas I had simply made a piece which was involved with *falls*, the idea of bodies falling.[7]

The lighting and sound accompaniment undoubtedly contributed to the dance's dramatic effect. (When parts of *Winterbranch* were later performed without them, in Event performances, audiences often laughed, as at pratfalls, which never happened when the work was performed as a repertory piece.) Young's *2 sounds* was excruciating: one of its elements was "the sound of ashtrays scraped against a mirror, the other, that of pieces of wood rubbed against a Chinese gong,"[8] amplified up to or perhaps beyond the limit of human endurance. *Winterbranch* made no concessions to the audience, and was both more personal and more truly experimental than either *Story* or *Field Dances*, which were less the products of personal conviction, even if they reflected contemporary trends in avant-garde dance.

• • •

On 3 June 1964, a company of sixteen flew to Paris. There were nine dancers: Cunningham, Brown, Farber, Shareen Blair, Barbara Lloyd, Sandra Neels, William Davis, Paxton, and Albert Reid; the two musicians, Cage and David Tudor; the designer, Rauschenberg, and his assistant, the painter Alex Hay; Hay's then wife, Deborah Hay, who would be a tenth dancer in a few pieces; and two administrators, Lewis Lloyd and the present writer. The repertory on the tour consisted of *Æon*, *Antic Meet*, *Crises*, *Field Dances*, *Night Wandering*, *Nocturnes*, *Paired*, *Rune*, *Septet*, *Story*, *Suite for Five*, *Summerspace*, *Winterbranch*, and three of Cunningham's solos: *Changeling*, *Collage III*, and *Untitled Solo*.

The company's cash assets totaled some $40,000. In addition to the grants from the Foundation for Contemporary Performance Arts and the JDR 3rd Fund, there had been gifts from individuals, notably Mary Hayes Sisler, Judith Peabody, Philip Johnson, Rauschenberg, and Betty Freeman, a long-time supporter of contemporary music in general and of Cage in particular. The dancers (except for Cunningham) and the administrators were paid $165 a week. Cunningham, the musical director, the pianist, the designer, and the designer's assistant were each paid $185. There was no per diem for living expenses (most of the company members managed to save part of their salaries). It was hoped that performance fees would make up the deficit in the budget, though many of these were small enough in all conscience. The tour, to put it bluntly, was a real barnstorming operation.

In Europe, the company traveled mostly in a chartered bus. On arrival at Orly Airport on the morning of 4 June, after being greeted by Bénédicte Pesle and other friends, they drove to Strasbourg, where, on the 6th, the first performance of the tour took place at the Théâtre de la Comédie. The program was *Æon, Crises,* and *Nocturnes.* The most enthusiastic audience response that evening came from the young people in the upper reaches of the house, and this set the pattern for most of the tour. Strasbourg was a kind of out-of-town tryout for Paris, where three performances had been arranged by Françoise and Dominique Dupuy, animators of the Ballets Modernes de Paris. (The company also gave an *avant-première* lecture-demonstration in the Dupuys' Paris studio.) Three different programs were given at the Théâtre de l'Est Parisien, in the twentieth arrondissement, on 12, 13, and 14 June. The performances received critical notice of the most serious kind, especially from the veteran critic Dinah Maggie in *Le Combat.* Two days after this engagement ended, the company performed at the Maison de la Culture in Bourges.

While the company was in and around Paris, its activities were recorded by a French film crew headed by the young director Etienne Becker. Some remarkable footage was shot of both rehearsals and performances, as well as interviews with Cunningham, Cage, and Rauschenberg. Unfortunately, this material was reduced to about a quarter of an hour in the final cut—which was edited, moreover, to give it the look of some existentialist drama, emphasizing sweat and strain, the whole accompanied by what sounded like bongo drums.[9]

From Paris the company flew to Venice, for a single performance on 18 June at the Teatro La Fenice. That year Rauschenberg won the Venice Biennale's international grand prize. The Cunningham performance took place the day before the jury reached its decision, and was generally assumed to be part of a carefully orchestrated campaign by Leo Castelli, Rauschenberg's dealer, to secure the prize for his client.[10] Cunningham's program certainly displayed Rauschenberg's work for the company at its most brilliant and diverse: *Antic Meet, Summerspace,* and *Story.* (Rauschenberg's set for the latter involved the theater's stage elevators, its revolving stage, and even the stagehands, whom he instructed "to move about in the background, pushing brooms or carrying props."[11])

Four days later the company left by bus for its next date, in Vienna. Earlier in the year, Dr. Gerhart Rindauer, director of that city's Museum des 20.Jahrhunderts, had visited Cunningham in his New York studio and invited the company to perform in the museum, but there was no theater there, only a large room on the ground floor where a platform stage could be set up. Cunningham looked at photographs of the space and decided that a repertory program would not be feasible. A platform stage would not allow the hanging of scenery, and intermissions would present a problem, since it would be awkward for the audience to leave and reenter the room. He therefore proposed a different kind of presentation, a continuous performance lasting about an hour and a half, without intermission, consisting of excerpts from the repertory—parts of dances or even

Below: Left to right, top row: Carolyn Brown, MC, John Cage, Doris Stockhausen, David Tudor, and Karlheinz Stockhausen. Bottom row: Steve Paxton, Michael von Biel, and Robert Rauschenberg, Cologne, July 1964. Opposite: Rehearsal at Les Baux, Provence, July 1964. Left to right: Viola Farber, Sandra Neels, Shareen Blair, William Davis, Deborah Hay, Barbara Lloyd, Steve Paxton, Carolyn Brown, and Alex Hay.

complete works—put together in a new sequence. These could overlap or even be performed simultaneously in different parts of the space. The title would be *Museum Event No. 1.*

The performance took place on the evening of 24 June. The accompaniment was a continuous performance of Cage's *Atlas Eclipticalis*, which was not the usual music for any of the pieces performed except *Æon.* It was played by Cage, Tudor, and members of the ensemble "die Reihe," who were situated around the performing area. The audience sat on three sides of the space and in a gallery above it. The fourth side was a glass wall looking out on the museum's sculpture garden, where people could be seen until dusk (the performance began at 7:30 P.M.), when the glass began to reflect back the lights that Rauschenberg had directed onto the performing area. At one point Rauschenberg himself walked across the back of the space, festooned with umbrellas.

This was the first of Cunningham's Event performances. In a sense the concept derived from that of Cage's Black Mountain theater piece twelve years before, and satisfied better than *Story* Cunningham's desire to allow for a degree of indeterminacy in performance.[12]

The next day the company moved on to Germany, where it performed in Mannheim on 27 June,

in Mies van der Rohe's Nationaltheater. Owing to the haphazard, not to say amateurish planning of the tour, the company was next scheduled to wait for two weeks in Cologne, where a single performance had been booked for 12 July. Here, however, Cunningham, Cage, and Rauschenberg met the great choreographer Kurt Jooss, who invited the company to give a performance at the Folkwang Hochschule in Essen. The fee was minimal, but Cunningham was happy to accept since the date broke up an unwelcome period of inactivity. He was also sensible of the honor of being invited to perform in the home of the Ballets Jooss.

The stage proved to be tiny—more like a shelf, as Cunningham said. He chose works that could be adapted without too much difficulty to such a space: *Suite for Five, Winterbranch, Untitled Solo,* and *Story.* The local dancers were puzzled by what they saw, but there was a vociferous, presumably friendly response from a group of art students, devotees of Joseph Beuys, from the nearby town of Düsseldorf, who at the end of the show banged their chairs on the floor while moving them up toward the stage.

The Cologne performance had been arranged with the help of Todd Bolender, then the director of the Opera ballet company, who had also arranged for Cunningham to have the use of a studio in the opera house during his stay in the city. Much of the audience was loud in its disapproval, but the performance was reviewed enthusiastically by Horst Koegler and Gerhard Brunner.

The following day the company drove south in its chartered bus, heading for Avignon on what would turn out to be a two-and-a-half-day trip. The next performance, on 16 July, was in a dance festival at Les Baux-de-Provence, again under the aegis of Françoise and Dominique Dupuy. Conditions at Les Baux were primitive. It was much too hot to rehearse during the day, so the company rehearsed on the night of their arrival. The mosquitoes were virulent. Rauschenberg augmented the lighting for *Story* with the headlights of two or three automobiles.

Having driven all the way from the Rhineland to Provence for one performance, the company then had to make its way north again, first to Paris and then, after a one-night stopover, to Calais and on by boat to Dover. Here a bus was waiting to take most of them to Devonshire, for performances at Dartington College of Arts, near Totnes. Cage, Cunningham, Rauschenberg, and I took a train to London, where there was to be a press conference the next day, at Sadler's Wells Theatre.

The invitation to Dartington had come about partly through the good offices of Dorothy Whitney Elmhurst, the American widow of the school's founder, Leonard Elmhurst. She had been closely connected for many years with the Cornish School in Seattle, and knew Cunningham from his time there. (Dartington had been the English home of the Ballets Jooss during the 1930s.) Dartington Hall, with its ancient buildings and exquisite gardens, seemed idyllically peaceful after the company's arduous journeys, and the dancers had a couple of days' rest before they gave an open dress rehearsal for students on 22 July, followed by performances on the two succeeding days. Dartington's Barn Theatre offered another tiny stage, but the company managed to perform a good portion of its repertory during the three evenings.

On 25 July, a Saturday, there was another long bus ride, to London. On the 27th the company opened at Sadler's Wells. The London producer Michael White had originally booked it sight unseen, but he had gone to see one of the Paris performances, after which he wrote, "I'm completely bowled over. Everything is fantastic, the intellectual expression, dancing, music and decor."[13] The theater director Peter Brook had also attended a performance in Paris, and wrote a foreword for the London program:

Merce Cunningham's work is of the highest quality and of great importance. It searches in new directions, it is free, it is open to the play of all the forces which the artists involved sense without being able to control—and yet it is precise, classical and severe. This is a mysterious marriage brought about by an intense creativity. The work of Merce Cunningham's group is in the tradition of Martha Graham in many ways, but in one most of all. The very things that are criticised, laughed at and ignored will only a few months later be imitated everywhere.[14]

To coincide with the London season, an exhibition of photographs of the company by Jack Mitchell opened at the American Embassy in Grosvenor Square, organized by Francis S. Mason, then deputy cultural attaché, who also gave an opening-night party in his London home. During the week the full repertory was performed, with the exception of *Field Dances* and *Collage III*, and with the addition of a new dance, first performed on Friday 31 July:

CROSS CURRENTS

This was a small work, a trio danced by Cunningham, Brown, and Farber. The title could have been interpreted narrowly and literally, since the dancers' paths frequently intersected, but it also referred to the piece's rhythmic qualities:

In the original version there was some freedom in the rhythms, but I couldn't remember them when I brought it back. There were things when suddenly the rhythms would go off among the three of us, and then we'd come together at the end. Now it's like a set piece. But the idea was that there were these three people who often had quite different rhythms and then they would come together at the end of the phrase. Originally the differences were more emphasized. But it has remained amazingly exact in time: it was 7½ minutes when we did it, and it still is.

Cross Currents received few performances as a separate work, but later became part of the material used in Events.

Cunningham adds that four pieces—*Winterbranch, Open Session* (a solo), *Paired,* and *Cross Currents*—were "made for the tour." Although *Cross Currents* was not given until London, he had worked on it in New York: "I got these hints that we could be performing in odd places—which came true," and

Cross Currents, 1964.
MC and Viola Farber.
Photograph: Douglas
H. Jeffrey.

all the pieces could be adapted to any situation. (*Open Session*, in fact, was done only in Hartford before the tour started.)

• • •

"Alexander Bland" (Nigel Gosling) had seen the company in Venice and wrote an advance notice in the *Observer*. "Everything is measured, calm, distilled. . . . [Cunningham] is unpretentious, relaxed, abstract, throw-away."[15] He followed this with an even more enthusiastic review at the end of the first week:

> At a blow, ballet has been brought right up in line with the front-rank experimenters in the other arts—something which has hardly happened since the days of Diaghilev. Here is heart-warming proof that it is an art with a future, opening up ranges of possibilities which stretch out of sight. . . .
>
> Diaghilev would have loved Cunningham. Besides admiring him as an artist he would have respected the seriousness and discipline of his company, the spare wit and style of Rauschenberg's costumes and lighting, the consistent

invention of the choreography and the provocative strangeness of John Cage's musical accompaniments. Above all, his acute artistic antennae would have tingled at the sense that Cunningham was talking in the language of today. . . .

> Instead of a steady beat he uses a sense of time. Like experienced runners completing a track-circuit his dancers (who rehearse with a stopwatch) can perform a sequence to split-second accuracy. . . .
>
> We are not so far here from the world of Petipa and Balanchine, and the total effect has the aloof conviction of the best classical dance. The element of ritual, so vital to a theatrical performance, is strong and the dancers themselves exude a powerful stage presence. . . .
>
> [The dances] are austere to the point of monotony . . . but they are so full of invention that they will be a mine for imitators for years. And they are beautiful in the disturbing way which makes you feel your angle of vision has been permanently shifted, which is a kind of beauty you don't get often.[16]

Even more of a problem than the two weeks of inactivity in Cologne was the lack of any engagement at all in August. Cunningham thought it essential to keep the company together, either in England or in Sweden (the next booking was in Stockholm early in September). Michael White came to the rescue: the Phoenix Theatre in the Charing Cross Road was empty, and White proposed an immediate transfer there for a further two-and-a-half-week run. Business at Sadler's Wells had steadily improved, and White thought it worth gambling on a continuation of this trend, particularly in a theater in the center of London. From the company's point of view, this proposal solved the problem of the hiatus in the tour (they would close at the Phoenix on 22 August), and even if the extended run did not sell out, any income was better than none, which was what they faced.

The company accordingly opened at the Phoenix on Wednesday, 5 August, and during the engagement gave four programs, performing each one on four successive evenings. *Field Dances*, which had not been given at the Wells, was on the second program. The combined engagements, lasting four weeks, added up to the longest so far in the company's history. Though not to the extent White had hoped, audiences did in fact build during the run; the company had begun to attract a following, and there were many who came night after night.

As in other European cities, these audiences included many artists and art students attracted by Rauschenberg's participation, as well as musicians interested in Cage. In the dance world the company's strongest supporter was Marie Rambert, long an advocate of dancing's right to exist independently of music. Ninette de Valois, Frederick Ashton, Margot Fonteyn, Rudolf Nureyev, and Kenneth MacMillan all attended performances. Ashton and Fonteyn both went backstage to see Cunningham: Ashton said he liked *Nocturnes* ("All those nuns' veils," he said, referring to the headdresses) and even *Winterbranch*, and said, "You are a poet, and I like poetic ballets." MacMillan, on the other hand, left before the end.

Cunningham's most devoted following was among theater people. Directors like Lindsay Anderson, George Devine, William Gaskill, and Peter Gill, the designer Jocelyn Herbert, actors like Irene Worth and Harold Lang returned several times to see the company. The London season was exciting for the dancers, but exhausting, not only in the unprecedented number of performances (with a daily schedule of class and rehearsals) but in the number of parties given for them by dance and theater people who became their friends. One party celebrated an unexpected event: Shareen Blair got married, and left the company at the end of the engagement. Cunningham took Deborah Hay into the company to replace her, at least for the rest of the tour.

The Stockholm engagement was arranged by Pontus Hultén, then director of the Moderna Museet, who planned a series of "5 New York evenings" in conjunction with an exhibition of works by Rauschenberg, Jean Tinguely, Niki de Saint-Phalle, Per Ultvedt, Claes Oldenburg, and Öyvind Fählstrom. Cunningham agreed to do two performances in a large room at the museum, to be called *Museum Event No. 2* and . . . *No. 3*, on 8 and 14 September. In between, there would be a concert of piano music by Tudor and two further dance concerts, one by Yvonne Rainer and Robert Morris and one by Rauschenberg. In addition, three pieces by the Cunningham company, also danced at the museum, would be filmed for Swedish television, under the direction of Arne Arnbom. As in Vienna, the first Stockholm event was accompanied by Cage's *Atlas Eclipticalis*. The music for the second was Cage's *Variations IV*. In both, Cage and Tudor were joined by local musicians.

At the last minute, the company was invited to perform at the Opera—not a whole program, but one piece in a program by the Royal Swedish Ballet, who had to cancel Antony Tudor's *Ekon av Trumpeter* because of a leading dancer's illness. The Opera asked for *Night Wandering*, first performed there six years before, but Cunningham decided to give *Winterbranch*, which, naturally, scandalized some ballet patrons. Before leaving Stockholm, Cunningham received a medal from the Society for the Advancement of Dancing in Sweden, of which the only previous recipients were the Queen of Sweden and Rolf de Maré, animator of the avantgarde Ballets Suédois in the 1920s.

The company's only other scheduled performance in Scandinavia was in Helsinki, on 18 September. However, while they were in Stockholm a telephone call came from Sara Strengell, director of the Åbo Svenska Teater in Turku, in the Swedish-speaking part of Finland, asking if they could perform there on the way to Helsinki. This at first seemed impossible, but after discussion it was agreed that it could be done on the 16th. Strengell could only pay $500, but she could arrange free first-class passage on the night boat. The company accordingly left Stockholm a day early, sailing on the late afternoon of the 15th, and arriving the next morning in time to go straight to the theater, set up, and rehearse.

Next day the company went by bus to Helsinki. The performance there, done before an audience, was also broadcast live on television, in a transmission directed by Heiki Seppala. The dances were *Story*, *Septet*, *Night Wandering*, and *Antic Meet*. (The film and videotape version of *Story* distributed by the Cunningham Dance Foundation was taken from a kinescope of this performance.)

After a couple of free days the company left on what was in many ways the tour's strangest leg: for the first time, an American avant-garde dance company was to visit Eastern Europe. From Helsinki it flew to Prague, via Stockholm, Copenhagen, and East Berlin. David Tudor had performed in Prague, and his contacts there included the musician Petr Kotík and his mother, Pavla Kotíková, who was able to persuade the authorities to invite the Cunningham company to perform there and in Ostrava. It was also agreed that the ensemble Musica Viva Pragensis, of which Kotík was a member, would accompany the Prague performance.

Although the Kotíks understood the nature of the company's work—in fact they had seen the June performance in Venice—it would, of course, be new to the general public. Posters advertising the performance in Prague's "Park of Culture" on 22 September described it as "in the style of *West Side Story*," presumably the nearest thing the sponsors could come up with. The posters did not mention Cage or Rauschenberg, apparently because of an official edict. Word of their presence, however, must have spread via the grapevine.

The hall was vast—there were about 2,000 spectators—but the stage was small and ill equipped. Cunningham decided to substitute *Story*, which could be done anywhere, for *Æon*, scheduled as the first work. The rest of the program, *Crises* and *Antic Meet*, was unchanged. The audience was probably confused, and the sightlines were so poor they could not in any case have seen much, but the reception was tumultuous all the same.

Prague at first seemed depressing—it was raining on the company's first two days there and the hotel was old and run-down—but on the free day after the performance the sun came out and the city was revealed in all its beauty. The next morning the company flew to Ostrava, where a pleasant surprise awaited them: a comfortable, modern hotel with fast service in the restaurant and plenty of hot water, and also an equally well-run theater, where that evening, the 24th, they danced *Suite for Five, Crises, Untitled Solo*, and *Story* (the Kafkaesque performance mentioned in the previous chapter).

The next day the company traveled by train to Warsaw, to make a single appearance at the Teatr Dramatyczny at noon on 27 September, as part of the eighth Warsaw Autumn Festival of contemporary music. The program was *Antic Meet, Story, Night Wandering*, and *Rune*, again with the participation of Musica Viva Pragensis. Between the last two pieces Cage and Tudor were to perform Cage's *Variations II* and *III*. Here tickets were available only to festival subscribers, many of whom had no interest in dance. The consequences were many empty seats and a large crowd of young people without tickets, banging on the locked doors of the outer lobby, trying to get in. Although the Americans wanted to let them do so, the sponsors considered such a spontaneous action unthinkable.

The next day the company traveled, again by train, to Poznan. The Miami-style hotel here was no architectural gem, but as in Ostrava the water was hot, the restaurant was efficient, and laundry got done in a flash. This was a pleasant surprise, particularly after the dreadful accommodations and service the company had experienced at the Hotel Warszawa, a hideous pile. In Poznan there was again a single performance, on 19 September, at the Paustwowa Opera; the program consisted of *Æon, Winterbranch*, and *Antic Meet*.

On the evening of 1 October, the company took a luxuriously comfortable train to East Berlin. There, in the middle of the night, they had to change trains to go on to Cologne. As the new train pulled out of East Berlin, everyone was appalled to see the theater baggage still piled on the platform. Farber, who speaks German, protested to a guard, and was told there was no through baggage

car and the trunks would follow on a later train. There was nothing for it but to go on to Cologne, and from there by bus to Krefeld, where a performance was scheduled imminently in conjunction with a Rauschenberg exhibition at the Museum Haus Lange.

All day long at Krefeld we called the Cologne station every time a train was due to have arrived. Each time the answer was negative. Finally Cage consulted the *I Ching*. The result was the hexagram "Waiting," which he interpreted as advising us not to worry, but to sit back and relax, have a good meal—everything would be all right. So we had an excellent dinner, then called the station again. "Yes," came the answer, "your baggage has arrived."[17]

The Krefeld performance (*Æon, Winterbranch, Nocturnes*), on 3 October at the Stadttheater, went off without a hitch. The European part of the tour, which had lasted four months, was almost over. On the morning of 4 October the company drove to Brussels, where the next day there was a television transmission of *Crises*. On the following three days the company gave three more performances, each one in a different city: Brussels (6 October), Antwerp (7 October), and Scheveningen, Holland (8 October). This last, the final performance in Europe, was on the smallest and worst-equipped stage (the Kurzaal) of any on which the company had performed during the tour.

On the 10th there was one more endless bus ride, back to Paris. After two days there we took off for India, arriving in Bombay on the morning of 14 October.

With barely a day to recover from severe jet-lag, the dancers had to give the first of two programs at the Bhulabhai Desai Auditorium on 15 October. They had been booked there by something called the Bombay Madrigal Singers' Organization, an agency whose name may conjure up visions of ladies and gentlemen singing heynonny-nonny, but that ran a "Foreign Artists' Division" to book concert tours of Western classical musicians. Still, the Merce Cunningham Dance Company may not have been quite what they or their patrons had bargained for.

On the evening of the 17th the company boarded the night train, the Gujarat Mail, to Ahmedabad, where the Sarabhai family were to be our hosts. For the next few days we were entertained in princely fashion. Limousines met us at the train on the morning of the 18th and drove us to "The Retreat," the Sarabhai "compound," where we were greeted by a military band like the one in Satyajit Ray's *Pather Panchali*. The compound, surrounded by a wall, was like the Garden of Paradise. Gorgeously plumed birds flew among flowering trees, and there was classical statuary, both Indian and Greek, everywhere. Each member of the family had his or her residence; that of the father and mother, where Cage stayed, was like a palace. Manorama Sarabhai, a daughter-in-law, had a pavilion designed by Le Corbusier, with an adjacent swimming pool with a chute that descended from the roof. (Brown, Tudor, and I stayed there.) Only Vikram Sarabhai and his wife, the dancer Mrinalini Sarabhai, with whom Cunningham and Viola Farber stayed, lived away from the compound.

Every evening when the company was not performing, there was a banquet, followed by an entertainment of some kind: a puppet show, folk-dancing, music, fireworks, or a performance by Mrinalini Sarabhai's company, Darpana. The dancers also visited her school and rehearsed there, and Cunningham later gave a lecture-demonstration there. The company performed on the 21st and the 22nd in the rather musty Mangaldas Town Hall.

> Mr Sarabhai from Ahmedabad in India, after seeing a performance by the Cunningham company, asked Merce whether his dancing was popular in the United States. Merce explained that programs were given principally in universities and colleges. Mr Sarabhai said, "That isn't what I mean. Do people do it after dinner?"[18]

On the 23rd the company, carrying bouquets of lotus, rose, and jasmine from the Sarabhais, flew to Delhi. Before performing there, however, they had a date in Chandigarh, capital of the Punjab, arranged by the Sarabhais chiefly because they wanted us to see the Corbusier buildings there. This entailed a long bus journey. We had been assured that the bus would be modern and air-conditioned, which actually meant that there was one feeble fan rotating slowly in a corner. We drove through villages and farms—an extraordinary journey, on which we saw more of India than we could ever have seen from a night train or plane.

On our arrival there was considerable confusion over the hotel. The first accommodations we were shown were quite unsuitable; the local sponsors seemed surprised that we had not brought our own bedding. This was finally resolved satisfactorily, but the next day there were further fights over the theater arrangements. The only posters to be seen advertised "American Ballet by Artists from New York," and no programs had been printed. The Tagore Theater itself was modern and well equipped, but it became necessary for the company's administrators to issue a list of requirements.

Two performances were given, on 25 and 26 October. It is safe to say that most of the audience had never seen anything like the Cunningham company's dancing. It is equally true that they appeared to be spellbound. Whenever a man lifted—or even touched—a woman, there were gasps. No doubt Rauschenberg's costumes seemed like the equivalent of nudity. But, as Cunningham observed, "You felt that if they hadn't liked it they would have come at you with knives." When the company left the next morning for Delhi, the bureaucrat who had been in charge of our arrangements said, "If we had known how good you are, we would have treated you better."

In Delhi, the company gave two performances, presented by the Delhi Music Society, in a hall called by the acronym AIFACS. A review of the first performance appeared on the following morning, 30 October, and began, "The Merce Cunningham Dance Company danced for a Delhi audience . . . on Thursday night and unless forcibly prevented will do so again on Friday night."[19] The review went on to describe *Winterbranch* as "a delicious lampoon

of the anaemically sentimental sequences one sometimes comes across in classical ballet."

The Sarabhais had arranged that before leaving India the company would visit Agra. On Sunday 1 November we flew there, seeing Fatehpur Sikri and, of course, the Taj Mahal. The following day we flew on to Bangkok, via Lucknow, Benares, and Calcutta. The engagement in Thailand became a Royal Command Performance, given before Their Majesties King Phumiphon and Queen Sirikit on 3 November 1964, and as soon as the curtain fell on the last piece, a scratchy tape recording of the Thai national anthem was played. The audience rose and turned their backs on the stage to face the king and queen, who sat in the front row of the balcony. Realizing there would be no curtain call, the dancers were told to go around to the lobby to be received by Their Majesties. This meant that, still in costume, they had to run around the outside of the building in the damp night air. In the lobby, the dancers were received graciously, and with more than polite interest, by the king (himself a composer) and queen, who gave each of them a bouquet.

On 5 November we flew on to Tokyo, via Hong Kong. Although we were to be in Japan for the rest of the month, only six performances were scheduled, plus an open dress rehearsal. This created a problem for Cunningham. The dancers were exhausted, and some were disaffected. And relations between Cunningham and Cage on the one hand, and Rauschenberg on the other, were strained almost to the breaking point; it was clear that their collaboration could not continue after the end of the tour. Following his triumph at the Venice Biennale, Rauschenberg had in any case become an artist of international stature, and it was unlikely that he would have been able to devote the time and energy to the company that he had in preceding years. If Rauschenberg went, it was obvious that Alex and Deborah Hay and Steve Paxton would go too. William Davis also said he was planning to leave, and Viola Farber had already told Cunningham that a foot injury she had sustained in Paris was causing her so much pain she would have to leave soon after returning to the United States.

Cunningham's immediate problem was to find a way to hold things together somehow until the end of the tour. Since the dancers were still on salary, he had the right to call them for class and rehearsal, and did so every day they were in Tokyo. However unwillingly, the dancers were obliged to attend. Paxton made his feelings very clear in one of these rehearsals: Cunningham asked each of the dancers to perform a slow phrase from *Story*, one by one. When Paxton's turn came, he did the phrase so slowly that it took about half an hour. Cunningham and the rest of the company watched, Cunningham expressionless, the others in an agony of embarrassment.

Cunningham himself, of course, was probably more exhausted than anyone, but he least of all would show it. As well as being a great dancer and a choreographer of genius, he is what is called in show business a trouper. However much of a strain, physically and otherwise, the tour was for him, he was as always never happier, never more alive, than on stage.

Backstage at Sankei Hall, Tokyo, November 1964. Above: David Vaughan and Lewis L. Lloyd. Right: David Tudor and John Cage.

As it was, there was the open rehearsal on 6 November, the day after the company's arrival, with a crowd of photographers clicking away at every moment, and then a break of three days before the first performances, on the 10th and 11th. Immediately after the second performance, the company flew to Osaka, then went by bus to Kobe, where they performed the following day. The next day we returned to Osaka and then were taken to Nara to see a performance of Bugaku dancing organized by the composer Toshiro Mayazumi. Finally, late in the evening, we were taken to a very long and mysterious Buddhist ceremony that took place in the dark, in a very cold temple. When that came to an end, we were driven for what seemed miles to a hotel on a mountain top near Kyoto. Fortunately this hotel was modern, warm, and comfortable, and proved in the morning to have a glorious view.

After two days of sight-seeing in Kyoto and Osaka, the company performed in the latter city on the 16th. The next day there was time to return to Kyoto to visit the Zen garden of Ryoan-ji before taking the fast train back to Tokyo. There followed another six days of inactivity, during which we were able to see performances of Noh and Kabuki, as well as the

Takarazuka dancers. The Japanese critic Eiryo Ashihara took Cunningham to see the Kabuki, and told him that in a few days the great onnagata Utaemon would be appearing in a rarely performed play, one of his greatest roles. That was a performance day for the Cunningham company, but between the rehearsal and the performance Cunningham and Carolyn Brown rushed over to see it. It was almost unheard of for Cunningham to go to another performance on a day when he was dancing himself.

This occasion was in fact the company's last performance of the tour; the last two shows took place on 24 and 25 November. There were, however, two more performances at the Sogetsu Art Center: a concert by Cage and Tudor on the 27th, and a Rauschenberg program on the 28th. On the afternoon of the latter performance, Cunningham and Cage went on a pilgrimage to Kamakura to visit Daisetz Suzuki. They got to Rauschenberg's performance late, and left before the end, which only made matters worse. The next day, most of the company left for New York.

Cunningham flew separately to Hawaii (as did Rauschenberg) to lie on the beach for a few days. The deficit for the tour amounted to $85,000, and there was an unresolved dispute with Air France, which had decided that the company had forfeited its group rate in all the rerouting and reticketing that had occurred. This had first erupted when we were in Helsinki, when Rauschenberg had temporarily bailed us out.[20] Eventually the question was resolved in the dance company's favor, after Cage personally took on the task of negotiating, or pleading, with the airline.

Looking back over the tour, I wondered whether the disasters did not outweigh the triumphs—and if they did, whether that was my fault, since I had done the planning. Cunningham told me one day soon after his return that he would leave again tomorrow if given the opportunity, so I felt to some extent vindicated; but the company would never be the same again. The time when the dancers and artistic personnel could live together like a family was over. That situation, however, could not in any case last. The company was inevitably to become a bigger operation. There was no longer any doubt that it was a major dance company, and that in future years Cunningham's work would have an enormous influence on contemporary dance, not only in the United States but in Europe, especially in France and Britain. The company would often return to France, and less frequently to Britain; dancers from both countries would make their way to New York to study at the Cunningham Studio, and on their return to their native countries would make work of their own that showed the influence not only of Cunningham's technique but of his aesthetic as well.

1965

News of the company's successes abroad had of course filtered back to the United States—had in fact been reported in the *New York Times* and *Time*.[1] The company was immediately booked into a dance series at Hunter College Playhouse in New York, where so many of Cunningham's early concerts had been given. The performance, on 12 February 1965, was sold out long in advance, so a second and then a third were added, on the 13th and 14th. At the first two, Cunningham opened the program with a brief talk, during which four of the dancers began to do *Field Dances*, followed immediately by Cunningham's solo *Collage III*. The rest of the program consisted of *Crises, Night Wandering*, and *Nocturnes*. None of these except the last had been seen in New York before.

Viola Farber had agreed to stay with the company for the rest of that season. There was one new dancer, Gus Solomons, Jr., who made his debut in *Nocturnes*. Beverly Emmons was engaged as lighting designer. The Hunter performances were not the dancers' first after their return from touring: two days before, they had appeared at Skidmore College in Saratoga Springs, giving *Field Dances, Collage III*, and the first American performance of *Cross Currents* as part of a "continuous event." This was also the first time a company performance was supported by the newly formed New York State Council on the Arts.

Cunningham's introductory talk began, "Dance is concerned with each single instant as it comes along."[2] The talk was punctuated by sounds made by Cage and David Tudor, an arrangement that foreshadowed Cunningham's future lecture-demonstrations, which came to resemble the Events he had begun to do on the tour.

The New York State Theater at Lincoln Center had recently opened, and once again there was an attempt to form a modern-dance repertory company, to be called the American Dance Theater (also funded by the New York State Council on the Arts). There had been two performances in November 1964; now there was to be a further week during which outside companies were invited to perform works by their own choreographers: José Limón, Pearl Lang, Alwin Nikolais, and Cunningham, who elected to perform *Winterbranch* on one program and *Summerspace* on another. Predictably, the critics who had enthusiastically greeted the company's return at Hunter College were outraged by *Winterbranch*. (*Summerspace*, on the other hand, had become acceptable.) Both Allen Hughes in the *New York Times* and Walter Terry in the *New York Herald Tribune* followed up their negative reviews with Sunday articles; Hughes claimed to be responding to protests "from within and without the Cunningham company," and Terry too said that he had received a letter in defense of *Win-*

terbranch from Carolyn Brown.[3] Both writers, however, continued to assert that the work constituted an unwarranted attack on a defenseless audience.

Before this uproar died down it was announced that the Cunningham company would appear again at Lincoln Center in July, this time at Philharmonic (later Avery Fisher) Hall, as part of a French-American Festival whose artistic director, Lukas Foss, had commissioned a new work from Cunningham and Cage, *Variations V*.

As a kind of postscript to the *Winterbranch* controversy, George Beiswanger published an article in the May 1965 issue of *Dance News* entitled "No Dolt Can Do It." Beiswanger had reviewed early Cunningham concerts sympathetically in *Dance Observer*, and he had attended the company's opening night at Sadler's Wells in July 1964. His appraisal of Cunningham brought the voice of reason into the discussion. Beiswanger divided Cunningham's works into four categories: the solos, which "present the anti-hero" familiar from contemporary literature "from Joyce and Kafka to Beckett"; group dances that present a kind of ordered serenity, "where beings touch without hurting and impinge without joining" (Beiswanger gave as examples *Night Wandering, Nocturnes*, and *Suite for Five*); "Happening"-type works presenting "common experience and the human scene" (*Story, Field Dances*); and works "concerned with final things—heaven, purgatory, hell, the end of the world." In this final category he placed *Summerspace*, "the human paradise in the here and now"; *Antic Meet*, "a modern fête champêtre"; *Crises*, which "encompasses the purgatorial ordeals which humans incontinently set themselves"; *Winterbranch*, in which "the dark scene, the phantom souls, the inquisitor eye suggest . . . the day of judgment and the world of the damned"; and *Æon*, which shows "the end of the world—the universe wrenched at the center and coming apart at the seams."

"That these dances are dead serious is patent," wrote Beiswanger—in contrast to those who took *Winterbranch* as a "joke" or "prank".[4] (After a performance in London in 1966, Brown spoke to a group of secondary-school students, one of whom asked if Cunningham were not "just pulling our leg." "I think I was quiet for rather a long time, and finally I said, 'Do you really believe that a man would spend his life working this hard, even going into debt, merely to pull your leg?'"[5])

VARIATIONS V

The French-American Festival commissioned Cage to prepare a score and me to make choreography to this score. John decided to find out if there might not be ways that the sound could be affected by movement, and he and David Tudor proceeded to find out that there were. Several in fact, only two of which finally worked out for us in the piece, the rest being impractical due to cost, or requiring machines not usable in the theater, or simply too clumsy. The two ways that were used were not different as to my work, but different for the technicians and the stage set-up. The first was a

Above: *Variations V,*
1965. Left to right,
foreground to back-
ground: John Cage,
David Tudor, Gordon
Mumma, Carolyn
Brown, MC, and
Barbara Dilley Lloyd.
Photograph: Hervé
Gloaguen.
Right: *Variations V,*
1965. Left to right:
MC, Gus Solomons Jr.,
Barbara Dilley Lloyd,
and Peter Saul. Photo-
graph: Nicolas Treatt.
Pages 148–49: *Varia-
tions V,* 1965. Left to
right: Sandra Neels,
Gus Solomons Jr.,
Peter Saul, and Carolyn
Brown. Photograph:
Oscar Bailey.

series of poles, twelve in all, like antennae,
placed over the stage, each to have a sound
radius, sphere-shaped, of 4 feet. When a dancer
came into this radius a sound would result.
Each antenna was to have a different sound,
and some had several. The poles were 5 feet
high and ½ inch in diameter. None of this put
me off. But I did wonder about our feet and the
wires which would be running from the base of
the poles to the machines which controlled all
this, and for no reason as they turned out to be
easily surmountable.

The second sound source was a series of
photo-electric cells, figured out by Billy Klüver
of the Bell Laboratories, which were to sit on
the floor along the sides of the stage. The stage
lights would be focussed in such a way as to hit
them, and when a dancer passed between a
sound could happen. This didn't work out
exactly as the stage lights were too distant to
strike strongly enough to the sides of the stage.
After all, they were focussed on us, and we were
more prone to be in the middle of the area. So
at the last minute the cells were put at the base

147

of the 12 poles throughout the area and this seemed to function. The general principle as far as I was concerned was like the doors opening when you go into the supermarket. The dancers triggered a sound, but the kind of a sound, how long it might be, or the possible repetition of it, was controlled by the musicians, who were at the various machines behind us—tape-recorders, oscillators, short-wave radios—there were about 8 men on the platform, where the electronic equipment was placed behind the dance area. There was a fairly constant scuttling among them—they were quiet about it—back and forth on the platform to fix things, wiring that had come out, a plug, etc. The effect was of a countdown when they count down to three and then stop.

There was another element involved in this piece, the use of film. Behind the platform with the musicians was the large Philharmonic Hall movie screen—it's very large. Stan VanDerBeek and his assistant Tom Dewitt had in the weeks ahead of this made a number of reels of film of us, myself dancing, my company doing moments out of the piece. Stan came to the studio one day when we were rehearsing and without disrupting the dancers at all shot through and around them. He shot my hands and feet several times. He said the feet would look marvelous blown up to such a size, like an army; when I saw them, more like elephants—at least they are light animals. Stan used other images, still shots and shots from movies, a montage of contemporary scenes, automobiles, a man in space, nature, buildings. Nam June Paik, the Korean composer [*sic*] who has developed ways of changing the images on a television screen, used some of these ways to change the images.

There were a number of non-dance activities that I had figured out for the dancers to do. I potted a large plant and Carolyn Brown re-potted it. The plant had a cartridge microphone attached to it so that any quiver could produce sound. Barbara [Dilley] Lloyd put a towel on her head which had a contact microphone attached to it, and proceeded to stand on her head and was moved gently back and forth by Gus Solomons, while upside down. At the end of the piece, I rode a bicycle through the space, around the poles and the photo-electric cells, and then exited.

Landscape of the dance

Everything worked out to allow for these and when you got there it wasn't what you expected.[6]

Variations V was a big piece, "with lots of things in it, and if I had only so many people all doing things, then it was harder to figure out how you could allow for the indeterminate part, because there wasn't anybody to be indeterminate with, they were all busy." The indeterminate elements included changes in the order of the events, largely dictated by the complicated technical setup. (The "electronic devices" did not always work.) As Cunningham has said, "There was so much technology involved that out of necessity I had to leave some of it indeterminate since we didn't know until we got there what these things were going to be."

Of the categories into which Beiswanger had divided Cunningham's work, *Variations V* belonged to the third—"happening"-type works that present "the human scene." But the dance sequences were formal and technically demanding, and their difficulty was increased by the need for the dancers to negotiate around the vertical metal rods. Just before Cunningham's bicycle ride, the dancers unwound a long cord, taking it from each other and stretching it across the stage.

The dancers wore basic leotards and tights (no costume designer was credited), over which the women sometimes wore clothes they had picked out themselves, such as cotton dresses in bright floral patterns.

Above: MC and John Cage, ca. 1965. Photograph: Jack Mitchell. Opposite: *How to Pass, Kick, Fall and Run*, 1965. Photograph: James Klosty.

• • •

At the end of the spring tour that year, Farber had finally left the company. Cunningham did not replace her right away, but in the fall, Valda Setterfield became a regular member. In November, the company went to Chicago to perform for a week in the Harper Theater Dance Festival, during which another new dance was given for the first time:

HOW TO PASS, KICK, FALL AND RUN

I am a practical man (the theater demands it). We had to have one simple dance in terms of sets and costumes, setting up and rehearsing—and the sound, which is variable, stories by John Cage read one per minute regardless of length by John or David Vaughan and sometimes both.[7]

The stories originally came from Cage's lecture "Indeterminacy," first given in Brussels in 1958, with musical accompaniment by Tudor. Later, other stories were added from various writings of Cage's.

How to Pass, Kick, Fall and Run was performed before the unadorned back wall of the stage. The costumes were tights and sweaters that the dancers chose themselves. As the title suggests, the piece's flavor was sportif, though without any specific references to games—huddles or football formations or whatever. The construction was by chance, but the order of the sections was invariable. The process used was similar to that of *Summerspace*:

. . . about where you came in, how many people came in at that moment, with some indication about the speeds, whether it changed to fast or slow, and something about level. There were two or three things going on at once, and that was all done that way—the directions they took. The lines were like *Summerspace*—through the space, sometimes in a circle. You don't come in and stay facing a given place for a long time, you keep shifting. You start with the idea that it could be seen from any angle, rather

than in a proscenium, and then you have someone coming in from a certain point, and following a certain route, but in a gymnasium that could be in any direction.

We'd go there and stop, instead of going offstage. A lot of the movement, even as you do it, could turn from side to side. If it were on stage, I didn't do that, but in an Event I could. And there's a structure by minutes, which I gave to John—his is minute by minute, but mine was like 2½, then 5, or whatever.

• • •

This year saw the creation by the federal government of the National Endowment for the Arts. Cunningham was an early member of the agency's dance panel.

1966

Early in the year, Cunningham began rehearsing *Summerspace* with the New York City Ballet, at the invitation of Lincoln Kirstein. The piece was adapted for classic ballet—that is, the women were on pointe; otherwise the choreography was the same. The ballet dancers predictably found Cunningham's approach to music problematic after working with George Balanchine, and his swift changes of weight and rhythm were not easy for them either. (This was the occasion previously mentioned when Cunningham asked Carolyn Brown to demonstrate movements to the ballet dancers, and afterward said that they had been astonished at her command.) The City Ballet first per-

formed *Summerspace* during its spring season, in April, then danced the piece four more times in New York and twice in Saratoga in July—only seven times in all. It was reported that Balanchine, after watching a performance, pronounced Morton Feldman's music "a fraud" and dropped the ballet from the repertory.

The company returned to Europe twice in 1966. Once again, funding was a problem. The State Department refused to help. The summer tour was to begin in Sitges, Spain; to continue to the Fondation Maeght, Saint Paul-de-Vence, France; and conclude with the filming of *Variations V* in Hamburg. The airfares were covered by the gift of a painting by Joan Miró, who had seen the company in Paris in 1964.

Before the tour there was a summer course at the 14th Street studio. Clearly, however, it was time to leave these premises, which had a badly leaking roof. The Living Theater had already vacated the lower floors. Some artist friends were willing to sublet, sub rosa, their loft at 498 Third Avenue, below 34th Street. There were two floors, with space upstairs for a large studio and downstairs for an office, dressing rooms, bathrooms, and even another, small studio. There was also a room upstairs where Cunningham could live and, behind folding doors in the main studio, a kitchen where he could make dinner when the students had left for the day. Although the rent was $450 a month (on 14th Street it had been $100), it was decided that 498 Third Avenue would be the temporary home of the Merce Cunningham Studio.

As soon as the move had taken place (immediately after the summer course), the company left for Europe. After performing in Sitges, they moved on by train to the south of France for four performances

Above, left: *How to Pass, Kick, Fall and Run*, 1965. Left to right: MC (in background), David Vaughan, and John Cage. Photograph: Fred W. McDarrah. Above, right: *How to Pass, Kick, Fall and Run*, 1965. Left to right: Carolyn Brown, Valda Setterfield, Gus Solomons, Jr., Barbara Dilley Lloyd, Sandra Neels, and Albert Reid. Photograph: Nicolas Treatt. Opposite: Rehearsal of *Place*, Foundation Maeght Saint-Paul, France, summer 1966. Foreground to background: John Cage, Sandra Neels, and MC. Photograph: Hervé Gloaguen.

at the Fondation Maeght. By a miracle, the first of these, on Monday 1 August, took place more or less on schedule although the theater baggage had been tied up in customs at the Spanish border over the weekend. Lewis Lloyd managed to get it out by noon on Monday, load it into two taxis, and take it to the Perpignan airport, where a Corsican plane was supposed to be waiting. "The ride," Lloyd would write, "was about 1½ hours, down twisting, hairpin-turn roads along the coast." There was in fact no plane, but Lloyd found another and loaded as much of the luggage as he could on to it, after taking out most of the seats:

> A crowd had gathered by now . . . to watch the traditional scene where the company manager hands out greenbacks to all the assembled foreigners. This time the number distributed was $570, cash, on the wing of the plane. In I get to the cockpit, next to the dapper pilot, and off we not too steadily go. Once up the pilot takes out a large loose-leaf binder entitled "Operational and Directional Manual," several maps, props them on his knees and begins poring through them. The trip continued this way with the plane weaving slightly to the left there while the pilot went over the maps and peered out the side windows. We did reach Nice by 7:20 though, and after bouncing three times (the pilot had the grace to say merde at this) we were free, so to speak.[1]

The performances at the Fondation Maeght were given on a stage erected in the courtyard, where there were several sculptures by Alberto Giacometti. According to Cunningham, this platform was so small that "we almost fell off." On the third evening, a new piece received its first performance:

PLACE

Place was begun during January (?) of 1966. I was working on *Summerspace* with the NYC Ballet, and commuting during the transit strike between the NY State Theater and my 14th Street studio, longer en route than the rehearsals. Working intermittently through the winter and into the spring, I amassed a number of separate sections. One day I sat down and juggled them and put them together. I had to add one short sequence for Albert Reid and Valda Setterfield to get them from stage left to stage right for the following sequence.[2]

Above: *Place*, 1966. Left to right: Sandra Neels, Jeff Slayton, Valda Setterfield, Gus Solomons, Jr., MC, Mel Wong, and Barbara Lloyd. Photograph: James Klosty. Opposite: MC in the final moments of *Place*, 1966. Photograph: James Klosty.

The piece was designed by Beverly Emmons, whose decor, an assemblage of bits of wooden crates and old newspapers, illuminated in part by light instruments on the stage floor, suggested a cityscape. The women wore brief tunics of clear colored plastic over their leotards.

The score was by Gordon Mumma, who at the time was traveling with the company as sound technician. "A duo for bandoneón and computer," it was in a sense composed by David Tudor as well as by the composer:

The bandoneón, named for its inventor Heinrich Band, of Krefeld, Germany, resembles a large accordion with two keyboards. This is played by David Tudor, who makes his own decisions concerning the sounds he plays; the computer, specially devised by Gordon Mumma, then makes its own decisions regarding the electronic distortion of these sounds on the basis of its reaction to them.[3]

Mumma had no doubts about the "meaning" of *Place*, writing in the magazine *Impulse,*

Place is a drama of human anxiety, the anxiety of failure to establish identity. Some people

have seen *Place* as a clinical panorama of the schizophrenic experience, the narrative of a degenerative sydrome which culminates in stark, outright withdrawal. In this work, performed with eight dancers, Mr. Cunningham has a rather predominant solo role: an individual who repeatedly attempts and fails to establish relationships with the people and events of his world.[4]

After seeing *Place* in an early performance in Stockholm, Cage seemed to recognize a somewhat similar mood, saying the work was "like Greek tragedy." At the very least, Cunningham's own role in *Place* had something of the neurotic intensity of his "dark" solos. At the beginning he entered and, as it were, claimed the scene as his territory. After that he never left the stage. "The other dancers join him and progress very slowly across the stage moving from one sculptural pose to another."[5] Later, Cunningham "asserts his control . . . by moving [the] group of lights [on the floor] from spot to spot."[6] "Each time Cunningham moves the [lights] a bit farther across the stage, the group becomes galvanized into violent activity only to freeze again like a . . . sinister game of 'statues.'"[7] At the end, Cunningham thrashed about inside a large plastic bag that had lain hidden on the floor near the lights.

> It was a terrifying, exhausting piece to do. It was terrible for me, it never stopped. It was hard to do and keep clear, because it ranged from sudden big things to something quite small and quick, sharp. And that last thing with the plastic—I was never sure I would be able to get into it. I was supposed to climb into a sack, and plastic sometimes sticks, and I couldn't get it open.

Much of the choreography was for the ensemble, sometimes working in couples. Valda Setterfield remembers learning one such section without a partner, and only realizing when Cunningham joined the group that she would be dancing with him. There were also duets for Cunningham and Carolyn Brown, and for Sandra Neels and Albert Reid. In their duet, Reid carried Neels onto the stage upside down in a spread-eagled position, then lowered himself into a "bridge" position with Neels balanced across his body, her arms outstretched.

• • •

The final performance at the Fondation Maeght, on 7 August 1966, was an Event—*Museum Event No. 4*. The dancers moved about in the galleries as well as in the courtyard. Part of the time, they were followed by paparazzi.

In Hamburg, as *Variations V* was being filmed (again under the direction of Arne Arnbom), a documentary crew directed by Hans Wildenhahn was making another film focusing on Cage and his work with the company. Both films were produced by Norddeutscher Rundfunk, Hamburg, the one on *Variations V* being coproduced with Sveriges Radio/TV, Sweden.

At the end of October another European tour was scheduled, beginning in Stockholm. Before leaving, the company went to Illinois for ten days. (The new studio at 498 Third Avenue opened on 19 September.) There was first a series of lecture-demonstrations at the Francis W. Parker School, Chicago, under the auspices of the Chicago Committee on Urban Opportunity and the Illinois Arts Council. The audiences were mostly children aged from seven to twelve, bussed in from "poverty areas"—by definition, mostly black and uninitiated into the mysteries of avant-garde dance. Cunningham, introducing the programs, spoke with his usual clarity and lack of pretension:

> Dancing is just as interesting as anything else, but you have to look at it differently. Some things can be understood in different ways than through the mind. They can be understood through the eye, and this we call the kinesthetic sense.[8]

One Chicago critic called the venture "very well-meaning, but completely unrealistic. The wrong people are invited at the wrong time."[9] In fact, however, the children were on the whole quiet and attentive. As Shirley Genther, a local dance educator, said, "Audiences, even if they don't know very much about dancing, sense very quickly whether or not you know what you are doing. And if they sense that they are likely to accept it even if they don't know what you are doing."[10]

The company next went to Champaign-Urbana to be in residence for a week at the University of Illinois, ending with a performance on Saturday 29 October. The first performance in Stockholm was to be on Monday the 31st. After the Saturday-evening show, then, the company drove through the night to Chicago. From there they flew to New York and on to Stockholm, arriving on Monday morning. A stage rehearsal was necessary, of course, and by the time of the performance the dancers were dizzy with fatigue.

Next the company went to Paris to perform at the Théâtre des Champs-Elysées, in the Quatrième Festival International de Danse de Paris. Cunningham had insisted on giving two programs, an arrangement that Jean Robin, the director of the festival, accepted only "under duress," adding that "in any case, you will have only ten more people to see the additional ballets. So the effort is useless." In fact *le tout* Paris came to the opening night, on 9 November. A newspaper headline described the audience's different factions: "*Mini-jupes contre smokings au Théâtre des Champs-Elysées.*"[11] Subseqent performances were sold out. At the end of the festival, the jury awarded Cunningham a gold medal for "choreographic invention."

On the day after the fourth performance, 13 November, the company flew to Portugal for a short tour, starting in Lisbon and proceeding to Coimbra and Porto. From Portugal they went to London for this European tour's last stop: again presented by Michael White, a ten-day engagement (23 November to 3 December) at the Saville Theatre.

The tour again resulted in a deficit, of some $15,000. Cunningham expressed some thoughts on the economics of the dance world at a dance-management seminar held in New York on 14 December 1966:

> Dancers have a strength of community that they are not aware of, and that consists of the human interest of the people who have been involved [in], or whose lives have in some way touched, the dance. I was furious at the Rockefeller Brothers report that said that dance is in a state of chaos. That is not true. Despite being ignored, we have made a forceful and handsome art come alive. The American dance has brought glory to this country around the world. Chaos indeed![12]

The company was again invited to perform in the Hunter College Modern Dance series when it returned to New York. As before, a third performance had to be added to those originally scheduled (on 9 and 10 December).

MC in the studio at
498 Third Avenue,
New York, 1967.
Photograph: Hervé
Gloaguen.

1967

Early in the year, the New York State Council on the Arts invited Cunningham and Cage to join a group of seven artists on a tour of college campuses in the state, under the rubric "Contemporary Voices in the Arts." The other artists were Robert Creeley, Billy Klüver, Len Lye, Jack Tworkov, and Stan VanDer-Beek. The idea may have been that the artists would conduct conventional symposia, but this did not appeal to them; instead, they presented a series of "happenings" (reminiscent, once again, of the Black Mountain theater piece of fifteen years before). There was a certain amount of dialogue among all seven, and Cunningham danced, Cage made sounds, Creeley read poems, and Lye and VanDerBeek showed films. They also met individually with groups of students.

The finale of this tour took place on the evening of 25 February at the YM/YWHA on Lexington Avenue and 92nd Street in New York. Tworkov had suggested that since the meals that the group ate together had been among the tour's most enjoyable events, they should eat one in public. Accordingly, they met on the stage of the Y for a program called "TV Dinner," subtitled "Homage to E.A.T. (Food for Thought)."

The evening began with Cunningham dancing in front of a white screen. This was followed by Lye's film. Then the screen was raised and the members of the group were seen milling about on stage. VanDer-Beek's films were projected on the walls of the hall, rather as they were in *Variations V*. The group sat down at a table and were served dinner. Their conversation, and the sounds of their eating, were supposed to be made audible to the audience through microphones, some of them attached to dishes, glasses, and cutlery. Unfortunately these microphones failed to work. As the meal progressed, the audience grew increasingly restive. Their complaints became vocal. The evening was a disaster.

The lecture tour was preceded and followed by out-of-town dates for the dance company. No Event performance had previously been given in the United States, but on 3 June, at a benefit for the Cunningham Dance Foundation at Philip Johnson's estate in New Canaan, Connecticut, the company performed *Museum Event No. 5*, on a platform erected in the grounds (rather than in Johnson's adjacent underground museum). Cage made a score in collaboration with Gordon Mumma, David Tudor, and Toshi Ichiyanagi. The performance ended with the dancers piling into a station wagon and driving off, Cunningham at the wheel. Dancing for the guests followed, to the music of the Velvet Underground, which could be heard for miles around, causing many complaints from the neighbors and eventually a visit from the local police.

The following month the company performed for the first time at the Ravinia Festival in Highland Park, outside Chicago. The second program included a new work:

SCRAMBLE

To make a dance without flavor
Scramble the fleet
Scramble the code
Scramble uphill
Scramble eggs
Scramble in fight
space or scientific jargon[1]

Scramble comprised eighteen sections of varying lengths, each of them self-contained. They could be

Below, left: *Scramble*, 1967. Left to right: Jeff Slayton, Valda Setterfield, Carolyn Brown, and Chase Robinson. Photograph: James Klosty. Below, right: *Scramble*, 1967. Left to right: Gus Solomons, Jr., Barbara Dilley Lloyd, MC, Sandra Neels, Chase Robinson, and Carolyn Brown. Photograph: Hervé Gloaguen. Opposite: *Scramble*, 1967. Left to right: Carolyn Brown, Gus Solomons, Jr., Valda Setterfield, Albert Reid, Sandra Neels, Yseult Riopelle, MC, and Barbara Dilley Lloyd. Photograph: Oscar Bailey.

done in different orders on different occasions. Not all the sections would be danced each time—generally about fifteen were. A complete performance would last about twenty-eight minutes; as usually given, the length was about twenty minutes.

Once again the sections were named for purposes of identification in rehearsal. Some of these names were simply descriptive of the sections' content: for example "Fast Dance," "Slow Entrances," "Slow Walk," "Slow Trio," "Fast Trio," "Circle," "Fall/Leap," "Huddle," "Air." In "Fall/Leap," the dancers ran across the stage in pairs, the first leaping and falling headlong to the floor while the next leaped over him or her. In "Slow Walk" the dancers gradually filled the stage; some stepped forward into a lunge, others extended one leg and fell onto it, hands clasped behind the head with elbows beating like wings. Sometimes one or other of the men lunged to the side, supporting a woman who braced her knee against his thigh. All these movements, Cunningham once said, "must be even, without accent, absolutely level." In "Slow Trio" three women began by standing on one foot, the other raised slightly off the floor and being moved by a sidewise movement of the hip. The head tilted from side to side in opposition. Originally the dancers had some freedom in terms of where they would move in the space, but things tended to become set with repeated performances.

Another section was called "Separate Movements." As the name suggests, each of the nine dancers performed a different phrase, repeated continuously and very slowly. Each dancer learned all of these phrases, rather than keeping the same one all the time.

Both Cunningham and Carolyn Brown had solos, hers characterized by slow, swimming movements. Cunningham's was one of his clownlike numbers, during which at one point he held his hands up flat in front of his face, then suddenly opened them and yelled (a reference, perhaps, to both *Sixteen Dances* and *Septet*).

Since the end of the 1964 tour, the company had been without a resident designer. None had been named for *Variations V* or *How to Pass, Kick, Fall and Run*; *Place* had been designed by the lighting designer, Beverly Emmons. In August 1967, however, Jasper Johns was named artistic advisor, in which capacity he would select

designers for new pieces as well as designing some himself. Unlike Robert Rauschenberg, Johns did not enjoy working in the theater, but was able to conquer his distaste because "Merce is my favorite artist in any field. Sometimes I'm pleased by the complexity of a work that I paint. By the fourth day I realize it's simple. Nothing Merce does is simple. Everything has a fascinating richness and multiplicity of direction."[2]

The first artist Johns chose was Frank Stella, for *Scramble*. Stella has recalled, "Merce said he was working on a dance, and I went along and watched a rehearsal. I made a sketch on yellow paper; John Cage said he liked it because it didn't have anything to do with anything."[3] The set consisted of six strips of canvas in the colors of the spectrum. The strips were eighteen inches high, and were mounted on vertical frames mounted on a movable base. Stella's idea was to make something simple and flexible that could be moved around to "define the stage space in relation to the dancers and the nature of their gestures—a kind of measurement device that was adapted to any size of stage space."

Stella has said that he did not think of this set as an extension of his concerns in his own paintings, though clearly a relation could be seen to his striped and shaped canvases of the period. "But I didn't think of it as a painting problem." He wanted the longest strip of canvas to be set at the front of the stage at the beginning of the dance, so that the dancers would first be seen cut off below the knees. "I thought this would be a dramatic effect, but they only did it once like that, they didn't like it." Cunningham would decide on arrival at a performing space whether it was possible to move the pieces around, and if so, when and by whom. Stella had little to do with the costumes beyond specifying their colors: the men wore jumpsuits, the women leotards and tights.

The score, by Ichiyanagi, was called "Activities for Orchestra." The "activities," as might be expected, were unconventional. Ichiyanagi himelf took part in the first performance, playing piano and celeste, together with Cage, Tudor (on bandoneón), Mumma (French horn), and two additional musicians from the Chicago Symphony Orchestra on percussion. "The musicians," Mumma later wrote,

> . . . each perform multiple activities: either several instruments simultaneously or a single instrument with complex electronic sound manipulation. Though scored for western instruments . . . , the music for *Scramble* has a sound texture reminiscent of Japanese classical theatre music. Quiet, transparent bands of sustained sound, some steady and some sliding, are punctuated with abrupt percussive timbres. The score is composed in cued sequences which are scrambled by the musicians in performance.[4]

• • •

On 12 August Cunningham and Cage gave the first of a number of performances called "Dialogues," at the Skowhegan School of Painting and Sculpture, in Skowhegan, Maine. Cage read from his

text "Diary: How to Improve the World (You Will Only Make Matters Worse)" and "used several tape recorders, amplifiers and a grand piano to fill the Old Dominion Fresco Barn with a consistently changing array of sounds."[5] Meanwhile Cunningham warmed up and danced excerpts from various of his solos. Unlike later Dialogues (in which no actual conversation took place between the two men), this first one was followed by a question-and-answer session.

In October Cunningham visited Stockholm for the final rehearsals of *Summerspace* in its staging by Margaret Jenkins for Birgit Cullberg's company, the Cullbergbaletten. Cullberg's son, Niklas Ek, who had briefly been an apprentice in the Cunningham company the year before, danced Cunningham's role in the first performance, on 22 October. The scenery and costumes were borrowed from the New York City Ballet.

In November, as part of a symposium entitled "University in Motion: Matrix for the Arts," held as part of the centennial celebrations of the University of Illinois, Cunningham took part in a panel discussion on the subject "Theater and the University: Amusement or Art?" The other panelists were the actor Joseph Chaikin, the actress June Havoc, the mime Claude Kipnis, and the director Wilford Leach. The filmmaker Dore Schary was the moderator. Cunningham made the following statement:

> I don't understand the antithesis between art and entertainment. . . . Dancing is entertainment. I don't understand the idea that art is opposed to entertainment. My feeling about theater and dancing is that they provide a contemporary experience. My work is not to make a special thing of the theater but to let it be what it is.
>
> It has to be part of the life you are living. . . . In all our work, it has not been our intention in any way to change the world, but to see that it is as it is and do with it what we may.[6]

The dance company performed in these celebrations, and Cage, who was in residence at the university that year, directed a "Music Circus."

1968

From the middle of February to the middle of March, the company was in residence at the Buffalo campus of the State University of New York and Buf-

falo State University College. The residency culminated in three performances in the Second Buffalo Festival of the Arts Today, when two new works were given for the first time:

RAINFOREST

"There were five sections. It's too close to pin down." So Cunningham wrote in his notes for his 1968 book *Changes*. "It meant," he said later, "that I couldn't tell her [Frances Starr, the editor of *Changes*] any more than that because I'd just made it." *RainForest* differed from other Cunningham dances in that, except for Cunningham himself, each of the six dancers performed his or her role, then left the stage and did not return. Cunningham was on stage at the beginning (with Barbara Lloyd) and returned at the end. During the duet, Albert Reid entered; Cunningham went off, and "that was the second part, Albert and Barbara . . . and then the third one, which Gus [Solomons] did, that was a separate thing; and then it was Carolyn, I considered that a single thing even though she did a duet with Albert; and then the final one, which was Sandra [Neels]. So it's more complicated, because they overlapped, it wasn't strict."

As the title suggests, *RainForest* is one of Cunningham's "nature studies," though there is of course no literal depiction of a natural habitat. Cunningham had been reading Colin Turnbull's book *The Forest People*: "He was a tall man, and he lived with these pygmies for a long time, so that some kind of relationship developed. He gives this marvelous picture of himself trying to follow them in the forest, and they would go under everything, and he would constantly be hung up by a branch some way, and they would turn and laugh at him." Cunningham thinks the idea of having something hanging above the stage came from this description. "And the title came from my childhood memories of the Northwest, of the rainforest in the Olympic Peninsula."

Cunningham had seen Andy Warhol's installation *Silver Clouds* at the Leo Castelli Gallery—a number of Mylar pillows filled with helium, so that they floated freely in the air. He asked Jasper Johns if he thought Warhol would let him use it as a set. Johns asked Warhol, who agreed. When asked about costumes, Warhol said he would like the dancers to go naked. Cunningham felt this wouldn't work, so he put them in flesh-colored leotards and tights, and asked Johns if the texture could be roughened in some way. Thinking of an ancient pair of practice tights Cunningham wore that was full of holes and

Pages 160–61: *Rain-Forest*, 1968. Left: MC and Meg Harper. Center and right: Carolyn Brown and Jeff Slayton. Photographs: James Klosty. Above: *RainForest*, 1967. MC and Meg Harper. Photograph: James Klosty. Right: Andy Warhol showing MC a Polaroid of himself taken by Warhol. Photograph: James Klosty.

tears, Johns cut and ripped the fabric of the dancers' costumes with a razor blade.

RainForest was the first repertory piece with a score by David Tudor. When Cunningham told him the title, Tudor said "Oh, then I'll put a lot of raindrops in it." The music also evokes the chattering and crying of birds and animals. (Later, Tudor was to make further versions of this score, in the form of an elaborate sound installation.)

WALKAROUND TIME

There's something interesting in it. I don't know yet. I think it's about time. The title comes from computer language. You feed the computer information then you have to wait while it digests. There's some argument as to whether the computer is walking around or those who are waiting.[1]

Cunningham and Cage first met Marcel Duchamp in 1942, when Cage and his wife Xenia stayed at Max Ernst's and Peggy Guggenheim's apartment after moving to New York from Chicago. But it was not until

the mid-'60s that they became close friends of Duchamp and his wife Teeny (Alexina), by which time Duchamp had long since retired (or given out that he had done so) from active involvement with art.

One evening at dinner at the Duchamps', Johns asked Cunningham if he would like a set based on one of Duchamp's best-known works, *The Large Glass*. Cunningham said he would, so Johns asked

Duchamp if it could be done. Duchamp was willing as long as he did not have to do the work. It was therefore Johns who supervised the screen printing of the images in *The Large Glass* onto seven inflatables.[2]

Walkaround Time, Cunningham's dance for this set, differs from others of his works in that all the elements are related to a central idea—a kind of *hommage à Duchamp*. The title of the music, for example, by David Behrman, was " . . . for nearly an hour . . . ," referring not only to the duration of the piece (about fifty minutes) but to a Duchamp work related to the *Glass, To be looked at (from the other side of the glass) with one eye, close to, for nearly an hour* (1918). The full title of the *The Large Glass* is *The Bride Stripped Bare by Her Bachelors, Even (La Mariée mise à nu par ses célibataires, même)*. (This of course is the source of the title of Calvin Tomkins's collection of *New Yorker* profiles, *The Bride and the Bachelors: Five Masters of the Avant-Garde*, its subjects being Duchamp, Cage, Cunningham, Robert Rauschenberg, and Jean Tinguely.) But Cunningham pays homage more to aspects of Duchamp's work in general than to the specific, erotic content of the *Glass* itself. Such content is rarely to be found in his dances, and in any case a literal approach to subject matter is alien to him. Cunningham told the British dance educator Ruth Foster how he worked on the dance:

And then I began to think about movement, and I tried out some simple things. I tried out

Opposite: *Walkaround Time*, 1968. Left to right: Carolyn Brown, Valda Setterfield, Meg Harper, Gus Solomons, Jr., and MC. Inset, left: *Walkaround Time*, 1968. Inset, right: Carolyn Brown in *Walkaround Time*, 1968. Photographs: James Klosty. Above: Opening night curtain call of *Walkaround Time*, 1968. Left to right: Barbara Dilley Lloyd, Gus Solomons, Jr., Carolyn Brown, Marcel Duchamp, MC, David Behrman, and Sandra Neels. Photograph: Oscar Bailey.

very, very slow things; nothing relating to previous notions, just movement ideas. I decided to make it very long, a long piece divided into two parts. There would be an entr'acte in the middle. I put in lots of things about Duchamp and his work which I never tell anybody because this confuses people. Like ready-mades, for instance, because a ready-made is something that is already done, and you can re-use it. So the piece has things that appear, not often, but over again. . . . I placed a kind of striptease in this, but that's because of Marcel's *Nude Descending the Staircase*. All those things that have been in his life, but not to imitate them; they always come out as movement things, not as ideas *about* movement. . . .

I went into a studio and I wanted to—I didn't want, I just did it. I asked one of the dancers to do a back fall, and I showed her something about it, but I let her find it for herself; then I asked one of the men to fall over her, and I asked another girl to fall over them. Then that didn't quite work, but that was because I hadn't explained it quite clearly. But I could see and I said: "Sandra, don't fall *that* way, fall the other way so that you can see where you're going." That was *one* thing; I didn't continue from there. Then I went away and made something with two other dancers. I also wanted to put in a kind of continuing thing for Carolyn Brown, particularly in the second half. I suppose I was thinking of Duchamp's interests, but not at all "This is meant to be. . . ."

The main thing, I think, is the tempo. Marcel always gave one the sense of a human being who is ever calm, a person with an extraordinary sense of calmness, as though days could go by, and minutes could go by. And I wanted to see if I could get that—the sense of time.[3]

Walkaround Time was divided into seven sections, each about seven minutes long. The opening section consisted of various movements taken from the warm-up exercises in a Cunningham technique class—a form of choreographic "ready-made." According to Valda Setterfield, Cunningham choreographed her solo in what was then an unusual way for him: instead of showing her the movement, he sat in front of her in the studio and described what he wanted.

Cunningham did not, as might have been expected, use everyday movement as an element in the dance proper, but between the third and fourth sections there was an intermission, when the houselights were brought up. Here the dancers strolled onstage, clad in robes and the assorted woollen garments that dancers wear offstage to keep warm. They did the kind of things they might do during an intermission with the curtain down: sit and chat, practice steps, lie down. Behrman's score gave way to recordings of popular music—Argentine tangos, a Japanese soprano singing "Tristesse," wildly off-key. This episode referred to the cinematic *Entr'acte* (by René

Clair) from the Dadaist ballet *Relâche*, presented by the Ballets Suédois in 1924, in which Duchamp appeared playing chess with Man Ray. He also appeared in the ballet itself, almost naked, as Adam in a tableau vivant after Lucas Cranach.[4]

The passage in which a male dancer (originally Gus Solomons, Jr.) was picked up and carried across the stage by the others like a figurehead was interpreted by Cunningham as follows: "You have an object—or a person if you like—and then that object is transported, and you see it, or him, in another circumstance—it's the same, but the situation has changed." Cunningham sees this as a Duchampian idea. Besides his own striptease, Cunningham also saw a reference to *Nude Descending a Staircase* in Brown's solo, its alternation of stillness and swift, large movement being intended to convey "the sense of stopping and moving at the same time."

An important aspect of the *Glass* is that the spectator looks not only at it but through it, to see, perhaps, another viewer on the other side, whose presence changes his or her own perception of the piece. Similarly, at various moments in the dance, the dancers are seen behind the pieces of the set, particularly at the end, when, in fulfillment of a stipulation of Duchamp's, these pieces were assembled in an approximation of the original work.

• • •

In July the company went to South America, following a month's residency in Boulder, Colorado. By the time they left, Solomons and Reid had left the company, and Dilley was to leave at the end of the tour. So three new dancers, Susana Hayman-Chaffey, Chase Robinson, and Mel Wong, went south. The tour included Mexico City, Rio de Janeiro, Buenos Aires, and Caracas, thanks to Lewis Lloyd, who salvaged that much of the tour after the original one collapsed when the impresario failed to fulfill his promises. Frank Stella designed a poster, proceeds from the sale of which went toward the tour's expenses.

Although the company this time received some assistance from the State Department's Office of Cultural Presentations, and was made welcome by the cultural attaché at the American Embassy in Mexico, American officials elsewhere were less helpful. In Buenos Aires, in fact, the company encountered "overt hostility," amounting almost to sabotage. It appears that members of the cultural staff contacted American organizations that had shown interest in supporting the company, and warned them that the performances presented "sex play on stage." When

Assemblage, 1968, MC in Ghirardelli Square, San Francisco. Photograph: James Klosty.

the people at the San Martin theater heard this, they "got cold feet," and did nothing to promote the company, which was "the best kept secret" in Buenos Aires, according to Lloyd.[5] Several long and serious articles did appear in local publications after the company's departure, however, both in Buenos Aires and in other cities visited on the tour.

ASSEMBLAGE

During the South America tour, a local television company filmed part of *Walkaround Time* at the Teatro Novo, Rio de Janeiro, on 2 August. Pieces from the repertory had been filmed or televised at various times in the company's history, though never with any supervision by Cunningham himself;

except in the case of the Helsinki program in 1964, in fact, the Foundation had never succeeded in acquiring kinescopes of these telecasts.

In 1961, as has been noted, Cunningham had made a short piece specifically for television, commissioned by Société Radio-Canada. In the fall of 1968 he had the opportunity to create a more extended work for the medium, in collaboration with the filmmaker Richard Moore. Done for the KQED television station in San Francisco, *Assemblage* was made on location in Ghirardelli Square in that city. It represented the amalgamation of two distinct ideas: one, a film about the place itself, and the other, a film about the dance company. Ghirardelli Square was one of the first of those urban environments that now exist in many large cities, where a sometimes run-down market or manufacturing area has been restored, prettified, and made into a mall-like precinct with restaurants, boutiques, galleries, and promenades. (Other examples are Covent Garden Market in London and the South Street Seaport in New York.) The film would show the dancers disporting themselves in this environment, as a kind of fanciful extension of the relationship between it and the people who normally visited it.

Cunningham had gone out in February to look the place over. He and the company then spent three weeks there in late October and early November, rehearsing and shooting. The project was funded by the National Endowment for the Arts and by the Ford Foundation.

In an interview, Cunningham told the San Francisco critic Robert Commanday that his idea was that "the finished film will deal not so much with dance in the narrow sense, but with various motions—boats moving, people walking, and, of course, groups dancing."[6] Meanwhile Moore, himself a former dancer, told an interviewer that Cunningham and his dancers were to make a number of "movement modules," and that he (Moore) would "arrange the sequences and edit the final . . . product." All the dances were to be shot in Ghirardelli Square or "in a special effects studio established in an industrial loft, nearby." Moore planned to use "extensive optical illusion and process photography," such as "the filming of the dancers as silhouettes ('travelling mats') which can be superimposed on other backgrounds."[7]

Cunningham's notes for the film not only include ideas for movements ("Yoga on roof-top," "Dancer doing complicated fall/unable to get up/pedestrian lifts him") but indicate his desire to explore the possibilities of the medium ("MC: segmented fall— 5 different angles," "Possibility of same shot in dance clothes and in street clothes"). He also wrote out in some detail his ideas for the "modules" mentioned by Moore:

Module #6
C[arolyn] B[rown] doing slow (slow motion) promenade [or CB and others (interchange)].
Camera in & out.
Scene [area] could change

in panorama view are people—dancers (can pedestrians enter this?)—there is no attention paid to CB (or who?)—dancers like static figures on cages (or near her) who face different ways (chance) in different positions— sometimes alone, sometimes grouped (chance)—a single dancer is seen in the space at different points (or same point in scene is caught with different dancer)

Commanday also visited the company musicians, Cage, Tudor, and Gordon Mumma, who were working, independently of course, on the sound score that would accompany the final 59-minute film, which was to be edited from some six hours of footage:

Specifically, they were assembling a sound track on tape of concrete sounds recorded by Mumma, mostly around San Francisco. . . . Cage had originally suggested the work's structural format based on a topographical map of the U.S., which they were to cross, keying different sounds to the changing colors on the map. They were using six sound categories, sounds near sea level, at high altitude (transformed through Tudor's *Rainforest* equipment that literally passes the sound through other substances, sheets of metal, wood, etc., changing its quality accordingly), animal life ("untransformed because they are poetic by themselves"), any sound materials modulated electronically to pulse and sound percussive, speech, Cage's thunder recording.[8]

• • •

Over the years, the Cunningham company had often given single performances at the Brooklyn Academy of Music, most recently in 1966 and 1967. In May 1968 it had given there its first extended New York engagement since its run at the Theater de Lys in 1953–54. This began on 15 May with a benefit to support the upcoming South American tour. Both *RainForest* and *Walkaround Time* had their New York premieres at Brooklyn; *Nocturnes*, *Variations V*, and *Untitled Solo* were all given for the last time during that season, which had ended on 26 May.

In November, Harvey Lichtenstein, director of the Brooklyn Academy, announced that the Merce Cunningham company, Alvin Ailey American Dance Theater, and a new company, Eliot Feld's American Ballet Company, would all be resident companies there. Each of the companies was assured of two engagements each year, beginning with the 1969–70 season.

1969

In 1967, the Ford Foundation had given a grant of $7 million to the New York City Ballet and its affiliate, the School of American Ballet, and to a number of other schools across the United States that George Balanchine had approved. This grant was the subject of some controversy, only somewhat allayed by a further grant of $485,000 that the Ford Foundation gave to underwrite, in part,

Canfield, 1969. Left to right: Meg Harper, Carolyn Brown, and MC. Photograph: James Klosty.

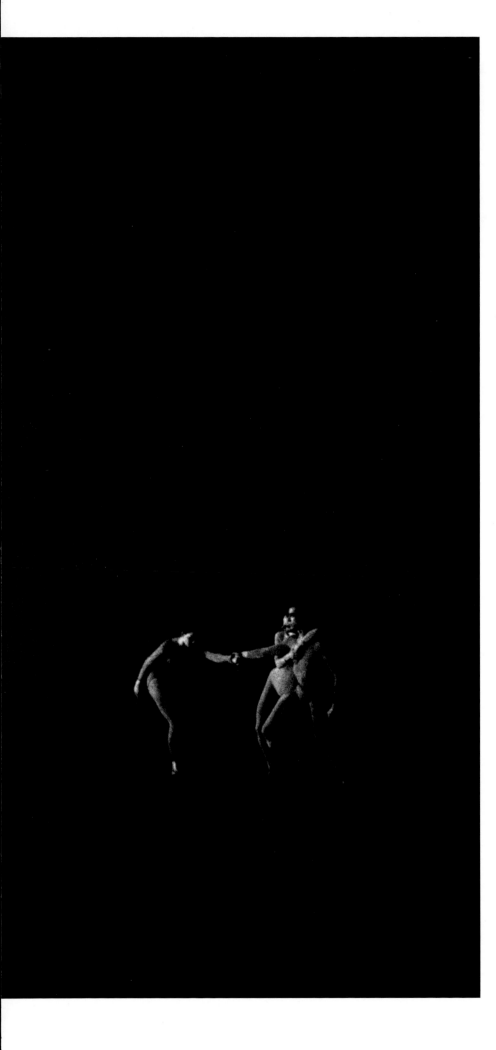

Festival of Dance 68–69, which took place at the Brooklyn Academy of Music and the Billy Rose Theater in Manhattan.

The festival included the companies of Martha Graham, Anna Sokolow, Erick Hawkins, Paul Taylor, Alwin Nikolais, José Limón, Alvin Ailey, and American Ballet Theatre, as well as Cunningham's. There were even some less established choreographers—Twyla Tharp, Meredith Monk, Yvonne Rainer, and Don Redlich—sharing the final week. The Cunningham company opened at the Billy Rose on 13 January 1969, its first engagement in a Broadway theater. Richard Nelson had taken over as lighting designer.

In February and March the company again toured colleges in New York State, with support from the New York State Council on the Arts. Some of these performances were "Gym Events." *Gym Event #5*, in the Elting Gymnasium of the State University College at New Paltz, on 27 February, was actually a preview, without decor and with an improvised electronic score by David Tudor and Gordon Mumma, of a new work:

CANFIELD

The dance's title refers to a game of solitaire invented by a gambler named Richard Canfield at the casino in Saratoga Springs, New York. Cunningham had played the game on vacation in Cadaqués, and it occurred to him that it could serve as the basis for a chance process to determine the sequence of movements in a dance. He assigned a word indicating some kind of motion (e.g. jump, kneel, perch, slide) to each card in the deck. The red and black suits denoted fast and slow movements respectively. "When two or three face cards came up in succession, they referred to the possibility of duets and trios."[1]

There were therefore fifty-two possible movement indications, and each time Cunningham played the game these came up in a different order. Since there are thirteen cards in a suit, he made thirteen strictly formal dances, or "hands." He also made fourteen "deals"—twelve between the "hands," plus one to begin and another to end the dance. These deals comprised simpler movements, in the performance of which the dancers were given certain freedoms—to do them or not, for instance, or to drop out for part of them.

The order was changed at each performance, and was posted in the wings for the dancers to read. A complete performance of all twenty-seven "hands" and "deals" would last about seventy-five minutes,

Opposite: MC with his notes for *Canfield*, 1969. Photograph: James Klosty. Above: Jasper Johns spray-painting Carolyn Brown's costume for *Canfield*, 1969. Photograph: James Klosty.

and such performances were given on occasion, sometimes under the title "Theater Event." More often, though, when the dance formed one part of a repertory program, only a selection of sequences was given, the shortest being some twenty minutes long.

Pauline Oliveros's score, *In Memoriam: Nikola Tesla, Cosmic Engineer*, was in homage to the Yugoslav physicist, who came to the United States in the early twentieth century and worked with Thomas Edison. He later moved to Colorado, where he experimented with artificial thunder and lightning. Oliveros instructed the musicians to find the "resonant frequency" of the building in which the performance was taking place. They would discuss the theater's sound qualities, testing them with whistles, bugles, cap pistols, and electronic instruments. When they had found the resonant frequency, they tried to match it with their instruments. If they succeeded, the air in the hall would vibrate, producing a deep pulsing sound. The musicians would tape these proceedings, then play them back later in the perfor-

mance. At a memorable Cologne performance in 1972, when *Canfield* was given in its entirety, the company encountered the most boorish audience of its entire history. The recording of their catcalls, laughter, and shouted comments was played back to them, and they gradually became silent as they realized what it was they were listening to.

Robert Morris's set featured a gray vertical beam, the height of the proscenium arch, which moved back and forth across the front of the stage. Lights in the back of this beam shone on to the backcloth, intensifying the illumination in the area over which they passed. Morris had intended the backcloth and costumes to be covered with a paint that would reflect this light, making them luminescent, but the paint wore off as the costumes were washed.

The first performance of *Canfield* as a piece (rather than a Gym Event) was at Nazareth College, Rochester, New York, on 4 March; the first New York performance was at the Brooklyn Academy of Music on 15 April. The decor was not used until the Brooklyn performance—which, on the other hand, was danced in silence, owing to an electricians' strike. The music was played at three subsequent Brooklyn performances (part of a further installment of Festival of Dance 68–69, again including the Ailey and Limón companies), the first in which all the elements were used.

• • •

After Brooklyn, there was a brief visit to Rome for two performances in the festival Premio Roma, at the end of April.

In September the company went to Minnesota for a ten-day residency, the first of many sponsored by the Walker Art Center, Minneapolis, with support from the National Endowment for the Arts, the Minnesota State Arts Council, and the schools involved in the residency. As well as repertory and event performances, there were other activities such as master classes and lecture-demonstrations.

That fall, the Rockefeller Foundation gave the Brooklyn Academy of Music a $350,000 grant toward developing new works by its three resident dance companies.

During the year, Something Else Press, New York, published Cunningham's *Changes: Notes on Choreography*. The book was edited by Frances Starr, who arranged Cunningham's notes, both written and graphic, and other illustrative material in a nonlinear, collagelike fashion intended to approximate the nature of the dances themselves.

1970s

Pages 172–173: *Inlets*, 1977. Left to right: Robert Kovich, MC, Ellen Cornfield, Chris Komar, and Karole Armitage. Photograph: Charles Atlas. This page, above: *Tread*, 1970. Left to right: MC, Meg Harper, Mel Wong, Jeff Slayton, and Carolyn Brown. Photograph: James Klosty. This page, left: *Tread*, 1970. Left to right: Douglas Dunn, Valda Setterfield, Mel Wong, Jeff Slayton, Carolyn Brown, and Meg Harper. Photograph: James Klosty.

1970

The Cunningham company's first season in the Brooklyn Academy of Music residency was from 5 to 16 January 1970. For this engagement, in addition to reviving *Crises* with Viola Farber returning as a guest artist, Cunningham made two new works, funded by the Rockefeller Foundation grant:

TREAD

Tread was one of Cunningham's lighter works, described by Patrick O'Connor as a "sometimes hilarious and always good-humored piece" in which "the dancers get into some extraordinarily complicated physical entanglements and Papa Cunningham comes along and straightens them out."[1] At one point the dancers huddled together and Cunningham stretched his arms over them like a mother hen gathering her chicks. Don McDonagh described rehearsals of the piece:

> Cunningham is sharpening the situation in which dancers form "gates" through which one or another of them will pass. Meg Harper slithers under Jeff Slayton's legs with virtually no clearance room and wraps herself around him. The general frame of the dance has been set: it begins quietly, with the company seated, and then works up to a humorous set of catches, lifts, and fast exits and entrances which resemble a French bedroom farce. At the finish, the work returns to its original, tranquil state.[2]

Bruce Nauman's set consisted of ten large industrial fans that stood in a row across the front of the stage, alternately stationary and turning from side to side. Nauman thought such fans would be available anywhere the company traveled, but this turned out not to be the case, and the fans had to be carried in the theater freight wherever the piece was performed. Cunningham himself designed the costumes—stylized sports clothes, the women in playsuits and leg-warmers, the men in sweaters and pants. The colors were in the range of brown to gray.

The music was an existing piece by Christian Wolff, *For 1, 2 or 3 people.*

SECOND HAND

One of the earliest of my solos, called *Idyllic Song* (1944), was made to the first movement of the *Socrate* of Erik Satie. Cage had arranged the music for two pianos [*sic*—actually it was for piano solo]. Over the years he had suggested I choreograph the other two movements, as he had planned to arrange them for piano also.

On one of our tours in the late sixties in the Middle West, David Tudor and Gordon Mumma, the musicians with us, explained to me that it was difficult for them to make different electronic set-ups for each of three separate dances for the performances and what could be done about it? Cage suggested I choreograph the *Socrate*. He had completed the two-piano arrangement [in collaboration with Arthur Maddox]. I worked on the dance, remembering the early solo to the first part, making a duet for Carolyn Brown and myself for the second, and a full company dance for the final movement. [Cunningham himself never left the stage.] A month before the scheduled first performance, Cage telephoned from Davis, California (where he was in residence at the University of California) to say that Satie's publisher had refused permission for his two-piano arrangement (and even for the use of Satie's own reduction of the score for piano and voices), but not to worry as he was writing a new piece for one piano, keep-

Second Hand, 1970, third part. Left to right: MC, Meg Harper, Ulysses Dove, Carolyn Brown, Mel Wong, Sandra Neels, Douglas Dunn, and Susana Hayman-Chaffey. Photograph: James Klosty.

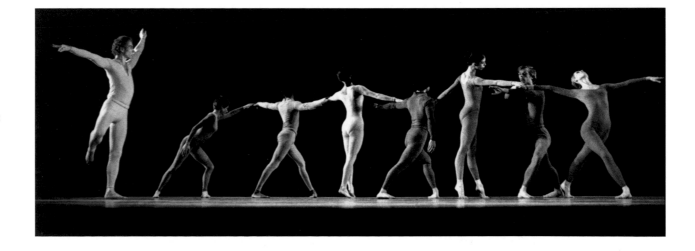

ing the structure and phraseology of Satie's music but otherwise using chance operations to change the continuity so there would be no copyright problem. When he told me this, I replied, "But you will have to rehearse with us and play the music so we can learn the new continuity." "Don't worry, I will," he answered. "I'm calling my version *Cheap Imitation*." "Well, if you're doing that, I'll call mine *Second Hand*." It was the last time I made a work following the phraseology of a musical score.[3]

Nevertheless, Cunningham taught the choreography to the dancers in the usual way, in silence. That he followed the musical structure of *Socrate* (as transformed by Cage) is certain. What is less clear is how much of its dramatic content he incorporated into the dance. Both Brown, his partner in *Second Hand*, and James Klosty have written that that content is implicitly if not explicitly present,[4] but Cunningham himself has discussed the piece only in formal terms:

> In the final movement, "Mort de Socrate," in an attempt to keep the space from being static, I decided to choreograph it in such a way that the dancers would have made a complete circle by the end of the piece. I began the movement standing alone at the back of the stage, and the dancers gradually entered and throughout the dance we make this spiraling circle before the final exit of the dancers leaving me on the stage alone.
>
> The circle is in no sense explicit. Dancers break off and move in different directions as the dance continues, but the diffused circular pattern is present.[5]

There was one small element of indeterminacy in the third movement: each of the dancers was given a number of hand or finger movements that he or she was free to use at will during the performance.

Second Hand had no set. Jasper Johns designed and dyed the costumes; both men and women wore leotards and tights, "each of a single color except for the edge of one side on the arm or the leg where another color enters. This second color is the major color of another of the costumes. This becomes apparent [only] when the dancers line up to bow. Jasper asked that the bow be arranged in order to show the color succession."[6]

· · ·

After a domestic tour in the spring, there was an extensive European tour in June and July, beginning

Left: Jasper Johns's "paper doll" costume design for *Second Hand*, 1970. Opposite: Rehearsing *Museum Event* at the Musée d'Art Moderne de la Ville de Paris, 31 May 1970. MC and John Cage. Photograph: James Klosty.

with two weeks in Paris at the Théâtre de France (Odéon) under the auspices of the Théâtre des Nations. There followed two performances in or near Amiens, a repertory program at the Maison de la Culture in that city and an Event at the Château de Ratilly; an eight-day tour of Holland under the auspices of the Holland Festival; a week at the Festival of Two Worlds in Spoleto, Italy; and finally another series of performances in St. Paul de Vence as part of the Nuits de la Fondation Maeght.

The second program at the Odéon included the first performance of a new work:

SIGNALS

Signals is really like a little traveling group of players that come out, place their chairs, sit down and do their parts. We've danced it in many places. Each has a kind of role, each does his little thing, then they pick up their chairs and leave. In fact some sit and some go away. I had an idea about a set that was really picked up chairs. It could happen in a French park, or in a theater, so working at it, I tried to think of something that you could do in a very simple circumstance. *Signals* is also an example of a piece that could change.[7]

This is made evident in the titles of the various sections: "Solos for 1, 2 or 3," "Duet for 2," "Trio for 3 or 4," "Sextet for 5 or 6."

Originally there was to be another solo, which would have given more flexibility. I tossed coins to determine the order of the dances; once it came up that the piece began with the Trio, which I thought might not work—the problem was, what happens next? When there are fewer

possibilities, it's harder to shift things around. But I think we tried it anyway.

Originally there were to be six chairs, in a clump upstage right. I wanted to put them in a different place each time, but most of the stages we were performing in were too small. As for the ending, there are two main divisions in what the dancers can do: if the chair is turned around and the dancer leans on it, then the dancer who goes to him or her is to have some contact with the other one—either to sit down, or fall into his/her arms. But if the chair is moved away, then the other dancer knows to exit. Those are "signals"—the piece is full of them.

In the sextet, when the dancers hold up a number of fingers, that's a signal to indicate what is their place in line. Then when they move out into the space they do one movement or another according to where they are in the line.

Another signal, in the last section, was the noise of breathing (originally by Cunningham himself):

The men start the specific movement and the girls come to it. Well, we couldn't figure out how to cue it, so the girls would know when to come. So I said I'll make the signal and I remember thinking and trying a number of things. And I thought, "Oh!" saying it with a nasal sound. Well, I took it as the signal for that part, and it works well except you have to make the sound on the intake of breath. . . .

The moment with the man with the stick: originally I had wanted it to be a quartet as it is now. When I was first making it, Mel Wong, who was holding the stick, was to pass it from time to time to me. Valda Setterfield was the girl in it, she was so nervous about the stick— "If you get hit you get hurt"—so I stayed out of it to make it simpler. Then eventually when I gave Mel Wong's part to Chris Komar, I remembered what I had originally planned, so that now there are two men who pass the stick back and forth.[8]

Patricia Lent, who danced in *Signals* in later years, has added another detail to this information: in the last section, who gets to stay on stage for the final moment with the chairs depends on where the dancers end up just before, and there is always a certain amount of "jockeying for position" as they all try to be in the right place.

Cunningham himself designed the costumes for *Signals*, sweat suits bound with tape to give the figure more definition. There was no set; Richard Nelson designed the lighting.

The music could and did change, and this was reflected in its title: for the first performance the title was *First Week of June*, the composers being given as Tudor-Mumma-Cage. As further performances were given, the title changed to *Second Week of June*, *Third Week of June*, and so on, and the order of the composers' names was switched. (Later, the program listing was often simplified so that only the musicians' names were given.)

• • •

In November, the company gave its second two-week season as a resident company at the Brooklyn Academy of Music. *Signals* received its first American performances, and there was yet another new work:

OBJECTS

The idea for this dance appears to have been based on the rhyme "Something old, something new, something borrowed, something blue." Much to Carolyn Brown's surprise, Cunningham says, a section from *Septet* (the "Virginia Reel") was incorporated into the piece—"that was something borrowed—I don't know what the something blue was." At another point Cunningham and other dancers mimed playing a game of jacks ("something old"?). This section was later revived for Events.

Neil Jenney's set provided the objects of the title: large sculptures of metal tubing and black cloth, with casters that enabled them to be wheeled about the stage during the piece. Cunningham had seen some sculptures by Jenney that he thought very beautiful, so Jasper Johns invited the artist to design a set. Cunningham liked the idea, but the actual objects turned out to be too big: "they were unmanageable, cumbersome in the wrong way for the theater." The cos-

tumes were tights and various kinds of tops, in black, white, and assorted colors.

The music was an existing work by Alvin Lucier, *Vespers.*

• • •

It had become increasingly evident that the company would have to move out of the studio at 498 Third Avenue. The building was to be torn down, if it did not fall down first—the floor sagged and creaked ominously when the dancers jumped. And in the winter months the heat was erratic at best. I was then still the studio administrator, and one day I read an article in the *New York Times* about Westbeth, the artists' housing and studio complex that would occupy the converted Bell Telephone Labs building in the West Village. I called and asked if there would be studio space for a dance company, and was told that there was such a space on the eleventh floor, the former auditorium. Cunningham and I went over to look at it. The space was ideal, with superb views across the Hudson River and and of the New York skyline. The rent was utterly beyond our means, but the J. M. Kaplan Fund, which was underwriting the Westbeth project together with the National Endowment for the Arts, offered us a subsidy that would enable us to pay it, at least for a couple of years. Accordingly, the decision was made to vacate the Third Avenue studios, which had served us well, and to move into Westbeth.

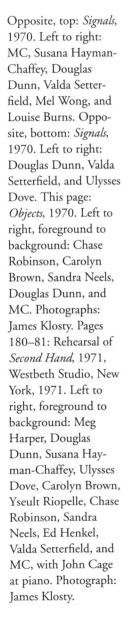

Opposite, top: *Signals*, 1970. Left to right: MC, Susana Hayman-Chaffey, Douglas Dunn, Valda Setterfield, Mel Wong, and Louise Burns. Opposite, bottom: *Signals*, 1970. Left to right: Douglas Dunn, Valda Setterfield, and Ulysses Dove. This page: *Objects*, 1970. Left to right, foreground to background: Chase Robinson, Carolyn Brown, Sandra Neels, Douglas Dunn, and MC. Photographs: James Klosty. Pages 180–81: Rehearsal of *Second Hand*, 1971, Westbeth Studio, New York, 1971. Left to right, foreground to background: Meg Harper, Douglas Dunn, Susana Hayman-Chaffey, Ulysses Dove, Carolyn Brown, Yseult Riopelle, Chase Robinson, Sandra Neels, Ed Henkel, Valda Setterfield, and MC, with John Cage at piano. Photograph: James Klosty.

1971

The Westbeth studios opened on 25 January, while the company was on tour. Cunningham and Cage had taken an apartment around the corner, on Bank Street.

Much of 1971 was taken up with domestic touring. Having performed twice at the University of California, Berkeley, in January, the company returned there in July for a month-long residency, with further performances at the beginning and the end. The two final ones were Events, the second of these unique in that Cunningham allowed the dancers to supply material of their own, "partly at Cage's suggestion," according to Carolyn Brown:

> [Cunningham] told us that his contribution would be to design the structure in skeleton. Otherwise, he would participate choreographically as one of the eleven dancers. He organized the stage space in three separate ways, but what went on in the space and how long it went on was indeterminate. . . . Merce ended up contributing two or three movement ideas, but this was more to encourage activity than to usurp control.[1]

Although the performance was well received, Cunningham did not repeat the experiment.

In contrast to the previous year, only one new dance, a solo for Cunningham, was performed in 1971:

LOOPS

Described by Cunningham as an "Event for soloist," Loops was performed by him at The Museum of Modern Art, New York, on 3 December. The music, by Gordon Mumma, was entitled *Biophysical and Ambient Signals from FM Telemetry*. By means of these signals, "the respiration and heart [beats] of Mr. Cunningham were heard live as part of the performance."[2] The piece was performed in front of Jasper Johns's large painting *Map, after Buckminster Fuller's Dymaxion Airocean World*, in the Founders' Room on the museum's sixth floor; there were also slides by Charles Atlas. Richard Nelson did the lighting. *Loops* was performed again at New York's Whitney Museum of American Art on 18 May 1973 (as *Loops and Additions*), and it also gave Cunningham material for his appearances in Event performances, such as the solo in which his hands move through the air around his head and torso, fingers flickering and twitching. Another section in which he pantomimed putting on

makeup was repeated later in some of the Dialogues he performed with Cage. At the end of this, he would hold his hands up flat in front of his face and then suddenly open them, revealing his face with his mouth wide open—a quotation from both *Septet* and *Scramble*.

Above: *Landrover*, 1971. Left to right: Ulysses Dove, Sandra Neels, Chris Komar, and Meg Harper. Photograph: James Klosty.

1972

In February the Cunningham company gave its third and, as it turned out, last two-week repertory season at the Brooklyn Academy of Music. Three new works were presented during the season:

LANDROVER

Landrover, first given on opening night (1 February), was a large-scale work, over fifty minutes in length.

> The dance is in four parts. The original conception was to change the playing area from section to section, that is, stage to hall to gymnasium to out-of-doors; or to have a constantly shifting landscape surround it.[1]
>
> My image for it was people moving in different landscapes. American perhaps in the sense that we move in our country—across varied spaces—with varied backgrounds.[2]

Cunningham even had the idea of performing the piece in front of a film of "a continuously changing landscape, like driving across the country; the landscape changes slowly but continuously." In the perfor-

Above: *Loops and Additions*, 1972, Whitney Museum of American Art, New York, 8 May 1973. Gordon Mumma and MC. Photograph: Tom Brazil.

Above: *TV Rerun*, 1971. Left to right: Morgan Ensminger, Susana Hayman-Chaffey, and MC. Photograph: Mark Lancaster. Below: *Borst Park*, 1971. MC and Sandra Neels. Photograph: James Klosty.

mance, though, there was no decor. Jasper Johns designed the costumes—tops and tights in various colors.

> This was just prior to my working on television, and the piece still employs space in a large way. When I began to work on television I changed that. I did think of doing at least part of *Landrover* as a video, but it's so spread out.

The second section was a long duet, originally danced by Cunningham and Carolyn Brown. The music, like that for *Signals*, was a collaborative effort by Cage, David Tudor, and Gordon Mumma, *52/3*, the figures representing respectively the piece's duration and the number of musicians involved.

TV RERUN

TV Rerun, first given the following night, was an indeterminate piece, "a dance," according to Brown, "in which everyone learns the same material but is free to choose spontaneously in performance what parts of it she or he wishes to perform. It is a dance which can be done by any number of dancers, and the whole is never jeopardized by the departure of any one dancer."[3] Brown put this principle to the test one evening in Belgrade, where she arranged to be replaced by Susana Hayman-Chaffey in *RainForest* and exercised her option not to appear in *TV Rerun*. Since she was not in the middle dance, *Signals*, this meant she had the evening off.

> I wanted to find some way to deal with shifting focus on stage. Jasper suggested having cameramen moving around so that the dancers could

do that—not necessarily facing the camera, but being aware of a nonfixed focus. If they left they "went off camera" and were supposed to go and stand near one of the cameramen, not in the usable space, and to move with him.

The design of *TV Rerun* was credited to Johns. The one or more persons on stage photographing the performance, with a still, movie, or television camera, constituted the "decor." (On occasion, Cunningham himself was a camera operator.) The costumes were white or black leotards and tights. A performance in Belgrade later that year was to be televised, and the television cameraman was offered the option of being on stage with the dancers, but refused it.

Mumma's score, *Telepos*, was described as "a collaboration between the composer and the dancers. . . . [who] wear telemetry belts, designed by Mumma, which transmit signals related to the dancers' motions and their positions with respect to gravity. . . . The composer then arranges the interactions of these signals for the audience, who hear the result from loudspeakers."[4]

BORST PARK

This dance was named for a small park in Centralia, Washington, Cunningham's hometown. "It used to be on the edge of town, but now the town has spread out beyond it. There's an Indian blockhouse there. We used to go for picnics." The dance indeed seemed to depict the kind of activity one might see in such a place—a picnic, games. It was a light piece; Meg Harper remembers a solo in which she seemed to be watching a crawling bug, which she finally picked up and gave to Cunningham. At the end of the picnic scene, the tablecloth and the objects spread out on it were pulled into the wings by a string.

The music, *Burdocks*, was an instrumental piece by Christian Wolff.[5] The six musicians, who performed this piece on stage, were listed alphabetically in the program together with the six dancers. (These six plus Brown, who was not in *Borst Park*, were the dancers in the first part of *Landrover*.)

The costumes were credited to "The Company," who chose for themselves what to wear.

• • •

At the end of April, Cunningham received one of that year's Brandeis University Creative Arts Awards. In June he received an honorary degree, Doctor of Letters, from the University of Illinois in Urbana-Champaign. (This degree had been assiduously pro-

Inset, top: *Events*, 1972, Persepolis, Iran, 1972. Left to right: Douglas Dunn, Susana Hayman-Chaffey, and MC. Inset, bottom: *Events*, 1972, Théâtre de la Ville, Paris, 1972. Left to right: Susana Hayman-Chaffey, Sandra Neels, Brynar Mehl, Barbara Lias, Meg Harper, Chris Komar, Ulysses Dove, Valda Setterfield, and Nanette Hassall. Photograph: James Klosty. Right: *Events*, 1972, Piazza San Marco, Venice, 1972. Photograph: James Klosty.

moted by Margaret Erlanger, head of the dance department there.)

As in 1970, the first part of the year's touring was all in North America—a performance in Toronto, and another residency in Minneapolis sponsored by the Walker Art Center. In May, the dance company gave its first series of Studio Performances at Westbeth. Early in September, however, foreign touring resumed. The company went first to Iran, to take part in that country's sixth Festival of Arts. They gave two Events in the open air, one in Shiraz and one in the Persian ruins in Persepolis, the latter in the presence of what was then the royal family.

From Iran the company flew to Venice for the 35th International Festival of Contemporary Music, part of that year's Biennale. Besides two repertory performances in the Teatro La Fenice and one in a theater (or cinema) in Mestre, on the mainland, the company performed another open-air Event, this one in the Piazza San Marco. Cunningham "procured a chair for each of the dancers; they began by sitting in a small circle and gradually pushed back until they had cleared enough space to work in. They also used brooms to sweep the space. . . . "[6]

The next stop was Belgrade, Yugoslavia, for the international theater festival BITEF 6: the company performed an Event in the modern-art museum, and two performances, one of them of *Canfield* in its entirety, in the Atelier 212 theater. There followed a performance in the 16th Warsaw Autumn Festival, Warsaw, where the company had been promised that it would this time be housed in a new and modern hotel. The hearts of those who had been on the 1964 world tour sank when the bus pulled up outside the Hotel Warszawa, where they had stayed eight years before. The new hotel, it was explained, was not finished yet. Cage set out to find other accommodations, but one of the guides ran after him and brought him back, assuring him that anything he might find himself would be worse.

It was a relief to fly to London for a week's run at Sadler's Wells, again under the auspices of Michael White. The following week—the first week of October—came two performances in Germany: the first the previously described Cologne performance of *Canfield*, in the opera house, at which the audience was so ill-mannered and hostile, the second an Event in an enormous hall (actually a restaurant) in Düsseldorf. The contrast in the reception in these two places could not have been greater: the Düsseldorf audience was wildly enthusiastic.

A week in Grenoble followed, with performances in two different spaces in the Maison de la Culture, two of them in the Théâtre Mobile, where the entire theater revolved. The company then drove by bus across the mountains to Milan, where it stayed for a week, performing in the Teatro Lirico as part of an international festival called "Milano aperta."

The tour ended in Paris, where the company performed for the first time at the Théâtre de la Ville (the former Sarah Bernhardt), under the auspices of the Festival d'automne. This theater was to become almost a second home for the company for nearly twenty years. The season, however, ended sadly: after nearly twenty years, Carolyn Brown had told Cunningham that she had decided to leave the company, and her last performance was on 29 October, in a program that included, appropriately, the elegiac *Second Hand*. It was the end of an era.

Above: John Cage performing *Child of Tree* (music for *Solo*, 1973), 1975. Opposite: MC performing *Solo*, 1973. Photograph: Jack Mitchell.

1973

For the next two years, all of the company's performances were Events or lecture-demonstrations (the distinction between the two was not always clear); there were also several of Cunningham's and Cage's Dialogues. Cunningham consequently did not have to address right away the question of a full repertory program without Carolyn Brown, whose departure, he said, made "a profound change." The excerpts from repertory works that were included in Events omitted her parts. Even so, the program for a series of four Events at the Brooklyn Academy of Music in March 1973 specified which dances were to be given on each evening, and these included a new work for the company's remaining members:

CHANGING STEPS

Changing Steps consisted of ten solos, five duets, three trios, two quartets, and two quintets, which could be performed in any order, <u>in any space</u>, in any combination.

> [I wanted] to make a piece which could have a different order from performance to performance. If it were done in sequential fashion, one dance after another, whatever the order, the whole piece would take forty-three minutes. If overlapped to the extreme degree, as many of the individual dances [as possible] taking place at the same time, compacted, they could all take place in twelve and a half minutes.

Cunningham deliberately designed the solos to display each dancer's individual qualities. (In later years, however, as the company grew, these solos were of course taken over by other dancers, and indeed might be danced by more than one dancer in the course of a given performance.) Chance procedures were used, but only "in a very broad sense," to define a dance's different sections rather than to specify its steps.

Cunningham made the dances separately so that each one could occupy a small space—it was, in fact, choreographed in the small studio at Westbeth ("We were beginning to think about the camera"). The piece could therefore be performed almost anywhere. It has frequently been used in Events. For the Brooklyn performance in March 1973, the music was by David Behrman, Cage, Gordon Mumma, and David Tudor. The costumes—jumpsuits in various colors—were designed by Charles Atlas.

The first theater performance of *Changing Steps* was in Detroit in 1975, when it was given with Cunningham's solo *Loops*; the music was now Cage's *Cartridge Music*. New costumes were designed by Mark Lancaster. On other occasions the piece was combined with *Loops* and one or other of the various "Exercise Pieces" Cunningham choreographed.

At another of the Brooklyn Events, Cunningham performed a new solo for the first time:

SOLO

This dance was based on Cunningham's observation of animals in the San Diego Zoo. "The dance images go from one kind of animal to another, bird, snake, lion, in eight minutes."[1] The observation was often detailed: his tongue flicked out between his lips like a snake's; on his exit, he pulled his head back into his neck just a little.

The costume was the one made for Cunningham to wear in *Dromenon*: Sonja Sekula had painted designs on a woollen unitard while Cunningham wore it. As with *Changing Steps*, the music at the first performance was by Behrman, Cage, Mumma, and Tudor. Also as with *Changing Steps*, the first theater performance took place two years later in Detroit, when the music was Cage's *Child of Tree*—another title out of Joyce's *Finnegans Wake*.

• • •

During the summer Cunningham went to Paris to choose dancers from the Paris Opéra ballet for an important commission, arranged by Michel Guy:

UN JOUR OU DEUX

In the fall of 1973 I spent nine weeks in Paris working with dancers from the Opéra Ballet. The Festival d'automne and the Paris International Dance Festival had jointly commissioned this work to be choreographed utilizing dancers from the Opéra on the Opéra stage. I asked Cage if he would compose the music, and Jasper Johns if he would design the decor. They agreed. It was to be an evening-

length work without intermission and would involve the full Opéra facilities.

Cage had originally wanted to use the works of Satie in various juxtapositions, to make a circus of Satie's music, but Salabert, the publisher, refused permission. So he composed the work "Etcetera," for orchestra, which involved twenty musicians and three conductors. Cage arrived in Paris a month before the first performance, and proceeded to have consultations with Marius Constant, the principal conductor, and the other two, Catherine Comet and Boris de Vinogradow. When the first musical rehearsal came, there was a problem. From what I understood, the musicians, upon learning that they were to make choices about which sounds they played, as indicated in Cage's score, asked for more money, pointing out also that it was chamber music. Rolf Liebermann, the then director of the Opéra, spent a good part of the day with them, eventually solving the difficulty by giving them two marks (double pay) for each rehearsal and performance. Cage was worried about setting a precedent. Constant said, "Don't. It's the Opéra. It would have happened anyway."

Each day I was in the top of the building working in the ballet studio with the dancers, many of whom were worried about dancing without musical support, and what would happen when the two came together? This fear increased as the piece grew longer, one or two of the soloists becoming quite upset at times. I thought it had to do mainly with an idea about their image, and assured them they were strong enough as dancers not to be thrown off by it.

At the first rehearsal of the music in the theater without the dancers, a sound like rain on a number of roofs came out of the pit. The large handful of spectators rushed forward to see what was producing it. Each musician had, as a supplement to his instrument, a French cardboard carton

Opposite: *Changing Steps* and *Loops*, 1975. Left to right: Jim Self, Karole Armitage, MC, and Lise Friedman. Photograph: Johan Elbers. Above, left: Rehearsal for *Un jour ou deux*, 1973. Left to right: Michaël Denard, MC, and Jean Guizerix. Photograph: François Hers. Above, right: Jasper Johns's set design for *Un jour ou deux*, 1973.

which he used as a drum at various moments during the piece.

Several days later, at the first full rehearsal of the work with the dancers on the stage and the musicians in the pit, I had to repeatedly calm several dancers as to their dancing with the music. Finally the rehearsal began. I was nervous enough trying to keep track of the dance and the timings within it and what was working and what wasn't, so any difficulties they might be having with the music were not immediately apparent to me. Afterward, upon my questioning, they said, "The music? No, we didn't have any trouble."[2]

Before rehearsal each day, Cunningham taught a company class; the *étoiles* Michaël Denard, Jean Guizerix, Wilfride Piollet, and Claude Ariel had spent some time in New York taking classes with him before the rehearsals began. Guizerix and Piollet especially were his enthusiastic supporters in the project. *Un jour ou deux* was first performed on 6 November, with a cast of twenty-six dancers. One of Cunningham's epic works, it lasted over ninety minutes without an intermission.

A program note for the ballet read,

Soirée de Ballet de Merce Cunningham
A Day or two is the title of this ballet.[3]

The dance will be comprised of a number of separate dance events—solos, duets, trios, quintets and larger groups—sometimes seen as a single entity, and sometimes in multiple with several going on at once.

There are no predetermined characters and there is no prearranged story, so the characters of the dance become the characters of the individual dancers themselves, and the story is the continuity of the events as they succeed one another.

The dance is made separately from the music, and is not dependent on it. The three elements—the music, the dance and the décor—appear simultaneously, but independently of each other, particularly in the case of the dance and the music. You as spectator can share this complexity of experience, but how you feel about what you see and hear is not determined by us. We present it, and allow each of you to receive this Day or two in your own way.[4]

Cage's score, an orchestral piece, allowed twelve string and wind soloists to move from one conductor to another. They also had the option of silence. There were also two pianists and six percussionists, who played independently of a conductor. Underlying the orchestral music as a constant was an environmental tape recorded at Stony Point, where Cage had lived before coming back to New York, of natural and man-made sounds, bird song, cars, factory sirens, and so on.

Johns's setting consisted of two scrims, one at the front of the stage and one halfway back. The space behind them could be made either visible or invisible by backlighting. The scrims shaded from almost black at the left to almost white at the right. When the lights went up behind the second scrim one saw the shadowy outlines of the stage's back wall, like the portals of a great cathedral. The dancers were dressed in leotards and tights that also shaded from dark to light gray at the top; they wore shoes, though the women were not on pointe. Later some put on sweatpants or leg warmers. The realization of Johns's designs was carried out under the supervision of a young British painter, Mark Lancaster.

• • •

Before returning to the United States, Cunningham and Cage went to Rome to perform in the Festival d'autunno there—another Dialogue, presumably, though the program described the performance as "Silence/Teatro concerto."

Charles Atlas, the company's stage manager and also a filmmaker, had completed the editing of a film of *Walkaround Time*. He has said of his work,

> The first three sections were shot in Berkeley, California, with a single hand-held camera during an afternoon stop-and-start rehearsal. The attempt was to record the complete choreographic material in actual time with a variety of points of view, and yet to keep the integrity of the movement.
>
> The last four sections were shot a year later in Paris, France, with three cameras during a live a performance. My concern here was to capture the actual performance quality of the dancers, and in the last two sections to make a filmic approximation of the experience of seeing a dance.[5]

Cunningham himself was beginning to be interested in the possibilities of choreography for the camera. He had been dissatisfied with the way his work had been shown on film and video, as for example in the 1968 piece for television *Assemblage*, but it seemed likely to him that in the future there might be more opportunities for his work to be seen in those media. Remembering the example of Fred Astaire, who learned about film technique so that his dances would be seen properly on the movie screen, he spent some time on his return to New York working with a video camera. "We bought one camera to begin with, I had to learn how to switch it on and off; that was my level."[6]

1974

By early in 1974, the Cunningham Dance Company had not performed since a brief series of Events in the Westbeth Studio the previous May. They reassembled for a longer series of such performances, which began in February and ran until the first weekend in May, except for the first weekend in March, when they gave two Events in the Lepercq Space at the Brooklyn Academy of Music. Cage invited a number of composers to provide music for the series—more or less a different composer each weekend, including Yasunao Tone, Jackson Mac Low, Annea Lockwood, Jacques Bekaert, Christian Wolff, Robert Ashley, Maryanne Amacher, Alvin Lucier, Joel Chadabe, Phill Niblock, Frederic Rzewski, Tony Martin, Garrett List, Philip Corner, and Nam June Paik, as well as David Behrman, John Cage, Gordon Mumma, and David Tudor, the company's regular musicians at the time.

That spring Cunningham was working on a new piece, which was shown in parts as a work in progress at some of these Events. Still untitled, it was eventually to be called *Sounddance*.

In April an exhibition entitled "Diaghilev/Cunningham" opened at the Emily Lowe Gallery, Hofstra University, Hempstead, Long Island, New York. Curated by Robert R. Littman and myself, the exhibition compared the collaborative processes of Diaghilev's Ballets Russes and the Cunningham Dance Company. In conjunction with this show, the Cunningham company performed another Event at the Nassau Veterans Memorial Coliseum, with music by Yoshimasa Wada.

Meanwhile Cunningham was pursuing his new interest in choreographing for the camera. He and Charles Atlas took an active part in the preparation of a two-part program for CBS Camera Three, *A Video Event*, directed by Merrill Brockway. The music was by Christian Wolff. Part I began by showing a company class, then moved into parts of *Winterbranch*, the Cunningham solo at the beginning of *Second Hand*, an excerpt from the work in progress that was to become *Sounddance*, and finally part of *TV Rerun*. For the latter, the screen was split into four parts, one of them showing a half-inch tape Cunningham himself had shot during a Studio Event. Part II began with further footage of a rehearsal of *Sounddance*, then continued with *Changing Steps*, *Landrover*, and *Signals*. *Changing Steps* was also shown on four screens. The program was shot in the CBS studios in May 1974, and was broadcast on 27 October and 3 November the same year.

After that, the dancers were again laid off while Cunningham worked with another company, this time The Boston Ballet, which opened its November season with productions of *Summerspace* and *Winterbranch*. (Margaret Jenkins again staged *Summerspace*, as she had in Stockholm in 1967.) Sandwiched between ballets by Birgit Cullbert (*Medea*) and David Lichine (*Graduation Ball*), the two dances were greeted by the audience with blank incomprehension and, in the case of *Winterbranch*, outright hostility. There were two performances, after which the dances were consigned to oblivion as far as Boston was concerned.

In the fall, the Cunningham company returned to work on another video project, the first to be made in the Westbeth Studio, which gave the piece its title. The music was by Cage and the costumes were by Mark Lancaster, from a design (for *Un jour ou deux*) by Jasper Johns. (Lancaster was becoming the company's de facto resident designer, though he was not named as Johns's successor as artistic advisor until 1980.)

The piece, for eleven dancers (not including Cunningham), was in six sections. Karen Carreras writes,

> Dancers introduce themselves in the first section by staring directly into the camera. In Section II the camera obscures the dancers' relationship to space through the use of close-ups. In the third section, the viewer's attention is continually re-centered upon a new dancer who has entered the group. Section IV investigates the possibilities of deep focus and its relationship to movement. Section V employs an elaborate use of multiple cameras. And lastly, in Section VI, separate movement segments were joined together in the editing process, thus creating the effect of physical and spatial discontinuity.[1]

For each dancing section of *Westbeth* we asked questions about video. The first one, for example, was concerned with the changing distance from the camera of each dancer, ranging from close-ups to long shots. These changes were made involving movement so that the dancing did not stop. In another section we asked how to cut from one camera to the other, making these cuts on the dance rhythms in such a way as not to interrupt the flow of the dancing; a cut is at a single instant. Or another question: how to tape five dancers each doing different movements in different directions and keep all five in full figure.[2]

Some of the choreography for this last section was based on the Quintet in *Suite for Five*.

1975

During February the Studio Events resumed, again with guest composers—Robert Ashley, Meredith Monk, and David Rosenboom and Mr. J. B. Floyd. On 14 February there was a screening of *Westbeth* preceded by a live performance of the piece. As well as *Westbeth* there was a new work, *Exercise Piece*.

In March, two New York gallery and art publishing establishments, Multiples Inc. and Castelli Graphics, published *A Portfolio of Seven Prints Recording Collaborations with Merce Cunningham and Dance Company, with a Text by Calvin Tomkins*. The seven artists represented were John Cage, Jasper Johns, Robert Morris, Bruce Nauman, Robert Rauschenberg, Frank Stella, and Andy Warhol. The works were exhibited first at the Leo Castelli Gallery and then at Multiples. In the portfolio, the prints were interleaved

MCDC on tour, 1970. Left to right: Gordon Mumma, Meg Harper, Carolyn Brown, Charles Atlas, Susana Hayman-Chaffey, Mel Wong, Jeff Slayton, Ain Gordon (Valda Setterfield's son), Jean Rigg (administrator), Valda Setterfield, MC, John Cage, Douglas Dunn, Jim Baird (technical director), Sandra Neels, and Chase Robinson.

with photographs by James Klosty of dances in which the artists concerned had collaborated with Cunningham. (Klosty's book of photographs and essays by various hands, *Merce Cunningham*, was published at about the same time.)

The company also began to tour again. After a brief residency at Williams College, Williamstown, Massachusetts, it gave three repertory performances at the Music Hall in Detroit, Michigan—the first since the end of 1972. Four works that had been previously given in Events received their first theater performances with their scores: *Changing Steps, Solo, Rebus,* and *Sounddance.*

REBUS

Rebus is a dramatic dance lasting thirty-one minutes, with me as protagonist, in opposition to the young dancers of my company acting as chorus.[1]

This was in fact the first piece in which the generational difference between Cunningham and the rest of his company, implicit in such different works as *Tread* and *Second Hand*, was not only acknowledged but exploited: he appeared as a detached, controlling presence, setting choreographic puzzles and equations for his dancers to solve.

Because of this difference between me and the dancers . . . , I am obliged to spend more time in rehearsals watching their work and answering their questions than in practicing my own parts. It becomes increasingly difficult, as I grow older,

for me to dance with them as one of them. As a matter of course a separation happens. . . .

The structure is made of a number of long sequences with quite long rhythms; some of them go all the way to seventeen. That was a suggestion by Pat Richter, the pianist who used to play for our class every day, and who observed me trying out these long phrases. I asked her what the rhythm would be the next time, and she jokingly said seventeen. So that's what it was the next day. . . .

The dance emerged from working on these long sequences.[2]

Rebus had been performed in the last two Studio Events that February; the first performance in Detroit was on 7 March. The music was David Behrman's *Voice, with Melody-Driven Electronics*, with Joan La Barbara as the vocalist. The design was by Mark Lancaster.

The costumes . . . are tights and leotards with splashes of color on them. I wear a gray shirt and brown pants with brilliant red unitard underneath, and at one point in the dance, I take off the shirt and pants to reveal the red unitard.[3]

(There was a clothes rack onstage on which the discarded garments hung.)

SOUNDDANCE

Sounddance had been shown as a work in progress in Event performances in 1974, and also in the television program *A Video Event* the same year.

I made *Sounddance* . . . after returning from nine weeks at the Paris Opéra. . . . The work had been so difficult, and trying, that when I got back to my own dancers, it was like an explosion, a tremendous release. I felt like doing something vigorous, fast, complex. The title is taken from *Finnegans Wake*: "In the beginning was the sounddance." The rehearsal room at the Paris Opéra had been very small. I felt like doing something in the same type of space, something compact, in which to keep up the energy level constantly. It's a very strenuous piece to dance though it takes only seventeen or eighteen minutes. The entrances and exits take place through a tentlike opening in the back, in a canvas decor. At the end, the dancers are swept back into it, as though into a wind tunnel.

The movement itself follows from the fact that the classical dancers had been so rigid, so

Opposite: Andy Warhol's *Merce Cunningham I*, 1974, screenprint on Japanese gift-wrapping paper, 30 x 20″, made for a 1975 portfolio using a photograph by Richard Rutledge of MC in *Antic Meet*, 1958. Below: *Sounddance*, 1975. Left to right: Robert Kovich, Karole Armitage, Chris Komar, Ellen Cornfield, Alan Good, Louise Burns, Lise Friedman, Jim Self, MC, and Lisa Fox. Photograph: Johan Elbers.

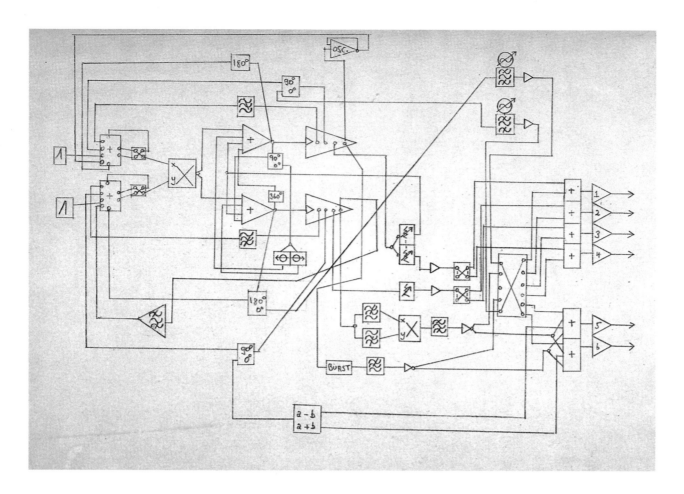

straight in their bodies. I wanted a lot of movement, twists in the torso. . . .

The structural idea is to have the ten dancers enter and exit from upstage center in different ways, one after the other. The footwork and torso movements are complex. The general impression is of a space observed under a microscope.

In fact Cunningham had been given a microscope as a gift, and the movement and groupings in *Sounddance*, such as those in which the dancers formed a mass of writhing or waving limbs, were sometimes derived from his observation of organisms under it.

The music is by David Tudor [*Toneburst*], sustained and powerful. It's an electronic music that provides a charged environment. The costumes by Mark Lancaster are light yellow and gray, his decor across the back is tent-like and sand colored.[4]

• • •

The rest of the month was taken up with residencies in Chicago and Minneapolis, both of which included Events and a repertory performance. In Minneapolis there was also another performance of *Westbeth* both live and on screen. The tour continued into April with performances in Saint Louis, Missouri; Tempe, Arizona; and at the University of California in both Los Angeles and Berkeley.

Returning east, the company performed a single Event at the State University of New York at Purchase, after which Studio Events resumed, continuing until the beginning of June. The composers for this new series included Linda Fisher (at Purchase, with Tudor), Anthony Braxton, Maryanne Amacher, Annea Lockwood, Shudo Yamato, Charlemagne Palestine, and Stuart Dempster. In the meantime, the Cunningham Dance Foundation had received a New York State Award for 1975.

• • •

In October there was another video project. Cunningham was invited to make a work at the WNET/TV Lab, in New York City, "an extremely small space":

BLUE STUDIO: FIVE SEGMENTS

If I raised my arms I touched the lights, there was a cement floor, and we had two days in which to do it. Everything we had planned there didn't work. *Blue Studio* was for a thirty-minute program that Nam June Paik had asked me to share with him, each of us having fifteen

Above: David Tudor's diagrammatic score for *Toneburst*, the music for *Sounddance*, 1975. Opposite: Playing-card illustrations using stills from Charles Atlas's video, *Blue Studio: Five Segments*, 1975, with MC, as manipulated by Nam June Paik in his video *Merce by Merce by Paik*, 1978.

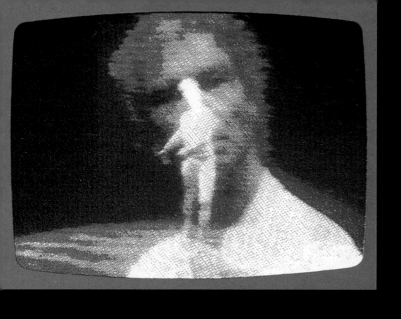

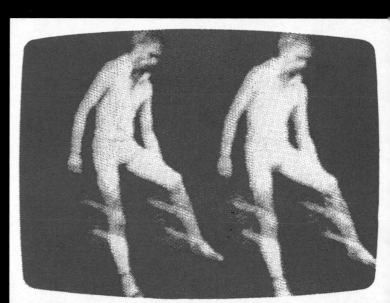

minutes. I originally wanted two dancers, but when I saw the studio and the conditions, I decided to do it myself.[5]

In this piece Cunningham and Charles Atlas experimented with the Chroma-key process, which enables a figure to be seen against a changing background, an effect reminiscent of the dream sequence in Buster Keaton's *Sherlock Jr.* The final section of *Blue Studio* eventually included five Merce Cunninghams, all moving simultaneously. As Cunningham has described it, the section had to be shot five times, during which he tried to remember what he had been doing and where in the space he had been doing it, so that he would not occupy the same space more than once.

• • •

The year ended with yet another series of Events, this time presented by Dance Umbrella at Roundabout Stage One in New York. Again, each had music by a different composer: Cage, Amacher, Tudor, Paik (with Cage and Tudor), Christian Wolff, and Monk. On the last two weekends of the year the company gave four more Events at Westbeth, with music by Jon Gibson and Yasunao Tone.

The company had not shown repertory in New York since early in 1972, prompting dance critic Arlene Croce to ask in *The New Yorker*, "What kind of dance capital of the world is it which confines the presentation of a new Merce Cunningham work to his downtown loft studio . . . ?"[6]

1976

On the first two weekends of January there were more Studio Events, with music by David Behrman and Liz Phillips. On 13 and 15 January the company gave two performances at the McCarter Theater in Princeton, New Jersey, reviving *Rune* and presenting another new work that, like its predecessors, had been given in Events as a work in progress:

TORSE

The choreography of *Torse* utilizes the numbers 1 to 64, taken from the *I Ching, The Book of Changes*. These numbers are used both in the spatial plan, conceived as a square 8 x 8, and the movement phrases, which constitute the language of *Torse*. All aspects of the continuity were chance-determined, the sequence of phrases, the number of things happening at once and the number of dancers involved in a

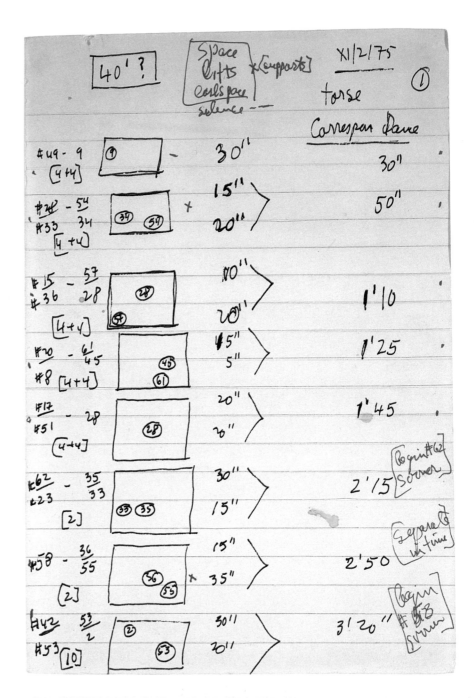

given phrase. The rhythm is sometimes metric and sometimes not. *Torse* refers to the use of the torso throughout the dance. There are five basic positions utilized—upright, arch, twist, tilt, and curve. The dance in live performance is ordinarily given in 22-minute sections.[1]

Excerpts from *Torse* had been given during the Event series at the Roundabout Theater the previous December. Only Part I was given at Princeton; Parts II and III were first danced in Caracas, Venezuela, soon afterward. Cunningham's subsequent practice was to alternate the three sections.

In a sense, the subject of *Torse* was Cunningham technique itself, especially the five basic back positions described, and his version of the directions of the body that are found in ballet, and the sequences of foot exercises done in those directions. (An important difference is that in ballet the eight directions are always taken in relation to the front, while in Cunningham technique the dancer's center shifts, so that anything can be "front.") From this material Cunningham made the purest kind of visual music, with solo "voices" emerging from the ensemble's complex antiphonal patterns, like a choreographic concerto grosso.

The music was by Maryanne Amacher, and had a complicated title:

(Remainder. 18.] R[]D[=An afterimage. (Also used as a classifier of seeds). *

*Hollis Frampton, A STIPULATION OF TERMS FOR MATERNAL HOPI

Mark Lancaster designed the costumes: the women wore black leotards and yellow tights, the men yellow leotards and black tights.

• • •

For the first time since 1972, the company went abroad later in January, to Caracas, for four performances. On returning, the dancers gave two more weekends of Studio Events (with music by Jim Burton and Ivan Tcherepnin) in February before leaving for Australia, via Berkeley, California, where they gave two performances on 1 and 2 March. The Australian tour, from 9 March through 1 April, included Perth, Sydney, Adelaide, and Canberra. In Adelaide another new work was given, on 24 March:

SQUAREGAME

Squaregame was finished while we were on tour in Australia. [The Adelaide Festival of Arts] had asked me to make a new dance. The idea was to define the space, as the title suggests, a sort of arena, with four stuffed duffel bags. The situations are very playful, on what seems to be an athletic court where there are participants who can also stop and watch. The dance starts with

Opposite, top: MC's movement and space notations for *Torse*, 1976, first of eighteen pages. Opposite, bottom: *Torse*, 1976. Left to right: Chris Komar, Ellen Cornfield, Morgan Ensminger, Robert Kovich, Susana Hayman-Chaffey, and Catherine Kerr. Photograph: Thomas Victor. This page, inset: *Squaregame Video*, 1976, Charles Atlas's version of *Squaregame*, 1976. Left to right: MC (behind duffel bag), Julie Roess-Smith, Robert Kovich, and Jim Self. Photograph: Herb Migdoll. This page, right: *Squaregame*, 1976. Left to right, foreground to background: MC and Karole Armitage, Morgan Ensminger, Meg Harper, Jim Self, Julie Roess-Smith, Robert Kovich, Chris Komar, Lisa Fox, and Ellen Cornfield. Photograph: Charles Atlas.

a quartet, there is also a trio, another couple of quartets. I worked on it during the tour, which I had never done before. I never was quite happy with such a situation, because it was not a comfortable way to work, given everything else I had to do, and the general fatigue and rigors of touring. And it was not finished when we arrived.[2]

There was also a duet, danced by Cunningham first with Susana Hayman-Chaffey and later with Karole Armitage and Catherine Kerr, in which he watchfully guided the woman's movements.

A recurring motif in the dance was that of people hanging on to others and being carried or dragged along by them. The first thing Cunningham did after emerging from behind a duffel bag, where he had been sitting playing peek-a-boo, was to hang on to one of the other men, who then dragged him and one of the women down to the front of the stage. At other moments, two men carried Cunningham around and tossed him into the air; a line of three dancers moved across on a diagonal, with a woman hanging between two of them; a man lunged from side to side doing a series of contractions, with one of the women hanging on to his waist.

Squaregame was the first work for which Takehisa Kosugi wrote a score; he joined the musicians' group for the Australian tour. The set, designed by Mark Lancaster, consisted of a white floorcloth surrounded by bands of green Astroturf. Otherwise the stage was bare—no wings, the lights exposed, the back wall visible. The costumes were slightly formalized practice clothes, with sweatpants and ankle socks.

The duffel bags (there were more than four) that defined the space played a part in the choreography: dancers not active in the dancing area sometimes sat on or behind them on the sidelines, watching; a man jumped across the stage in a diagonal with a bag held between his legs like a pogo stick; in the finale, the dancers tossed them around, before assembling in a tableau, as for a family portrait. (This finale has frequently been used in Events.)

• • •

From Australia the company went to Japan, where they performed in Kyoto, Tokyo, and Sapporo. *Squaregame* had been conceived with video adaptation in mind, and this was realized when the company returned to New York, that May. "Cunningham designed the choreography," Karen Carreras writes, "so that it would fit in a square area measured upon the larger rectangular space of the stage. [When it was] videotaped two months later in the Westbeth studios, little restructuring was necessary to insure filmic continuity."[3]

Michel Guy, director of Paris's Festival d'automne, had long wanted to bring the Cunningham company to France for a long teaching residency. This took place in the summer of 1976, in Villeneuve-lès-Avignon, a small town on a hillside overlooking Avignon. The studio was in a former Carthusian monastery. There were classes for professional dancers and open rehearsals, and the month-long residency culminated in four Events in the Cour d'Honneur of the Palais des Papes, in Avignon, as part of that year's Avignon Festival.

From Avignon the company traveled to Israel for performances in Tel Aviv, Caesarea, and Jerusalem. They next went to Greece, giving four Events in the Herod Atticus Theater in Athens, and finally to Dubrovnik, Yugoslavia, for two more Events.

That fall, again with the assistance of Margaret Jenkins, Cunningham staged *Summerspace* for Jacques Garnier's dance company Théâtre du Silence, based in La Rochelle. The dancers came to New York to rehearse the piece, which was first given in La Rochelle at the end of October.

Meanwhile Cunningham was working on an important video project. The New York public television station WNET/Thirteen had received funding from the National Endowment for the Arts, the Exxon Corporation, and the Corporation for Public Broadcasting for a $3 million series called "Dance in America." The Cunningham company was one of the first to be invited to take part.[4] Cunningham and Charles Atlas would once again be working with Merrill Brockway, director of *A Video Event* for CBS Camera Three two years before. The new program also followed the Event format, and was called *Event for Television*.

Our Event for Television, presented on the National Educational Television's "Dance in America" series, was a collaboration among the dance company, John Cage and David Tudor. This was an hour program which in this instance became fifty-eight minutes and forty-five seconds. Charles Atlas . . . and I spent four weeks working out the dances and excerpts from dances we planned to present. The excerpts that were from the repertory were remade and angled for the camera; in some cases they were shortened, as I feel one receives information quicker and more directly on television than on the stage.

Cage and Tudor decided to share the hour, Cage having the first section for which he played *Branches*, music for plant materials. He was interested in sounds from nature and had found that the spines of cacti, when touched and amplified, produced resonant sounds. At the point in the program when the dance *RainForest* appeared, Tudor's music for it began, and this continued through the balance of the hour. Both musics were introduced into the program after the taping and editing had been completed—that is, several weeks after the actual shooting of the dances.

Working with dance in video requires a constant adjustment in terms of space, often on a small scale. A six-inch shift can seem large on the camera. This also can cause a displacement in the timing, requiring a change in rhythm, or the amplifying of a dance phrase, sometimes necessitating a cut or speed-up of the movement. In the conventional music-dance relationship, this could require a constant recomposing or rearranging of the sound. But since I work separately from the music and not on a note-by-note

relationship, I was free to adjust the dance phrases and movements through the camera in a visual sense.[5]

Early in November the company went to Nashville, Tennessee, for the shooting. The program included some reconstructed fragments of *Minutiae* (using a replica of Robert Rauschenberg's set; the original had been returned to the artist); *Solo*; excerpts from *Westbeth* (including footage from the Cunningham/Atlas video version); *Septet*, *Antic Meet*, and *Scramble*. *RainForest* was given almost in its entirety. After an excerpt from *Sounddance* there was a short new work made for the program, *Video Triangle*. The original designs were used for each excerpt; Mark Lancaster designed *Video Triangle*.

Above: Mark Lancaster's designs for *Video Triangle*, 1976. Below: Robert Rauschenberg's sketch for *Travelogue*, 1977.

1977

The time was ripe for Cunningham and his company to have a New York season. It was five years since the last repertory performances in Brooklyn, and there were several important new works to show. At the very beginning of January there were two more weekends of Studio Events, with music by Jon Hassell and Joan La Barbara. During the week, *Event for Television*, the Dance in America program, was broadcast for the first time, and an exhibition of Cunningham's notes and notations on dance opened at the Carl Solway Gallery.

The season took place in a Broadway theater, the Minskoff, from 18 to 23 January. There were two programs; *Solo*, *Rebus*, *Torse*, *Signals*, *Sounddance*, and *Squaregame* were all seen for the first time in the city, together with a revival of *Summerspace* and an entirely new work:

TRAVELOGUE

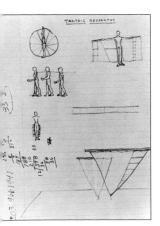

Travelogue reunited Cunningham and Cage with Robert Rauschenberg, who made his first design for the company since the 1964 tour. The main feature of the decor—which had its own title, *Tantric Geography*—was a row of wooden chairs mounted on white platforms separated by bicycle wheels; at the beginning this was dragged on stage by a rope, with the dancers seated on the chairs. Later, two large collage banners (related to the sail-like "Jammers" that Rauschenberg was making at the time) descended from the flies. As the dance went on, various garments and accessories were added to the dancers' basic costumes of brightly colored leotards and tights. One of these was a fanlike appendage that the dancers wore between their legs in one number, inhibiting any movement beyond opening and closing the fans or shaking them slightly. Michelle Potter has described these as being "like life-size color-wheels. Images of color-wheels (or flattened umbrellas whose sectioning recalls that of a color-wheel) are recurring ones throughout Rauschenberg's oeuvre, beginning perhaps with his painting *Charlene* in 1954."[1]

Robert Kovich performed a solo with festoons of tin cans attached to his legs. Meg Harper danced languorously in a loose chiffon blouse and matching leggings. Behind her, two men held a rope with scarves tied to it; when she exited, she left behind her own scarf, and Cunningham, faunlike, curled up on the floor with it. Next, the dancers entered in a slow procession, holding two long strips of white fabric, which closed up concertina-fashion when they bunched together. They opened up again, and Chris Komar dropped to the floor. The others lifted him up and he disappeared behind the fabric veil.

The structure of *Travelogue* was similar to that of *Antic Meet*—a series of "turns," as in vaudeville. There were bits of ballroom dancing, Balanchinian tangles, a high-stepping cakewalk. At one point Cunningham played dead and the dancers jumped over and around his supine body. At another, he executed a sort of "boomps-a-daisy" routine with two of the women, at the end of which they went off like a miniature chorus line. Cunningham repeated the image from *Tread* in which he gathered the dancers under his outspread arms like a mother hen. (In later performances this section was cut.) Other material had been used in *Video Triangle* shortly before.

Cage's score, *Telephones and Birds*, used recordings of bird song by Norman Robinson, from the Australian National Collection of Recorded Bird Calls. The program also listed telephone numbers that were dialed during the performance (according to a chance process), and the results played over the sound system: the Rare Bird Alert network, Horse Race Results, Sports News, Dial-A-Prayer, and (from New York Telephone) Dial-A-Money-Saving-Tip, Dial-A-Plant, Weather, Time, Dial-A-Joke, and Dial-Your-

Travelogue, 1977. Left to right: Ellen Cronfield, Lisa Fox, Morgan Ensminger, MC, Robert Kovich, Meg Harper. Photograph: Charles Atlas. Inset, left: MC in *Travelogue*, 1977. Photograph: Johan Elbers. Inset, right: *Travelogue*, 1977. Left to right: Julie Roess-Smith, Morgan Ensminger, and MC. Photograph: Lois Greenfield.

Stars, plus arrival and departure information courtesy of Pan-American World Airways.

• • •

In February the company left for a United States tour that again included a Minneapolis residency sponsored by the Walker Art Center. But its New York performances were not over for the season: in March there was a further week of Events sponsored by Dance Umbrella. These were to have been at Roundabout Stage One again, but the theater proved to be unavailable, and the performances were moved to the Barnard College Gymnasium. As before, a number of composers were involved: Joan La Barbara, John Cage (for two Events), Meredith Monk, Annea Lockwood, and David Tudor. The following week, Cunningham received the Capezio Dance Award for that year.

At the end of May and the beginning of June, the company gave four repertory performances and an Event in Vienna. The program did not fail to point out that the Event format had been born in that city, thirteen years earlier.

From 22 August to 11 September, the company was in Seattle for a residency sponsored by the Cornish Institute (as it was then called), Cunningham's alma mater. As usual, there were classes and workshops, including a videodance workshop conducted by Charles Atlas. The Foster/White Gallery exhibited sets and costumes designed for Cunningham by Rauschenberg, Jasper Johns, Frank Stella, and Andy Warhol, together with paintings by the artists, photographs by James Klosty, and scores and manuscripts by Cage; there were Rauschenberg shows at both the Cornish Institute Gallery and the Linda Farris Gallery downtown. Performances included Events in Tacoma and Seattle, a Cunningham and Cage Dialogue, a Cage concert in the Cornish theater, and two performances at the University of Washington, when a new work commissioned for the residency was performed:

INLETS

With *Inlets*, Cunningham and Cage finally fulfilled their old wish to collaborate with Morris Graves, who had withdrawn from the Ballet Society project *The Seasons* thirty years before. Graves sketched a design concept, which was realized by Suzanne Joelson. The set consisted of a large Mylar disk that moved slowly across the back of the stage. At the front was a pale scrim, which remained in place throughout the piece, so that the dancers were seen dimly at first, as though in a mist. When the disk reached stage center, the lights shone brightly for a moment. (A poster for the

residency reproduced Graves's lithograph *Waning Moon*.) To everyone's surprise, the reclusive artist showed up for the premiere.

The costumes were leotards and tights (except for Cunningham, who wore sweatpants) in variegated black and white (the men with one leg white and one black, and with patchwork tops, the women with tops divided between black and white). Everyone wore a rhinestone choker.

Cage wrote the music, which he wanted to link with nature, "one of Morris Graves's most important affinities."

I visited a friend in Long Island who had the most beautiful shells. . . . Some of them were huge—around eighteen inches long. I tapped the shell with my finger and knew it belonged in water, so I went to the sink and filled it with water. When I tipped it, it made the most beautiful gurgle.

The gurgle must be amplified to hear it properly. It gives an effect related to the sound you hear when you place a shell over your ear. During the course of *Inlets*, the players will

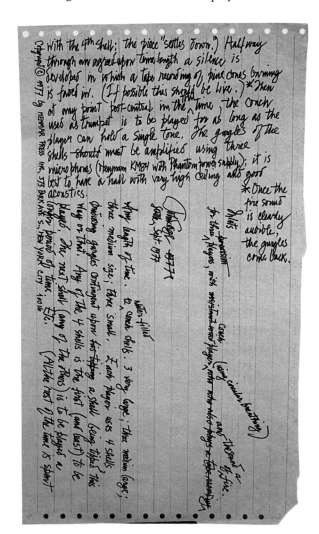

Left: John Cage's written instructions for the score for *Inlets*, 1977. Opposite: *Fractions*, 1978, stage version. Left to right: Meg Eginton, Robert Kovich, Ellen Cornfield, Lisa Fox, Joseph Lennon, Karole Armitage, and Louise Burns. Photograph: Johan Elbers.

make a predetermined number of gurgles with one shell, and then pick up another. Three players will perform simultaneously.

If we can get clearance from the authorities, the performance will also include the burning of crackling pine cones in a fire and the sound of a conch shell being blown. This will unite the elements of air, fire, and water.[2]

The authorities did not give permission, and the sound of burning pinecones had to be recorded. The tape also picked up the sound of an airplane flying over.

Similarly, the dance seemed to be "about" the climate and topography of the Northwest—its very title evoked the landscape of Puget Sound. The disk's passage across the back of the stage inevitably suggested the passing of time. As in earlier dances, Cunningham made great use of stillness; one or another of the dancers was almost always holding a static, archaic pose. Cage once said that the opening pose held the germ of all the subsequent movement. (It has been suggested that two "signature" stances in *Inlets* referred to well-known photographs of Nijinsky, one in *L'Après-midi d'un faune*, the other in *Tyl Eulenspiegel*.) Toward the end, a group suddenly coalesced downstage left in a small apotheosis, with one woman (Ellen Cornfield) lifted above Cunningham, who was on the floor in a "bridge" position.

• • •

While in Seattle the company filmed *Torse*, under Atlas's direction, in Meany Hall, at the University of Washington, where the repertory performances also took place. The film, Karen Carreras wrote,

> was designed as two synchronous hour-long films to be projected simultaneously on adjacent screens, providing a complete archival record of the choreography and approximating the spectator's experience of the dance. The contrapuntal structure of the dance and Cunningham's asymmetrical use of space also suggested a two-screen presentation. Either film may be viewed separately; but their combination provides a more complete record and experience of the dance.[3]

There was one more major engagement in 1977: a two-week season at the Théâtre des Amandiers, in the Maison de la Culture at Nanterre, a suburb of Paris, from 4 to 16 October. Here the latest repertory works were shown in France for the first time. On returning to New York, Cunningham and Atlas began work on another video project to be shot in the Westbeth Studio in November and December:

FRACTIONS

Fractions, for eight dancers (not including Cunningham), played with the idea of fragmenting images among a number of screens. Action taking place simultaneously in different areas of the studio was seen on the main screen and also on monitors set up within the range of the main camera. Carreras wrote,

> As many as four video monitors share the screen space with the dancers. Projected on these monitors are both images of dancers absent from the central dance space and close-ups of dancers who are present in that space. Thus dancers just outside one camera's range could be viewed by another camera and seen in smaller scale on one of the monitors-within-the-screen. The division of the frame into parts or "fractions" allowed . . . Atlas to group more dancers into the frame, while still achieving greater depth and fluidity of movement by alternating between the monitors and the studio space.[4]

Mark Lancaster's decor, a journalist wrote, consisted of "two 6′x4′ painted panels which he placed at right angles to the floor. Between takes, he moved the panels, so that sometimes they appeared behind the dancers and other times, between them."[5] The costumes were multicolored leotards and tights.

1978

The company's first performances of the year were again weekend Studio Events, in which the participating musicians were Ronald Kuivila, Nicolas Collins, and Yasunao Tone. The last of these performances was on 3 February, after which the company left for a five-week residency in Massachusetts. As with the Seattle residency in 1977, there was a full schedule of exhibitions, screenings, open classes and rehearsals, and formal and informal performances, in Boston and elsewhere in the state. The residency was also marked by a terrific blizzard that kept the company marooned in their hotel for several days.

Fractions received its first stage performances in repertory programs at Boston English High School from 25 February through 1 March. Mark Lancaster designed eight rectangular panels that descended from the flies at certain moments—a variation on his set for the video. "'They appeared singly, or in pairs,' says Lancaster, 'and floated in quite gently, so that you were not distracted from the dance.'"[1] The stage was divided into different areas in which different actions took place, as an equivalent of the original video piece's division of the video screen by monitors.

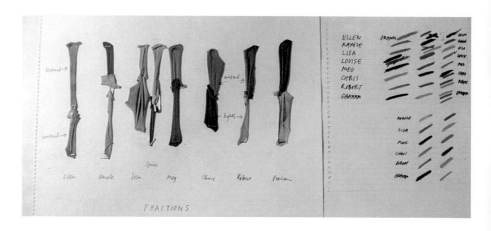

FRACTIONS

Soon after returning to New York, the company performed another two-week Event series at the Roundabout Theater (which was available this time). For some of these, music was provided by the company musicians, a group now comprising Cage, David Tudor, Takehisa Kosugi, and Martin Kalve. The extraordinary Greek vocalist Demetrios Statos performed Cage's *Mesostics re Merce Cunningham* on two evenings; David Behrman, Jon Gibson, and Meredith Monk also performed. At the end of May there were still further Studio Events, with Tudor providing the music. In the meantime Cunningham and Cage had been in Paris, where they performed a Dialogue at the American Center.

In September the company opened its first repertory season at the City Center Theater, New York, from 26 September to 8 October. (From 1980 to 1995, a Cunningham season at the City Center was to be an annual early-spring event.) For most of this first season, unfortunately, the newspapers were on strike, so the company received limited press coverage. A major company work and a new solo were presented for the first time at the City Center:

EXCHANGE

Exchange . . . was a long, large-scale piece. It was 37 minutes long, divided into three parts, with half of the company in the first part, the other half in the second and all involved in the third. I appeared in all three sections. I've often been struck by the idea of recurrence, ideas, movements, inflections coming back in different guises, never the same; it is always a new space and a changed moment in time. So I decided to use it in *Exchange*.

After making the gamut of movements for the dance, I used chance operations to find the order of the phrases for each section, then again to find what phrases might reoccur in Section

Above: Mark Lancaster's costume swatches for *Fractions*, 1977. Opposite: *Exchange*, 1978. Left to right: Meg Eginton, Joseph Lennon, Alan Good, Catherine Kerr, Rob Remley, Lise Friedman, and MC. Photograph: Johan Elbers.

II, again in Section III. When phrases came up as repeats, they would of course occur in a different context in a different space and time and also with different dancers. Further, phrases that had been done completely in one section might only have parts repeated. Again, a phrase done in parallel position in Section I would be redone in turned-out position in Section II, and if appearing in Section III, could have the element of leaping added to it. . . .

The dance ends with the entire company on stage moving in separate groups of two or three. It does not stop; it stays in process.[2]

Exchange, choreographed for the newly enlarged company (fourteen dancers plus Cunningham himself), was the first piece in which he divided the dancers into two groups, roughly speaking the "old" company members and the "new," or younger ones. Section I was danced by Cunningham and the new dancers, followed by a transitional passage in which the older dancers gradually replaced them for Section II. This was one of the dance's forms of "exchange." In a recurring sequence, four women moved around, under, and over Cunningham as he lay on the floor;

in the second section this was repeated and elaborated by a single woman and another man.

If *Summerspace* and *Inlets*, for example, were "outdoor" pieces, *Exchange* seemed irrefutably urban. The grisaille of *Inlets* was that of mist and soft rain; *Exchange* also featured grays, in Jasper Johns's backcloth and costumes, but they were gritty, like slag and anthracite, with touches of sooty color. (Johns said he wanted "polluted" colors.) Some dancers wore sweatpants at certain points in the action; Cunningham wore sweatpants throughout. Johns had made a costume for him with many pockets, cut from black nylon stockings, sewn onto it, with the idea that various small objects could be put into them, but Cunningham decided that it would be too obtrusive.

The overall impression of *Exchange* was stark, even tragic. As Alastair Macaulay wrote, "Its grand plan unfolds like pages of history."[3] Cunningham's own movement was becoming increasingly limited with time, yet he found new ways to be expressive—in the tilt of his torso, or a kind of slow ripple through the chest. Whether fortuitously or not, all the elements contributed to the work's effect. Tudor's music, *Weatherings*, sounded like industrial noises.

TANGO

Tango was a solo for Cunningham—or perhaps more accurately a duet for Cunningham and a television set. (He may have had in mind the lyric of the popular song, "It takes two to tango.") Cunningham, in a baggy yellow-ocher sweater and sweat pants, seemed to be performing his morning chores while the color TV showed whatever was playing at the time. He passed a red or blue cloth from hand to hand, as if he were cleaning and polishing the air around him. Some of the material was familiar from what he had been doing in Events. At a certain moment he stopped dead and gazed out into the audience, as if to say, Are you still there? Finally he picked up a raincoat that had been lying on the floor and thrust one arm into a sleeve, then stood motionless. The television continued to play throughout; for a few moments the sound was turned up. But it didn't upstage him in the least, though he sometimes met stiff competition—once from a Laurel and Hardy movie, once from Fred Astaire himself.

Cage's music, *Letter to Erik Satie*, began with Cage vocalizing the letters of Satie's name.

• • •

A few days after the City Center season, the company took off on a cross-country tour, starting in Buffalo, moving on through Minneapolis out to California for performances in Berkeley and San Jose, and performing on the way back east in Boulder, Colorado, and Greensboro, North Carolina. In Berkeley, *Exchange* was filmed. In the Walker Art Center in Minneapolis and at the Denver Art Museum, and then in New York, Cunningham and Cage again performed Dialogues. Besides doing the makeup pantomime at the Walker, Cunningham did a new bit in which he crawled out under a large sheet of black plastic, moving slowly across the stage and disappearing through a door—a reference, no doubt, to *Winterbranch* and perhaps to *Place*. At the Denver Art Museum he repeated the makeup pantomime, only this time he seemed to be painting not only his face but his body and limbs; he also did the crawling entrance, but under a red blanket, finally ascending a staircase at the back of the space.

1979

LOCALE

The year began with the making of *Locale*, Cunningham's first dance for film (as opposed to video). Curtains, a Marley floor, and screens on the windows transformed the Cunningham Studio at Westbeth into a black box. Once again the company (fourteen

Left: MC in *Tango*, 1978. Photograph: Nathaniel Tileston. Opposite, top: *Locale*, 1979, stage version. Left to right: Rob Remley, Catherine Kerr, Lise Friedman, Joseph Lennon, Alan Good, and Meg Eginton. Photograph: Johan Elbers. Opposite, below: *Locale*, 1979, stage version. Left to right: Catherine Kerr, Joseph Lennon, Susan Emery, Rob Remley, and Meg Eginton. Photograph: Linda Vartoogian.

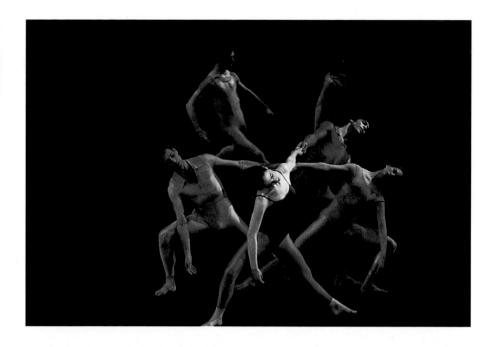

Three kinds of camera were used: a Steadicam, a Movieola crab dolly, and an Elemac dolly with a crane arm. This equipment was expensive to rent, limiting the amount of rehearsal and shooting time with the dancers. So the logistics were figured out as far as possible on paper beforehand. Atlas had one weekend to practice with the equipment, but without the dancers. After that he rehearsed along with them, setting the paths he would follow with the Steadicam. When the time came to shoot, certain adjustments had to be made—as Cunningham said, there are things the camera "just won't do"—but for the most part things went according to plan.[1]

In the first section of *Locale* the camera moves back and forth and up and down the length and breadth of the studio space, sometimes at dizzying speeds. Different groups of dancers appear in its field of vision (instead of entering as they would have to do on stage). Perhaps to avoid forcing the spectator to register too many kinds of movement at once, Cunningham choreographed this first section mostly in terms of stop-motion poses. It was shot virtually in one take; what cuts were necessary were made as unobtrusively as possible, usually when the camera passed a blank wall.

The second section begins with a sequence of short passages separated by cuts, during which the movement becomes more fluid. In a later section, the camera moves again, at one point executing a complete 360-degree revolution, finding dancers in corners or catching their reflections in a mirror. The final section is a kind of coda, a recapitulation of everyone's material.

The costumes were designed by Atlas, "choosing the same hues," Karen Carreras wrote, "as are seen on the television adjustment color-bars, and combining these with gradations of the corresponding gray-based tones used in tuning black and white television monitors."[2] Atlas also recorded the making of *Locale* in a documentary called *Roamin' I* (which can be read as "Roman One" or "Roaming Eye"), using some material shot during the filming as well as outtakes from *Locale* itself. *Roamin' I* provides often hilarious glimpses behind the scenes—the dancers scuttling around to reenter on another side, climbing over cables, or jumping out of the way of the dolly or crane. Atlas's assistant, Elliot Caplan, devised an elaborate system of pulleys to pull cables out of the shot as the camera pursued its restless path, and this is seen in operation, in response to shouted cues to the technicians.[3]

dancers not including Cunningham) was divided into two, partly for economic reasons: only one group had to be called at a time for its part of the shooting.

As before, Cunningham and Charles Atlas spent several weeks on advance planning, since the project was especially complicated. Their previous video-dances had dealt principally in movement *within* the frame rather than in movement of the frame—that is to say, they had mostly used a stationary camera and had foregone any fancy editing. Now they were ready to investigate the possibilities of a moving camera. Because they wanted the camera to move not only along with but around and among the dancers, and at different speeds, its movements would have to be choreographed as precisely as those of the dancers.

• • •

There was no New York repertory season in 1979, and there were fewer Event performances than in previous years, though there were two weekends in April. (The musicians were Martin Kalve and Robert Rutman.) But there was extensive touring abroad. In May the company traveled around the French provinces, with a side trip to Berlin, then in June performed in the Holland Festival in the Hague. They returned to Paris in the fall.

In the meantime, however, there was an engagement at the American Dance Festival at Duke University, Durham, North Carolina, which had commissioned a new work:

ROADRUNNERS

I wanted to make a piece that was closer to TV than anything I had made before in the way it was cut up from moment to moment: short things that happen and disappear, and other things that come in. The abruptness and swiftness with which they change could be construed as humor, also as a clarity of forms.

The idea for the images in *Roadrunners* came from a visit to the antique Greek museum in West Berlin which I made when we were touring there. The shapes of the figures on the vases were lively and active and I wondered what they could provoke going one to the other. I copied a number of them in stick figure form and added enough hoping to have sixty-four. To get from one of these shapes in its space to another in its allotted space brought about the abruptness and change of pace. I kept the space in horizontal lines, that is, the figures primarily move right and left from one side of the stage to the other, something like a shadow play.[4]

The reference to the number sixty-four indicates that Cunningham was once again using a chance process derived from the *I Ching*.

Notwithstanding the Greek derivation of the dance, Cunningham again appeared in the guise of a clown. As in *Squaregame*, he was lifted and carried by the other men. In one sequence he tried to put on socks, running shoes, and a pair of pants, but was prevented by Lisa Fox, who chased him from one part of the stage to another. At the end of this section and elsewhere, Cunningham again seemed to refer to one of Nijinsky's poses in *L'Après-midi d'un faune*.

There were further sight gags involving both Cunningham and the other dancers. One by one, for instance, three of the women jumped up onto Alan

Good until they all hung from him in a cluster; then the whole group collapsed in a heap. In one exit, Cunningham was surrounded by three of the dancers, all swatting at him with their white berets. In another, Good carried off Meg Eginton stiff as a board, like a battering ram.

Roadrunners was designed by Mark Lancaster, who dressed the dancers in white leotards and tights, to which other garments were sometimes added—skirts for the women, vests for the men, and the abovementioned berets (one of which was black). The costumes, Cunningham said, had "a certain sharpness about them."[5] The piece was performed against black curtains.

The music [*Geography and Music*] is by Yasunao Tone, a Japanese living in New York, for viola and piano, or two pianos, electronics and ancient Chinese tales which are recited live in English using two separate microphones that gate the musical instruments. Sometimes a recording of the stories in Chinese is heard.[6]

These "tales" were "Tone's translations of 8th century Chinese texts which are read while instrumentalists

Opposite: MC's movement and space notations for *Roadrunners*, 1979, first of six pages. This page, above: *Roadrunners*, 1979. Left to right: Joseph Lennon, Louise Burns, and Chris Komar. Photograph: Johan Elbers. This page, right: *Roadrunners*, 1979. MC and Meg Eginton. Photograph: Lois Greenfield.

perform music derived from 8th century pipa (an ancient Chinese string instrument) music. By means of a voice-controlled delay line, the amplification of the instrumentalists is electronically controlled by the readers' voices, wedding the instrumental elements to the voice part."[7]

• • •

Early in August the company performed at Artpark, in Lewiston, New York. There they were also filmed, in rehearsal and in performance, by a crew from London Weekend Television's *South Bank Show*, for a documentary directed by Geoff Dunlop. Some filming had also been done at the Cunningham Studio. Excerpts from *Exchange*, *Squaregame*, and *Travelogue* were included in the program, as well as interviews with Carolyn Brown and with current company members.

The company next did a series of Events—in September, four at the Edinburgh Festival (the first Events performed in Great Britain), and in October, three in New York under the auspices of Dance Umbrella, this time on a large sound stage at Camera Mart/Stage One. The third of this latter series included one of the rare complete performances of *Torse*. The company then left right away for a season in Paris, as part of the Festival d'automne. There were repertory performances at the Théâtre de la Ville and ten extraordinary Events in the Forum of the Centre Georges Pompidou. At the Théâtre de la Ville, the

stage version of *Locale* was given for the first time (that is to say, as a discrete work; it had been performed as part of an Event in Angers during the French tour earlier in the year). In one Event at the Centre Pompidou, the company was joined by the Théâtre du Silence in a performance of *Changing Steps*, which the French company had first performed (at the Théâtre de la Ville) in April, in a staging by Chris Komar. After rehearsal one day, Merce Cunningham was told that Greta Garbo had been watching from above.

1980s

1980

In 1980 the Cunningham company initiated its annual early-spring repertory seasons in New York (in some years there were also Event performances during these seasons). During this first run, at the City Center Theater from 19 February to 2 March, *Locale* and *Roadrunners* received their first New York performances, *Landrover* was revived, the filmdance *Locale* had its first screening, and two new works were given: *Exercise Piece III*, given as part of *Changing Steps et cetera* (together with Cunningham's solo *Loops*), and *Duets*, which had been included as a work in progress during Event performances the previous year, starting with those at the Edinburgh Festival.

DUETS

It began with the idea of making a duet for Susan Emery and Rob Remley to be included in the Events. Having finished that one, I decided to make a second, and then a third, for other dancers in the company, until there were six. I don't remember the order they were made in, but gradually in working on them, the thought to have two dancers do distinct and separate phrases, although in proximity to each other, came up. After the six dances

were finished, I decided they could be a work by themselves. I added a brief entrance and exit by one of the other couples in each of the duets; then the ending, involving all six couples. The ending is comprised of three short phrases, each followed by a brief stop, as though a still photograph were being taken. Following the third stop there is a blackout. The music is by John [Cage], his *Improvisation III*. The material for it is cassette recordings of traditional Irish drumming, Bodhrans played by Paedar and Mel Mercier.[1]

The Merciers, father and son, had played in *Roaratorio*, a work that Cage had completed the previous summer at IRCAM in Paris. The Cunningham musicians manipulated and modified their recordings during performances of *Duets*.

The costumes were designed by Mark Lancaster, who put the women in short skirts. Each dancer wore a color that was picked up in the costume of a dancer in one of the other couples.

• • •

Only three weeks after the close of the City Center season the company gave a series of six Events on consecutive evenings at the Westbeth Studio, with music by Martin Kalve, before going on a brief domestic tour. In the summer the company was again in Britain, first at the Everyman Theatre in Liverpool, then at Sadler's Wells in London. Here another new dance was given, which had been included as a work in progress in the recent Events at the Studio:

FIELDING SIXES

In the *Sixes*, the sixty-four phrases used were all in six and all in the same tempo—rapid. They varied only in terms of movement and accent. Repetition was allowed for. Chance operations gave the continuity, and the spaces to be used, and the number of dancers to appear at any moment. A great many of the phrases involved leaping and rapid crossing of the stage space and sudden reversals of direction. My impres-

sion, as I have seen the dancers perform it, is of a country dance in which the formal shapes open out in unexpected ways, the dancers appearing and disappearing and exchanging groups and partners in a fluid manner.[2]

Cage's music, *Improvisation IV*, like *Improvisation III* for *Duets*, was derived from recordings for *Roaratorio*: cassette tapes of flute and violin duets by Matt Molloy and Paddy Glackin, again subjected to modification by the Cunningham musicians, who used means devised by John Fullemann, company sound consultant, for changing the speed of the cassette players.

Monika Fullemann's decor featured three macramélike weavings suspended above the stage and a white backcloth with three colored blotches on it—purple, green, and red. The women wore white shorts over pale green tights and leotards, the men purple tank tops and long pants. In certain passages some of the men put on white quilted jackets like those worn by fencers.

• • •

Still in London the week after the season at the Wells, Cunningham and Cage pursued residency activities at both Riverside Studios and the Laban Centre for Movement and Dance at University of London, Goldsmiths' College. Cunningham and Cage performed a Dialogue at both places; there were film and video showings; an exhibition at Riverside; and, at the Laban Centre, where Bonnie Bird was on the faculty, master classes, a panel discussion, a lecture by Cage on music for dance, and a concert of his early music.[3]

After the London season Cunningham underwent a knee operation, but had recuperated sufficiently to take part in the company's next performances—two Studio Events early in October, with music by Ralph Jones, followed by a brief European tour (Strasbourg and Milan). In the Events, Cunningham performed something he called "The Bed-ridden Hop," which he had composed while recovering from his operation. After limping across the floor he lay down on his back and then slowly and painfully rose first to one knee, then to both feet, all the while executing a series of arm movements. Finally he marched about the room and came to a halt in a heroic attitude, arms thrust out to the side. The Studio was immediately invaded by the other dancers, walking, running, skipping, falling to the floor—and all performing the same gestures.

That September, Lancaster had been appointed the company's artistic advisor, succeeding Jasper Johns, who had held the title since 1967—though

As far as dancing is concerned I find it more lively to look for something awkward rather than something beautiful. Happy New Year![4]

1981

CHANNELS/INSERTS

The year began with the shooting of a new filmdance, *Channels/Inserts*, again at the Westbeth Studio. The action was divided among the main studio, the small studio, and the office area. In the latter two spaces, no attempt was made to cover up the windows, moldings, and peeling plaster—these areas are "real" while the main studio, again transformed into a black box, is anonymous. Charles Atlas compared the film to a party going on in different rooms: "It's as if you have two movies going on at once—both have a total continuity, but you have to make a choice between which you want to show at any given moment."[1]

To achieve the effect of simultaneity, Atlas devised some elaborate transitions. At moments when the action shifts from the main studio to another space, the picture seems to disintegrate, revealing another behind. Atlas has explained,

> The conception of *Channels/Inserts* suggested we make use of cross-cutting, a classic filmic device developed by D. W. Griffith, to indicate a simultaneity of dance events in different spaces; such simultaneous presentation is particularly well suited to Cunningham's choreographic aesthetic. In addition, I have designed animated travelling mattes as transitions between some scenes as a rhythmically irregular alternative to a straight cut. These serve as another way to show, however briefly, different simultaneous events in a precise way that is related to the dance movement (as opposed to the more generalized device of a "dissolve").[2]

Lancaster had been de facto resident designer since 1974.

At the end of the year, Cunningham was invited by Jennifer Dunning of the *New York Times* to contribute to a feature in which "a sampling of luminaries in theater, movies, dance, music and the visual arts [expressed] their wishes for 1981." He wrote,

> I don't want anything artistic next year, farthest thing from my mind, just some energy and maybe a little spirit thrown in. A chance to work with dancers, make a few pieces, find some way to have them shown and wish we'd all get along.

In planning the work, Cunningham and Atlas drew up two columns, one for the main action and one for the "inserts." The action was conceived as continuous and was initially rehearsed in one space. The various spaces were numbered; the order in which they would be used, whether action would occur in more than one location at a time, and how many dancers would be involved, were all determined by chance. Once again, three cameras were used; one fixed, one on a dolly, and a Steadicam.

Cunningham divided the piece into sixteen sections, varying in length from ten seconds to three minutes. As before, the fourteen dancers were divided into two groups, at the beginning at least.

> In this work . . . the partners stay constant, particularly Lise Friedman and Alan Good. The same couples are seen together whenever they appear in the piece. It's like a constant reminder while going along an unknown path.[3]

One of the most brilliant sections was the series of brief virtuoso solos for the men of the company, filmed in the main studio with a stationary camera. After each had danced, there was a wipe to a shot of the women in the small studio, laughing and talking among themselves; then back to the main studio for a second series of solos.

At the end, after the credit titles, there was a shot filmed with a stop-motion camera in the small studio, which became flooded with light as the sun rose over the New York skyline outside the windows. Some viewers took this as a simulation of a nuclear explosion, though Atlas thought of it as nothing more than a sunrise. Even so, Cunningham was surprised by the dramatic effect of the finished film.[4]

• • •

The City Center season took place from 17 to 29 March, but once again there were Studio Events a couple of weekends before, with music by Philip Edelstein. At the City Center, *Fielding Sixes* received its first New York performances, the stage version of *Channels/Inserts* was given, and on opening night there was another brand-new dance:

10'S WITH SHOES

10's with Shoes was a kind of companion piece to *Fielding Sixes*. Just as the earlier dance was built on phrases of six, so the new one was built on tens, at least at first:

> The title comes from the original phrases which were counts of tens, later changing to include eights, and my decision that the seven dancers should wear shoes.
>
> The steps are precise; the movement relates in my memory to the "shuffles" that Mrs. Barrett taught, and to the look of young people now when I see them dancing in the streets, bobbing and shifting. There is a use of the hips, and the shoulders, turned-in feet, and stretched heels, the arms are often down at the sides of the body, but when in use, are articulated at the joints, the shoulder, the elbow and even the

wrist in precise counts. The rhythm should look free and exact at the same time.[5]

The music was by Martin Kalve, a company musician at the time, and was called *All Happy Workers Babies & Dogs*—crying babies and barking dogs could be heard in it, along with other sounds, including those of the dancers' feet striking the stage, which was miked.

Mark Lancaster dressed the dancers in black unitards, with white jazz shoes, as specified by Cunningham. The set consisted of cloth panels in colors ranging from Prussian blue through viridian and lime green to yellow, sprinkled with white squares. These panels could be hung in different arrangements as backcloth and wings, according to the size of the stage.

• • •

The stage version of *Channels/Inserts* differed more radically from the film than in the case of previous adaptations such as *Fractions* and *Locale*, because the action had to be contained in a single space. If anything, however, the dramatic effect was intensified, since there could now be closer contact (including eye contact) between dancers who, in the film, had been divided among different spaces. The sequence in which there was a cut, or wipe, to the women in the small studio halfway through the series of men's solos had to be handled differently: during the first series the women walked on and sat down in the upstage right corner, watching the men dance; then, as the second series of solos began, they all stood up and walked off again. The effect, intentionally or not, was more humorous. The stage version ended with the leading couple's exit after their final duet.

David Tudor's score, *Phonemes*, was "a solo piece for electronics. In this work, electronically generated vowels are transformed into fricatives and these percussive sounds go back to vowels in electronic alteration."[6] Design and lighting were credited to Atlas—the costumes consisted of tights plus sweaters and other store-bought garments.

Following the City Center season, in April, the company had another residency in Minneapolis, sponsored as before by the Walker Art Center, with performances (both Events and repertory), classes, open rehearsals, film screenings, a music concert, and workshops. On returning to New York they gave a weekend of Studio Events, with music by Ned Sublette, before leaving for a European tour, visiting Portugal, Switzerland (Lausanne), and, for the second year in succession, London—another American Dance Season at Sadler's Wells, shared with Twyla

Above: *10's with Shoes*, 1981. Left to right: Alan Good, Neil Greenberg, and Chris Komar. Photograph: Lois Greenfield. Opposite: *Gallopade*, 1981. Left to right: Ellen Cornfield, Judy Lazaroff, and MC. Photograph: Johan Elbers.

Tharp Dance and an ad hoc group called Ballet Stars of America. Once again, a new Cunningham work received its first performance:

GALLOPADE

Gallopade, made in 1981, is a series of non-sequitur situations. It deals with referential movement, in a nonsensical way, made nonsensical by the use of chance operations. At one point, for example, a series of small gestures with the hands and the face are used. These are gestures ordinarily used by various peoples as accents with speech or as derisive gestures. Here, the gestures are removed from context, and further fragmented by using chance to find the continuity. Humor and the unexpected get along together.[7]

Unusually, there were titles for the various sections of the piece: "Street Fair," "50 Looks with Poses,"

"The Bed-ridden Hop and Chess Game," "L'Amour and the Bounce Dance," and "Gallop." "The Bed-ridden Hop" was a version of the sequence that had first been performed in a Studio Event the previous October.

As Atlas had done for *Channels/Inserts*, Lancaster gave the dancers store-bought clothes (Cunningham a brightly checked flannel shirt). The music, by Take-hisa Kosugi, was *Cycles*, "a work which employs tiny, battery-operated electronic devices designed and built by the composer."[8]

• • •

The company returned to Europe in July, to perform for the first time in the International Dance Festival at Chateauvallon. Three Events were given, and there were film and video screenings.

For a number of years, an International Dance Course for Professional Choreographers and Composers had been held at the University of Surrey in

Guildford, England. Cunningham and Cage had been invited to direct the 1981 course that August, assisted by Chris Komar, who taught technique classes and a repertory class (*Torse*).[9]

The year ended with another week of Studio Events, with music by Pauline Oliveros.

1982

To celebrate the year of John Cage's seventieth birthday, at the beginning of March there was a John Cage Week at the University of Puerto Rico, Rio Piedras, where the Cunningham company performed twice. In New York, on Saturday 13 March, there was an all-day tribute, "Wall-to-Wall John Cage and Friends," at Symphony Space, where the company performed *Changing Steps* and Cunningham danced *Solo*. Nearer Cage's actual birthday (5 September) there was a further celebration at the Walker Art Center, Minneapolis, though the Cunningham company did not take part.

On 16 March the company's annual season at the City Center opened with the first performance of a new work:

TRAILS

The idea of having two people who are dancing together do two things rather than one, is carried further in *Trails*. . . . I made the phrases for each dancer separately. Then, in the rehearsal, I put them together, keeping each phrase as distinct as possible, at the same time allowing for any cooperation between the dancers that was possible—a lift, or as in one of them, a leaning of the woman on the man.[1]

The music, Cage's *Instances of Silence*, was "a live sound collage featuring pre-recorded tapes. The sounds of traffic from Sixth Avenue [which Cage said he liked better than any music], the interior of a taxicab and a venetian blind in Puerto Rico will evolve as the dance is performed."[2] The costumes, by Mark Lancaster, were in combinations of red and gray, against a blood-red backdrop.

• • •

The City Center season included two Events—the first in a proscenium theater in Manhattan. *Gallopade* received its first New York performance and the film of *Channels/Inserts* was screened for the first time, at the Carnegie Hall Cinema around the corner from the City Center. The first Event introduced new material (some of it previously performed as a work in progress) that, although it was only done in Events, had a title:

NUMBERS

This was a section for seven dancers, in three parts:

I Accumulation: one man began in a solo, to be joined by two other dancers in a trio; another entered, making it a quartet; the other three entered, making it a septet.
II Group dance.
III First part in reverse order, i.e. subtracting dancers instead of adding them.

• • •

The season was followed by a tour that took the company to California (Los Angeles and Berkeley), Texas (Austin), New Jersey (Montclair), and Mexico. Meanwhile American Ballet Theatre presented Cunningham's *Duets*, staged for them by Cunningham assisted by Chris Komar, during its spring season at the Metropolitan Opera House. Lancaster designed new costumes for this revival, similar to his originals but with a different color scheme. Though performed only three times that season, *Duets* was to become a staple in the ABT repertory.

At the end of May the Cunningham company performed at the Holland Festival in both Rotterdam and Amsterdam. Returning to New York, they gave a week of Events at the Westbeth Studio, three with music by Ron Kuivila and three with music by Richard Lerman (with Tom Plsek).

In 1981 the Samuel H. Scripps American Dance Festival Award had been established "to honor those great choreographers who have dedicated their lives and talent to the creation of our great American modern dance heritage." The recipient that year had been Martha Graham. In 1982 the award was given to Cunningham, who wrote the following acknowledgment:

To the dancers who have shared these experiences with me over the years, whether briefly or those who have given me of themselves for longer periods, I extend my gratitude. It is with their backs and legs and energies and spirits that any arrival point has been reached, and I am indebted to all of them.[3]

The company danced a short Event before the award presentation (by Joan Mondale), the first performance by the Merce Cunningham Dance Company in which Cunningham himself did not appear. The company then gave three repertory performances in the American Dance Festival itself.

The fall season opened in September with two more weekends of Studio Events, with music by Jerry Hunt performed live in Canton, Texas, and received in New York by telephone. Two further

Opposite: *Trails*, 1982. Left to right, in foreground: Louise Burns, Chris Komar, and Catherine Kerr. Photograph: Lois Greenfield. Right: MC, ca. 1987. Photograph: Peter Hujar.

Events followed at the University of Maryland in early October. A European tour began two weeks later in Switzerland (Geneva and Basel) and continued in France until 1 December. In Basel, a new production of *Rune* was given, with new costumes by Lancaster. The Geneva performance included a "preview," without decor, of a new work that was soon danced in complete form at the Théâtre des Champs-Elysées in Paris:

QUARTET

Quartet . . . has five dancers in it. The title was prompted by two possibilities. The first is that two of the dancers act as one in the sense that they do the same movements at the same time; the second is my role in it which again sepa-

rates me from the others. I am on stage at the beginning, the shapes I present are different from the others, although occasionally I mirror their movements and interact with them. Essentially there is a different gamut for each dancer, but at times they share phrases. The nature of the work is on the dark side. The action is all confined within a relatively small area. The phrases were planned to have as few and as short transitions as possible from one movement to another.[4]

"On the dark side" indeed: many people have said that *Quartet* seems a meditation on profound, even tragic matters—the piece is full of foreboding. At the rise of the curtain Cunningham was discovered standing at the stage rear, his body bent to one side. Three women and another man entered. They moved for the most part independently of him, though occasionally they mirrored his movements, or he was caught between two of them. Toward the end, after a small paroxysm, he passed unnoticed from the scene, but in the few remaining moments the other dancers' movements reverted to the restricted, almost robotlike shifts of weight with which they began, as though their independent existence still depended on his presence.

David Tudor's music, *Sextet for Seven*, was a live electronic composition for "six homogeneous voices and one wandering voice," performed by the composer.[5] Lancaster dressed the dancers in sooty crimson, blue, and green; the lighting was somber.

After five repertory performances at the Champs-Elysées, the company moved to the Centre Pompidou for two Events in the Forum, like those given in 1979. (The Paris performances were once again under the auspices of the Festival d'automne à Paris.) For the rest of the tour the company performed Events at Maisons de la Culture all over France. To coincide with these, a documentary on Cunningham by Benoît Jacquot, made for the Institut National de l'Audiovisuel (INA), was shown for the first time on French television. Also during the tour, Cunningham was named Commander of the Order of Arts and Letters by the French Minister of Culture. (Cage too had received this award, in 1982.)

1983

Once again the year began with a filmdance, shot this time at the Synod House of New York's Cathedral Church of St. John the Divine. The location was chosen because it allowed camera movements (crane shots) that were impossible at the Cunningham Studio, and also because Cunningham and Atlas wanted a change of venue.

COAST ZONE

The fluidity of waves, the shifting of sands, the changing landscapes a coastal area can present, specifically the rapidity of changes in such an atmosphere are the images that came to mind as I worked on the piece. The choreography and the camera movement were made with chance operations. That is, the sequence and overlapping of movements and the number of dancers to be seen at any given moment, and the space the dancers were to be in as well as the changes

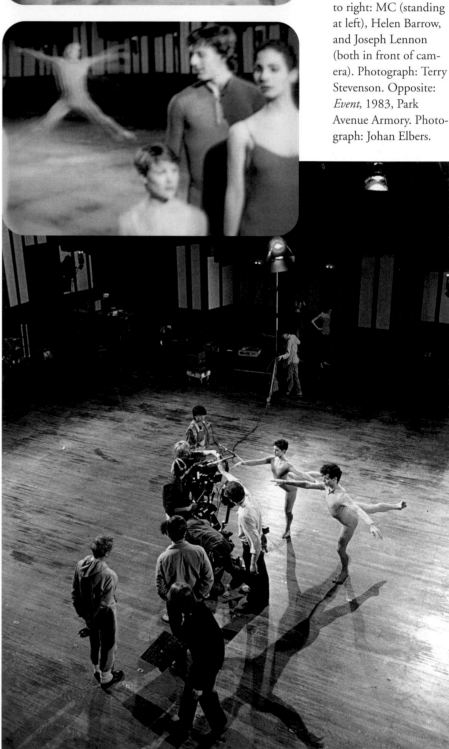

This page, top: Still from *Coast Zone*, 1983. In foreground: Rob Remley and Lise Friedman. This page, center: Still from *Coast Zone*, 1983. Left to right: Rob Remley, Susan Quinn Young, Neil Greenberg, and Lise Friedman. This page, bottom: Filming of *Coast Zone*, 1983. Left to right: MC (standing at left), Helen Barrow, and Joseph Lennon (both in front of camera). Photograph: Terry Stevenson. Opposite: *Event*, 1983, Park Avenue Armory. Photograph: Johan Elbers.

of camera positions were initiated by chance means. We used close-ups as an integral part of the film. My starting point for the division of the space was to plan it in three areas, rear, middle and front, that is, full figure to be seen in the rear, full or partial figure in the middle and close-ups in front. . . .

The music is by Larry Austin. It is called *Beachcombers*. Computers were used in its composition and the realization of the tapes, some of which enter as part of the music; others act as conductors for the performers.[1]

I used chance process to determine the camera positions, how many closeups, middle range and back shots there would be and what the dancers do from the closeups—whether they go to the middle, back or exit.[2]

The constant, Cunningham told Jennifer Dunning, "was that there would be no more than five dancers [of the twelve in the cast] in each shot and nine possible camera positions."[3] As Cunningham had wanted, the camera at one point circled the action "one and one-half times in a single, smooth trajectory; rarely does the camera shoot from a fixed position." Another important new element, Karen Carreras wrote, was the use of deep focus, "contrasting background figures (often in motion) with those in the foreground (sometimes in extreme close-up)."[4]

Charles Atlas once again collaborated with Cunningham on *Coast Zone*; he also collaborated with Mark Lancaster on its design. No attempt was made to disguise the ecclesiastical nature of the setting.

• • •

The British choreographer Richard Alston, who had lived in New York for two years in the mid-'70s in order to study at the Merce Cunningham Studio (where he also gave a concert of his work), had recently been appointed resident choreographer of the Ballet Rambert. Through his efforts, the Rambert company acquired its first Cunningham work in *Fielding Sixes*, in a version "derived by Chris Komar from a number of sources including his experiences performing the work, videotapes, choreographer's notes, and conversations with Merce Cunningham."[5] Komar went to England to stage the work, and Cunningham was present at the final rehearsals and the first performance, at the Royal Northern College of Music, Manchester, on 11 February. The Rambert production featured new designs by Lancaster. The first London performance was at Sadler's Wells a month later, during a season dedicated to the memory of the company's founder, Marie Rambert. Cunningham had agreed to give the Rambert company one of his works because Madame Rambert had enthusiastically supported his early London seasons, and he remembered her with gratitude and affection.

The company's annual season at the City Center ran from 15 to 27 March. Once again it included two Events. *Quartet* received its first New York performances, as did the revival of *Rune* danced in Basel the year before. (As always, *Rune* did not stay long in repertory; the two performances at the City Center were the last this revival received.) The stage version of *Coast Zone* was given on 18 March:

> Of the dances I have made for film or video, this was the most difficult to transfer to the stage. To attempt to keep the sense of rushing, constantly transforming movement along with the large image the close-up presented in the camera, I found it necessary to add to and in some instances enlarge the "close-up" movement into held shapes for the stage to make them appear against the continuous flow of the dance.[6]

There were five further Event performances in Rome at the end of April, and another week of them in New York in June, at the Park Avenue Armory. The first three in the latter series had music by Liz Phillips, the last three by the company musicians.

In May, Cunningham received the Mayor of New York's Awards of Honor for Arts and Culture. The award was presented by Louise Nevelson, an old friend and a member of the board of the Cunningham Dance Foundation.

In October the company returned to Europe for the Klapstuk 83 International Dance Festival in Leuven, Belgium. Toward the end of the month, at the Festival de Lille in Roubaix, France, they gave a major new work:

ROARATORIO

In 1979, on commission from the Cologne radio station Westdeutscher Rundfunk, Cage had composed his *Roaratorio, an Irish Circus on Finnegans Wake*. In the early summer of that year, he and two assistants, John and Monika Fullemann, had traveled through Ireland recording sounds in places mentioned in Joyce's novel. Then Cage and John Fullemann, who had worked as a sound engineer with the Cunningham company, spent a month in the studios of the Institut de Recherche et de Co-ordination Acoustique-Musique (IRCAM), Paris, assembling these sounds, together with others contributed by radio stations all over the world, on sixteen-track tapes, each thirty minutes in length. The piece that resulted was an hour long.

When *Roaratorio* was performed live, Irish musicians took part, as did Cage himself, reading his

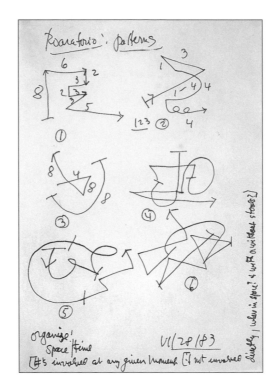

mesostics on the name "James Joyce." The recordings used in Cage's scores for *Duets* and *Fielding Sixes* had been made by some of these musicians, originally for *Roaratorio*.

Although Cage conceived the piece for radio, he had always envisaged it as eventually to be choreographed by Cunningham. Attending a performance of the work in Toronto in February 1982, Cunningham had found in it the feeling of dance that permeates Joyce's book. The first things he made for *Roaratorio* were a series of jigs that he began to include in Events. Then he choreographed other short dances, including duets, "in which the partners change, then come back to the original couples," to convey the idea that there are characters in *Finnegans Wake* who are transformed into other characters.[7] Joe Heaney, a singer who performed in *Roaratorio*, described different kinds of jigs and reels to Cunningham, including both slow and fast ones. Cunningham also did some research in the Dance Collection of the New York Public Library for the Performing Arts at Lincoln Center, New York, and found that the differences had mostly to do with meter.

Lancaster's costumes were basic gray tights and leotards, to which other garments were added during the piece. There was no set, but the dancers sat on or moved a number of stools around the stage; sometimes they tied a scarf or other garment to one of the stools.

Since *Roaratorio* lasted an hour, without intermission, there was a need for a curtain-raiser that also did not involve the company musicians:

INLETS 2

Inlets 2 is a variation of *Inlets*, made in 1977. The same gamut of sixty-four movements was subjected again to other chance operations, this time for seven dancers instead of six, to produce a different continuity and to allow for the appearance of movements not present in the original *Inlets*.[8]

Cunningham did not dance in *Inlets 2*. Lancaster designed new costumes—leotards and tights in gray, blue, or brown, over which two of the women wore short skirts of tulle.

After the first performances at the Festival de Lille, there were further performances of the two new works at the Alte Oper in Frankfurt at the beginning

of November. Cunningham and Komar then taught another version of *Inlets 2* to the dancers of the Groupe de Recherche Chorégraphique de l'Opéra de Paris (GRCOP), directed by Jacques Garnier (a kind of reincarnation of his Théâtre du Silence, which had had two Cunningham works in its repertory). This was performed at the Opéra-Comique (Salle Favart) in Paris at the beginning of December.

1984

On New Year's Day Cunningham and Cage took part in a telecast entitled *Good Morning, Mr. Orwell*, a Paris/New York satellite linkup conceived and coordinated by Nam June Paik, directed by Emile Ardolino, and produced by WNET/TV Lab and FR 3. Immediately afterward the Cunningham company left on a tour of Asia, beginning with Event performances in Madras, Bombay, and New Delhi. From India the tour proceeded to Hong Kong, Taipei, and Seoul, where it finished at the end of January.

Before the City Center season opened (on 6 March), there was an exhibition of drawings by Cage and Cunningham at Margarete Roeder's gallery at 545 Broadway in New York. On opening night at the City Center the company showed an extraordinary new dance:

PICTURES

This was a work for the full company, including Cunningham, who entered toward the end of the piece.

As choreographic material, Cunningham had made drawings of stick figures in various poses (or "pictures," as in tableaux vivants), varying from two to five people. There were sixty-four of these poses, plus an equal number of kinds of movement that could be used to get from one to another. The sequence of the tableaux and of the transitional movements was determined by chance. The "negative space" defined by Cunningham's sculptural groupings had always been an important element of his choreography; in *Pictures* it became almost the subject of the piece.

Arlene Croce has observed that "*Pictures* may have evolved from *Coast Zone* (1983), which may in turn have come from *Trails* (1982),"[1] and it is true that groupings in *Coast Zone* may have foreshadowed those in *Pictures*. Cunningham himself has written that "finishing a dance has always left me with the idea, often slim in the beginning, for the next one."[2] Croce adds that "*Trails* is a succession of entries in which no fewer

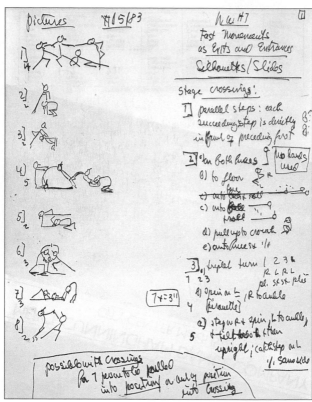

than two and no more than five dancers are on the stage at one time."[3] As we have seen, the limit of five dancers at a time onstage also held good for *Coast Zone*, and it did for *Pictures* as well.

David Behrman's music, *Interspecies Smalltalk*, was a set of compositions for instrumental performers and a computer system designed and assembled by Behrman. The piece was performed by Takehisa Kosugi (or sometimes Behrman himself), on an electric or acoustic violin, and another musician operating a Casio keyboard and an Apple II computer.

Mark Lancaster dressed the dancers in gray or black leotards and blue sweatpants. The backcloth was a white cyclorama. The design's most striking element was the lighting, which threw the tableaux into silhouette against the cyclorama, "fixing" them like photographic images—an effect requested by Cunningham. In the last of these changes of light, Cunningham lifted the inert body of Patricia Lent, then the newest member of the company, and held her horizontally.

In the seven years that *Pictures* remained in the repertory, it was performed over 200 times.

• • •

Also during the City Center season, *Inlets 2* received its first New York performances, and *Torse* was performed for the last time as a repertory piece. (Excerpts from it were often still given in Events.)

In the spring, Cunningham went on a short lecture tour, talking on "Dance and the Camera" and showing the film of *Coast Zone*. The last in this series of lectures was at the Metropolitan Museum of Art in New York; later, during the summer, there was a further lecture in San Francisco. On 16 May, Cunningham was made an Honorary Member of the American Academy and Institute of Arts and Letters. Toward the end of the month there was another series of Studio Events, with music by Pauline Oliveros and David Behrman. There followed a brief engagement in Copenhagen, featuring two more Events. (It rained heavily, and the rain came in through the roof of the theater, a former gasworks.)

In Lyons the next week, on 4 June, the company inaugurated the 1984 Biennale Internationale de la Danse with a special Event. There were repertory performances on the four succeeding nights, followed by a week-long season in Paris, at the Théâtre de la Ville.

The 1984 season of the American Dance Festival marked its fiftieth anniversary. Cunningham was one of the choreographers from whom a new work was commissioned as part of the celebrations:

DOUBLES

Cunningham told Jack Anderson that this dance consisted of "solos with duets and trios superimposed upon them so that two things are always going on at once," which partly explains the title.[4] But also there

Above, left: *Pictures*, 1984. MC and Patricia Lent. Above, right: MC's notations for *Pictures*, 1984, first of fourteen pages. Opposite: Takehisa Kosugi's diagrammatic score for *Doubles*, music for *Spacings*, 1984.

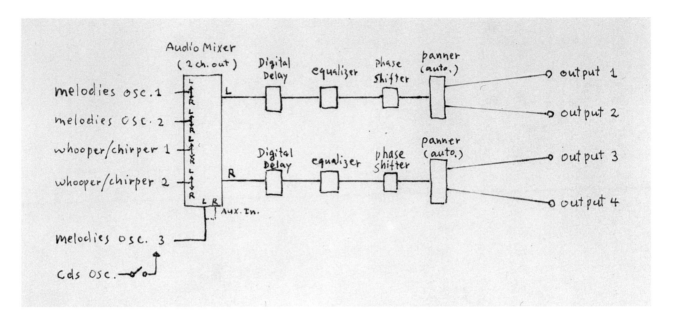

were two casts, of seven dancers each. Cunningham taught the choreography to the two casts separately, so that there were in fact two versions of the dance that differed slightly from one another.

The dance was constructed according to a complex chance process. The first solo, for instance, for a woman, was made according to a square-root system, with seventeen phrases of seventeen counts each. Chance determined on which of these counts the dancer would move in space, on which she would move her arms, her torso, and so on. All of the piece's solos were made similarly, though they differed in length and tempo. *Doubles*, Cunningham told another interviewer, "is based on rhythm, on time more than space, although space enters into it, too." Rhythmic phrases were organized by chance: "Say the numbers come up to be 2, 7 and 5. The phrase consists of a short movement in 2 counts, and movements in 7 and 5 counts."[5]

Kosugi's music, *Spacings*, was a composition for custom-made light-sensitive oscillators and electronics. In performance, the composer varied the amount of light that shone on the oscillators with a tensor lamp, triggering the various sounds.

Lancaster's costumes were similar to but more brightly colored than those of *Pictures*—leotards and sweatpants. The backcloth was purple.

• • •

An ambitious arts festival was held in Los Angeles that summer in conjunction with the Olympic Games, and the Merce Cunningham Dance Company was among those invited to participate. The company also performed at the Jacob's Pillow Dance Festival (August) and the Berliner Festwochen (Sep-

tember). From Berlin, Chris Komar went to Rotterdam to stage *Cross Currents* for Werkcentrum Dans.

At the end of September the Cunningham company performed a series of nine Events at the Joyce Theater in New York, all with music by the company musicians—Cage, Kosugi, and David Tudor. Cage had designed a set of Event costumes, using chance processes to decide on the colors; these were worn in some of the Joyce Events.

From early in October the company was in residence at the Centre National de Danse Contemporaine, Angers, where Cunningham choreographed a new work that was presented at the end of the residency, early in December:

PHRASES

Phrases was a work for the full company, including Cunningham, who danced a duet with Catherine Kerr. The title, Cunningham told Robert Greskovic, "is actually quite descriptive—the piece is made up of 64 phrases."[6] As usual, the sequence of these phrases was determined by chance.

This one wasn't made for the camera, but I worked on it as though using the camera. It was divided into four sections, and in each section I thought about the camera. For section A, I wrote "seen in huge confusion," because there was so much activity.

Section B was "seen in segments"; section C "seen in detail," like a hand, or whatever; section D "seen in huge non-confusion." I'm not sure I followed this, but still.

Using chance operations, I made movement categories for each section—a gamut. Also

I allowed for possible crossings from one section to another, also done through chance operations. And there was a possibility of variation if a phrase repeated—there were about five variations.

Lancaster had returned to England, and therefore had resigned as the company's artistic advisor. William Anastasi and Dove Bradshaw were appointed jointly in his place. *Phrases* was the first work they designed, Anastasi handling the set and lighting, Bradshaw the costumes. "William Anastasi," Anna Kisselgoff wrote, "has designed a backdrop with a rope-like line that cuts from top to bottom and then rises upward at a diagonal. The lighting creates a luminous grayish backdrop against which fourteen of the fifteen-member cast initially [stand] out in bright solid-colored leotards by Dove Bradshaw. After Mr. Cunningham joins in [dressed in a gray jumpsuit], the dancers add black ankle- or leg-warmers to their red, white, yellow or greenish costumes and some later add trousers, sweaters and shirts."[7]

1985

Once again Cunningham began the year with a video project, though of less ambitious scope than the preceding film works. Charles Atlas had left the Cunningham Dance Foundation, and his place as filmmaker-in-residence was taken by Elliot Caplan, who had worked as his assistant since 1977. Caplan's first collaboration with Cunningham was a videodance shot in the Cunningham Studio in January 1985:

DELI COMMEDIA

This short piece, lasting only eighteen minutes, used a student group of three women and two men. (Two of the women subsequently joined the company). Cunningham had actually begun work on the piece in the summer of 1983. As with *Coast Zone*, there was no attempt to disguise the architecture of the setting; the dancers used both the floor and the small stage at the studio's west end, and made entrances and exits through the doors and arches to the right and left of the stage. Cunningham, Caplan wrote,

Opposite: *Phrases*, 1984. Left to right: Kevin Schroder, Susan Quinn Young, Megan Walker, Robert Swinston, Alan Good, Patricia Lent, Rob Remley, Chris Komar, and Helen Barrow. Photograph: JoAnn Baker. Above: *Deli Commedia*, 1985. Left to right: Kristy Santimyer, Frey Faust, Bill Young, and Carol Teitelbaum. Photograph: Tony Cucchiari.

wanted to create a sense of different spaces or scenes within his studio, and incorporate into the development of the choreography the various possibilities presented by its physical layout. . . .

Cunningham had wanted to shoot the entire work in one continuous take. After several days we agreed on specific cuts which would allow the editing to share in the rhythm of the dance.[1]

According to Karen Carreras, the dance was "conceived as a slapstick comedy, Cunningham's nod to the improvised farces of the Italian 18th-century commedia dell'arte," and to the two-reel comedies of the silent screen. The score—*I Can't Go On to the Next Thing, Till I Find Out More about You*, by Pat Richter, Cunningham's favorite class accompanist—functioned like the piano accompaniments to silent films. Sight gags, "comic kinetic jokes, cakewalking, tango, lindy hop and imaginative juxtapositions of bodies, props and special effects" figured in the choreography. "A film screen in the background produces the illusion of a movie within a movie."[2]

During the year Cunningham and Caplan also collaborated on an instructional tape, *Cunningham Dance Technique: Elementary Level*, demonstrated by four students, with Cunningham himself giving the commentary.

• • •

The first event of the year for the Cunningham company proper was a residency at the University of Illinois at Urbana/Champaign, from 20 to 23 February. There were video screenings even before the company's arrival. During the residency, Cage conducted a composers' forum and Cunningham a "Conversation" with students of the dance department; these two events were simultaneous, but later on the same day the two men performed a Dialogue, which was followed by a concert by the University's New Music Ensemble. There were master classes, and finally two performances, one an Event, the other a repertory program.

The annual season at the City Center ran from 5 to 17 March. On opening night *Phrases* received its American premiere, and on the second *Doubles* was performed for the first time in New York. The second week included the premiere of another new dance:

NATIVE GREEN

This dance for three couples was made possible in part by a gift in memory of the dance critic Edwin Denby, who had died in 1983. Cunningham has said that in devising the movement he divided the body into four parts: legs, torso, arms, head. In this respect the process was reminiscent of such early chance pieces as *Untitled Solo*, except that here the movements for the different parts were not arbitrarily combined, but moved from one part to another sequentially (though the sequence was determined by chance). This gave a quivering, birdlike quality to the movement. At the end, the dancers picked up a length of plastic tubing that had lain at the back of the stage, and came to rest clinging to it, as though to a branch of a tree. Cunningham had wanted this object to be flexible, "so that it looked almost alive."

John King's music, *Gliss in Sighs*, used an electronic violin, custom-made by Max Mathews, and three prerecorded stereo cassettes; the tapes were started at the beginning of the piece, but punched out (not faded out) at the times written on them. According to a program note, "The idea of 'preparing' this electronic violin with lead, cork, and rubber objects came to Mr. King while he was fishing in Maine."[3]

The set and costume designs were by William Anastasi, with lighting by Dove Bradshaw. Spreading the backcloth out on the floor, Anastasi worked directly on it with red and black Magic Markers. It was also bisected by a diagonal line. (This design was related to the "blind" drawings that Anastasi was making at the time, in India ink with a fine-point pen.) The costumes were made similarly, with marks being made directly on the fabric of the leotards and tights and the women's skirts.

• • •

Concurrently with the City Center season, choreographic notations by Cunningham were exhibited at Margarete Roeder's gallery at 545 Broadway, together with scores by Cage, Takehisa Kosugi, and David Tudor.

The company went on tour soon after the New York season, first to Washington, D.C., Berkeley, and Chicago, then to Italy (Rome, Naples, and Modena) and England (Sadler's Wells Theatre, London). In June, it was announced that Cunningham had received one of that year's MacArthur Fellowships. (Paul Taylor was another recipient). Cunningham had intended to present *Roaratorio* that month at the Park Avenue Armory in New York, where the company had performed Events two years earlier, but the Armory was preempted for military maneuvers. There was further touring abroad in July: to Istanbul, Montpellier, Avignon (where the company performed *Roaratorio* in the Cour d'honneur du Palais des Papes), and Barcelona.

Through the National Choreography Project, which existed to make it possible for ballet companies to commission works from outside choreographers, the Pennsylvania Ballet commissioned a new dance from Cunningham, first given at the Academy of Music in Philadelphia in September 1985:

ARCADE

Cunningham choreographed the dance on his own company; Chris Komar then taught it to the Pennsylvania Ballet. The choreography, divided into quartets, duets, solos, and so on, was made with the ballet dancers in mind, the rhythms, for example, being very defined: "I counted out the phrases in a way I don't often do." (When he worked on the piece with his own dancers, Cunningham "stretched" the rhythms and "let kinds of freedom take place.") In the opening section, the slow extensions of a group of four women were contrasted with an almost acrobatic series of lifts and catches performed by a female soloist and three male partners. Later there was a more sustained adagio sequence for a man and a woman, their movements echoed by two subsidiary couples. Cunningham used musical notations alongside his own choreographic notations, "so they [the ballet dancers] wouldn't look stunned." Even so, the dancers of the Pennsylvania Ballet did not hear the music (Cage's *Etudes Boreales I–IV*, played by Michael Pugliese) until the final rehearsal.

Dove Bradshaw's set featured a single white pillar in front of a white backcloth on which were painted three gray rectangular panels of unequal size. The idea for this design, Cunningham has said, came from being in Barcelona that summer: "I went to look at the Gaudi architecture, and there was this beautiful

series of archways, very long, very elegant—they didn't get in the way of what you were looking at." Bradshaw's costumes were slate gray or blue leotards and tights, daubed with white X's.

• • •

The Cunningham company continued its touring in September with performances at Pennsylvania's Swarthmore College, at the Festival International de Danse in Ottawa, the Festival International de Nouvelle Danse in Montreal, and St. Johnsbury, Vermont. In October the company was back in Spain, this time in Madrid for the Festival de Otoño, and then in six cities in Germany. In November there were performances in Stamford, Connecticut; Philadelphia, where the company gave its own first performance of *Arcade*, at the Annenberg Center, University of Pennsylvania; and Detroit.

Returning to New York, the company gave another series of Events at the Joyce Theater. For the first of these, Cunningham taught Rob Remley one

Above: *Arcade*, 1985, MCDC version, 1985. Left to right: Karen Radford, Neil Greenberg, Patricia Lent, Robert Swinston, Rob Remley, and Megan Walker.

of his solos from *Suite for Five*, which had not been performed since 1972 (though the Trio and Quintet from the piece were frequently danced in Events).

On Saturday 7 December, Cunningham was a recipient of the Kennedy Center Honors, at a dinner at the Department of State in Washington, D.C. In the gala performance the following evening, members of his company danced part of *Native Green*, the company's hundredth performance of the year. Just before the performance, Cunningham was handed a message that told him that *Pictures* had just won a Laurence Olivier Award in London for the Outstanding New Dance Production of the Year.

1986

At the beginning of the year, Cunningham and Chris Komar traveled to Paris to work with the Paris Opéra Ballet on a revised version of *Un Jour ou deux*, which was first performed on 31 January. The ballet was somewhat shorter—more because it was tightened than because anything was cut—and was given this time in a dou-

ble bill with either *Washington Square* or *Manfred*, ballets by Rudolf Nureyev, now the Opéra's *directeur de la danse*. Apart from two of the principals, Jean Guizerix and Wilfride Piollet, only three of the original cast were still in *Un Jour ou deux* (and both Guizerix and Piollet had alternates). Laurent Hilaire replaced the third principal, Michaël Denard.

On Cunningham's return to the United States, the company left for a domestic tour that included performances in Cleveland, Ohio; Jacksonville and West Palm Beach, Florida; Santa Fe, New Mexico; and Austin, Texas. The tour was followed by the annual season at the City Center, from 11 to 23 March. Here *Arcade* received its first New York performances and *Fielding Sixes* was revived with new designs by William Anastasi, though these were in fact the company's last repertory performances of this dance. There was also one new work:

GRANGE EVE

Like *Native Green* in 1985, *Grange Eve*—a work for fourteen dancers, including Cunningham—was "in memory of Edwin Denby." It may be remembered that as a teenager Cunningham had danced in grange halls; the title of *Grange Eve* refers to these. Reviewers seized on this rare personal reference, saying, as one put it, that the dance "recalls a typical Saturday night remembered from Cunningham's youth in Centralia."[1] Anna Kisselgoff, in the *New York Times*, went into detail on the subject:

> Its source of inspiration was obviously Mr. Cunningham's childhood and adolescence in Centralia, Wash., a period when . . . Mrs. Maude Barrett, took the young charges from her dancing school into movie houses and granges to perform the tap-ballroom-acrobatic numbers that she had taught them. . . .
>
> The childhood snapshot images come alive on stage as a formal exercise. . . . At the same time it is clearly anecdotal. That is, we see the barn dances of the granges around Centralia. The dancers perform stylized, almost abstract, renderings of do-si-dos and allemandes left. They actually perform social dances, the rollicking polka variety. And in a brilliantly theatrical sequence, Mr. Cunningham, Alan Good, Chris Komar, Rob Remley and Kevin Schroder all dance with canes. . . .
>
> *Grange Eve* incorporates social dances and floor patterns associated with hoedowns although they are made to look mainly geometrical. . . . At one point, two women move while ringed by a huge rubber band. Mr. Cunningham used a similar rubber band in *Crises* (1960). Is it relevant that Mrs. Barrett . . . would put "a big rubber band" (Mr. Cunningham's words) over her skirt and then walk on her hands in some of her shows? . . .
>
> The women fill the stage in a quieter sequence. As they stand, [Helen] Barrow pushes Remley about. He could be just staggering about—but he could also be the town

drunk. There are other sketched-out vignettes: Mr. Cunningham repositions Mr. Good from one "photo" grouping to another. Mr. Good shadowboxes as Mr. [Robert] Swinston has his back to him and then turns his back as Mr. Swinston boxes.[2]

Cunningham had used elements of different social dances in both *Roaratorio* and *Deli Commedia*. When he was working on *Grange Eve*, he had been reading a book called *A Time for Dancing* (he forgets the name of the author), which dealt with such folk forms as clog and buck dancing. "I tried to figure out the steps, and write them down, but I began to add my own steps and mix them up, so that the women, say, might start to do something different." As usual, he used chance procedures to do this. None of the steps he used came from Mrs. Barrett—"she didn't do country dances"—but he did remember seeing square dances at a place called Woody's Nook, in the country outside Centralia.

Grange Eve was designed by Anastasi. His backcloth suggested no reference to the dance's autobiographical content—indeed, at one performance, on 22 March 1986, it was performed with his new back-

cloth for *Fielding Sixes*. At the Théâtre de la Ville in Paris the following year, and thereafter, the *Fielding Sixes* backcloth was used again (the original one having been damaged). The costumes for *Grange Eve* were thigh-length T-shirts worn over tights.

For Kisselgoff, the music, Takehisa Kosugi's *Assemblage*, added "to the down-home atmosphere," with its suggestions of "jars and cans being struck"[3] in what another critic called "the style of a shivaree."[4]

• • •

After the New York season, Cunningham embarked on his most ambitious videodance project so far, a coproduction with the British Broadcasting Corporation, once again in collaboration with Elliot Caplan:

POINTS IN SPACE

The title comes from Albert Einstein's statement "There are no fixed points in space," a favorite quotation of Cunningham's. The phrase also refers to Cunningham's perception of the nature of the space in video, which, he feels, offers the possibility of multiple points of view instead of a single one.

In its original, video version, *Points in Space* was a work for the full company, including Cunningham

Opposite, top: *Points in Space*, 1986. Left to right, foreground to background: Helen Barrow, David Kulick, MC, Chris Komar, Catherine Kerr, Alan Good, and Megan Walker. Photograph: Robert Hill, B.B.C. Opposite, bottom: *Points in Space*, 1986. Left to right: MC, Catherine Kerr, and Alan Good. Photograph: Robert Hill, B.B.C. This page: Dove Bradshaw's costume designs for *Points in Space*, 1986.

(the first time he had taken part in one of his company dances for the camera). The piece was divided into seven parts, their tempo alternating between fast and slow. Cunningham and Caplan planned the work in New York and rehearsed it first in the Westbeth Studio. The company then moved to London and worked in the BBC studios, recording the piece there in May. The first part of the program in which the piece was broadcast was a half-hour documentary on Cunningham made by the producer Bob Lockyer. This documentary focused especially on the creation of *Points in Space.*

The music, *Voiceless Essay* by Cage, was realized at the Center for Computer Music at Brooklyn College of the City University of New York, and at Synesthetics, Inc. Using computer-generated chance operations, Cage chose groups of words from his text "Writings through the Essay: On the Duty of Civil Disobedience [by Henry David Thoreau]," a section from his lecture "The First Meeting of the Satie Society." (Like many of Cage's writings, this text takes the form of a series of mesostics—a kind of vertical acrostic—on the title of Satie's *Messe des pauvres.*) The words were recorded, then synthesized and analyzed by computer; only the sounds of the consonants were retained. Each of the company musicians who performed the score played a cassette tape of the recording, muting it during the performance for varying durations of between thirty seconds and two minutes.

Anastasi's decor, a panoramic backcloth in three sections, was adapted from drawings he had made in the 1970s. (In the documentary section of the video, Anastasi says that Cunningham told him to "think of weather.") The costumes, by Dove Bradshaw, were tights and leotards dyed in one of two ways: either in colors divided horizontally, or swabbed with a sponge to give a *tachiste* effect, with clear areas created by patches of masking tape that were then peeled off.

• • •

The company, which had given almost one hundred performances in 1985, performed only forty times in 1986. Touring abroad was much curtailed: there were five performances in Munich in May (following the video recording in London), and three at the Singapore Festival of the Arts in June. Between these excursions, the company performed once again at the American Dance Festival at Duke University in Durham, North Carolina, though this time there was no new work.

Cunningham and Cage together received a Special Achievement Award at the "Bessies" (the New York Dance and Performance Awards), presented by Carolyn Brown at the Brooklyn Academy of Music on 17 September. The next month, the company gave the first American performances of *Roaratorio* there, as the opening event in that year's "Next Wave" Festival (again coupled with *Inlets 2*).

1987

The number of performances in 1987 was closer to that in 1985: ninety-three in all, at various venues in New York and on tour at home and abroad. A three-year, three-commissions project with the Walker Art Center, Minneapolis, was begun, and the first of these works (co-commissioned by the Northrop Auditorium and the Cunningham Dance Foundation with the Walker) was presented there on 21 February.

FABRICATIONS

According to Cunningham, the title refers to both meanings of the verb "to fabricate": to combine parts to form a whole, and to invent or concoct, even to lie.

Fabrications was a work for the full company, including Cunningham. Once again, Cunningham used a chance process based on sixty-four phrases of varying lengths, from one count to sixty-four counts (sixty-four being the number of hexagrams in the *I Ching*). The continuity of the phrases was determined by chance, as was the number of people who would perform each phrase. The duration of each phrase remained constant, though the phrases could overlap.

Such was the structure of *Fabrications*. Yet the dance also had an undeniably dramatic, elegiac quality, even though there was of course no narrative content. (As the Russian ballerina Yelizaveta Gerdt is reported to have said to someone who criticized a lack of narrative in George Balanchine, "The plot is in the plotlessness."[1]) To some, *Fabrications* seemed to be a memory piece, like certain works by Antony Tudor or Frederick Ashton (*Enigma Variations*).[2] Certainly the dance gave the lie to those who claimed that Cunningham's dancers made no connection with one another: In *Fabrications* they looked like lovers, or friends, and Cunningham's own role seemed to be that of a revenant, revisiting scenes of the past. In an especially potent passage, he stood gazing into the eyes of Victoria Finlayson for a long moment.

The music, *Short Waves 1985*, by the Brazilian composer Emanuel Dimas de Melo Pimenta, was an electronic composition on tape, combined with short-wave radio sounds, also on tape. (No doubt fortuitously, the sounds of muffled voices or snatches of music added to the dance's dramatic effect.) The mixing was done in performance by David Tudor. The music actually consisted of two separate compositions, the first about fifteen minutes long. There followed a silence of about six and a half minutes; the second piece began at the end of a solo entry by Cunningham. The timing of the first part of the dance was not planned in relation to the music, but was later made precise in performance.

Unusually, Dove Bradshaw costumed the company's women in dresses for this piece; the men were in shirts and trousers. The dresses were silk, in prints or solid colors; these too added to the "period" sense of the dance. This too was unplanned, though when Bradshaw told Cunningham that she wanted to put the women in dresses sometime, he replied that this would be as good

Above: *Fabrications*, 1987. Left to right: Chris Komar, Alan Good, Susan Quinn Young, Helen Barrow, Catherine Kerr, Kristy Santimyer, and David Kulick. Photograph: Tom Brazil. Right: *Fabrications*, 1987. Victoria Finlayson and MC. Photograph: Johan Elbers.

a time as any. Her backdrop was taken from drawings derived from medical and mathematical diagrams, and thus did not contribute to the effect.

• • •

The company's annual season at the City Center, from 3 to 15 March, began soon after its return from Minneapolis. The repertory included *Fabrications*, the stage version of *Points in Space*, revivals of *Septet* (not seen in its entirety since 1964) and *Signals* (not

seen in repertory since 1981), and yet another new work, given on the second night:

SHARDS

Shards was a work for eight dancers (originally those not in the revival of *Septet*). Cunningham had thought to make a dance in which both the movements and the dancers were isolated from one another. "I made a gamut of movements which are static . . . although when I look at *Shards*, it doesn't seem static. There's always something moving; you catch it out of the corner of your eye."[3] Even so, there was a great deal of stillness in the piece; sometimes only one dancer would be moving while the others remained immobile.

As always, Cunningham used chance procedures, which determined in the first place that there would be no exits or entrances—all the dancers would remain on stage until the last moments, when they would begin to leave the stage. Nor was this intended as an exit: the last phrase that came up in the chance procedure was a walking phrase, and since it was also indicated that all the dancers would go to one side except one, some of the dancers began to go off because of where they already were in the space.

Cunningham made a gamut of movements, mostly very short phrases, that could be repeated or not. These movements were passed from one dancer to another; one began a phrase, another picked up part of it (this was also determined by chance), and so on. The title, *Shards*, referred to this kind of fragmentation, but also seemed to have another significance:

> It seems to me the way we work—although I may be stretching it—is a lot . . . the way that society exists now. . . . Being able to take fragments, long and short, and put them together in different ways—we have to, in a sense, do that in our lives all the time, although we don't think about it. Society is split into so many directions. Look at the disintegration. So many things are falling apart, so many people are having troubles of multiple kinds. There is no center. I think that the center lies in one's self. Each person has to find it for himself. I think *Shards* must come from all that kind of thinking. Not explicitly, of course. But no matter what you do, whatever you make, it comes from whatever you are.[4]

For whatever reason, the piece had a somber, tragic feeling, so much that it made some people feel that it was taking place in some nuclear winter of the future.

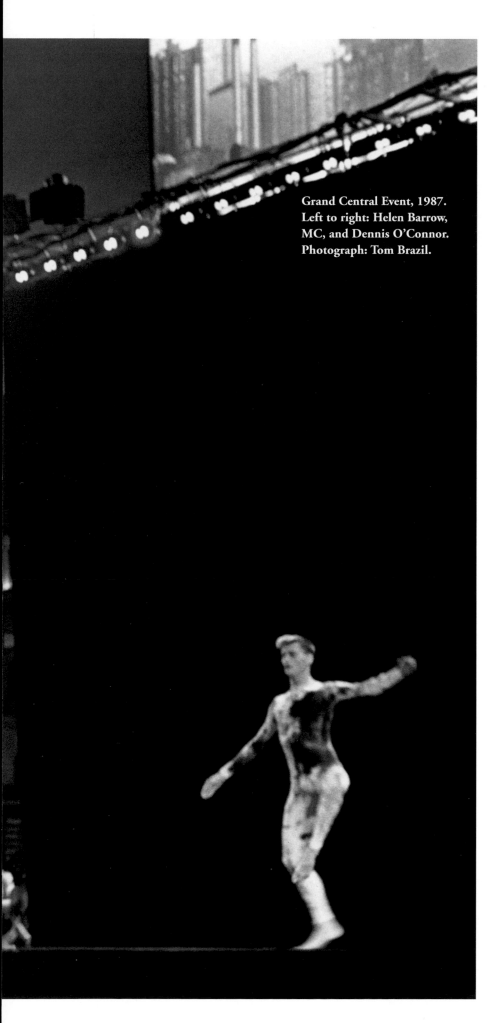

**Grand Central Event, 1987.
Left to right: Helen Barrow,
MC, and Dennis O'Connor.
Photograph: Tom Brazil.**

Concerning his music, Tudor wrote,

> The sound source for *Webwork* is obtained from
> sea-sounds recorded under water, which are
> subsequently fragmented to give the most
> minute impulses. These impulses activate a
> chain of electronic components producing a
> variety of sound transformations, which can be
> changed instantaneously. The performance
> process is, in part, like weaving through a warp
> having many colors.[5]

William Anastasi designed an abstract backcloth.
At the first performance the dancers wore brightly
colored costumes; these seemed unsuitable, and were
quickly replaced by sweatpants over leotards, in
greenish gray.

● ● ●

During the season's first week there was a festival organized by Patricia Kerr Ross, then director of programs
in the arts at the State University of New York, under
the rubric "Merce Cunningham and the New
Dance/The Modernist Impulse in Dance." There
were symposia, open rehearsals and classes, screenings,
and performances at various locations in the city; present and former dancers and artistic collaborators,
scholars, and critics all took part.[6]

Points in Space received its first stage performance
at the beginning of the season's second week. The
stage version differed from the original more than
other video and film pieces that Cunningham had
adapted for the stage. Cunningham's own role and
those of two dancers who had left the company in the
interim were omitted. The sequence was changed—
the original finale was cut and replaced with choreography from an earlier section. The duet originally
danced by Catherine Kerr and Alan Good was
extended with material added from elsewhere in the
piece, and also from a duet that Kerr had danced with
Joseph Lennon in *Exercise Piece III* (1980). There
Kerr had done a backward fall, to be caught by
Lennon; this fall resembled a movement in the *Points
in Space* duet, and she suggested to Cunningham that
he might incorporate it. The duet was divided into
several sections, one of which replaced Cunningham's
solo in the sixth part of the original. The decor for
the stage version was one section of the panoramic
backcloth that Anastasi had made for the video.

Touring began soon after the season ended, first to
the Midwest, then, in a second trip, to California and
on up to Portland and Seattle. (The bus stopped in
Centralia, Cunningham's hometown, where his

235

brother Dorwin greeted the group. They then drove around the town, with Cunningham pointing out landmarks, such as the house the family had lived in.)

About a week after returning from the Northwest, the company left for Europe: Salzburg, Munich, and Paris. Between this tour and a visit to Japan there was another domestic date (at the Spoleto Festival USA in Charleston, North Carolina), and by mid-July the company was in London, where *Roaratorio* was performed at the Royal Albert Hall in the ninety-third season of the "Proms" (the Henry Wood Promenade Concerts). It shared its program with Stravinsky's *Les Noces*, thus repeating a pairing from the festival at Brandeis University thirty-five years before when Cunningham had choreographed both the Stravinsky ballet and Pierre Schaeffer's *Symphonie pour un homme seul*. On the day before this single performance, the video version of *Points in Space* was shown on BBC2. The following week, the company opened a two-week season at Sadler's Wells. Cunningham and Elliot Caplan had somehow squeezed in a short visit to Aarhus in Denmark, where American Ballet Theatre was taping a *Dance in America* program consisting of Balanchine's *La Sonnambula* and Cunningham's *Duets*. Thomas Grimm was credited as the program's director, with Cunningham and Caplan as consultants.

Less than three weeks later, the company was back at the Jacob's Pillow Dance Festival in Lee, Massachusetts, where the programs included *Septet*, which the company had performed there in 1955, and the first performances, on 18 August, of a work commissioned by Liz Thompson, then the festival's director:

CAROUSAL

Carousal, a work for thirteen dancers (not including Cunningham), was made with the small stage of the barn theater at Jacob's Pillow in mind. It was like a little circus or sideshow with the possibility of two or three rings, delineated by the dancers with lengths of tubing, for which Cunningham devised a series of "turns," their order determined by chance. Other props included a partly inflated beach ball and a pink cloth that could be held up to conceal or at least partly reveal dancers behind it. (This may have referred to a similar device used by Bonnie Bird in her *Imaginary Landscape* at the Cornish School in 1939.) At one point, the men joined hands like acrobats to form a fan-shaped grouping at the back of the stage, with one woman (Helen Barrow) running in and out. It has been suggested that this grouping echoed a pose seen in a photograph of a dance choreographed by Ted Shawn for his company of men dancers at Jacob's Pillow in the early 1930s, but it also resembled a grouping in Balanchine's *Card Game*.

Carousal began with two men (Chris Komar and Dennis O'Connor) alone on stage, as though warming up before the performance. Another male duet had David Kulick and Rob Remley "tumbling tightly around each other on the floor, like two wrestlers looking for holds."[7] A quieter passage was the long duet for Kerr and Robert Swinston. The piece ended with three women being lifted to mime

climbing ropes, or hauling upon them hand over hand, as though lowering the curtain—which at that point closed.

Takehisa Kosugi's *Rhapsody* used acoustic sounds made with pieces of bamboo, balloons, Tibetan finger-cymbals, and other small objects. These sounds were electronically processed, creating an electro-acoustic blend.

The dance was performed before the back wall of the stage. Dove Bradshaw's costumes were clothes from thrift shops and cheap stores on Canal Street in New York, and from her own closet; some of them were turned inside out. (The idea came from her observation of scarecrows in various parts of the world.) Cunningham wanted the possibility of changes of costume; Bradshaw left the dancers free to choose among the range of things she provided for each one of them. At Jacob's Pillow, she noticed a string of Christmas-tree lights used to help dancers find their way backstage in the dark. During one of the "turns," when dancers became visible through the pink gauze cloth, she had these lights turned on momentarily, an effect reproduced in other theaters where the dance was performed.

• • •

Although the company had toured in California in the spring, they returned to Los Angeles early in September for an Event subtitled "Cage and Colleagues (II)," part of a "Celebration for John Cage" presented by the Los Angeles Festival. ("Cage and Colleagues (I)" was a concert by the company musicians, Tudor, Kosugi, and Michael Pugliese.) A few days later the company returned to Europe for dates in Italy (Rovereto) and Belgium (Antwerp). October was also extremely busy. Back in New York at the beginning of the month, the company took part in the AIDS benefit performance "Dancing for Life" at the New York State Theater, performing an excerpt from *Fabrications*. (Cunningham did not appear.) A few days later there were two Events in Grand Central Terminal, as part of the "Grand Central Dances" presented by Dancing in the Streets. A stage was erected in the station's main concourse, and the performances were seen by hundreds of people, including commuters.

The company next went to Philadelphia for an Event in the Philadelphia Museum of Art in connection with the show "Apropos of Marcel Duchamp," a celebration of the artist's centenary. The set for *Walkaround Time* was used, and Cunningham reconstructed some excerpts from the piece. The performance "took place at the Great Stair Hall, with the audience sitting on the steps and standing in the gallery overlooking the floor on which the company performed."[8]

Cunningham had been chosen to be the fifth recipient of the Algur H. Meadows Award, given by the Meadows School of the Arts of Southern Methodist University in Dallas, Texas, "for Excellence in the Arts." This was the occasion of another symposium, "About Merce Cunningham," from 19 to 24 October, accompanied by an exhibition, panel discussions, and master classes, and culminating in a performance at which the award was given.

On 29 October *Points in Space* had its first American television showing, on the Arts and Entertainment cable network.

The year ended with a further revival of *Septet*, staged by Komar for the Rambert Dance Company (formerly the Ballet Rambert). Cunningham had been in Frankfurt to help Cage rehearse his *Europeras 1 & 2*, but the first performance of that work, scheduled for 13 November, was canceled when the opera house burned down. Cunningham attended the first performance of *Septet*, at the Theatre Royal, Glasgow, on 20 November, after another flying visit to Denmark to supervise the editing of the videotape of *Duets* by American Ballet Theatre. He then returned to Frankfurt for the rescheduled premiere of *Europeras 1 & 2* on 12 December.

During the year, Cunningham and Caplan completed another instructional tape, *Cunningham Dance Technique: Intermediate Level.*

1988

The *Dance in America* program in which American Ballet Theatre performed *Duets* was first shown on Public Television in February.

In place of its annual Manhattan season at the City Center, the Cunningham company was this year invited to perform a four-week season at the Joyce Theater, on Eighth Avenue at 19th Street. On opening night, 1 March, a revival of *RainForest* was presented. *Carousal* had its first New York performances during the same season, and there was a brand-new work:

ELEVEN

Eleven, so named because of the number of dancers in the piece, was choreographed specifically for the stage of the Joyce. Cunningham divided the space into eight equal areas: "I wanted to see whether, given the size of this stage, one could not get a sense of different proportions by dividing it this way." Chance operations determined which dancers would perform each section, and in which area of the stage. Each phrase had to stay within the square in which it began; then the dancers could move to another square. Cunningham sometimes had to make an adjustment if the chance process demanded that the dancers move into a space that was already occupied, but he found the limitations interesting—"how to refocus the movement so that it works within the space." Elliot Caplan observed that much of the movement in space in *Eleven* was lateral, and speculated that this might reflect the influence of video on Cunningham's work. Cunningham agreed that this might be the case.

The music, by Robert Ashley, was called *Problems in the Flying Saucer*, and involved two speakers (Takehisa Kosugi and Michael Pugliese) narrating an excerpt from the screenplay for Ashley's 1987 opera *Odalisque*. The musical arrangement for this text was

commissioned by the Cunningham Dance Foundation. A note by Ashley on his score was printed in the program:

> Late 1940s. Flying Saucer. Captain and Lieutenant in concerned discussion about what they have on board—a musician, apparently American (probably "in exile"), on his way to a concert in the South of France. His imagination about the music, which is pretty narrative by Flying Saucer standards, and about other things, is contagious to the Saucer. Personnel seeing things. The Captain, confined to the bridge, has to have it explained to him by the Lieutenant. After not too long the Captain's concern gives way (or contagion spreads), he gets into the spirit of the music and they try out a few tunes.

Eleven was performed in front of the theater's bare back wall, with costumes and lighting by William Anastasi. The men wore leotards and pants, the women shirts and tights; the men's pants and the women's shirts were decorated with blotches of paint.

• • •

Touring abroad resumed the following month. (The company had had one out-of-town date before the Joyce season, an Event at Wellesley College in Massachusetts.) The company was one of six performing in the Carlton Dance Festival in Brazil, circulating among São Paulo, Rio de Janeiro, and Belo Horizonte from 8 to 15 April.

Cunningham had received commissions for new work from both Werkstatt Berlin 1988 and jointly from the Festival d'Avignon and the Paris Festival d'automne. Rather than make two separate dances, Cunningham decided to make one long piece. The first part, *Five Stone*, was performed for the first time at Freie Wolksbühne Berlin on 16 June. The complete work, with the addition of the second part, *Wind*, was first given at the Festival d'Avignon, in the Cour d'honneur du Palais des Papes, on 30 July.

FIVE STONE WIND

The title refers to Cunningham's delineation of the space for *Five Stone* by five focal points indicating the direction in which the dancers would enter or exit, and in which they would face in relation to the audience. Ninety-two phrases were organized around these five points.[1] As Cunningham put it, these five points were "like camera positions" in a video piece. The "wind" in the title was the mistral that was likely to be blowing during summer performances in

Below: *Five Stone Wind*, 1988. Left to right: Kimberly Bartosik, Patricia Lent, Emma Diamond, and Carol Teitelbaum. Photograph: Michael O'Neill. Opposite: Mark Lancaster's costume designs for *Five Stone Wind*, 1988.

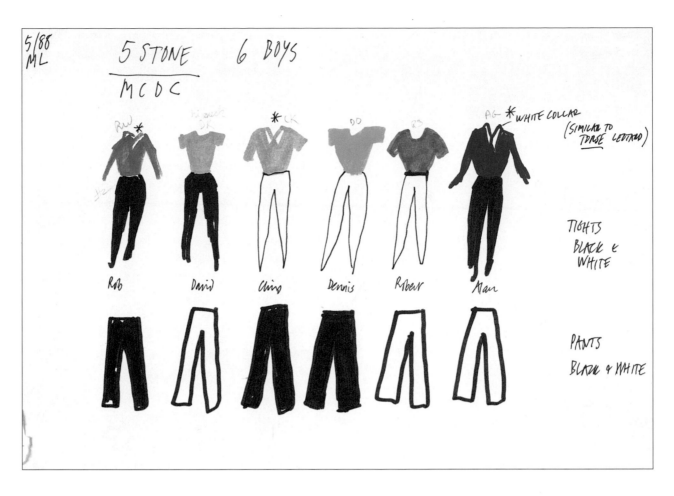

5/88
ML

5 STONE   6 BOYS

MCDC

AG ✳ WHITE COLLAR
(SIMILAR TO TORSE LEOTARD)

Rob   David   Chris   Dennis   Robert   Alan

TIGHTS
BLACK &
WHITE

PANTS
BLACK & WHITE

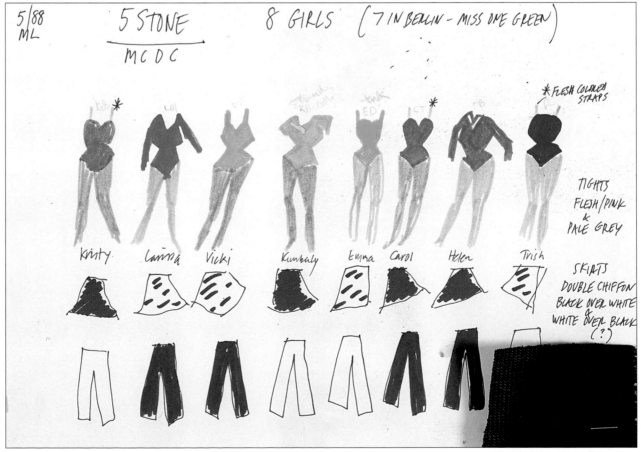

5/88
ML

5 STONE   8 GIRLS   (7 IN BERLIN - MISS ONE GREEN)

MCDC

✳ FLESH COLORED
STRAPS

Kristy   Larissa   Vicki   Kimberly   Emma   Carol   Helen   Trish

TIGHTS
FLESH/PINK
&
PALE GREY

SKIRTS
DOUBLE CHIFFON
BLACK OVER WHITE
&
WHITE OVER BLACK
(?)

Avignon; in the work's second part, Cunningham said, the dancers "go every which way."

The Berlin space was enclosed in such a way that it was necessary for the dancers to enter, then pause a moment before beginning to dance. The Cour d'honneur, on the other hand, is a wide, open space, with no wings, which the dancers could enter from far offstage.

Five Stone featured thirteen dancers, including Cunningham himself. Most of the phrases in this first part were slow. Two more women (Kimberly Bartosik and Emma Diamond, who had both recently joined the company) entered for *Wind*, with swift movements—"like the wind"—and as the dance went on, it increased in virtuosity, complexity, and rapidity, with jumping phrases and others that moved through the space, "breaking open the sense of enclosure," Cunningham has said, "so that there is a kind of metamorphosis, an opening out."

As usual, Cunningham used chance to determine the length of the individual sections (which varied in length from fifteen seconds to two minutes), the sequence of the dance phrases, their location in the performing space, and their distribution among the dancers. Cunningham composed sixty-four phrases, with an additional twenty-nine alternates that could be used in case of a repetition, or if other movement possibilities were needed. This involved voluminous charts: "I call it paperwork, but John Cage calls it composition."

The music for *Five Stone* was by Cage and David Tudor, joined by Kosugi for *Five Stone Wind*. Unlike previous scores by three composers, such as those for *Signals* and *Landrover* (by Cage, Tudor, and Gordon Mumma), and those for Event performances in which the musicians had played either together or sequentially, that for *Five Stone Wind* was "somewhat composed," according to Cage.

Cage described his overall organization of the score as follows:

Using chance operations I composed a framework of time-brackets with flexible beginnings and endings for three players, one who did not begin playing until after 30 minutes (Takehisa Kosugi). I did not in any way give details to David Tudor or Kosugi for the realization of their parts. However, for Michael Pugliese's part I made specific plans with him for the use of the clay drums within particular brackets and the subsequent alternation of these plans for performances on tour. These included . . . the

use or not while improvising of electronic feedback produced by moving the drum closer to the microphone.[2]

Tudor described his contribution as follows:

Five Stone Wind . . . is an electronically generated work, basically percussive in nature. The sounds are derived from recordings of earth-vibrations (not earth-quakes) passed through an electronic "gate." The gate can be "tuned," both as to frequency and duration. The resulting sounds are further treated by other electronic components, which produce a variety of timbres.

In the second part of the work, *Wind*, the action of the gate is sometimes reversed, controlling the release of the sounds rather than the attack, allowing the sounds to have a more continuous character.[3]

Kosugi joined Pugliese and Tudor at the beginning of Wind, thirty minutes into the overall piece:

I begin my performance playing alternatively with violin (pizzicato), "piezzo tree" for sound transducer (percussion) and bamboo flute (blowing). The sounds are processed occasionally through a sampling machine (time modulation), and all the time through digital multi-effector (reverberation).[4]

The instrumentation of Kosugi's part consisted of violin, voice, and bamboo tubes, and varied with each performance, using chance operations. The tubes could be played with a saxophone mouthpiece

Five Stone Wind, 1988, Avignon, France. Left to right: MC, Alan Good, and Helen Barrow. Photograph: Colette Masson.

or blown into, like the Australian didgeridoo. The vocal element was a kind of shamanistic incantation, ranging from low register to falsetto, with male or female sounds in a yin-yang relation.

Cunningham asked his former artistic advisor Mark Lancaster to design *Five Stone Wind*. (Since the first performances would be in Europe, it was easier for Lancaster, now resident in Britain, to be present.) For the set, a number of ropes hung against a purple backdrop, moving occasionally. Although this set was used in Berlin and later on tour in Germany, in Avignon *Five Stone Wind* was performed against the wall of the Cour d'honneur. The complete work, therefore, was not given with its full scenic investiture until it was performed on tour in France toward the end of the year, and finally at the Théâtre de la Ville in Paris in December.

While *Five Stone Wind* was a full-company work, Cunningham asked Lancaster to think of it, as he himself did, "as one in which the dancers are individual 'characters.'" Lancaster accordingly designed shirts and leotards in various colors and cuts; there were also skirts and pants that the dancers could put on at different moments. Cunningham's own costume, a jumpsuit, was in the same shade of purple as the backdrop, so that he sometimes merged with it.

• • •

During the German tour that followed the engagement in Berlin, an injury to one of the dancers, Alan Good, necessitated a change of program in Duisburg and Cologne. Casting about for a substitute, Cunningham hit on the idea of performing *Scramble* as a repertory piece. Although it had not been done as such since March 1971, almost all of the choreography was included in the material for the Events being performed on the tour, so Cunningham decided it could be performed in repertory, though without its original score (by Toshi Ichiyanagi) and decor (by Frank Stella). Pugliese, Kosugi, and Tudor provided the music, and the dancers wore Events costumes by Lancaster.

On 9 and 10 July, between returning to New York and leaving for Avignon, the company gave two preview performances of *Five Stone Wind*, still in incomplete form, in an open-air theater at Battery Park City, New York, during the First New York International Festival of the Arts. They also performed at the American Dance Festival at Duke University in Durham, North Carolina.

In Avignon, *Five Stone Wind* was performed with either *Points in Space* or *RainForest*. The run opened on 1 August; the performance on 3 August had to be canceled because the mistral, as Cunningham had predicted, was indeed blowing and there was a storm with enormous hailstones. This was the first such cancellation in the company's history. The following night, *RainForest* had to be performed without decor, because the wind would have blown the Warhol pillows away. (One audience member asked for his money back, complaining that the company was putting on an incomplete show.)

On 10 September Cunningham took part in another of Nam June Paik's public-television extravaganzas, *Wrap around the World*, in which he and Tudor performed something called *Transpacific Duet*. Domestic touring resumed in the fall, with performances in Boston; Stanford, California; and Colorado Springs. The company then took up residence at Sundance, Utah, for a videotaping directed by Caplan. When this short residency became a possibility, Caplan and Cunningham had decided that there was not enough time to create a new work for the camera, but that *Changing Steps* could be adapted for the purpose.

> For the video production of *Changing Steps*, Merce and I spoke of breaking up the frame, allowing dancers to pass through it on their way to somewhere else, even to leave the frame and return again, allowing the camera an independence not previously explored.
>
> *Changing Steps* was a piece of choreography already made for the stage. The dance company knew it and because of its structure of overlapping sections, Merce said I could do whatever I wanted to with the camera. That flexibility allowed me to shoot stage rehearsals of the piece on the road [on tour in Germany], and look for different settings to put the dancers in. The sequence of what comes after what was decided in the editing room after the shooting. Each section of dance was approached separately with the number of dancers determined by the space. . . .
>
> The music was added later. . . . John Cage sent me finished recordings that I could lay in where I felt it would work best.
>
> What made *Changing Steps* unique was the fact that it had a history, since Merce first made the piece in 1973. Black and white half-inch open reel videotape had been made during rehearsals in 1974 and I thought it would be interesting to use it, where possible. Sections are repeated in both the black and white archival material and the current color material, allowing the viewer to see the historic layers of the transfer of the choreography from dancer to dancer.[5]

In mid-November the company returned to France to perform in Toulon, Grenoble, Caen, Le Havre, and Brest—either Events or repertory programs, some of them including *Five Stone Wind*. The tour ended on 7 December in Brest, but the company returned to France for a holiday season at the Théâtre de la Ville, from 20 to 29 December, with a break over the Christmas weekend.

1989

CARGO X

Cargo X was the first product of what was intended to be another three-year, three-commission project like that sponsored in Minneapolis by the Walker Art Center, this time in cooperation with the Sharir Dance Company at the University of Texas, Austin, directed by Jacov Sharir. During the Cunningham company's res-

idence in Austin to complete the work, the company also performed in Houston and San Antonio, and in Austin there was a conference, "Merce Cunningham: Critical Perspectives," concurrently with the performances there at the end of January.

Cargo X was a work for seven dancers; there were two, alternating casts. The title had no particular significance, Cunningham told an interviewer: "It's made up. It can mean anything. Cargo means something going around and moving around, although it doesn't have anything to do with the dance. And I thought that if I added an X that would confuse it all even further."[1]

The most important decorative element was a ladder, which stood at the back of the stage and also played a part in the choreography: the dancers moved it during the piece, tilting it, laying it on its side, or carrying it from one place to another. They left the stage only to fetch plastic flowers, which they attached to the ladder. The audience was free to interpret the significance of these actions, and props, as it wished. Although the prevailing mood of the

dance was lighthearted, the activity around the ladder also gave the piece an eschatological feeling.

My idea was a ladder about 6 or 7 feet tall. We've got one in our studio in New York to work with—it's a ladder with a top and one of those things you let down and put the paint bucket on. But we were touring in France in Toulon in November and I walked into the theatre and there was a beautiful ladder—it was like a children's idea of a ladder. I looked at it and I thought, "That's marvelous—I want that ladder."

[The theater's technical crew] were a little puzzled by this to begin with, and then the chief of the crew said that he didn't think we should have it because it's an heirloom. It had been built around 1900 and it's handmade. He didn't feel it should leave Toulon. Their liaison explained to the crew leader, "But you have to understand that this would mean that a bit of Toulon would go all around the world." They

Cargo X, 1989. Left to right: Kristy Santimyer, Robert Wood, Larissa McGoldrick, Emma Diamond, and Dennis O'Connor. Photograph: Beatriz Schiller.

thought about that and they decided they liked that, so they agreed to let us have the ladder if we got them another one. We got them a blue metal ladder. We played two performances, and after the second performance, the crew decided that they liked what we did so they were glad that we had the ladder.[2]

The dance had three possible endings; Cunningham originally planned five, but only three were ever finished. He would decide which ending to use when he saw the stage on which the performance was to take place. If there were no room in the wings, an ending in which the ladder was carried offstage could not be used.

Dove Bradshaw costumed the dancers in leotards and tights, selecting the colors from the palette she was using in her painting at the time, including dark gray, green, purple, intense pink, chartreuse, and gold. She decided which dancers would wear which colors after watching rehearsals.

Takehisa Kosugi's music was entitled *Spectra*. "My meaning for the word spectra," he told an interviewer, "is the kind of after-image or echo. That idea includes the after-image of sounds."[3] The writer added, "In the work, Kosugi brings together very simple, natural sounds and very sophisticated electronics. He runs various sound sources through digital processing equipment."[4] Among the objects used to produce the sounds were several small tops and some highly polished pebbles. Kosugi also used tape recordings of a flamenco singer, and vocalized himself during the performance, in imitation of them.

FIELD AND FIGURES

On 17 February, soon after the Texas performances, the company was in Minneapolis for another premiere, the second of the Walker Art Center co-commissions. *Field and Figures* was made for fourteen dancers, who were divided into four groups, two of three and two of four. Cunningham acknowledged that he had in mind the idea of the four elements, earth, air, fire, and water. Each group had its own set of phrases, and each group began by dancing alone, then with each of the other groups in turn. Alone, they performed their material in its original form; with the other groups, they performed variations of it. The piece thus had a more clearly evident structure than most of Cunningham's work.

The music, by Ivan Tcherepnin (grandson of the Nicholas Tcherepnin who composed music for Diaghilev's Ballets Russes), was entitled *The Creative Act*, with the subtitle "Heterophonies of a Text of Marcel Duchamp." It was performed by Kosugi, Rob Miller, Michael Pugliese, and David Tudor, then the company musicians. One musician played an acoustic instrument called the boo-bam, a chromatically tuned membranophone; this sound was electronically processed independently from the sounds produced by the other musicians. Tapes of the text by Duchamp, read by Duchamp and Cage, were played; Kosugi recited the same text in broken English, and played the harmonica. These sounds too were electronically processed and manipulated.

The design was by Kristin Jones and Andrew Ginzel, two artists who had collaborated since 1983, creating tableaux that "deal with the physical and spiritual forces of the universe, existing simultaneously in the realms of physics, philosophy and poetry."[5] Anna Kisselgoff described the decor as follows:

> The backdrop was a scrim curtain horizontally striped in shades of gray. The same shades of gray appeared on the costumes for the 14 dancers in the cast. Behind the scrim, small lights occasionally twinkled like stars. At stage left, a set of motorized red poles kept tilting from side to side. Above the stage, on the right, hung a moonlike disk that brightened and faded during the course of the action. A diamond-shaped object was suspended from it and the moon also cast its shadow on the scrim.[6]

• • •

The company returned to New York for its annual City Center season, which opened on the last day of February. *Five Stone Wind*, *Cargo X*, and *Field and Figures* were all shown for the first time in New York, and *Native Green* was revived after a three-year absence from the repertory. The season was immediately followed by a brief visit to Britain for a series of four Events with decor (from *RainForest* or *Walkaround Time*) at the Leicester International Dance Festival, held in the Haymarket Theatre in that city. Another Event, also with the *RainForest* decor, was given at Arizona State University in Tempe on the first two days of April.

The company's performances in Washington, D.C., had hitherto been given on the inadequate stage of the Lisner Auditorium (except for the excerpt from *Native Green* performed at the Kennedy Center Honors Gala in December 1985). In the first week of May, the company finally performed a full week of performances at the Kennedy Center, in the Eisenhower Theatre.

In July the company returned to Europe. After two Event performances in Turin, they took up a week's residency as part of that year's Festival d'Arles. Again the performances coincided with a conference, on the topic of "*L'Instant, la mémoire et l'oubli*." In keeping with this subject, the Cunningham company performed a retrospective "Arles Event" including excerpts from *Story, Winterbranch, Cross Currents, Loops, Walkaround Time, Canfield, Signals, Un jour ou deux, Torse, Locale, Roaratorio,* and *Five Stone Wind*, some of them specially reconstituted for the occasion. The Event was performed in the *Walkaround Time* set. A repertory program included a preview of another new work, *Inventions*. These performances were given in the beautiful Roman Théâtre Antique, where the Rambert Dance Company and GRCOP (the Groupe de Recherche Chorégraphique de l'Opéra de Paris) also danced, both performing programs that included Cunningham works (*Septet* and *Inlets 2*, respectively). There was also a midnight showing of Cunningham films. Before returning home, the company gave a single performance at the Palais des Festivals in Cannes, as part of a Festival Américain.

• • •

Left: *Field and Figures*, 1989. Left to right: Emma Diamond, Dennis O'Connor, Larissa McGoldrick, Robert Swinston, and Patricia Lent. Photograph: Tom Brazil. Inset: *Field and Figures*, 1989. Left to right: Chris Komar, Helen Barrow, Carol Teitelbaum, David Kulick, Victoria Finlayson, and Robert Wood. Photograph: Johan Elbers.

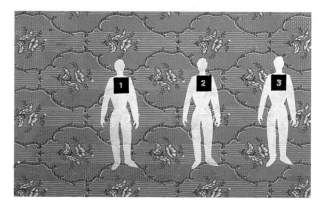

1989 was an astonishingly productive year for Cunningham. For the third week of September, the company was in residence at the University of California in Berkeley, with performances and yet another symposium, the whole under the title "Celebrating Merce Cunningham." During a public interview with Cunningham and Cage conducted by the present writer, an audience member asked, "What is your personal life like at home?" "There was a hushed silence and then, smiling broadly, Cage replied, 'Well, I do the cooking.' Pause. 'And Merce washes the dishes.'"[7]

Not only was *Inventions* given its first full performance, but another new dance, the fourth of the year, was given for the first time on 22 September:

AUGUST PACE

August Pace was a dance for full company, not including Cunningham. The title refers to the fact that the piece was choreographed in August 1989, shortly after the company had returned from Arles and before they left for Berkeley. "The pace," Cunningham has said, "was hectic." Because some dancers were absent with injuries during part of the rehearsal period, he had to work with whomever was free: "I just had to begin making duets."

As so often, Cunningham used a chance process based on the *I Ching*. The structure was a series of seven duets, with interruptions, as in the earlier *Duets*, with the difference that here each of the fifteen dancers had a different continuity of movement. "When they do something together," Cunningham said, "it's because the numbers came up." For instance, he began by giving Victoria Finlayson "almost all of her continuity," then gave Robert Swinston his, and then saw what possibilities there were of their coming together. At various moments, one or the other of the dancers was off-balance, introducing a recurrent movement motif. At one point, for example, a woman was supported by her partner in an off-balance position, and "if they let go, they would both fall down."

The "interruptions" were more than simple crossovers by another couple, as in *Duets*. Cunning-

Clockwise from top: *August Pace*, 1989. Left to right: Larissa McGoldrick, Emma Diamond, Michael Cole, and Randall Sanderson. *August Pace*, 1989. Victoria Finlayson and Robert Swinston. Photographs: Tom Brazil. Sergei Bugaev's (a/k/a Afrika) costume design for *August Pace*, 1989. Opposite: John Cage, MC, and Jasper Johns, 1989. Photograph: Allen Ginsberg.

John Cage, Merce Cunningham & Jasper Johns among others at Spring meeting & induction ceremony to American academy of arts & letters. For John Brow aleen Xtarberg Poet. Meeting was may 17, 1989.   A·G· 1/20/90.

ham originally figured them out separately, not in continuity but in terms of (for example) how many dancers each of them involved. These passages were then inserted into the piece.

The music, *Peace Talks*, was Pugliese's first score for a repertory piece (as distinct from Events to whose accompaniment he contributed). It was based, according to Pugliese, "on the concept of a global union of socially and politically troubled nations." Percussion instruments from such nations were chosen to illustrate peaceful communication through primitive rhythms. The instruments included Chinese tom-toms, Native American drums, the Brazilian beribau, and the sitar. Some were recorded on audiotape, others were played live by Pugliese and Kosugi.

On a visit to Russia in May 1988 for performances of his music by members of the Bolshoi Ensemble, Cage had met the Leningrad painter and performance artist Sergei Bugaev, who used the sobriquet "Afrika." Visiting New York in March 1989, Bugaev had expressed interest in working with Cunningham,

who had agreed to let him design a new work. The design was executed on the back of a sheet of wallpaper that the artist sent to New York in a mailing tube. On the right-hand side of the backcloth were a number of colored pictographs—a fish, an automobile, a rising sun, etc.—executed in folk-art style and arranged in two vertical lines. Each image was numbered. There were also official-looking (but not actually authentic) rubber-stamp imprints. The costumes were turtleneck sweaters and trousers, the men's in white and the women's in black, with stenciled numbers on their backs (the "odd woman out" wore half black, half white). The numbers did not correspond to those against the pictographs.

INVENTIONS

Inventions was given the following evening, 23 September. This was another work for the full company of fifteen (not including Cunningham), of whom no more than seven appeared at one time. Cunningham has described the structure as follows:

Opposite: John Cage, Jasper Johns, and MC, 1989. Photograph: Timothy Greenfield-Sanders. This page: Jasper Johns's *Dancers on a Plane*, 1980–81.

The dance is comprised of sixty-four separate phrases, the continuity of the phrases arranged by chance operations with the further chance possibility of additions or inventions added to any single phrase.

Cage's music was called *Sculptures musicales*, a title, like the music's process, derived from a note by Duchamp in the *Green Box for a Sculpture musicale*: "Sounds lasting and leaving from different places and forming a sounding sculpture, which lasts." The music, realized by the company musicians, consisted of a number of sounds "coming out of the silence and lasting, like a sculpture, and then disappearing," according to Cage. "Then there is silence except for the sounds made by the dancers themselves." The nature of the sounds was left to the performers.

The design for *Inventions* was by the Philadelphia artist Carl Kielblock: costumes (leotards and tights) in shades of green against an orange backdrop. The choice of green, Kielblock has said, arose from his observation of colors in the world, where there are more greens than any other color. Orange was chosen for the backdrop as a complementary color to the green. The lighting design was suggested to the artist by an ancient text, *The Yellow Emperor's Book of Internal Medicine*, the philosophy of which is based on five elements. The idea that there are concordances between the seasons and colors led Kielblock to light the dance according to the cycle of seasons,

with a red phase, a yellow, a white, a black, and a green. (For the black, the stage was darkened.) At the first performance, the cycle began and ended with spring, but the lighting plot was designed to change at each performance according to the time of year when it took place.

• • •

At the end of October the company returned to England for the second time that year, for a two-week season at Sadler's Wells. At the same time, an exhibition at the Anthony d'Offay Gallery, London, celebrated the friendship and collaboration of Cage, Cunningham, and Jasper Johns, under the rubric "Dancers on a Plane"—the title of a series of paintings by Johns, one of which belonged to Cunningham, the letters of whose name are interspersed (in reverse) with those of the series' title along the bottom edge of two of the works. ("Jasper came to dinner one night carrying something wrapped in brown paper; he said, 'be careful, it's still wet.'" It was the painting.) Cage was represented by the score of "Solo for Piano" from *Concert for Piano and Orchestra*, and Cunningham by a number of videos. The exhibition traveled to the Tate Gallery Liverpool early in the following year.

Over two years had passed since the company had performed repertory in Britain, and there were several recent works to show for the first time there, including the four made that year. Cunningham even decided to change the program originally announced: in the third program, *August Pace*, not originally scheduled at all, replaced *Fabrications*, which was already included in the first program. This meant that the series included two programs in which he did not appear—a first. Although some observers assumed that this would become a common occurrence, it did not, certainly not for three or four years.

The company's travels were still not over for the year: in mid-November they were back in France for the first engagement in a brief tour of France and Germany, a single Event at the Opéra-Comique in Paris, under the auspices of the Théâtre Contemporain de la Danse/MARS International. There were also single performances in Friedrichshafen, Frankfurt, and Metz. Before this tour, Chris Komar had gone to Seattle to stage *Septet* for the Pacific Northwest Ballet.

1990s

1990

The year began with a tour of the Midwest and New England. The annual season at the City Center ran from 13 to 25 March, and included the first New York performances of *August Pace* and *Inventions*, as well as yet another new work:

POLARITY

Cunningham had agreed to serve during the upcoming summer on the jury of the Concours International de Bagnolet, which had commissioned a work from him, in conjunction with MC 93/Théâtre de Bobigny and the Cunningham Dance Foundation. Like *Cargo X*, the new dance, *Polarity*, was a work for seven dancers and with alternating casts. Cunningham had been intrigued by the fact that the dictionary definition of "polarity" refers not only to the separation of two poles but also to their attraction. There were, then, two distinct types of movement in the piece, one static, the other active. For the static movement, Cunningham divided the body into its different parts and noted the ways each part could move: the lower arm, for example, is more limited in movement than the upper arm, which can move in larger arcs from the shoulder. He used chance processes to determine which part of the body would be moving at any given moment. (To some extent,

therefore, he was returning to the process he used in his earliest chance solo, *Untitled Solo*, of 1953.) These static movements were usually performed by two dancers, or sometimes three or four, who remained in place; only rarely were they executed by a single dancer.

David Tudor's score, *Virtual Focus*, depended on the interaction among strips of metallic material on the dancers' costumes, metal screens behind the backdrop, and radar and ultrasonic frequencies controlled by the composer. Like a feedback system, any interference in the path of the frequency transmission created a signal, which activated the music. The results were the products of chance. Since Tudor chose the dancers to whom he sent out the radar and ultrasonic signals, and the moments at which he did so, the score varied from performance to performance.

William Anastasi's backdrop consisted of two enlarged drawings by Cunningham: at stage right, an owl and a bird that looked like a cross between a crow and a cormorant; at stage left, a cross between a hare and a rabbit. The costumes, designed by Anastasi, were black tights and leotards, over which the dancers wore see-through shirts decorated with strips of the metallic material used in the music. The lighting was designed by Carl Kielblock, designer of *Inventions* in the previous year.

• • •

Pages 250–51: *Trackers*, 1991. Left to right: MC, Randall Sanderson, Helen Barrow, Michael Cole, and Emma Diamond. Photograph: Johan Elbers. This page: *Polarity*, 1990. Left to right: Carol Teitelbaum, Chris Komar, Victoria Finlayson, and Helen Barrow. Photograph: Tom Brazil. Opposite: *Polarity*, 1990. Left to right: Victoria Finlayson, Robert Swinston, Chris Komar, Alan Good, Patricia Lent, Helen Barrow, and Carol Teitelbaum. Photograph: Colette Masson.

253

There was one revival for the City Center season: *Trails*, with its score by Cage and its design by Mark Lancaster. This was given only twice during the season, and then returned to its previous status as Event material.

At the Merce Cunningham Studio, an apprentice program that had been in existence for some time was formalized as the Repertory Understudy Group (RUG), under the direction of Chris Komar. These dancers learned past repertory and worked alongside the company during rehearsal periods. When a dancer left the company, his or her replacement was customarily chosen from among the RUG dancers.

Foreign touring for the year began in mid-April with three performances at the Muziektheater in Amsterdam. Here Cunningham's notations for *Pictures* of 1984 were displayed in a foyer. This engagement was followed by a tour of five Italian cities: Cremona, Modena, Bari, Reggio Emilia, and Ferrara.

In June Cunningham went to France to fulfill his obligation to serve on the jury at Bagnolet. At the same time, Komar and Catherine Kerr were in Paris teaching *Points in Space* to the ballet of the Paris Opéra, for a series of ten performances beginning on 6 June. Cunningham never saw this staging, since he was also busy rehearsing his own company for a performance at the end of the competition at the Maison de la Culture de la Seine Saint-Denis in Bobigny, at which the European premiere of *Polarity* was to be given. Following this, the company went to the Canary Islands for Event performances in Las Palmas and Tenerife, with enough days off to enable them to enjoy the sun and sea. Before returning home, they went back to Italy for two more Events at the Florence Dance Festival.

Back in New York, there was another single, and singular, Event performance in Damrosch Park, New York, on 18 August, as part of the Lincoln Center Out-of-Doors series. Augmented by the members of RUG, the company danced before an audience of about 5,000, certainly its largest audience at any single performance in the United States. On 10 September Cunningham and Jasper Johns were recipients of the National Medal of Arts from President George Bush at a White House ceremony.

American dance was the theme ("An American Story") of the fourth Biennale de la Danse at Lyons in September and October; the Cunningham company performed three Events with decor (from *Walkaround Time*, *RainForest*, and *Five Stone Wind*) at the Théâtre National Populaire in Villeurbanne, and a fourth at Le Cargo in Grenoble. There followed a season in Paris at the Théâtre de la Ville, from 25 September to 6 October, with an accompanying series of classes and lectures at the Théâtre Contemporain de la Danse. During the Paris engagement, Cunningham went to London for one day to receive the 1990 Digital Dance Premier Award, a prize of £30,000 awarded each year to a person who had made an outstanding contribution to British dance, the prize money to be handed over to a dance project of the winner's choice. Cunningham gave his prize to the Rambert Dance Company, to commission a new work from him. (The commission was not fulfilled until two years later.)

At the beginning of November, the Cunningham company began a four-city tour of India (New Delhi, Calcutta, Bangalore, and Bombay) under the auspices of the Indian Council for Cultural Relations and the Indo-US Subcommission on Education and Culture. Two performances were given in each city, always with the same program: *RainForest*, *August Pace*, and *Pictures*.

One last touring date remained at the end of this busy year: five performances in Toronto, Ontario. (Another date in Montreal was canceled owing to a stagehands' strike at the theater.)

1991

Ten years after the last performance of *Exchange* (at Sadler's Wells in London), Cunningham revived the dance for the company's annual season at the City Center, in March. His own role was given to Alan Good, for whom Cunningham elaborated the choreography somewhat. *Exchange* was performed three times, only once more than the revival of *Trails* had been in 1990, but it would be given more often later in the year. There were also two completely new dances:

NEIGHBORS

Neighbors was a work for three women and three men, whom Cunningham described as "three neighborhood couples, probably from the suburbs." When asked if that were all he had to say on the subject, he replied, "Isn't that enough?" Mark Lancaster once again designed the piece, creating for the backdrop a geometric design that was related to a series of paintings he had made in 1990 and exhibited at the Mayor Rowan Gallery in London. Lancaster has written,

This is the first time in over twenty designs for the Cunningham company that a backdrop has had a direct relationship to a painting. Several of the 1990 paintings contain geometric patterns taken from eighteenth-century Nymphenburg figures of Harlequin and Columbine. It was

while working on one of these comparatively small paintings that the idea of using a similar pattern as a backdrop occurred to me, and I suggested the possibility to Merce Cunningham in Paris in September 1990. In early 1991 I was told that there would be six dancers in the piece, three women and three men. I decided that the colors on the drop would be a combination of yellow, blue, black, and off-white. . . .

[The costumes are in] a range of six different colors, related closely to, but not duplicating, those of the backdrop, between pale orange and pale lavender, each in combination with either silver or gold, and each bisected vertically. . . . The spatial ambiguities of the backdrop are subtly exploited by continuous lighting variations, against which the dance is seen in a clear, bright atmosphere lit to suggest an idyllic scene.[1]

The design scheme proved very appropriate to the piece, with its light and witty choreography, *à l'italienne*, in the Cunningham equivalent of ballet's petit

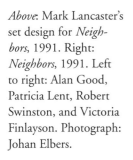

Above: Mark Lancaster's set design for *Neighbors*, 1991. Right: *Neighbors*, 1991. Left to right: Alan Good, Patricia Lent, Robert Swinston, and Victoria Finlayson. Photograph: Johan Elbers.

Left: *Neighbors*, 1991. Left to right: Larissa McGoldrick, Alan Good, and Patricia Lent. Photograph: Tom Brazil. Opposite, left: *Trackers*, 1991. Left to right: Michael Cole, Emily Navar, MC, Carol Teitelbaum, and Robert Wood. Photograph: Johan Elbers. Opposite, right: *Trackers*, 1991. Left to right: Michael Cole, Emily Navar, Carol Teitelbaum, Robert Wood, and MC. Photograph: Tom Brazil.

allegro. Takehisa Kosugi's music, *Streams*, was an electronic composition performed by the composer.

TRACKERS

Trackers was the first work that Cunningham developed in part by using a three-dimensional human animation system called LifeForms, devised by Dr. Tom Calvert, a professor of computing science and kinesiology at Simon Fraser University, Vancouver, British Columbia. Having previously produced programs for computerizing Labanotation scores, Calvert collaborated with two SFU choreographers, Catherine Lee and Thecla Schiphorst, on a program that could help in the creation of dance. Knowing of Cunningham's interest in new technology, they decided to make the program available to him. Schiphorst made several trips to New York to tutor him, and during their sessions Cunningham made several suggestions as to how the program might be improved.

The title [*Trackers*] comes from a button on the dance computer, called "Track." It also refers to tracking with a camera. On the screen, the body moves in relation to the space, as it does on the stage, but if you press "Track" you move in close, like a camera. The first thing I did on the computer was the walking sequence—so again it's like "tracking."

Twenty-five or thirty percent of the movement was worked out on the computer in some way; sometimes it was just a stance, which I would put into the memory like a photograph. I would put in one, then another, and I'd have to figure out how to get from one to the other. At that time the capability of making a whole phrase didn't exist.

Cunningham likened the process to his early work with chance. In fact a device had been incorporated into the LifeForms program to allow him to use

chance to extract movement sequences from the computer memory.

"The thing that interested me most, from the very start," Cunningham told an interviewer, "was not the memory—it wasn't simply notation—but the fact that I could *make* new things." In the same interview he said, "I look at some things and say, 'Well, that's impossible for a dancer to do.' But, if I looked at it long enough I could think of a way it could be done. Not exactly as it's done on the screen, but it could prompt my eye to see something I've never thought of before."[2]

Certain of the movements in *Trackers*—angular movements of the arms performed in a counter-rhythm to those of the legs—were of a kind that was to become instantly recognizable as having originated in the computer. (Cunningham's method was to make the movements of the legs first, then those of the arms and upper body, and finally to put them together. He taught the phrases to the dancers in the same way.) Movement of this sort had appeared in *Polarity* in 1990; though Cunningham had not used LifeForms to develop that dance, he had already begun to experiment with the program, and it seems likely that it had already begun to have some influence on him. At the same time, Cunningham made it clear that "I don't expect [the dancers] to look like the computer. . . . Do you expect dancers to look like Labanotation?"[3] Passages in *Trackers* when the dancers formed into cells and clusters were presumably not computer-generated; with this early model of the software, no more than one figure could be worked with at a time.

The work was for eleven dancers (originally those not in *Neighbors*), including Cunningham himself, who was discovered on stage at curtain-rise together with two of the women. A sweeping gesture from him cued the action to start. Later he reentered two or three times, at one point carrying a portable barre, which he then used as an aid in performing some of his movements, as he did in the studio. With its strange small incidents taking place at various points on the stage—such as one in which a woman took a "bridge" position, bending backward on all fours, while a man crawled into the space beneath her— *Trackers* sometimes had the look of a Surrealist artwork, or even of a proto-Surrealist one, such as Hieronymus Bosch's *Temptation of Saint Anthony*. Whether deliberately or not, this and the "computer" sequences gave it a character very different from that of previous Cunningham dances.

The music (*Gravitational Sounds*) and design for *Trackers* were by Emanuel Dimas de Melo Pimenta and Dove Bradshaw respectively, both of whom had worked on *Fabrications* in 1987.

• • •

It was twenty-five years since the Cunningham company had last performed in Stockholm; in April 1991 they returned there for four performances (three repertory programs, one Event) at the Dansens Hus. There were also a symposium, film screenings, and an exhibition at the Dans Museet, in the same building as the theater.

For the last several years, Elliot Caplan had been working on a documentary portrait called *Cage/Cunningham*, shooting the company in rehearsal and performance, interviewing Cage and Cunningham and many of their friends and associates, assembling archival material, and finally editing all of this, in part according to chance processes, as Cage wished. On 24 March the film had its first preview, at a benefit screening at the Alliance Française in New York.

After a brief engagement at the University of California, Los Angeles, in May, the company left for Europe in June, for appearances first in the Wachauer Theaterfestival (Donau Festival) in Krems, Austria, where the company gave two Events, then in the James Joyce/John Cage Festival in Zurich, Switzerland, an ambitious undertaking that included exhibitions, readings, music, theater, and dance. The company played for a week, during which another new work, commissioned by the city of Zurich for the occasion, was performed for the first time on 20 June:

BEACH BIRDS

"Between the river and the ocean, Beach Birds." This epigraph referred to James Joyce's projected next book after *Finnegans Wake*, which Joseph Campbell had once told Cage would be called *Ocean*. When it was first suggested to Cage that he and Cunningham create a new work for the Zurich festival, he had the idea of writing a large-scale piece with the same title, but no suitable space was available for such a project. *Beach Birds* was done instead.

As with all subsequent dances, *Beach Birds* was in part made through the use of LifeForms. Like *Trackers*, it was a work for eleven dancers, this time without Cunningham. The choreography of his dances is usu-

ally rhythmically strict, but here the rhythm was more fluid—there were almost no counts, so that the sections could differ in length from performance to performance. As Cunningham himself put it,

> It is all based on individual physical phrasing. The dancers don't have to be exactly together. They can dance like a flock of birds, when they suddenly take off. They are not really together; they just do it at the same time.[4]

Even so, Cunningham did not intend the title to be taken literally (though it frequently has been). Yet this was clearly another of his nature studies, based on his observation of birds and, for that matter, of people:

> I had three things in mind: one was birds, obviously, or animals or whatever, but also humans on the beach and also one of the things that I love so much on shores—the way you are looking at a rock and you go around it, and it looks different each time, as though it were alive too. Those three images are part of what I worked at. In dividing the structures the way I always do, I used those three things as something to think about. . . .
>
> It is not meant to be a particular bird, but I used the idea of a bird, and then since dancers are also human beings, I thought I might as well include that.[5]

Cage's music, *FOUR³*, is for four performers on one or two pianos, twelve rainsticks, violin or oscillator, and silence. It consists of "four activities for the

John Cage's score for *Four³*, the music for *Beach Birds*, 1991.

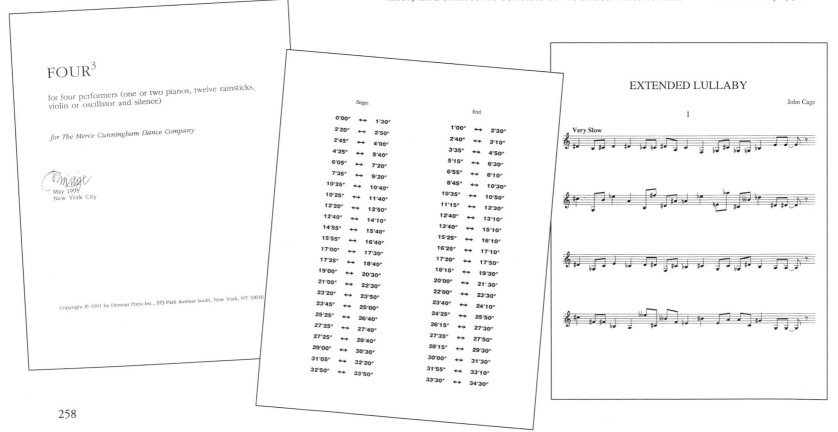

Marsha Skinner's drawing that served as the basis for the costume design for *Beach Birds*, 1991. Pages 260–61: *Beach Birds*, 1991. Left to right: Michael Cole, Randall Sanderson, Helen Barrow, Robert Swinston, Jenifer Weaver, and Carol Teitelbaum. Photograph: Johan Elbers.

four players that interpenetrate within the given time brackets," as follows:

1 Silence (each player may do nothing) within a single bracket.
2 The sound of a rainstick non-agitated simply tilted (each player has three rainsticks). Extensions of one tilt by that of another on the same stick should be virtually imperceptible.
3 One of the players has either the means to express a sine wave in the neighborhood of c'''' [four octaves above middle c] or to play in that frequency area, non vibrato, a violin harmonic with imperceptible bowing, very quietly.
4 Excerpts (any length less than twelve quavers) from *Extended Lullaby* 1–6 and 7–12 (chance-determined variations of the cantus firmus and the counterpoints of *Vexations* by Erik Satie) very slowly and quietly played on one or two widely separated pianos (one "in" the auditorium, the other "outside"). Two pianos playing at the same time must not be in the same tempo, nor as though playing together.

Marsha Skinner, a painter resident in Taos, New Mexico, who had often sketched the dance company

in performance, submitted a design idea for *Beach Birds* that Cunningham decided to use. The dancers were dressed identically in leotards and tights, white up to the collarbone, then black from fingertip to fingertip (the dancers wore gloves) and across the upper part of the chest. The backcloth was a white scrim on which the light varied in color and intensity, according to a lighting plot that Skinner devised using chance methods—the timings did not relate to the dance structure at all, though the changes of light have been interpreted to suggest those that might occur from dawn to dusk on a beach.

• • •

The company was to spend much of the fall in France, including two weeks back in Paris at the Théâtre de la Ville in September. *Exchange* was given at every performance in the first week, together with *Native Green* and a new work commissioned by the Festival d'automne de Paris in celebration of its twentieth anniversary and dedicated by Cunningham to the memory of Michel Guy (who had died the year before), as was the whole season:

LOOSESTRIFE

This was a work for the full company of sixteen dancers, including Cunningham. According to the *Oxford English Dictionary*, "loosestrife" is the name of "two small upright plants growing in moist places," one of them golden or yellow, the other red, purple, or spiked. The plant's botanical name is *Lysimachia*, from the name of the man who discovered it, Lysimachus. The English name "loosestrife" is a mistranslation of the Greek or Latin words that make up the name. "None of this," according to Cunningham, "has anything to do with the dance." He went on, "This dance, as it moves through time, is in a field, where the life may be wild and tame. The space for the dance was divided into thirteen separate sections, or 'territories,' as they were originally called, in any of which loosestrife might be found."

Loosestrife did not remain long in the repertory, though both its movement and its structure were extraordinarily beautiful. A structural device that Cunningham has often used is to break up a phrase into its component parts; while one or more dancers perform the phrase in its entirety, others perform only a part or parts of it. One long section in *Loosestrife* used this device to an extreme, as when Emma Diamond performed a long adagio phrase that was echoed in fragmented form by other dancers on stage. Sometimes she was supported by first one, then

another of the men; other dancers performed the movement without support. Finally, two of the men carried her off.

As for Cunningham himself, while it was true that he could do less and less, he found more and more ways to do it, and in fact his role in *Loosestrife* was longer than usual. The dance began with him alone on stage; he hunched his shoulders, made sweeping gestures from side to side, as if summoning the dancers, then paced back and forth as they entered one by one. As in some earlier dances (such as *Rebus*), he seemed to be controlling or conducting the younger dancers, demonstrating, as it were, movements that they then repeated, albeit with greater physicality.

The music, entitled *Mixed Signals*, was Michael Pugliese's second score for the Cunningham repertory, after *Peace Talks* for *August Pace* (1989). He has described the quality of *Mixed Signals* as "the surprise and discovery of thirty-two backward, forward, half-speed forward, and half-speed backward marimbula tones being channeled between eight to sixteen loudspeakers. Four marimbulas are improvised upon live during the performance."

Carl Kielblock, who had worked on *Inventions* (1989) and on the lighting for *Polarity* (1990), was the designer for *Loosestrife*. As always, Cunningham left him free to do whatever he wanted. The only decision Kielblock made in advance was not to use blue. The costumes were designed before the choreography was completed; they were painted by hand, starting with a gray background to which five colors were added: black, white, red, green, and yellow.

• • •

On the Monday of the Paris season's second week, when there was no performance at the Théâtre de la Ville, *Cage/Cunningham* was screened at the Ciné-mathèque Française in the Palais de Chaillot. *Beach Birds*, *Neighbors*, and *Trackers* all received their first performances in France during the ensuing week.

After four performances in Madrid in November, in that city's autumn festival, the company returned to Paris, where they were to stay during a tour of small towns in the Îles de France, under the rubric "Îles de Danse." A program consisting of *Neighbors*, *August Pace*, and *Trackers* was given in each place except the last, Combs-la-Ville, where the company gave an Event in a very small theater in the round. The European tour ended with two performances of the same repertory program in Blagnac, near Toulouse.

The year ended with another film project. Cunningham and Caplan wanted to make a 35-mm wide-screen film, and decided that *Beach Birds* afforded a suitable subject. The film adaptation, called *Beach Birds For Camera*, was slightly shorter than the original version, and Cunningham added three dancers who had not been in it. The film was shot on location, first at the historic Kaufman Astoria Studios in Queens, New York (the second half of the dance, filmed in color); then at Industria Superstudio in New York City (the first half, filmed in black and white).

1992

The second in the projected trilogy of works co-commissioned by the University of Texas, Austin, was first performed there on the last day of January 1992:

CHANGE OF ADDRESS

There was some speculation that the title of this piece referred to the fact that the street address of the Merce Cunningham Studio, and of the offices of the Cunningham Dance Foundation, changed from 463 West Street to 55 Bethune Street. Although both remained in the Westbeth building, the main office was now at the Bethune Street entrance rather than at West Street. Cunningham himself wrote, somewhat cryptically,

> Address is a fixed place. You change it by moving to a different fixed place. In the moving, you are discombobulated; your balance is upset; you boggle.
>
> The groups in the dance range from a single person to one accommodating 5 maximum, the sexes being mixed, ranging 1 sex to various numerical combinations of the 2.

The ingredients are phrases, 32 in all, that are combined, using chance operations, with unbalances, either by a single person, or in combination. The phrases are set; the unbalances have a certain freedom.[1]

The motif of "unbalances" recurred often in the piece, with people tilting, even to the point of falling. Near the beginning, two women (Kimberly Bartosik and Larissa McGoldrick) ran to stage center, where they hopped, turning in place; then each took the other's left hand and pulled away from the other until they both fell into a sitting position. Several times, three men leaned against each other until two of them fell to the floor. Dancers gathered in groups of three and stood on one leg until they collapsed to the ground. Frédéric Gafner walked backward, stiff-legged, until he nearly toppled over. Many Cunningham dances finish with the action apparently continuing; here the stage emptied, there was a pause, then a blackout, and then the curtain fell.

Walter Zimmermann's music, *Self-Forgetting*, based on a text by Meister Eckhart, was scored for violin, bandoneón or harmonium, glass harmonica, cowbells, and voice, to which other instruments, such as guitar, could be added. The score was performed by the company musicians; each played the same material, but the timing was free, Zimmermann's idea being that the piece "falls apart, then comes together at the end."

Change of Address was the second Cunningham dance designed by Marsha Skinner. The decor was based on one of a series of small chance landscapes (*No. VII*) she had recently completed, its materials being canvas, chokecherry-dyed silk, blue cornmeal, yellow cornmeal, fire, and oil, mounted on board and measuring thirteen inches square. The costumes were in the same earth colors as those on the backdrop;

each had a red stripe running down one side of the body and along one leg.

• • •

At the end of February, the company for the first time visited Alaska, for two performances at the Alaska Center for the Performing Arts in Anchorage. The annual City Center season, opening on 17 March, included the first New York performances of *Beach Birds*, *Loosestrife*, and *Change of Address*, and a revival of *Channels/Inserts* with new costumes by the original designer, Charles Atlas.

TOUCHBASE

In the spring, Cunningham finally had time to fulfill the commission of the new work for the Rambert Dance Company that had been paid for by his Digital Dance Award two years before. The new dance, *Touchbase,* would also enter the repertory of the Cunningham company.

This time Cunningham followed a different procedure from that used, for example, when *Arcade* was commissioned for the Pennsylvania Ballet, in 1985. Then, he had worked with his own company on the dance, which had been taught to the ballet dancers later; this time the Rambert company sent seven dancers to New York to rehearse alongside Cunningham's dancers in the Westbeth studio. The Cunningham company's version would have two casts, and *Touchbase* was created simultaneously on the three casts. Richard Alston, artistic director of the Rambert Dance Company, described the process as follows: "The intention [was] for Merce to create sections of the piece on each group—choreography which [was] then taught to the other groups in a sort of round-robin."[2] The Rambert dancers gave the first performances of the piece in their company's season at the Royalty Theatre, London, in June 1992, final

rehearsals having been supervised by Chris Komar. Once again Cunningham used the computer program LifeForms in devising the choreography.

As the title (and the costuming) suggested, *Touchbase* was playful in feeling, though not referring literally to any particular game. Much of the movement was athletic, but as always there were stillnesses; in the final moments, "the dancers [formed] a frieze with linked hands, then [scattered] to a last tableau in which the dancers downstage, suddenly in the dark, [were] silhouetted against those in the sunshine upstage."[3]

Michael Pugliese described his score, *Icebreeze*, as follows:

> This piece was inspired by my visit to Alaska with the Merce Cunningham Dance Company, and by the winds and sounds of the Pacific Ocean. Also, I had recently been studying the hand drum, which I use in the piece, though not to reproduce any particular sounds from the ocean. Hand drums, wind wands, surf drums, and the waterphone are used to evoke my response to the Pacific Ocean.

Mark Lancaster's design included a lemon-yellow backcloth, in front of which there was a white column with a double gate (modeled on a Chippendale design) attached to it. The dancers opened and closed this gate at various points in the dance. The costumes consisted of summer casual and sports wear that Lancaster and costume design coordinator Suzanne Gallo bought in New York during the initial rehearsal period.

• • •

On 12 August 1992, John Cage died, after suffering a stroke at the Sixth Avenue apartment that he and Cunningham shared. The company was in rehearsal at the time; Cunningham returned to work the next day, and over the rest of the summer completed a new dance. In July and August there was a series of concerts of Cage's music in the garden of The Museum of Modern Art, most of which Cage and Cunningham had attended; the final concert took place after Cage's death.

In September a series of European engagements began; the first was in Luxembourg, where the company had been invited to perform at the Second European Congress of Viscero-Synthesis. From there the company went to Frankfurt, to perform in a Cage festival that had been planned before his death to celebrate his eightieth birthday. They returned briefly to New York before going back to Germany for performances in Dresden and Cottbus at the beginning of October. The tour continued in France, at Clermont-Ferrand and Nîmes, then in Belgium, at Antwerp. Next the company went to England, first to Northampton and then to London; in both cities they performed Events. Apart from the fact that Cunningham and the dancers were mourning Cage's loss, this was a period of turmoil in the company, marked by deep divisions between the dancers and the administration—a situation that was not to be resolved for another year.

In the meantime the company again returned home, where, on the last day of October, a celebration "for John Cage" was held in the Westbeth Studio, to which people came from all over the United States and Europe.

ENTER

The dance that Cunningham was working on at the time of Cage's death was a commission from the Paris Festival d'automne, and was to be presented in a series of five performances at the Opéra de Paris Garnier, starting on 17 November. On the 15th, also in the Garnier, there was a first screening of the new film *Beach Birds For Camera*. *Enter* was a long piece, of one hour's duration, and was given each night with a different work from the repertory. ·

> *Enter*, the title for the dance, is derived from LifeForms, the dance computer with which I work.
> Nearly one-third of the phrases of movement that are utilized in this hour-long dance have been originally worked out on and programmed into the computer. The phrases have then been entered into the memory to be brought back when needed. . . .
>
> The structure of the dance, *Enter*, is based on a series of numbers, one through fifteen. The order in which they occur was arrived at by the use of chance operations. One through fifteen refers to the number of dancers in *Enter*, with the addition of one extra, myself.
> Also, one of the numbers, twelve, was divided again, using chance operations, into one through twelve subdivisions as an added possibility.
> The duration of each section, and the division and entrances and exits of the dancers in any given section, have been chance derived.
> The dance, *Enter*, is concerned with humans involved in different experiences of movement.[4]

Cunningham himself had two solo entrances during the dance; as he told an interviewer, "I stand still in one part, and in the other I try to move."[5] The three static positions that he took at different points on the stage in the first entrance were held for lengths of time that corresponded to the three "movements" of Cage's *4' 33"*. He also joined in the final ensemble before everyone left the stage except Michael Cole, Jean Freebury, and Frédéric Gafner, who were leaping around the stage as the curtain fell.

Other striking sections included a long solo for Gafner and a duet in which Emma Diamond and Robert Swinston slowly advanced from the back of the stage, with arms and legs interlocking (this was reminiscent of a duet sequence in *Roaratorio*).

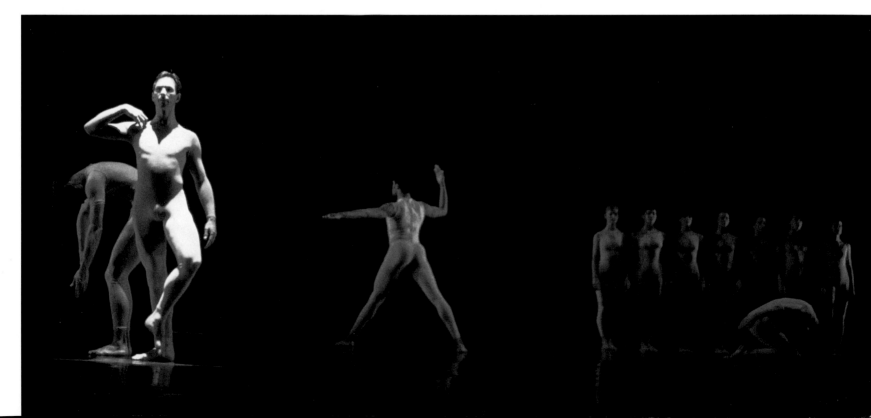

proceeded, the dancers gradually changed to black unitards, though at one point Chris Komar appeared in red shirt and pants before he too changed into black. Cunningham's costume consisted of pants and a shirt, in the same colors as the other dancers' costumes.

The *rideau de scène* (used for the whole engagement at the Opéra, but subsequently only for *Enter* itself) was taken from a drawing by John Cage (selected by him for this purpose before his death), "Where R=Ryoanji R/2—March 1990." (The same drawing had been used for the invitation to the Cage celebration at the end of October.)

• • •

The touring, and the turmoil, were not over yet: from Paris the company went to Douai to perform a single Event, and then to Israel for three performances in Tel Aviv at the end of November and one in Jerusalem on 2 December.

Throughout the year, screenings of *Cage/Cunningham* took place at dance and film festivals, museums and cinemas, in both the United States and Europe.

There were those who saw *Enter* as a dance about death, but the final leaping section certainly left the audience with a sense of continuing. Cunningham himself admitted that "I miss talking with [Cage], not necessarily about dance, but about so many things, because he always had a fresh way of seeing things"; yet he maintained that "the work has not been affected" by Cage's death.[6] Nevertheless, he did not deny "that even though his own work avoids narrative, he, or any dancer, can become a figure of drama."[7]

Concerning his musical score, David Tudor wrote:

Neural Network Plus is a first work incorporating a synthesizer designed around an analog neural network chip by Intel Corp. The musical process displays the device's ability to respond to external signals of many kinds which are gated by the performers, increasing the complexity and unpredictability of the sonic results.

Skinner's backdrop and costume design used photography from a computerized video still by Elliot Caplan. The dancers wore tan unitards; in the early part of the dance the women wore short jackets with a design similar to that on the backdrop. As the dance

1993

In February, the company began another residency in Minnesota with an Event devised by Cunningham for the tiny stage of the exquisitely restored Sheldon Theater, built in 1904 in Red Wing. Next they traveled by bus to Moorhead, in the northern part of the state, to perform another Event at Moorhead State University. That season the Walker Art Center in Minneapolis was showing an exhibition called "The Spirit of Fluxus," which was celebrated by an extravaganza called "FluxArenaRama" at the Arena Health Club, in the city's downtown Target Center; here too the company performed an Event, in the Blue Basketball Court, while the URepCo (University of

Left: *Enter*, 1992. Left to right: Michael Cole, Robert Swinston, and David Kulick. Photograph: Tom Brazil. Below, left: *Doubletoss*, 1993. Left to right: Kimberly Bartosik, Patricia Lent, Frédéric Gafner, and Alan Good. Photograph: Tom Brazil. Below, right: Takehisa Kosugi.

Minnesota Repertory Dance Company) gave a preview of its production of *Changing Steps* in the racquetball courts.

Finally, the company gave two repertory performances at Northrop Auditorium, on 26 and 27 February, which included the third work in the trilogy commissioned by the Walker Art Center, Northrop Auditorium, and the Cunningham Dance Foundation:

DOUBLETOSS

Doubletoss, a work for fourteen dancers, was created as two separate dances that Cunningham then merged, using chance procedures. The title referred partly to the double toss of coins involved in this process, but as usual with Cunningham its significance was ambiguous: duality was a basic concept of this dance.

The design was by Cunningham himself, whose ideas for the set and lighting and for the costumes were realized respectively by Aaron Copp, the company's production manager, and Suzanne Gallo. In front of the backcloth hung a black scrim, with space on either side for the dancers to pass around it, so that they could be seen both behind and in front of it. Cunningham gave Copp a list of chance-generated lighting cues. Each dancer had two costumes to wear, according to which of the two dances they were performing: one was practice clothing, the other more clearly a "costume"—responding to Cunningham's desire that the dancers look nude beneath some kind of transparent covering, Gallo dressed them in flesh-colored leotards and tights, over which they wore an outer garment, each of a different design, made of black net.

The sense suggested by this contrast in costuming that the dancers inhabited two different worlds was reinforced by the fact that they entered the area behind the scrim only when they wore the costumes of black net. As Deborah Jowitt wrote, "There must be rents in the veil that divides the two worlds/dances. Not only do dancers exit in one costume and reappear in another, but people from the two groups do see and touch one another."[1] In fact, the dancers actually supported one another—one section was a number of duets performed simultaneously by pairs of dancers, one in informal clothing, the other in black. (Unusually for Cunningham, in this section men supported other men, and women supported other women.)

Jowitt went on to say, "Through the unusual duets and sudden ensemble actions of *Doubletoss*, Cunningham constantly feeds our awareness of separate coexisting layers of reality. Whatever formal explorations may have prompted this dance, it is impossible not to feel it as a reassurance that what we call death may be simply an opening in the space-time fabric, and that the dead and living dance together on the same stage."[2] Needless to say, Cunningham disavowed any such intention on his part.

The music, *Transfigurations*, was composed and performed by Takehisa Kosugi, who had told Cunningham that the dance "reminded him of bears being attacked by mosquitoes."[3] To produce a desired sound, Kosugi tuned a radio receiver, broadcast with a radio transmitter, and processed the signal digitally—shifting the pitch, panning, etc. The resulting sounds were distributed among eight channels of audio. While performing the piece, Kosugi continued fine-tuning and altering the process, interacting with what the transmitter produced and what he heard in the hall; a certain degree of structure emerged.

• • •

Early in the year, Chris Komar was appointed assistant artistic director; his former position as assistant to the choreographer was assigned to Robert Swinston. Komar's last performances as a dancer would take place during the summer.

In March the company gave its annual season at the City Center. On this occasion one critic described them as "the finest collection of dancers ever assembled under one roof."[4] They performed *Touchbase* for the first time during this season, and *Enter* and *Doubletoss* for the first time in New York. During the summer the company performed at both the Jacob's Pillow Dance Festival and the American Dance Festival in Raleigh, North Carolina, which had commissioned a new work from Cunningham as part of its sixtieth-anniversary celebrations:

CRWDSPCR

Cunningham explained the title as follows:

The use of LifeForms, the dance computer, brought about the title. Computer technology is changing our language, condensing words.
    From its original form, Crowdspacer, I have utilized two variants—Crowd Spacer/Crowds Pacer.

The initial impression of the dance was one of nonstop, even frenetic activity, interrupted only by a long, slow solo for Patricia Lent (later danced by Banu Ogan) in which she passed diagonally from upstage left to downstage right. Frédéric Gafner also had a solo, a more vigorous one, in which he jumped up and down more than two dozen times.

The music, "*blues 99*," was composed by John King, who performed it at the premiere with John D. S. Adams and Kosugi. It is produced through electronic transformations of the sounds of a Dobro steel guitar, played slide. According to an interviewer, King said "Cunningham gave him three pieces of information about the dance: its length, its title, and that there would be groups of dancers on the stage. . . . King said he instantly got a picture of urban life, and knew what he had to do."[5]

Mark Lancaster's multicolored costumes divided the dancers' bodies into fourteen sections, vertically and horizontally; Cunningham had told Lancaster that that was what the LifeForms computer program did. Other influences were costume designs by the Russian Constructivist painter Kasimir Malevich. Having made a basic drawing of a dancer's figure, Lancaster had photocopies made, which he then colored in—originally thirty for men and thirty for women. He then reduced these to the required numbers, choosing those with the most variety in the colors and in the kinds of divisions. Suzanne Gallo assigned the designs to the individual dancers at random, cutting out the pieces, dying them, and then reassembling them. At first Lancaster used two colors, then added a third; he also gave some costumes white areas. He decided not to use primary colors, but those between the primaries; gray was also important. There was an aquamarine backcloth, and the lighting featured a dappled floor pattern.

• • •

From Raleigh the company flew straight to France, to perform in a festival at Chateauvallon, near Toulon. *Enter* was given on the open-air stage on 23 and 24 July, preceded by *Beach Birds* on the first evening and *Neighbors* on the second. The company returned to New York, then flew back to Europe a month later for performances at the Staatsoper Unter den Linden in Berlin; again *Enter* was given with a different piece each evening (*Beach Birds, Change of Address, Doubletoss*).

At the time of his death, Cage had been working with Julie Lazar, curator of the Museum of Contemporary Art, Los Angeles, on an exhibition to be called "Rolywholyover" (naturally, a word from Joyce), subtitled "A Circus for Museum." His idea was that parts of the exhibition would change from day to day, according to computer-generated chance operations. The show finally opened on 8 September. Later that

month the Cunningham company performed *Change of Address* in a benefit performance at the Joyce Theater in New York, to celebrate the twentieth anniversary of the Fund for Dance (which was, however, to go out of existence soon afterward). The program was shared with American Ballet Theatre, which danced Frederick Ashton's *Symphonic Variations*, and the Mark Morris Dance Group, which danced Morris's *Grand Duo*, a unique and marvelous combination.

Meanwhile Cunningham had two choreographic projects to work on. The first was a work for the Boston Ballet, under the auspices of the Kennedy Center's Ballet Commissioning Project, "a multi-year program to commission and produce new ballets by leading American choreographers for six of the nation's outstanding ballet companies. . . . *Breakers* [was] the fourth premiere to result from this project."[6] This time Cunningham reverted to his usual practice of creating the work on his own company, after which Komar and Swinston taught it to the dancers of the Boston Ballet. The premiere of the piece was to take place during the ballet company's October season at the Kennedy Center in Washington, D.C., but this season was canceled owing to a strike of musicians at the Opera House, and the premiere was postponed.

The second project was even more ambitious: it had become evident that the work Cunningham and Cage had had to shelve at the time of the James Joyce/John Cage Festival in Zürich two years before, to be called *Ocean*, could now be realized as a commission from festivals in Brussels and Amsterdam. Cunningham therefore began work on the choreography, with the plan of completing a third of it by the end of the year and the remaining two-thirds during the first months of 1994.

1994

Early in January, the company left for a tour of Japan. As he had planned, Cunningham had choreographed a third of *Ocean* before leaving on this tour. In two weeks the company visited four cities: Tokyo, Takamatsu, Osaka, and Kyoto. On their return from Japan Cunningham resumed work on *Ocean*, completing the second installment before the company's annual season at the City Center.

A week before that season started, Mikhail Baryshnikov's White Oak Dance Project opened a short season at the New York State Theater with a repertory

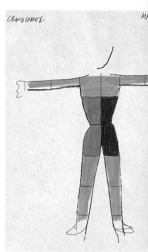

Above: Mark Lancaster's costume designs for *CRWDSPCR*, 1993. Opposite, top: Stills from the film *CRWDSPCR*, 1996, directed by Elliot Caplan showing MC using "LifeForms." Opposite, bottom: *CRWDSPCR*, 1993. Left to right: Jenifer Weaver, Jeannie Steele, Frédéric Gafner, Jean Freebury, and Alan Good. Photograph: Rebecca Lesher.

including a revival of Cunningham's *Signals*, staged by Chris Komar, with new costume and lighting design by Brice Marden. Baryshnikov generously offered to make the opening night, 1 March, a benefit for the Cunningham Dance Foundation, to celebrate Cunningham's seventy-fifth birthday (somewhat prematurely; it actually fell on 16 April.)

During the Cunningham season that followed, the company gave the first New York performances of *CRWDSPCR* and of a revival of *Sounddance*, staged by Komar and Meg Harper, which had not been performed since the summer of 1980. By arrangement with the Boston Ballet, it also gave the premiere of the new dance:

BREAKERS

Breakers was originally a work for the Kennedy Center's Ballet Commissioning Project for the Boston Ballet, unknown to me except as a company of classical dancers. I choreographed the dance on my company, continuing to utilize movement ideas that are interesting to me now, rather than being concerned with a dance intended for classically trained dancers.

The result may be two variations of the same dance, one made for my company, the other a translation [for] the Boston Ballet dancers by Chris Komar and Robert Swinston, the Boston dancers assuming the complexities of the ges-

tures in their way based on their training and commitments.[1]

Breakers was a dance for fourteen dancers, partly choreographed, like all Cunningham's recent works, with the use of the LifeForms computer program. The Boston Ballet version was performed for the first time at the Kennedy Center two weeks after the Cunningham company's premiere.

John Driscoll wrote an unpublished note on his music, *CyberMesa*:

CyberMesa focuses upon the use of acoustical resonance (from the microscopic to the architectural scale). It combines unique instruments (ultrasound trombones) which respond to small physical movement (resonant fishing pole microphones) which scan the resonant nodes of the performance space, along with other acoustically and electronically generated sound sources.

Also utilized in the piece are two custom-made CDs, with digital audio production by Tom Hamilton, which contain the recorded source materials. These source signals, played back on a dual CD player, allow the performers random access to any point within over two hours of recorded material along with 0–50% speed changes. A four-channel electronic panning device is also instrumental in creating a dynamic spatial sound architecture.

Left: *Breakers*, 1994. Left to right: Michael Cole, Jenifer Weaver, Glen Rumsey, China Laudisio, Emma Diamond, Thomas Caley, Cheryl Therrien, Frédéric Gafner, and Robert Swinston. Photograph: Johan Elbers. Opposite: Marsha Skinner's costume designs for *Ocean*, 1994.

The design was by Mary Jean Kenton, who wrote,

I am a painter who worked with rectangles on grids in the late 1960s and early 1970s and who then, in response to the changing artistic climate of that period, felt that literally taking the rectangles off the canvas, and using a number of them to form one work, was a more interesting and timely way in which to proceed.

In 1973 I began a large-scale piece titled *The Free Rectangles*, on which I am still at work. It is made with acrylic paint on heavy pressed board. In time I began similar groupings in watercolor on paper, one of which I gave to John Cage and Merce Cunningham, and to which I eventually added significantly so that it could be used in John Cage's *Rolywholyover A Circus*. Titled *The Floating Rectangles*, it contains a little over 400 pieces.

When Merce Cunningham asked me to do a design for the Dance Company I wanted to do something related to my already established painterly concerns, and I informally adapted *The Floating Rectangles Floating* as a working title for my designs. I envisioned the fabric panels on the dancers' clothing literally floating when activated by their movements.

In a production meeting, Aaron Copp, production manager of Merce Cunningham Dance Company, and Philip Jordan, director of production of Boston Ballet, developed the idea of using individually constructed rectangles in the background. . . . My sketches presumed a backdrop with the great arch of rectangles painted directly on it, but Aaron's idea . . . permitted the sort of painterly richness that my own paintings and drawings possess.

The relationship of the designs for *Breakers* to my own work is very clear and obvious. . . . Although the lighting is linear and remains the same from performance to performance, it adheres to my standard procedure of establishing a geometric understructure, . . . then exploring a variety of coloristic and textural variations within the basic scheme.

• • •

In April, the "Rolywholyover" exhibition came to the SoHo branch of New York's Solomon R. Guggenheim Museum. In the same month, "Cunningham on Camera," a retrospective of Cunningham's work in film and video, opened at the city's Walter Reade Theater as part of the series "Capturing Choreography: Masters of Dance & Film," while The Museum of Modern Art featured an installation honoring Cunningham on the occasion of his seventy-fifth birthday.

A weekend visit to Berkeley, California, at the beginning of May inaugurated one of the company's most extensive programs of foreign and domestic touring: no fewer than seven transatlantic crossings, back and forth, as well as a trip to Brazil. Before this began, Cunningham completed the third segment of *Ocean*, which received its first performance on 18 May at the Cirque Royal, Brussels, under the auspices of kunstenFestivaldesArts:

OCEAN

Cage's idea was that the dance be presented in the center in a circular space with the audience surrounding the dancers and the musicians further surrounding the audience on all sides so that the sound would come from multiple directions, the 112 musicians being separated around the space. There is no conductor. John Cage had discussed the project with Andrew Culver, who had put his ideas into the computer; this led Andrew to believe that the piece could be completed, using John's ideas. David Tudor [composed] the electronic component of the score, working with underwater sounds.

The piece is in nineteen sections, with fifteen dancers. In principle I have utilized the process based on the number of hexagrams in the *I Ching*, using 64 phrases as the source of movement, although due to the length of the dance, I decided to double the number so that a maximum of 128 phrases would be available. The dance is one and one half hours long, the same as one of our Events.

Choreography in the round has opened up a number of possibilities, particularly in terms of directions and facings. It is not flat space, but curved. The result is that, given the frequency of changes possible, it takes longer to choreograph. Often I find, after an hour's work, that I have covered 15 seconds. . . .

The form of the work allows for solos, duets, trios, and quartets, and group [dances], meaning any number of dancers from five to fifteen maximum. The Cirque Royal in Brussels has four entrance/exit passageways at one end of the circle. I labeled them #1, #2, #3, #4 and then, using chance operations, indicated to the dancers which of these they would use for each entrance or exit.

Each time we go over what has been worked on, I see possibilities missed; through chance operations I try to utilize them. It is amazing to be working in the round, in reference to the space, it brings up Einstein's work about curving space—we tend to think flat. I told the dancers: "You have to put yourself on a merry-go-round that keeps turning all the time." I use chance operations to determine where they face at each moment in a phrase. Difficult but fascinating.

After we have presented *Ocean* in Brussels, there will be another two weeks of rehearsal in New York, then three days to adapt the piece to the Muziektheater in Amsterdam. There the stage can be extended into the house, and there will be both musicians and audience on the back of the stage to complete the circle.[2]

The conception of *Ocean* was credited to both Cunningham and Cage. Cunningham himself was not in the dance, but he sat at a small table next to Tudor and his battery of electronic equipment, making notes and giving cues, so that he remained a presence in the piece. Tudor wrote of the electronic component of the music, *Soundings: Ocean Diary,*

Each performer uses different sound materials, derived from peripheral "ocean" sources: sea mammals, arctic ice, fish, telemetry and sonar, ship noises.

The sounds are preconditioned by a group of input modifiers, and then acoustically presented via a group of output modifiers, which substantially alter their characteristics.

The choice of electronic components effecting these alterations can differ with each performance.

The sound system employs a sophisticated electronic panning process, distributing the sounds among three systems: two clusters of four speakers each, which are moveable, hanging from the ceiling at either side of the space; and an encompassing group of four additional channels. Thus three different architectural spaces are defined.

It is envisioned by the composer that from time to time the sound materials will change with invited contributions.[3]

The music's orchestral component, Culver's *Ocean 1–95*, was played by the Nederlands Balletorkest, augmented by a number of Belgian student musicians. Culver wrote,

Ocean 1–95 consists of 32067 events spread over 2403 pages divided [among] 112 musicians. There is no score, no place where all that will sound simultaneously can be viewed simultaneously. There is no conductor, though two of them—Arturo Tamayo and Georges-Elie Octors—worked brilliantly to introduce the musicians to their individual responsibilities. Played throughout are 5 simultaneous but non-synchronous sequences of compositions, the players jumping from place to place, layer to layer, as they become available, each of the 5 layers having 19 compositions in sequence, hence the 95 compositions referred to in the title. Each time a player enters a new composition he or she will find it composed according to a different set of rules and parameters (1 of 20), and that it must be performed according to 1 of 7 sets of performance practices. . . . *Ocean 1–95* is my homage to John Cage.[4]

Above, left: *Ocean*, 1994, Teatro La Fenice, Venice, 1995. Left to right: Jeannie Steele, Thomas Caley, Matthew Mohr, Jean Freebury, Glen Rumsey, and Cheryl Therrien. Photograph: Claude Gafner. Above: Marsha Skinner's costume designs for *Ocean*, 1994.

Ocean was the third Cunningham dance designed by Marsha Skinner, who wrote,

> To go with James Joyce I've turned to *Moby Dick* for lighting inspiration and to Homer's "wine-dark sea" for the source of the costumes. A literary design for Merce.

> The warm waves blush like wine.
> The gold plow plumbs the blue.
> It was a clear steel-blue sky. The firmaments of air and sea were hardly separable in that all-pervading azure . . . the pensive air was transparently pure and soft . . . the contrast (between sea and sky) was only in shades and shadows.
> Muffed in the full morning light, the invisible sun was only known by the spread intensity of his place, where his bayonet rays moved on in stacks. Emblazonings, as of crowned Babylonian kings and queens, reigned over everything. The sea was as a crucible of molten gold, that bubblingly leaps with light and heat.
> (Herman Melville)[5]

> There are three sets of costumes; we didn't know until we worked with the dancers how and when the changes would be made, or whether there would be more than one set on stage at a time. Only when we came to the space could we begin to do the lighting.[6]

• • •

At the beginning of June, before taking *Ocean* to Amsterdam, the company went to Lisbon for five repertory performances. The performances at the Holland Festival were at the end of the month; for this engagement, the Muziektheater was transformed into a theater-in-the-round.

Briefly returning to New York, the company appeared for one night only (15 July) at Summer-Stage in Central Park, in a program entitled "4′33″ and Other Sounds Not Intended/A Tribute to John Cage." Irwin Kremen, to whom Cage dedicated the score of his famous (or notorious) "silent" piece, gave a talk on its history, and Cunningham and his dancers performed while David Tudor played it.

4′33″

Each of the dancers chose three positions to hold during the piece's three "movements"; a change of lighting indicated when each movement began.

• • •

Pages 274–75: Rehearsal at the Teatro La Fenice, Venice, 1995 for *Ocean*, 1994. Left to right: Robert Swinston, MC, Matthew Mohr, Frédéric Gafner, Cheryl Therrien, Banu Ogan, Jared Phillips, Lisa Boudreau, Jeannie Steele, Glen Rumsey, China Laudisio, Michael Cole, Thomas Caley, Jenifer Weaver, and Kimberly Bartosik. Photograph: Claude Gafner. (The Cunningham Company was the last to perform in the Fenice before it was destroyed by fire in January 1996.)

At the end of July the company was in Vienna, to perform in the festival called Im Puls•Tanz in Wien, part of the Internationale Tanzwochen Wien. It was, of course, in Vienna, thirty years before, that the Cunningham company had performed the first Event, *Museum Event No. 1*. To commemorate that anniversary, the second of the three performances (at the Volkstheater, not the Museum des 20.Jahrhunderts, as thirty years earlier) was an Event, and even included some passages that were probably given in 1964 (e.g., excerpts from *Suite for Five* and *Æon*).

A month later the company had again crossed the Atlantic to perform, for the first time since 1979, at the Edinburgh Festival. Back in New York two weeks later, they opened a week's season of Events at the Joyce Theater. Renewing his collaboration with Cunningham, Robert Rauschenberg created a large painting (titled *Immerse*) that was used as the decor. In the last two of these Events, *4′33″* was the finale. Immediately following this short season, the company left for a week's residency in Pittsburgh, which included panels, exhibitions, film screenings, lectures, and one repertory performance at the end of the week.

By the second week in October, the company was back in Europe, first in Saint-Médard-en-Jalles, near Bordeaux, and then in Antwerp, for a return visit to deSingel. There had been talk of further performances of *Ocean* in São Paulo, Brazil, but this had come to nothing; instead, at the end of October the company gave three Events there in the Teatro Sesc Pompéia, part of an extraordinary cultural complex.

There remained one final tour in this extraordinarily busy year, a long one encompassing several towns in France and one in Germany: Lyons, Ludwigshafen, Mulhouse, Valence, Nîmes, Aix-en-Provence, and finally Marseilles. The company finally returned home a few days before Christmas.

Queen Elizabeth II of England had characterized 1992 as an "annus horribilis" for the royal family. The year 1994 was an "annus mirabilis et horribilis" for the Merce Cunningham Dance Company. It was the year in which the internal strife that had plagued the company was finally resolved, not without anguish. But it was a year of triumphant progress through many cities at home and abroad. And fifty years after Merce Cunningham's first concert with John Cage in New York in 1944, which Cunningham has said marked the beginning of his career as a choreographer, their collaboration achieved its final manifestation in the production of *Ocean*.

FOUR EVENTS THAT HAVE LED TO LARGE DISCOVERIES (19 SEPTEMBER 1994)

During the course of working in dance, there have been four events that have led to large discoveries in my work.

The first came with my initial work with John Cage, early solos, when we began to separate the music and the dance. This was in the late forties. Using at that time what Cage called a 'rhythmic structure'—the time lengths that were agreed upon as beginning and ending structure points between the music and the dance—we worked separately on the choreography and the musical composition. This allowed the music and the dance to have an independence between the structure points. From the beginning, working in this manner gave me a feeling of freedom for the dance, not a dependence upon the note-by-note procedure with which I had been used to working. I had a clear sense of both clarity and interdependence between the dance and the music.

The second event was when I began to use chance operations in the choreography, in the fifties. My use of chance procedures is related explicitly to the choreography. I have utilized a number of different chance operations, but in principle it involves working out a large number of dance phrases, each separately, then applying chance to discover the continuity—what phrase follows what phrase, how time-wise and rhythmically the particular movement operates, how many and which dancers might be involved with it, and where it is in the space and how divided. It led, and continues to lead, to new discoveries as to how to get from one movement to the next, presenting almost constantly situations in which the imagination is challenged. I continue to utilize chance operations in my work, finding with each dance new ways of experiencing it.

The third event happened in the seventies with the work we have done with video and film. Camera space presented a challenge. It has clear limits, but it also gives opportunities of working with dance that are not available on the stage. The camera takes a fixed view, but it can be moved. There is the possibility of cutting to a second camera which can change the size of the dancer, which, to my eye, also affects the time, the rhythm of the movement. It also can show dance in a way not always possible on the stage: that is, the use of detail which in the broader context of theatre does not appear. Working with video and film also gave me the opportunity to rethink certain technical elements. For example, the speed with which one catches an image on the television made me introduce into our class work different elements concerned with tempos which added a new dimension to our general class work behavior.

The fourth event is the most recent. For the past five years, I have had the use of a dance computer, Life-Forms, realized in a joint venture between the Dance and Science Departments of Simon Fraser University in British Columbia. One of its uses is as a memory device: that is, a teacher could put into the memory of the computer exercises that are given in class, and these could be looked at by students for clarification. I have a small number of particular exercises we utilize in our class work already in the memory. But my main interest is, as always, in discovery. With the figure, called the Sequence Editor, one can make up movements, put them in the memory, eventually have a phrase of movement. This can be examined from any angle, including overhead, certainly a boon for working with dance and camera. Furthermore, it presents possibilities which were always there, as with photos, which often catch a figure in a shape our eye had never seen. On the computer the timing can be changed to see in slow motion how the body changes from one shape to another. Obviously, it can produce shapes and transitions that are not available on humans, but as happened first with the rhythmic structure, then with the use of chance operations, followed by the use of the camera on film and video and now with the dance computer, I am aware once more of new possibilities with which to work.

My work has always been in process. Finishing a dance has left me with the idea, often slim in the beginning, for the next one. In that way, I do not think of each dance as an object, rather a short stop on the way.

—MERCE CUNNINGHAM

Notes

Throughout this book, quotations of Merce Cunningham that are otherwise unattributed are from conversations between Cunningham and the author, dating from roughly 1978 on. Similarly, unattributed quotations of John Cage are from conversations between Cage and the author, dating from the same time.

Much of the documentary material quoted in the book comes from files in the Archives of the Cunningham Dance Foundation. Not all of this material is supplied with complete bibliographical information; many of the press clippings collected over the years, for example, are without page numbers, and some are even undated. It is equally impossible to date some of the interviews conducted by the author. The reader's patience is requested for what is hoped will prove a minor inconvenience.

A number of texts appear often in this book's notes, and constitute a highly selective Cunningham bibliography. They are:

John Cage, *Silence* (Middletown, Conn.: Wesleyan University Press, 1961).

Merce Cunningham, *Changes: Notes on Choreography*, ed. Frances Starr (New York and Frankfurt-am-Main: Something Else Press, 1968), n.p.

Merce Cunningham, "A Collaborative Process between Music and Dance," *TriQuarterly* 54 (Spring 1982): 173–86. Reprinted in Peter Gena and Jonathan Brent, eds., *A John Cage Reader* (New York: C. F. Peters Corporation, 1982), pp. 107–120.

Robert Dunn, *John Cage* (catalogue of compositions) (New York: Henmar Press, 1962).

James Klosty, ed., *Merce Cunningham* (New York: Saturday Review Press/ E. P. Dutton, 1975).

Richard Kostelanetz, ed., *John Cage* (New York: Praeger Publishers, 1970).

Jacqueline Lesschaeve, *The Dancer and the Dance*, rev. ed. (New York and London: Marion Boyars, 1991).

Calvin Tomkins, *The Bride and the Bachelors: Five Masters of the Avant Garde* (New York: Viking Press, 1965).

Calvin Tomkins, *Off the Wall* (Garden City, N.Y.: Doubleday, 1980).

David Vaughan, ed., *Merce Cunningham & Dance Company* (souvenir booklet) (New York: The Foundation for Contemporary Performance Arts, 1963), n.p.

The notes cite these books in abbreviated form.

1919–1939

1. Merce Cunningham, quoted in Lesschaeve, *The Dancer and the Dance*, p. 33.
2. Cunningham, quoted in Alan M. Kriegsman, "Merce Cunningham's Overdue Debut," *The Washington Post*, 30 April 1989, p. G10.
3. Cunningham, preface to Pierre Lartigue, *Plaisirs de la danse: Une Histoire du ballet* (Paris: Messidor/La Farandole, 1983).
4. See Ann Trout Blinks and Ann Thayer, "World-Famous Dancer First Began His Art in Centralia," *The Centralia Daily Chronicle*, 30 August 1986, p. B1.
5. Cunningham, quoted in Lesschaeve, *The Dancer and the Dance*, p. 33.
6. Cunningham, "The Impermanent Art," in Fernando Puma, ed., *7 Arts* no. 3 (Indian Hills, Colo.: Falcon's Wing Press, 1955), p. 76.
7. Ibid., pp. 76–77.
8. "Centralia Classmates Tell about Their Dancer," *Centralia Daily Chronicle*, 30 August 1986, p. B1.
9. Ibid.
10. Cunningham, quoted in Kriegsman, "Merce Cunningham's Overdue Debut," p. G10.
11. Bonnie Bird and Nina Fonaroff, interviews with the author.
12. According to Cunningham's application for admission to the Bennington School of the Dance at Mills College, Oakland, California, dated 21 March 1939, Cunningham studied music at Cornish with Ellen Wood Murphy and Stephen Balogh; he also took courses in costume design there. I am indebted to Susan Sgorbati of Bennington College for a copy of this document.
13. Bird, interview with the author.
14. J.R.R., "Moore Festival Night Pleases," *Seattle Times*, 7 May 1938, p. 8.
15. "Local Boy in Cornish Dance," *Centralia Tribune*, 11 March 1938, p. 1.
16. Program, Cornish Theater, 29–30 April 1938.
17. Cunningham, interview with the author.
18. Program, Cornish Theater, 4–5 May 1939.
19. Bella Lewitzky, interview with the author.
20. Larry Warren, *Lester Horton: Modern Dance Pioneer* (New York: Marcel Dekker, 1977), p. 87.
21. See Warren, ibid., and "Starting from Indiana," "The Dance Theater of Lester Horton," *Dance Perspectives* 31 (Autumn 1967): 15, 68.
22. Bird, interview with the author.
23. Cage, "Goal: New Music, New Dance," *Dance Observer*, December 1939, pp. 296–97. Reprinted in Cage, *Silence*, pp. 87–88.
24. Cunningham and Bird, interviews with the author.
25. "Seattle Prelude to Ballet Russe Planned by Symphony Group," *Seattle Times*, 15 January 1939, sect. 4, p. 1.
26. Lincoln Kirstein, in Klosty, ed., *Merce Cunningham*, p. 89.
27. Bird, interview with the author.
28. Program note for a performance of *Imaginary Landscape* at the Laban Centre for Movement and Dance, London, July 1980.
29. Cage, "Notes to the Recording of the 25-Year Retrospective Concert of the Music of John Cage, Town Hall, New York, 15 May 1958" (New York: George Avakian, 1959). Reprinted in Kostelanetz, ed., *John Cage*, p. 128.
30. See Dunn, *John Cage*, pp. 35–36. The program for the 1958 retrospective concert (see note 29) lists the original performers as Xenia Cage, Doris Dennison, Margaret Jansen (*sic*), and Cunningham. The 1939 dance performance is not listed in Dunn's catalogue, which gives the first (concert) performance as 9 December 1939, at the Cornish School.
31. Jane Estes, "Cornish Dance Group," *Argus* (Seattle) 46 no. 11 (18 March 1939): 5.
32. "Cornish Shows Surrealist Art," *Seattle Post-Intelligencer*, 22 January 1939, p. 6S.
33. Cage, *Silence*, p. xi.
34. Nancy Wilson Ross, "Why I Believe I Was *Born* a Buddhist," *Asia* 3 no. 5 (January/February 1981): 11.
35. Cage, contribution to "Essays, Stories and Remarks about Merce Cunningham," *Dance Perspectives* no. 34 (issue titled *Time to Walk in Space*, Summer 1968): 13.
36. *Bennington College Bulletin* 7 no. 3 (February 1939). Quoted in Sali Ann Kriegsman, *Modern Dance in America: The Bennington Years* (Boston: G. K. Hall, 1981), p. 82.
37. Schedule of courses attached to Cunningham's application for admission to the Bennington School of the Dance at Mills College, 21 March 1939.
38. See Kriegsman, *Modern Dance in America*, p. 87.
39. Louis Horst, "Modern American Percussion Music," *Dance Observer* 6 no. 7 (August–September 1939): 250–51.
40. Ethel Butler, quoted in Sali Ann Kriegsman, *Modern Dance in America*, p. 84.
41. Cunningham, quoted in ibid., p. 257.
42. Bird, interview with the author.

1939–1941

1. Cunningham, undated letter to Bonnie Bird.
2. Nancy Wilson Ross, undated letter to Bonnie Bird.
3. Joseph H. Mazo, "Martha Remembered," *Dance Magazine* LXV no. 7 (July 1991): 42.
4. Sali Ann Kriegsman, *Modern Dance in America*, p. 101.
5. Nina Fonaroff, interview with the author.
6. Kriegsman, *Modern Dance in America*, pp. 211–14.
7. Edwin Denby, "With the Dancers: Graham's 'El Penitente' and 'Letter to the World'; Balanchine's 'Balustrade,'" *Modern Music* XVIII no. 3 (March–April 1941): 197. Reprinted in Denby, *Dance Writings*, ed. Robert Cornfield and William MacKay (New York: Alfred A. Knopf, 1986), p. 73.
8. Kriegsman, *Modern Dance in America*, p. 221.
9. Denby, "With the Dancers: Ballet Theatre; Graham's 'Punch and the Judy,'" *Modern Music*, January–February 1942. Reprinted in Denby, *Dance Writings*, p. 85.

1942

1. Cunningham, conversation with the author.
2. Jean Erdman, interview with the author.
3. Erdman, quoted in Sali Ann Kriegsman, *Modern Dance in America*, p. 229.
4. Dunn, *John Cage*, p. 35.
5. Cunningham, *Changes*.

1943

1. Cunningham, quoted in Lesschaeve, *The Dancer and the Dance*, pp. 83–84.
2. The program for this event is reproduced in Kostelanetz, ed., *John Cage*, fig. 6.
3. Edwin Denby, "Graham's 'Deaths and Entrances' and 'Salem Shore,'" *New York Herald Tribune*, 27 December 1943, p. 8. Reprinted in Denby, *Dance Writings*, p. 187.

1944

1. Cunningham, *Changes*.
2. Cunningham, "A Collaborative Process between Music and Dance," p. 173.
3. Cunningham, quoted in Lesschaeve, *The Dancer and the Dance*, p. 39.

4. Cunningham, *Changes*.

5. Cunningham, "A Collaborative Process between Music and Dance," p. 174.

6. Cunningham, quoted in Tomkins, *The Bride and the Bachelors,* pp. 244–45.

7. Jean Erdman, "What *Is* Modern Dance?," *Vassar Alumnae Magazine* XXXIII no. 3 (February 1948): 24.

8. This description of the dance first appeared in the program for a performance by Cunningham and Cage at the Woman's Club, Richmond, Va., on 20 November 1944.

9. Dunn, *John Cage,* p. 16.

10. Denby, "Merce Cunningham," *New York Herald Tribune,* 6 April 1944. Reprinted in Denby, *Dance Writings,* p. 207.

11. Cunningham, "A Collaborative Process between Music and Dance," p. 174.

12. Ibid., pp. 174–75.

13. Unidentified clipping from Salt Lake City newspaper, n.d.

14. Cunningham, *Four Walls,* scene XIV. I am indebted to Els Grelinger for giving me a copy of the text.

15. The film, *Integration of Dance and Drama,* is in the Dance Collection of the New York Public Library. These excerpts are also included in Elliot Caplan's film portrait *Cage/Cunningham* (1991).

16. See Deborah Jowitt, "Saving Perry-Mansfield," *Dance Magazine,* January 1992, p. 67.

17. At the first performance, the melodic line was played by a solo flute, whose player happened to be available.

18. Program note, The Woman's Club, Richmond, Va., 20 November 1944. The words enclosed in quotation marks were omitted at subsequent performances.

19. In the dance *Second Hand,* 1970.

20. Nina Fonaroff, interview with the author.

21. Martha Graham, quoted in Robert Commanday, "The Great Force of Martha Graham," *This World* (San Francisco), 3 November 1974.

1945

1. Dunn, *John Cage,* p. 17.

2. Elliott Carter, "Scores for Graham; Festival at Columbia, 1946," *Modern Music* 23 no. I (Winter 1946): 54.

3. Edwin Denby, "Cunningham Solo," *New York Herald Tribune,* 10 January 1945. Reprinted in Denby, *Dance Writings,* pp. 279–80.

4. Denby, "Dudley-Maslow-Bales and Cunningham," *New York Herald Tri-*

bune, 29 January 1945. Reprinted in Denby, *Dance Writings,* pp. 283–84.

5. Denby, "Cunningham's 'Mysterious Adventure,'" *New York Herald Tribune,* 19 May 1945. Reprinted in Denby, *Dance Writings,* p. 317.

1946

1. Baby Dodds, as told to Larry Gara, *The Baby Dodds Story* (Los Angeles: Contemporary Press, 1959), pp. 90–91.

2. Program of second performance, Hunter Playhouse, New York, 12 May 1946.

3. Virginia Bosler Doris, interview with the author.

4. Ann Daly, "Dance in Pittsburgh: The First Fifty Years, 1910–1960," *Carnegie Magazine,* January/February 1985, p. 18.

1947

1. Cage, interview with the author.

2. Cunningham, *Changes*.

3. Ballet Society prospectus, schedule of events for 1946–47, n.d.

4. Dunn, *John Cage,* p. 33.

5. Note in the program for the Ballet Society dance concert at the Ziegfeld Theater, New York, 18 May 1947.

6. Cage, "[On Earlier Pieces]," in Kostelanetz, ed., *John Cage,* p. 129.

7. Lincoln Kirstein, quoted in Klosty, ed., *Merce Cunningham,* p. 89.

8. Dunn, *John Cage,* p. 33.

9. Cunningham, *Changes*.

10. Tanaquil Leclercq, quoted in Nancy Reynolds, *Repertory in Review: 40 Years of the New York City Ballet* (New York: Dial Press, 1977), p. 80.

11. Isamu Noguchi, *A Sculptor's World* (New York: Harper and Row, 1968), p. 130. Reprinted in Cobbett Steinberg, ed., *The Dance Anthology* (New York: New American Library, 1980), pp. 190–91.

12. Frances Herridge, "With the Dancers: Designer Noguchi Brings Sculpture to the Stage," *PM,* 13 July 1947, p. 26.

13. *The Ballet Society,* vol. I (1946–47) (New York: Ballet Society, Inc., 1947), p. 55.

14. Edwin Denby, "The American Ballet," *Kenyon Review* 10 no. 4 (Autumn 1948): 638–51. Reprinted in Denby, *Dance Writings,* p. 525.

15. Kirstein, quoted in Klosty, ed., *Merce Cunningham,* p. 89.

16. Anna Kisselgoff, "City Ballet Turns 30, Still a Different Drummer," *New York Times,* 19 November 1976, p. C22.

17. *The Ballet Society,* vol. I, p. 52.

18. Now Lady Lousada; no relation to Patricia McBride.

19. Note in the program for a dance concert at Hunter Playhouse, New York, 14 December 1947.

20. Dorothy Berea, interview with the author.

21. Lou Harrison, letter to Jonathan Sheffer (conductor of the Eos Ensemble), n.d. (ca. April 1996). I am indebted to Jonathan Sheffer for a copy of this document.

22. Harrison, letter to Sheffer, 14 April 1996, reprinted in the program for a concert by the Eos Ensemble at the Lincoln Center Festival '96, New York, 28 July 1996.

23. N. K. (Nik Krevitsky), "Merce Cunningham and Company," *Dance Observer* 15 no. 1 (January 1948): 5.

1948

1. E. K. (Ellen Kraft), "[Irwin] Shaw and Cunningham Analyze Isolation of Drama and Dance," *Vassar Miscellany News* 32 no. 18 (3 March 1948): 5.

2. "Cunningham," *Vassar Chronicle,* 6 March 1948.

3. Cunningham, "A Collaborative Process between Music and Dance," p. 175.

4. Martin Duberman, *Black Mountain: An Exploration in Community* (Garden City, N.Y.: Anchor Press, 1972), pp. 288–90.

5. "Campus News," *Black Mountain College Bulletin* 6 no. 4 (May 1948): 5. I am indebted to Mary Emma Harris for furnishing me with a copy of this publication.

6. "'New Arts Weekend' Starts Tonight with First Program in Series of Four by Experimentalists in Humanities," *The Stephens Life* (Stephens College, Mo.) XX no. 28 (7 May 1948): 1.

7. Dunn, *John Cage,* p. 7.

8. Buckminster Fuller, quoted in an unidentified clipping.

9. Elaine de Kooning, "De Kooning Memories," *Vogue* (New York), December 1983, p. 394.

10. Ibid.

11. Duberman, *Black Mountain,* pp. 301–4.

12. De Kooning, "De Kooning Memories," p. 394.

13. Cage, "Defense of Satie," in Kostelanetz, ed., *John Cage,* p. 81.

14. Duberman, *Black Mountain,* pp. 291–92.

15. Pat Grant, "Dance Recital Evaluated; Explained by Performers," *Vassar Chronicle* 6 no. 16 (12 March 1949): 3.

16. Herta Pauly, "Miss Pauly Finds Cunningham-Cage Performance Delightful," *Vassar Miscellany News* 33 no. 18 (16 March 1949): 3–4.

17. Dunn, *John Cage,* pp. 10–11.

18. Program of lecture-demonstration, Cooper Union, New York, 24 November 1950.

19. Dorothy Berea, interview with the author.

20. See Kostelanetz, ed., *John Cage,* plate 17.

21. Cage, *Silence,* p. xi.

1949

1. Sybil Shearer, letter to the author. Shearer's review, "Merce Cunningham," appeared in *Dance News* XIV no. 3 (March 1949): 9.

2. Cage, contribution to "Essays, Stories and Remarks about Merce Cunningham," *Dance Perspectives* no. 34 (issue titled *Time to Walk in Space,* Summer 1968): 19.

3. See Ellsworth J. Snyder, "Chronological Table of John Cage's Life," in Kostelanetz, ed., *John Cage,* p. 36.

4. Minna Daniel, interview with the author.

5. Cunningham, letter to John Heliker, March 1949. The letter remains in Heliker's possession.

6. Cunningham, "An American in Paris/A Report from Merce Cunningham," *Dance Observer* 16 no. 9 (November 1949): 132.

7. Information contained in a wall label in Heliker's retrospective exhibition "A Celebration of Fifty Years," at the Kraushaar Galleries, New York, in 1995. Another artist to use Cage's *Perilous Night* title, of course, was Jasper Johns, for a painting of 1982.

8. Cunningham, "An American in Paris," p. 132.

9. Ibid.

10. Cunningham, interview with the author. See also Cunningham, "An American in Paris," and Paul Ruhstrat, "The Dance Scene in Paris," *Dance Observer* 15 no. 8 (October 1948): 100–101.

11. Betty Nichols, interview with the author.

12. I am indebted to Pierre Lartigue for providing me with the exact date of the performance and with a copy of Cage's handwritten invitation to it.

13. Cunningham, "An American in Paris," p. 132.

14. Maurice Pourchet, "The 1948–49 Ballet Season in Paris," *Ballet Annual* no. 4 (London: A. & C. Black, 1950), p. 123. I have not succeeded in tracing the original review.

15. Nichols, interview with the author.

16. Merce Cunningham, "An American in Paris," pp. 131–32.

1950

1. R. S. (Robert Sabin), "Merce Cunningham Dance Recital," *Musical America* LXX no. 3 (February 1950): 353.
2. N.K. (Nik Krevitsky), "Merce Cunningham," *Dance Observer* 17 no. 2 (February 1950): 25.
3. Cage, *Silence*, p. 127.
4. Ibid., p. ix.
5. Ibid., p. 126.
6. Meyer Schapiro, *Modern Art/19th & 20th Centuries/Selected Papers* (New York: George Braziller, 1978), p. 219.
7. Calvin Tomkins, "The Antic Muse," *The New Yorker*, 17 August 1981, p. 80.
8. Adolph Gottlieb and Mark Rothko, "Statement," in Herschel B. Chipp, ed., *Theories of Modern Art: A Source Book by Artists and Critics* (Berkeley: University of California Press, 1968), p. 545. Quoted in Barbara Haskell, *Blam!: The Explosion of Pop, Minimalism, and Performance 1958–1964*; exh. cat. (New York: Whitney Museum of American Art, in association with W. W. Norton & Company, 1984), p. 89.
9. Calvin Tomkins, "The Antic Muse," p. 80.
10. Mary Emma Harris, author of *The Arts at Black Mountain College* (Cambridge, Mass.: The MIT Press, 1987), believes that this must have taken place in May of that year.
11. Remy Charlip, interview with the author.

1951

1. Tomkins, "John Cage," *The Bride and the Bachelors*, p. 105.
2. *The I Ching or Book of Changes*, the Richard Wilhelm translation rendered into English by Cary F. Baynes, with a foreword by C. G. Jung (New York: Pantheon Books, Bollingen Series XIX, 1950).
3. Cage, "Composition," *Silence*, p. 59.
4. Cunningham, "A Collaborative Process between Music and Dance," pp. 175–76.
5. Cunningham, "Two Questions and Five Dances," *Dance Perspectives* no. 34 (issue titled *Time to Walk in Space*, Summer 1968): 49/51.
6. Remy Charlip, "Composing by Chance," *Dance Magazine* XXVIII no.1 (January 1954): 17/19.
7. John Heliker, interview with the author.
8. Charlip, "Composing by Chance," p. 17.
9. Margaret Lloyd, "Novelties in the Dance," *Christian Science Monitor*, 9 January 1954, p. 4.
10. Pat Dunbar, "Modern Dance Recital at Meany Hall," *Seattle Times*, 13 April 1951, p. 29.
11. L. H. (Louis Horst), "Merce Cunningham and Dance Company," *Dance Observer* 21 no. 2 (February 1954): 26.
12. David Tudor, interview with the author.
13. Cunningham, quoted in Tomkins, "Merce at Seventy-Five," *The New Yorker*, 7 March 1994, p. 74.

1952

1. *Excerpts from Symphonie pour un homme seul* was later retitled *Collage*.
2. Cunningham, *Changes*.
3. Cunningham, unpublished notes.
4. Ibid.
5. Vicki Goldberg, "A 53-Year Bond between Breakers of Rules," *New York Times*, 5 March 1995, p. 32.
6. Donald McKayle, interview with the author.
7. Joan Brodie, "Choreographics," *Dance Observer* 19 no. 5 (May 1952): 70.
8. Tomkins, *The Bride and the Bachelors*, p. 117.
9. Anon, "The Summer at the Burnsville School of Fine Arts," *Dance Observer* 19 no. 9 (November 1952): 139.
10. Ibid.
11. See Mary Emma Harris, *The Arts at Black Mountain College*, p. 231.
12. Cunningham, "A Collaborative Process between Music and Dance," pp. 176–77.
13. See Richard Kostelanetz, "Conversation with John Cage," in Kostelanetz, ed., *John Cage*, p. 27.
14. Cage, "Foreword," *Silence*, p. x.
15. Francine du Plessix Gray, "Black Mountain, an American Place," *New York Times Book Review*, 31 July 1977, sect. 7, p. 3. A slightly different version is quoted in Duberman, *Black Mountain*, p. 352.
16. Calvin Tomkins, "Figure in an Imaginary Landscape," *The New Yorker*, vol. 40, 28 November 1964, p. 104. Reprinted in Tomkins, *The Bride and the Bachelors*, p. 117, and *Off the Wall*, p. 74. The account in *Off the Wall* itself differs slightly from the earlier ones.
17. Michael Kirby, "Introduction," *Happenings* (New York: E. P. Dutton, 1965), pp. 31–32.
18. Haskell, *Blam!*, pp. 31 and 110.
19. According to Dunn's catalogue of Cage's compositions for 1952, in his *John Cage*, p. 43, Tudor performed this composition at Black Mountain on 12 August 1952. The date given for Tudor's concert in a Black Mountain "calendar for august 1952," however, is Monday the 11th, not the 12th. According to this calendar, Cage was to give a concert on the 16th and Cunningham on the 17th. There seem to have been no programs for these performances. The exact date of the theater event is not known.
20. Mary Emma Harris, *The Arts at Black Mountain College*, pp. 226–28.
21. Harris, interview with Cage, 1974, in Kostelanetz, *Conversing with Cage* (New York: Limelight Editions, 1988), p. 104.
22. Cage, quoted in Duberman, *Black Mountain*, p. 351. Duberman quotes several other different descriptions of the performances; see pp. 350–58.
23. Cage, quoted in Tomkins, *Off the Wall*, p. 70.
24. Ibid., p. 77.
25. Carolyn Brown, untitled essay, *Dance Perspectives* 34 (issue titled *Time to Walk in Space*, Summer 1968): 29.
26. See Minna Lederman, "John Cage: A View of My Own," in Peter Gena and Jonathan Brent, eds., *A John Cage Reader*, pp. 152–53.
27. Brown, interview with the author.

1953

1. L. G. (Louise Gutman), "Merce Cunningham Lecture-Demonstration," *Dance Observer* 20 no. 7 (August–September 1953): 107.
2. Cunningham, *Changes*.
3. Cunningham, quoted in Lesschaeve, *The Dancer and the Dance*, p. 90.
4. Carolyn Brown, interview with the author.
5. Cunningham, *Changes*.
6. Ibid.
7. Remy Charlip, "Concerning Merce Cunningham and His Choreography: Composing by Chance," *Dance Magazine* XXVIII no. 1 (January 1954): 19.
8. Cunningham, *Changes*.
9. Program note, Marine's Memorial Theater, San Francisco, Calif., 15 November 1955.
10. Earle Brown, Remy Charlip, Marianne Simon, and David Vaughan, "The Forming of an Aesthetic: Merce Cunningham and John Cage," transcript of a panel discussion held on 16 June 1984, at the Dance Critics' Association Conference, in *Ballet Review* 13 no. 3 (Fall 1985): 38.
11. Carolyn Brown, interview with the author.
12. Dunn, *John Cage*, p. 8.
13. Cunningham, *Changes*.
14. Carolyn Brown, untitled essay, *Dance Perspectives* no. 34 (issue titled *Time to Walk in Space*, Summer 1968): 30.
15. Program note, Theater de Lys, New York, 29 December 1953–3 January 1954.
16. Cunningham, *Changes*.
17. Carolyn Brown and Marianne Preger-Simon, interview with the author.
18. I am indebted to Janice Ross for this information, and also for a copy of the text of Cunningham's talk on this occasion.
19. The subtitles and the program note first appeared in the program for a performance at Sarah Lawrence College, Bronxville, New York, on 18 October 1955.
20. Cunningham, *Changes*.
21. Cage, note on *Septet* in Vaughan, ed., *Merce Cunningham & Dance Company*.
22. I am using the names of the original interpreters here.
23. There is an extended description of *Septet* in Marcia B. Siegel, *The Shapes of Change* (Boston: Houghton Mifflin Company, 1979), pp. 324–32.
24. John Percival, "Originality to the Fore," *New Daily* (London), 14 August 1964.
25. Ibid.
26. Cunningham, *Changes*.
27. Cunningham, "Two Questions and Five Dances," *Dance Perspectives* no. 34 (issue titled *Time to Walk in Space*, Summer 1968): 51.
28. Carolyn Brown, untitled essay, *Dance Perspectives* no. 34 (issue titled *Time to Walk in Space*, Summer 1968): 29.
29. Cunningham, *Changes*.
30. Tomkins, *Off the Wall*, p. 102.
31. R. S. (Robert Sabin), N. K. (Nik Krevitsky), and L. H. (Louis Horst), "Merce Cunningham and Dance Company," *Dance Observer* 21 no. 2 (February 1954): 25–26.
32. Anatole Chujoy, "Merce Cunningham and Dance Company," *Dance News* XXIV no. 2 (February 1954): 10.
33. Doris Hering, "Merce Cunningham and Dance Company," *Dance Magazine* XXVIII no. 2 (February 1954): 69, 70, 73.
34. Program note, Marine's Memorial Theater, San Francisco, 15 November 1955.
35. Margaret Lloyd, "Novelties in the Dance," *Christian Science Monitor*, 9 January 1954, p. 4.
36. Carolyn Brown and Marianne Preger-Simon, interview with the author.

1954

1. A photograph of the final version of the set is reproduced in *Robert Rauschenberg*, exh. cat. (Washington, D.C.: National Collection of Fine

Arts/Smithsonian Institution, 1976), p. 80.

2. Cunningham, *Changes*.

3. Program note, Henry Street Playhouse, New York, 27 May 1955.

4. Cunningham, *Changes*.

5. Ibid.

6. Ibid.

7. Walter Sorell, "Dancer Gets Guggenheim Award," *Providence Sunday Journal*, 20 June 1954, sect. 7 p. 4.

8. Cage, contribution to "Essays, Stories and Remarks about Merce Cunningham," *Dance Perspectives* 34 (issue titled *Time to Walk in Space*, Summer 1968): 13.

9. "Merce Cunningham Receives Guggenheim Award," *Dance Observer* 21 no. 7 (August–September 1954): 107.

1955

1. Earle Brown, in "The Forming of an Aesthetic: Merce Cunningham and John Cage," *Ballet Review* 13 no. 3 (Fall 1985): 30–32.

2. Marianne Simon, Carolyn Brown, and Remy Charlip, conversations with the author.

1956

1. Program note, University of Notre Dame, 18 May 1956. Another version of this note appeared in a program for a performance at the Brooklyn Academy of Music on 12 January 1957: "The complexity of this dance and its music arises from the superimposition of disparate events which are related, as in nature, for instance, air, earth, fire, and water, acting at one and the same time are related, simply by their happening in the same time and place."

2. Earle Brown, in Klosty, ed., *Merce Cunningham*, pp. 76–77. See also "The Forming of an Aesthetic: Merce Cunningham and John Cage," transcript of a panel discussion held on 16 June 1984 at the Dance Critics' Conference, in *Ballet Review* 13 no. 3 (Fall 1985): 25.

3. Program note, University of Notre Dame, 18 May 1956.

4. Cunningham, *Changes*.

5. In another version, this section is called "Hatch the plot."

6. Program note, University of Notre Dame, 18 May 1956. "Ballet" was later amended to "dance."

7. Cage, note on *Suite for Five* in Vaughan, ed., *Merce Cunningham & Dance Company*.

8. Cunningham, "A Collaborative Process between Music and Dance," pp. 177–78.

9. Cunningham, remarks at a performance at Douglass College, New

Brunswick, N.J., 16 October 1959, quoted in part in *Changes*.

10. Cunningham, unpublished manuscript note.

11. Cage, note on *Suite for Five* in Vaughan, ed., *Merce Cunningham & Dance Company*.

12. Toward the end of his life, Erik Satie planned to write six *Nocturnes*, but completed only five. In the dance, the pieces were played in a different order from that in the piano score, as follows: 3, 5, 1, 4, 2.

13. Cunningham, *Changes*.

14. Cunningham, quoted in Lesschaeve, *The Dancer and the Dance*, p. 92.

15. P. W. Manchester, "Merce Cunningham and Dance Company," in "The Season in Review," *Dance News* XLVI no. 3 (March 1965): 8.

16. Cage, note on *Nocturnes* in Vaughan, ed., *Merce Cunningham & Dance Company*.

17. Cunningham, manuscript note, probably for lecture-demonstration, n.d.

18. Cage, note on *Nocturnes* in Vaughan, ed., *Merce Cunningham & Dance Company*, n.p.

1957

1. Cunningham, statement from the symposium "4 Choreographers Will Speak and Dance," Henry Street Playhouse, New York, 27 April 1957. Reprinted in "Close-Up of Modern Dance Today: The Non-Objective Choreographers," *Dance Magazine* XXXI no. 11 (November 1957): 22.

2. See "Choreographics," *Dance Observer* 24 no. 8 (October 1957): 116.

3. Cunningham, *Changes*.

4. See Nicholas Kenyon, "A Forgotten Revolutionary," *The New Yorker*, 22 October 1979, pp. 182–88.

5. Margaret Lloyd, "Merce Cunningham and His Dancers," *Christian Science Monitor*, 16 December 1957.

6. Carolyn Brown, interview with the author.

7. Brown, "On Chance," *Ballet Review* 2 no. 2 (1968): 18.

8. Cunningham, "Two Questions and Five Dances," *Dance Perspectives* no. 34 (issue titled *Time to Walk in Space*, Summer 1968): 51.

9. Brown, "On Chance," p. 18.

1958

1. Program note, Town Hall, New York, 15 May 1958.

2. See William Fetterman, "Merce Cunningham and John Cage: Choreographic Cross-Currents," in David

MC in *Minutiae*, 1954. Photograph: Danny Livingstone.

Vaughan, ed., *Merce Cunningham: Creative Elements, Choreography and Dance*, Volume 4 Part 2, London: Harwood Academic Publishers, 1997, in which Cunningham's movements as he conducted Concert for Piano and Orchestra are notated in the notation of Friedrich Zorn.

3. Cage, manuscript notes, n.d.

4. Program note, Eleventh American Dance Festival, Connecticut College, New London, Conn., 14 August 1958.

5. Cunningham, letter to Robert Rauschenberg, 12 July 1958, reproduced in *Changes*. I have left the spelling and punctuation unaltered.

6. Cunningham, "A Collaborative Process between Music and Dance," p. 178.

7. Cage, manuscript note, n.d.

8. Earle Brown, in Brown, Remy Charlip, Marianne Simon, and David Vaughan, "The Forming of an Aesthetic: Merce Cunningham and John Cage," *Ballet Review* 13 no. 3 (Fall 1985): 38.

9. Jill Johnston, "Merce Cunningham & Co.," *The Village Voice*, 24 February 1960, p. 6.

10. Jack Anderson, "Merce Cunningham and Dance Co.—Brooklyn Academy of Music—April 15, 16, and 18, 1969," *Dance Magazine* XLIII no. 6 (June 1969): 34.

11. Cunningham, manuscript note, n.d.

12. Cunningham, *Changes*. A more extended version of these notes was published in *Dance Magazine* XXXX no. 6 (June 1966): 52–54, under the title "Summerspace Story."

13. Ibid.

14. Cage, manuscript notes, n.d.

15. Nora Ephron, "3 Characters in Search of a Ballet, or the Genesis of 'Summerspace,'" *New York Times* (Paris), 14 June 1964.

16. Louis Horst, "11th American Dance Festival," *Dance Observer* 25 no. 7 (August–September 1958): 102.

17. P. W. Manchester, "Merce Cun-

ningham and Dance Co.," *Dance News* XXXVI no. 3 (March 1960): 11.

18. Cage, note on *Night Wandering* in Vaughan, ed., *Merce Cunningham & Dance Company*.

19. Cunningham, *Changes*.

20. Cage, manuscript note, n.d.

21. Walter Sorell, "Merce Cunningham: An Artist Creating a World All His Own," *New London Day* (New London, Conn.), 17 August 1963, p. 7.

22. Richard Buckle, "Invitation to the Chance," *Sunday Times* (London), 2 August 1964, p. 20.

23. Henry David Thoreau, *Walden*, 1854, reprinted in Carl Bode, ed., *The Portable Thoreau—Revised Edition* (New York: The Viking Portable Library, 1979), p. 282.

24. Margaret Erlanger, "Merce Cunningham at the University of Illinois," *Dance Observer* 26 no. 8 (October 1959): 121–22.

25. "College Correspondence/From University of Illinois," *Dance Observer* 25 no. 7 (August–September 1958): 110.

1959

1. "Music-Dance Program Set," *Champaign-Urbana Courier*, 24 February 1959, p. 7.

2. Lynn Ludlow, "Dance, Music Parting Ways: Independent Existence Cited by Cunningham," *Champaign-Urbana Courier*, 4 March 1959, p. 10.

3. Cunningham, *Changes*.

4. Margaret Erlanger, "Merce Cunningham at the University of Illinois," *Dance Observer* 26 no. 8 (October 1959): 122.

5. Cunningham, *Changes*.

6. Program note (an English paraphrase of the poems), 1959 Festival of Contemporary Arts, University of Illinois, 14–15 March 1959.

7. Cunningham, letter to Donna Horié, n.d.

8. Cage described the company's eating habits, and other adventures on tour, in his "Where Are We Eating? And What Are We Eating?," in Klosty, ed., *Merce Cunningham*, pp. 55–62.

9. Cunningham, *Changes*.

10. Ibid.

11. Cage, note on *Rune* in Vaughan, ed., *Merce Cunningham & Dance Company*.

12. Cunningham, "X.16.59," manuscript in the archives of the Cunningham Dance Foundation.

1960

1. Walter Terry, "Cunningham Dance Group Gives Avant Garde Works,"

New York Herald Tribune, 17 February 1960, p. 19, and "Theater Week End with the Moderns: Mr. Cunningham," *New York Herald Tribune*, 21 February 1960, sect. 4, p. 5. See also Jill Johnston, "Merce Cunningham & Co.," *The Village Voice*, 24 February 1960, p. 6; "How Strange," *Time* 75 no. 9 (29 February 1960): 44; and "Out—Way, Way Out," *Newsweek* LV no. 9 (29 February 1960): 62–63.

2. Cage, quoted in Dunn, *John Cage*, p. 42.

3. William Flanagan, "New Work by John Cage/A 3-Ring Circus of Lunacy Is This Musical Premiere," *New York Herald Tribune*, 8 March 1960, p. 13.

4. Anon, "Anarchy with a Beat," *Time*, 21 March 1960, p. 46.

5. Cunningham, *Changes*.

6. Cage, note on *Crises* in Vaughan, ed., *Merce Cunningham & Dance Company*.

7. Ibid.

8. Virgil Thomson, "Stravinsky—Gesualdo," *New York Times*, 2 October 1960, sect. 2, p. 11.

9. Yvonne Rainer, "Some Retrospective Notes on a Dance for 10 People and 12 Mattresses Called 'Parts of Some Sextets,' Performed at the Wadsworth Atheneum, Hartford, Connecticut, and Judson Memorial Church, New York, in March 1965," *Tulane Drama Review* 10 (T-30, Winter 1965): 168.

1961

1. Program of the Fourteenth American Dance Festival, Connecticut College, New London, Conn., 17 August 1961.

2. Cage, note on *Æon* in Vaughan, ed., *Merce Cunningham & Dance Company*.

3. Cage, manuscript note, n.d.

4. Ibid.

5. Cage, note on *Æon* in Vaughan, ed., *Merce Cunningham & Dance Company*.

6. Ibid.

7. Cage, in Dunn, *John Cage*, p. 30.

8. William Davis, in an unpublished interview with Sally Banes, 3 March 1980.

9. Cunningham, manuscript note on *Æon*, n.d. This is a longer version of the note that appears in *Changes*. Two of the "trial orders" and an order for the touring version are also reproduced there.

10. Cage, manuscript note, n.d.

11. Tomkins, *Off the Wall*, p. 223.

12. Cunningham, manuscript note, c. 1961.

1962

1. See Tomkins, *Off the Wall*, pp. 193–98, and John Wulp, "The Night They All Saw, at Last, What Was Happen-

ing," *Esquire* LX no. 5 (November 1963): 134–38, 184–87.

1963

1. Cunningham, manuscript notes, n.d.

2. Jasper Johns painted *Field Painting* about this time.

3. Cunningham, quoted in Ruth Foster, *Knowing in My Bones* (London: Adam and Charles Black, 1976), p. 29.

4. Cage, letter to Peter Yates, n.d.

5. Cage, manuscript note, n.d.

6. Ibid.

7. See Cunningham's three-part "*Story*/tale of a dance and a tour," *Dance Ink* 6 no. 1 (Spring 1995), no. 2 (Summer 1995), and no. 3 (Fall 1995), for Cunningham's account of the 1964 world tour and of the performances of *Story* during it.

8. Cunningham has said, however, that "we never did all of them, even at the first performance."

9. The composer's own detailed note on the music is reprinted in Cunningham, *Changes*.

10. Cunningham, manuscript note. This is a conflation of the slightly different accounts of *Story* given by Cunningham in *Changes* and in *Dance Perspectives* 34 (issue titled *Time to Walk in Space*, Summer 1968).

11. Flyer published by the UCLA Committee on Fine Arts Productions, July 1963.

12. Tomkins, *Off the Wall*, p. 230.

13. Carolyn Brown, "On Chance," p. 21.

14. See Sally Banes, "Merce Cunningham's *Story*," Proceedings of the *Twelfth Annual Conference Society of Dance History Scholars, 17–19 February 1989* (California: Society of Dance History Scholars, 1989), pp. 96–110. This paper was based on interviews Banes did with several former members of the Cunningham company on the subject of *Story*.

15. Ibid.

16. This note first appeared in the house program of the Arkansas Arts Center Theater, Little Rock, Ark., 23–24 October 1963.

1964

1. The list of cues is reproduced from one of Cunningham's notebooks in Cunningham, "*Story*/tale of a dance and a tour [Part 3]," *Dance Ink* 6 no. 3 (Fall 1995): 33.

2. Cunningham, *Changes*.

3. Ibid.

4. Cunningham, commentary for *A Video Event* (Part I), CBS Camera Three, May 1974.

5. Cunningham, *Changes*.

6. Cunningham, manuscript note, n.d.

7. Cunningham, quoted in Lesschaeve, *The Dancer and the Dance*, p. 105.

8. Program note, Sadler's Wells Theatre, London, 1 August 1964.

9. Etienne Becker, *Image et Technique: Merce Cunningham*; black-and-white film in 16 mm., 1964.

10. See Grace Glueck, "Leo Castelli Takes Stock of 30 Years Selling Art," *New York Times*, 5 February 1987, p. C19.

11. Tomkins, *Off the Wall*, p. 10.

12. See Katherine S. Lobach, "Definitely Not Three-Quarter Time/June 24, 1964," (previously unpublished?) reproduced in Cunningham, "*Story*/tale of a dance and a tour [Part I]," *Dance Ink* 6 no. 1 (Spring 1995): 18.

13. Michael White, letter to the author, 15 June 1964.

14. Program, Sadler's Wells Theatre, 27 July–1 August 1964.

15. Alexander Bland, "Farther Out Than Ever," *The Observer* (London), 28 June 1964.

16. Bland, "The Future Bursts In," *The Observer* (London), 2 August 1964. Reprinted in Bland, *Observer of the Dance 1958–1982* (London: Dance Books, 1985), pp. 65–67.

17. See David Vaughan, "Adventures on a World Tour," *New York Times*, 3 January 1965, sect. 2, p. 13.

18. Cage, contribution to "Essays, Stories and Remarks about Merce Cunningham," *Dance Perspectives* 34 (issue titled *Time to Walk in Space*, Summer 1968): 22.

19. "Our Music Critic," "Dance Recital by Cunningham Group," *Times of India*, 30 October 1964.

20. See Tomkins, *Off the Wall*, p. 232.

1965

1. See Clive Barnes, "U.S. Dancers Win Hearts in London," *New York Times*, 3 August 1964; "Pop Ballet," *Time*, 14 August 1964; and Francis Mason, "London Likes American Dancers," *New York Times*, 27 December 1964.

2. Cunningham, quoted in Allen Hughes, "Dance: Merce Cunningham Returns," *New York Times*, 13 February 1965.

3. The initial reviews included Frances Herridge, "American Dance Theater Adds an Experiment," *New York Post*, 5 March 1965; Hughes, "Dance: At Lincoln Center," *New York Times*, 5 March 1965; and Walter Terry, "Brash, Boisterous Guest," *New York Herald Tribune*, 5 March 1965. Hughes followed up with "Spotlight on Dance," *New York*

Times, 21 March 1965, and Terry with "Show a Little Mercy, Merce," *New York Herald Tribune*, 21 March 1965.
4. George Beiswanger, "No Dolt Can Do It: An Appraisal of Cunningham," *Dance News*, May 1965.
5. Carolyn Brown, untitled essay in Klosty, ed., *Merce Cunningham*, p. 30.
6. Cunningham, *Changes*. A different version of this note appears in Cunningham, "A Collaborative Process between Music and Dance," pp. 180–81.
7. Cunningham, *Changes*.

1966

1. Lewis L. Lloyd, letter to the author, 23 August 1966.
2. Cunningham, *Changes*.
3. Note in the program for the Quatrième Festival International de Danse de Paris, Théâtre des Champs-Elysées, Paris, 9/10 November 1966. Translated from the French by the author.
4. Gordon Mumma, "Four Sound Environments for Modern Dance," *Impulse: The Annual of Contemporary Dance* (issue titled *The Dancer's Environment*, San Francisco: Chapman Press, 1967), p. 14.
5. Mary Clarke, "Merce Cunningham and Company," *Dancing Times*, January 1967.
6. Anonymous (John Percival), "The Ballet of 'Interpret It Yourself,'" *The Times* (London), 24 November 1966.
7. Peter Williams, "Anything Can Happen," *Dance and Dancers*, January 1967.
8. Cunningham, quoted in Michael Williams, "Merce Breaks New Ground," *Chicago Daily News*, 19 October 1966, sect. 6, p. 53.
9. Ann Barzel, "Double Header for Dance Fans," *Chicago American*, 20 October 1966.
10. Shirley Genther, quoted in David Vaughan, "Performing for the Right People," *Ballet Review* 1 no. 6 (1967).
11. Patrice de Nussac, "*Mini-jupes contre smokings au Théâtre des Champs-Elysées*" (Miniskirts versus dinner jackets at the Théâtre des Champs-Elysées), *France-Soir*, 11 November 1966.
12. Cunningham, quoted in Lydia Joel, "Dance Management Seminar Held," *Dance Magazine*, February 1967.

1967

1. Cunningham, *Changes*.
2. Jasper Johns, quoted in Hubert Saal, "Merce," *Newsweek*, 27 May 1968.
3. Frank Stella, interview with the author.
4. Gordon Mumma, "Four Sound Environments for Modern Dance," *Impulse: The Annual of Contemporary Dance* (issue titled *The Dancer's Environment*, San Francisco: Chapman Press, 1967), p. 14.
5. "Unique and Exciting Event Held at School of Painting," *Somerset Reporter* (Skowhegan, Me.), 14 (?) August 1963.
6. Cunningham, quoted in Larry Finley, "Was Egghead a Stripper? U.I. Panel Debates Arts," unidentified newspaper, Urbana, November 1967.

1968

1. Cunningham, *Changes*.
2. A fuller account is given in David Vaughan, "'Then I Thought about Marcel': Merce Cunningham's *Walkaround Time*," *Art and Dance: Images of the Modern Dialogue, 1890–1980*, exh. cat. (Boston: Institute of Contemporary Art, 1982). Reprinted in Richard Kostelanetz, ed., *Merce Cunningham/Dancing in Space and Time* (Pennington, N.J.: a capella books, 1993), pp. 66–70.
3. Cunningham, quoted in Ruth Foster, *Knowing in my Bones* (London: Adam and Charles Black, 1976), pp. 39–40.
4. René Clair, *À nous la liberté* and *Entr'acte*, English transcription and description of the action by Richard Jacques and Nicola Hayden (New York: Simon & Schuster, 1970). See also Henning Rischbieter, ed., *Art and the Stage in the 20th Century* (Greenwich, Conn.: New York Graphic Society, 1968).
5. Lewis Lloyd, letters to the Cunningham Dance Foundation, 8, 9, 10, and 16 August 1968.
6. Cunningham, quoted in Robert Commanday, "Composing with the Camera," *This World*, 10 November 1968.
7. "Unique Dance Program," *San Francisco Chronicle*, 10 October 1968.
8. Commanday, "Composing with the Camera."

1969

1. Lesschaeve, *The Dancer and the Dance*, p. 115.

1970

1. Patrick O'Connor, "Enchanting *Tread* by Cunningham," *Jersey Journal*, 6 January 1970.
2. Don McDonagh, "The Quality of Merce," *Show*, April 1970.
3. Cunningham, "A Collaborative Process between Music and Dance," pp. 181–82.
4. See Carolyn Brown, untitled essay in Klosty, ed., *Merce Cunningham*, p. 25, and "Michael Snell" (a pseudonym for Klosty), "Cunningham and the Critics," *Ballet Review* 3 no. 6 (1971): 27–35.
5. Cunningham, quoted in Lesschaeve, *The Dancer and the Dance*, p. 89.
6. Ibid., pp. 89–90.
7. Ibid., p. 108.
8. Ibid.

1971

1. Carolyn Brown, untitled essay in Klosty, ed., *Merce Cunningham*, p. 27.
2. Press release, Detroit Institute of Arts, 25 February 1972.

1972

1. Cunningham, manuscript note.
2. Cunningham, narration for *A Video Event*, CBS Camera Three, 1974.
3. Carolyn Brown, untitled essay in Klosty, ed., *Merce Cunningham*, p. 26.
4. Press release, Detroit Institute of Arts, 25 February 1972.
5. See Christian Wolff, note in Klosty, ed., *Merce Cunningham*, p. 81.
6. Deborah Jowitt, "I've Just Got a Running Start," *The Village Voice*, 22 March 1973.

1973

1. Cunningham, quoted in Lesschaeve, *The Dancer and the Dance*, p. 83.
2. Cunningham, "A Collaborative Process between Music and Dance," pp. 182–83.
3. Cunningham's original working title was *Paris Collage*. *Un Jour ou deux* is a quotation from the French translation of a text by Cage on Joan Miró.
4. House program, Théâtre National de l'Opéra, Paris, November 1973.
5. Charles Atlas, program note for the first screening of the film *Walkaround Time*, 10 November 1973.
6. Cunningham, quoted in Lesschaeve, *The Dancer and the Dance*, p. 190.

1974

1. Karen Carreras, ed., *Films and Videotapes*, catalogue (New York: Cunningham Dance Foundation), n.d., p. 17.
2. Cunningham, quoted in Lesschaeve, *The Dancer and the Dance*, pp. 190–91.

1975

1. Cunningham, quoted in Lesschaeve, *The Dancer and the Dance*, p. 120.
2. Ibid.
3. Ibid.
4. Ibid., pp. 119–20.
5. Ibid., pp. 191–92.
6. Arlene Croce, "Look What's Going On," *The New Yorker*, 10 March 1975.

1976

1. Cunningham, note on *Torse*, 1976. The choreography and process of *Torse* are described in more detail in Lesschaeve, *The Dancer and the Dance*, pp. 17–24.
2. Cunningham, quoted in Lesschaeve, *The Dancer and the Dance*, pp. 120–21.
3. Karen Carreras, ed., *Films and Videotapes*, p. 14.
4. See Anna Kisselgoff, "$3-Million Dance Series on WNET," *New York Times*, 13 June 1975.
5. Cunningham, "A Collaborative Process between Music and Dance," p. 184.

1977

1. Michelle Potter, "A License to Do Anything," *Dance Chronicle* 16 no. 1 (1993): 18–19.
2. Cage, quoted in Melinda Bargreen, "Change and Cage," in an unidentified clipping (from the *Seattle Times*?), September 1977.
3. Karen Carreras, ed., *Films and Videotapes*, p. 16.
4. Ibid., p. 9.
5. Marguerite Feitlowitz, "What the Set Designer Needs to Know about Video," *Theatre Crafts* 18 no. 7 (August/September 1984): 72.

1978

1. Mark Lancaster, quoted in Marguerite Feitlowitz, "What the Set Designer Needs to Know about Video," p. 72.
2. Cunningham, quoted in Lesschaeve, *The Dancer and the Dance*, p. 155.
3. Alastair Macaulay, "Happy Hooligan," *The New Yorker*, 27 April 1992.

1979

1. See David Vaughan, "Merce Cunningham Talks," *Soho Weekly News*, 13 February 1980, p. 13.
2. Karen Carreras, ed., *Films and Videotapes*, p. 10.
3. See Lesschaeve, *The Dancer and the Dance*, pp. 195–99, and Vaughan, "*Locale*: The Collaboration of Merce Cunningham and Charles Atlas," *Millennium Film Journal* 10/11 (Fall/Winter 1981/1982). Reprinted in Richard Kostelanetz, ed., *Merce Cunningham/Dancing in Space and Time*, pp. 151–55.
4. Cunningham, quoted in Lesschaeve, *The Dancer and the Dance*, pp. 154–55.
5. Ibid.
6. Ibid.
7. Press release from Performing Artservices, New York, 1982.

1980

1. Cunningham, quoted in Lesschaeve, *The Dancer and the Dance*, p. 156.
2. Ibid., p. 157.
3. See Stephanie Jordan, "Cunningham and Cage at the Laban Centre," *Dancing Times*, October 1980, pp. 38–39.
4. Cunningham, quoted in Jennifer Dunning, "25 Cultural Wishes for the New Year," *New York Times*, 28 December 1980. Cunningham's contribution is quoted as he originally wrote it, not as it appeared in the article.

1981

1. Charles Atlas, conversation with the author.
2. Atlas, program note for screening of *Channels/Inserts*, Carnegie Hall Cinema, New York, 21 March 1982.
3. Cunningham, quoted in Lesschaeve, *The Dancer and the Dance*, p. 156.
4. See Cunningham, "Diary of a Cunningham Dance," *New York Times*, 15 March 1981, and David Vaughan, "*Channels/Inserts*: Cunningham and Atlas (continued)," *Millennium Film Journal* 12 (Fall/Winter1982/1983): 126–30.
5. Cunningham, quoted in Lesschaeve, *The Dancer and the Dance*, p. 157.
6. Press release from Performing Artservices, New York, 1982.
7. Cunningham, quoted in Lesschaeve, *The Dancer and the Dance*, p. 157.
8. Press release from Performing Artservices, New York, 1982.
9. See Cunningham, "A Collaborative Process between Music and Dance," pp. 119–20; also Stephanie Jordan, "International Dance Course," *Dancing Times*, November 1981, p. 102.

1982

1. Cunningham, quoted in Lesschaeve, *The Dancer and the Dance*, pp. 156–57.
2. Press release from Performing Artservices, New York, 1982.
3. Program, Page Auditorium, Duke University, Durham, N.C., 16 June 1982.
4. Cunningham, quoted in Lesschaeve, *The Dancer and the Dance*, pp. 157–58.
5. David Tudor, interview with the author.

1983

1. Cunningham, quoted in Lesschaeve, *The Dancer and the Dance*, p. 158. See also the interview with Cunningham in anonymous (Calvin Tomkins), "The Camera Looking," *The New Yorker*, 14 February 1983.
2. Cunningham, quoted in Jennifer Dunning, "New 'Adventure' Begins for Merce Cunningham," *New York Times*, 20 March 1983.
3. Ibid.
4. Karen Carreras, ed., *Films and Videotapes*, p. 5.
5. Program note, Ballet Rambert, Royal Northern College of Music, Manchester, 7–19 February 1983.
6. Cunningham, quoted in Lesschaeve, *The Dancer and the Dance*, p. 158.
7. Cunningham, in an interview with Pierre Lartigue. Translated from the French by the author.
8. Manuscript note by Cunningham, and program note, City Center Theater, New York, 8 March 1984.

1984

1. Arlene Croce, "Three Elders," *The New Yorker*, 26 March 1984, pp. 114–19.
2. Cunningham, "Four Events That Have Led to Large Discoveries," unpublished note, 19 September 1994.
3. Croce, "Three Elders."
4. Cunningham, quoted in Jack Anderson, "The Surprising Merce Cunningham," *New York Times*, 3 March 1985, sect. 2, p. 19.
5. Cunningham, quoted in Andrea Grodsky Huber, "Merce Cunningham Brings 'Unpremeditated Creation' to Dance," *Baltimore Sun*, 24 March 1985.
6. Robert Greskovic, "Cunningham Dares to be Different—and Dance World Loves Him for It," *Chicago Tribune*, 14 April 1985.
7. Anna Kisselgoff, "Dance: Merce Cunningham Presents a Premiere," *New York Times*, 6 March 1985, p. C19.

1985

1. Elliot Caplan, "Video Art/Producing Videodance," *Videography*, September 1985, p. 65.
2. Karen Carreras, ed., *Films and Videotapes*, p. 8.
3. Program note, City Center Theater, New York, 5–17 March 1985.

1986

1. Joseph Gale, "A Night on the Grange," *Independent Press*, 26 March 1986.
2. Anna Kisselgoff, "When Social Dance Meets the Avant-Garde," *New York Times*, 30 March 1986.
3. Ibid.
4. Tobi Tobias, "Measure for Measure," *New York*, 7 April 1986, p. 61.

1987

1. Yelizaveta Gerdt, quoted in Anna Kisselgoff, "For Balanchine, Her Dancing Was a Path to the Future," *New York Times*, 10 October 1993.
2. See Alastair Macaulay, "The Merce Experience," *The New Yorker*, 4 April 1988, pp. 92–96.
3. Cunningham, quoted in Donald J. Hutera, "Defining Merce Cunningham," *Los Angeles Times*, 5 April 1987.
4. Cunningham, quoted in Donald J. Hutera, "Glimpses into the Rehearsal Studio of a Master," *New York Times*, 1 March 1987, sect. 2, p. 8.
5. David Tudor, manuscript note, 1987.
6. See "Cunningham and His Dancers," transcript of a panel discussion, *Ballet Review* 15 no. 3 (Fall 1987): 19–40.
7. Deborah Jowitt, "So Many Gold Rings," *The Village Voice*, 1 September 1987.
8. Nancy Goldner, "The Merce Cunningham Dancers Present an Event," *Philadelphia Inquirer*, 17 October 1987.

1988

1. Cunningham, quoted in Simone Dupuis, "*Cunningham: le mouvement est superficiel*," *L'Express*, 29 July 1988.
2. Cage, liner notes for the record *Music for Merce Cunningham*, on the Mode label, 1989.
3. David Tudor, liner notes for ibid.
4. Takehisa Kosugi, liner notes for ibid.
5. Elliot Caplan, in conversation with Michael Stier, Cunningham Dance Foundation, 4 April 1990.

1989

1. Cunningham, quoted in Jerry Young, "Master of the Dance: Cunningham Builds Legacy of Style," *Austin American-Statesman*, 21 January 1989.
2. Ibid.
3. Takehisa Kosugi, quoted in Young, "Dance Company's Premiere in Austin a First for Texas," *Austin American-Statesman*, 27 January 1989.
4. Young, in ibid.
5. Kathleen Goncharov, curator, note for the Seventh Triennale—India 1991, Lalit Kala Akademi, Rabindra Bhavan, New Delhi.
6. Jack Anderson, "Fleeting Patterns Evoke an Ephemeral World," *New York Times*, 9 March 1989, p. C18.
7. Cage, quoted in Janice Ross, "Cunningham and Cage: A Creative Conversation," *The Oakland Tribune*, 20 September 1989.

1991

1. Mark Lancaster, unpublished note, 1991.
2. Cunningham, quoted in Robert Greskovic, "Dancing with a Mouse," *Los Angeles Times*, 5 May 1991.
3. Cunningham, quoted in Susan Mehalick, "Still a Modernist at 74," *Berkshire Eagle*, 4 July 1993.
4. Cunningham, quoted in Ursula Fraefel, "Dancing—Not Counting," *Der Tanz der Dinge* (Switzerland) no. 13 (September–November 1991).
5. Ibid.

1992

1. Cunningham, manuscript note, 24 December 1992.
2. Richard Alston, "The Rambert Riddle," *Dance Now* 1 no. 1 (Spring 1992): 24.
3. Marilyn Hunt, "Country Dances," *Dance Magazine*, November 1992.
4. Cunningham, original version of a note published in French translation in the program of the Opéra de Paris Garnier, 17/21 November 1992.
5. Cunningham, quoted in Janice Berman, "Cunningham Hurtles Forward," *New York Newsday*, 9 March 1993.
6. Ibid.
7. Ibid.

1993

1. Deborah Jowitt, "Merce Cunningham Dance Company," *The Village Voice*, 13 April 1993.
2. Ibid.
3. Cunningham, quoted in Janice Berman, "Cunningham Hurtles Forward," *New York Newsday*, 9 March 1993.
4. Nancy Goldner, "Merce Cunningham's 3 New Works Include an Hour-Long Dance, 'Enter,'" *Philadelphia Inquirer*, 11 March 1993.
5. Linda Belans, "Magical Merce," Raleigh (N.C.) *News and Observer*, 17 July 1993.
6. Program note, John F. Kennedy Center for the Performing Arts, Washington, D.C., 22–27 March 1994.

1994

1. Program note, City Center Theater, New York, 8–20 March 1994.
2. Cunningham, program note, kunstenFestivaldesArts, Brussels, May 1994.
3. David Tudor, program note in ibid.
4. Andrew Culver, program note in ibid.
5. Marsha Skinner, program note in ibid.
6. Skinner, note to the author, n.d.

Merce Cunningham's Dancers

*Armitage, Karole 1975–1981
*Attix, Karen 1975–1976
 Aul, Ronne 1952
 Bahn, Erin 1992–1994 (RUG)
 Backer, Phyllis 1952
*Barrow, Helen 1982–1993
*Bartosik, Kimberly 1987–1996
 Berea, Dorothy 1947–1950
 Berley, Helaine 1952
 Birch, Patricia 1944
*Blair, Shareen 1961–1964
 Bok, Marlise 1944
 Bond, Sudie 1950–1952
 Boomershine, Ty 1991–1993 (RUG)
 Bosler, Virginia 1946–1947
*Boudreau, Lisa 1994–
*Breceda, Maydelle 1996–
*Brodsky, Ethel 1953
 Bromer, Steven 1987–1988 (RUG)
 Broughton, Shirley 1947
*Brown, Carolyn 1953–1972
*Burdick, William 1958
*Burns, Louise 1970–1971/
 1977–1984
*Caley, Thomas 1992–1993 (RUG),
 1993–
 Canton, François 1950
 Carmody, Matthew 1989–1991
 (RUG)
 Case, Adelaide 1952
 Chamberlain, Keith 1989–1991
 (RUG)
*Charlip, Remy 1950–1961
 Churchill, Mili 1947–1951
*Cole, Michael 1987–1989 (RUG),
 1989–
*Conley, Graham 1977
*Cornfield, Ellen 1974–1983
 Cummings, Jean 1944
 Dana, Leora 1944
*Davis, William 1963–1964
*Dencks, Anita 1953–1955
*Diamond, Emma 1988–1994
*Dove, Ulysses 1970–1973
*Dunn, Douglas 1969–1973
*Dunn, Judith 1959–1963
*Eginton, Meg 1978–1980
*Ek, Niklas 1966
*Emery, Susan 1977–1984
*Ensminger, Morgan 1975–1978
 Erdman, Jean 1942–1943
*Farber, Viola 1953–1965/1970
 Farmer, Holley 1996– (RUG)
 Finkelor, Joanne 1952
*Finlayson, Victoria 1984–1992
 Folkman, Marjorie 1995–1996
 (RUG)
*Fox, Lisa 1977–1980

 Frederiksen, Joan 1944
*Freebury, Jean 1991–1992 (RUG),
 1992–
*Friedman, Lise 1977–1984
*Gafner, Frédéric 1990–1991 (RUG),
 1991– (aka Foofwa d'Immobilité)
 Garber, Ben 1952
 Goff, Eleanor 1947
*Good, Alan 1978–1994
*Greenberg, Neil 1980–1986
 Grelinger, Els 1944
 Hamill, Sara 1947–1948
 Harris, Julie 1944
*Harper, Meg 1968–1977
*Hassall, Nanette 1971–1972
*Hay, Deborah 1964
*Hayman-Chaffey, Susana
 1968–1976
*Henkel, Ed 1971

 Hindle, Martha 1944
 Hodges, Corinne 1993 (RUG)
 Jacobsson, Petter 1995–1996 (RUG)
*Kanner, Karen Bell 1957
*Kerr, Catherine 1974–1976/
 1978–1988
*King, Bruce 1955–1958
 Koerber, Betty 1944
*Komar, Chris 1972–1996
*Kovich, Robert 1973–1980
 Kuhni, Connie 1944
*Kulick, David 1986–1993
*Kurshals, Raymond 1975–1976
*LaFarge, Timothy 1953–1954
 Lang, George 1944
*Laudisio, China 1993–
 Lawrence, Patricia 1944
*Lazaroff, Judy 1981–1983
 LeClercq, Tanaquil 1949–1950
*Lennon, Joseph 1978–1984
*Lent, Patricia 1983–1984 (RUG),
 1984–1993
 Leonard, Florence 1992–1993
 (RUG)

 Lerner, Raissa 1987–1988 (RUG)
*Lias, Barbara 1972–1973
 Lippold, Louise 1948
 Litz, Katherine 1946
*Lloyd, Barbara Dilley 1963–1968
 Louisy, Lennard 1993–1994 (RUG)
 Lunick, Olga 1947
 Lynch-John, Rachel 1989–1992
 (RUG)
 Mann, Marc 1994–1995 (RUG)
 Martin, Judith 1947
 McBride, Pat 1950
*McGoldrick, Larissa 1987–1993
 McKayle, Donald 1952
*Mehl, Brynar 1972–1973
*Melsher, Jo Anne 1952–1954
 Miskovitch, Milorad 1949
*Mohr, Matthew 1994–
*Moore, Jack 1960

The dancers have been, and continue to be, the life of my work. It is to them that I am most indebted, for their dedication and energies and willingness under favorable or trying conditions, to work at something which was for long outside the experience of most people, whether players or public, and to be able to face indifferent or even hostile audiences with equanimity. And together, I hope they will agree, despite the unfamiliarity of the work, we have tried to hold a standard that for me is the balance of the tightrope. One side is to have the clarity, the strength, the virtuosity of movement and its demands of the body, like flexible steel. The other side is the abandon, if I may use the word, that allows you to be human. It is a wonderful performance koan.

—Merce Cunningham

*Moscowitz, Deborah 1953
*Moulton, Charles 1974–1976
*Navar, Emily 1989–1992 (RUG),
 1990–1991
*Neels, Sandra 1963–1973
 Neumann, Natanya 1952–1953
 Nichols, Betty 1949
*O'Connor, Dennis 1986–1989
*Ogan, Banu 1992–1993 (RUG),
 1993–
*Paxton, Steve 1961–1964
 Perry, Sabra 1995–1996 (RUG)
*Phillips, Jared 1993–
 Pickett, Fawn 1944
 Power, Fionuala 1991–1993 (RUG)
*Preger-Simon, Marianne 1950–1958
*Radford, Karen (Fink) 1983–1987
*Reid, Albert 1964–1968
*Remley, Rob 1978–1987
*Riopelle, Yseult 1966–1967
*Robinson, Chase 1968–1972
*Roess-Smith, Julie (Sukenick)
 1973–1977
 Roman, Leticia 1994–1995 (RUG)

 Rosenthal, Rachel 1950
 Rosenzweig, Greta 1952
 Rouillier, Florian 1994–1995 (RUG)
*Rumsey, Glen 1992–1993 (RUG),
 1993–
*Sanderson, Randall 1988–1990
 (RUG), 1990–1992
*Santimyer, Kristy 1985–1989
*Saul, Peter 1965–1967
*Schroder, Kevin 1985–1986
 Schmutz, Stanton 1944
*Self, Jim 1977–1979
*Setterfield, Valda 1961/1965–1975
 Skinner, Joan 1952–1953
*Slayton, Jeff 1968–1970
 Smith, Graham 1993 (RUG)
*Solomons, Gus, Jr. 1965–1968
 Squire, Daniel 1996– (RUG)
*Steele, Jeannie 1990–1993 (RUG),
 1993–
 Steinberg, Vivian 1944
*Stone, Cynthia 1957–1958
*Swan, Derry 1996–
*Swinston, Robert 1980–
 Tanner, Virginia 1944
*Taylor, Paul 1953–1954
*Teitelbaum, Carol 1984–1986
 (RUG), 1986–1993
*Therrien, Cheryl 1992–1994 (RUG),
 1994–
*Titus, George 1974
 Van Loon, Marc 1995–1996 (RUG)
*Wagoner, Dan 1959
*Walker, Megan 1980–1986
 Wallenrod (Prevots), Naima 1952
 Walter, Julie 1950
 Walters, Diane 1950
*Weaver, Jenifer 1988–1989 (RUG),
 1989–1996
 Webre, Septime 1991–1992 (RUG)
 Whiting, Rachel 1991–1994 (RUG)
 Widman, Anneliese 1950–1953
*Wong, Mel 1968–1972
*Wood, Marilyn 1958–1963
*Wood, Robert 1988–1991
*Young, Susan Quinn 1981–1987

Note: * signifies that the dancer is or was a member of the Merce Cunningham Dance Company; RUG signifies that the dancer is or was a member of the Repertory Understudy Group (individuals who joined the Company in the same year that they joined the RUG are not listed as members of the RUG); everyone else danced with Merce Cunningham either before the formation of the Company, or as part of some ad hoc group.

Chronology

Ch	Choreographed by
C	Costumes by
D	Danced by
FP	First performance
MCDC	Merce Cunningham Dance Company
L	Lighting by
M	Music by
NP	New production
R	Reproduced by
S	Scenery by
ST	Staging

(Staging implies a production substantially the same as the original; new production implies one with different elements.)

All solos danced by Merce Cunningham unless otherwise stated.

The date of the first performance is followed where applicable by the date of the first performance in New York.

1938
UNBALANCED MARCH
Solo **M** Paul Hindemith **FP** Elks' Club, Seattle WA 30 November 1938

JAZZ EPIGRAM
Ch D MC, Dorothy Herrmann **M** Ernst Toch **FP** Elks' Club, Seattle WA 30 November 1938
Unbalanced March and *Jazz Epigram* were given on a program presented "through the courtesy of the Cornish School, Seattle"

1939
SKINNY STRUCTURES
In four parts, the first **Ch D** Dorothy Herrmann **M** Jean Wiener; the second **Ch D** MC **M** Darius Milhaud; the third **Ch D** Syvilla Fort **M** Felix Petyrek; and the fourth **Ch D** Dorothy Herrmann, MC, Syvilla Fort **M** Alfredo Casella **FP** Cornish Dance Group, Cornish Theatre, Seattle WA 24 March 1939

COURANTE, CONTAGION
Solo **M** Zoe Williams **FP** Mills College, Oakland CA 11 August 1939
Performed in the "Final Demonstration of Student Work, I: Pre-Classic and Modern Forms and Music Group," under the direction of Louis Horst, Sixth Session of the Bennington School of the Dance at Mills College, Oakland CA

1942
SEEDS OF BRIGHTNESS
Ch D Jean Erdman and MC **M** Norman Lloyd **C** Charlotte Trowbridge **FP** Bennington College, Bennington VT 1 August 1942; Studio Theatre, New York NY 20 October 1942

CREDO IN US
"A dramatic playlet for Two Characters" **Ch** Jean Erdman and MC **M** John Cage **C** Charlotte Trowbridge **D** Husband-Shadow: MC; Wife-Ghoul's Rage: Jean Erdman **FP** Bennington College, Bennington VT 1 August 1942; Studio Theatre, New York NY 20 October 1942
After the first performance the subtitle was changed to "A Suburban Idyll"

RENAISSANCE TESTIMONIALS
Solo in two parts, "Profession-Confession" **M** Maxwell Powers **C** Charlotte Trowbridge **FP** Bennington College, Bennington VT 1 August 1942; Studio Theatre, New York NY 20 October 1942
According to Nina Fonaroff, this dance was originally to be titled *Auto-da-fé*

AD LIB
Ch D Jean Erdman and MC **M** Gregory Tucker **C** Charlotte Trowbridge **FP** Bennington College, Bennington VT 1 August 1942; Studio Theatre, New York NY 20 October 1942
NP M John Cage **FP** Arts Club of Chicago, Chicago IL 14 February 1943

TOTEM ANCESTOR
Solo **M** John Cage **C** Charlotte Trowbridge **FP** Studio Theatre, New York NY 20 October 1942

1943
IN THE NAME OF THE HOLOCAUST
Solo **M** John Cage **C** MC **FP** Arts Club of Chicago, Chicago IL 14 February 1943

SHIMMERA
Solo **M** John Cage **C** MC **FP** Arts Club of Chicago, Chicago IL 14 February 1943

THE WIND REMAINS
Zarzuela in one act, after Federico García Lorca's *Así que pasen cinco años*, adapted by Paul Bowles **M** Paul Bowles Produced and directed by Schuyler Watts. Dance director: MC **S** Oliver Smith **C** Kermit Love **Cast** 1st Figure: Jean Erdman; 2nd Figure: Barbara Brae; Harlequin: Romolo De Spirito; Girl: Jeanne Stephens; Clown: MC; Stenographer: Marcia Motherwell; Mask: Claude Alphand; Young Man: Clement Brace; Footman: Paul Sweeney; Butler: David Raher; Old Man: E Da Neres; Boy: Baby Riverita. Conductor: Leonard Bernstein **FP** The Third Serenade, Museum of Modern Art, New York NY 30 March 1943

1944
TRIPLE-PACED
Solo **M** John Cage **C** MC **FP** Studio Theatre, New York NY 5 April 1944

ROOT OF AN UNFOCUS
Solo **M** John Cage **C** MC **FP** Studio Theatre, New York NY 5 April 1944

TOSSED AS IT IS UNTROUBLED
Solo **M** John Cage (*Meditation*) **C** MC **FP** Studio Theatre, New York NY 5 April 1944

THE UNAVAILABLE MEMORY OF
Solo **M** John Cage **C** MC **FP** Studio Theatre, New York NY 5 April 1944

SPONTANEOUS EARTH
Solo **M** John Cage **C** MC **FP** Studio Theatre, New York NY 5 April 1944

FOUR WALLS
A dance play by MC, directed by MC and Arch Lauterer **M** John Cage **S C** Arch Lauterer **D** MC (boy), Patricia Birsh, Marlise Bok, Jean Cummings, Leora Dana (mother), Joan Frederiksen, Julie Harris (girl), Martha Hindle, Betty Koerber, Connie Kuhni, George Lang (lover?), Patricia Lawrence, Fawn Pickett, Stanton Schmutz (father?), Vivian Steinberg, Virginia Tanner **FP** Perry-Mansfield Workshop, Steamboat Springs CO 22 August 1944
The exact distribution of all the roles is unknown; the supporting group was divided into one group of "six nearpeople" and one group of "six mad-ones." **NP** excerpts only **D** Virginia Tanner, Connie Kuhni, Fawn Pickett **FP** University of Utah, Salt Lake City UT 9 September 1944
NP solo excerpts only **FP** Woman's Club, Richmond VA 20 November 1944
NP solo under the title *Soliloquy*

FP Hunter Playhouse, New York NY 9 January 1945

IDYLLIC SONG
Solo **M** Erik Satie (1st movement of *Socrate*, drame symphonique, 1919), arranged by John Cage **C** MC **FP** Woman's Club, Richmond VA 20 November 1944; Hunter Playhouse, New York NY 9 January 1945
See 1970, *Second Hand*

1945
MYSTERIOUS ADVENTURE
Solo **M** John Cage **C** and object after a design by David Hare **FP** Hunter Playhouse, New York NY 9 January 1945 **ST** Martha Graham and Dance Company **FP** National Theatre, New York NY 17 May 1945

EXPERIENCES
Solo in two parts **M** John Cage and Livingston Gearhart **C** MC **FP** Hunter Playhouse, New York NY 9 January 1945
NP M for both parts by John Cage; *Experiences II* is a setting for mezzo-soprano of a poem by e. e. cummings ("III," one of the "Sonnets-Unrealities" from *Tulips and Chimneys* (1923) **FP** University of California, Los Angeles CA 21 April 1948 (?)

1946
THE ENCOUNTER
Solo **M** John Cage **C** MC **FP** Hunter Playhouse, New York NY 12 May 1946

INVOCATION TO VAHAKN
Solo **M** Alan Hovhaness **C** MC **FP** Hunter Playhouse, New York NY 12 May 1946

'FAST BLUES'
Solo **M** drum improvisation by Baby Dodds **C** MC **FP** Hunter Playhouse, New York NY 12 May 1946

THE PRINCESS ZONDILDA AND HER ENTOURAGE
"A Theatrical Fantasy by Merce Cunningham" In three parts: Swift Prologue, Royal Procession, Swift Epilogue **M** Alexei Haieff **S C** MC **D** The Princess: Virginia (Winkie) Bosler; Courtiers: Katherine Litz, MC **FP** Hunter Playhouse, New York NY 12 May 1946

1947
THE SEASONS
Ballet in one act, divided into nine sections: Prelude I, Winter, Prelude II,

Morris Graves, *Waning Moon #2*, 1943; poster for the Merce Cunningham Dance Company's Seattle residency, 1977.

Spring, Prelude III, Summer, Prelude IV, Fall, and Finale (Prelude I) **M** John Cage **S C** Isamu Noguchi **D** MC, Tanaquil LeClercq, Gisella Caccialanza, Beatrice Tompkins, Dorothy Dushock, Fred Danieli, Gerard Leavitt, Job Sanders **FP** Ballet Society, Ziegfeld Theater, New York NY 18 May 1947
ST New York City Ballet **FP** City Center, New York NY 22 January 1949

THE OPEN ROAD
Solo **M** Lou Harrison **C** MC **FP** Hunter Playhouse, New York NY 14 December 1947

NP revised version **FP** YM&YWHA, New York NY 14 May 1950

DROMENON
M John Cage (*Three Dances*, 1945) **C** for MC: Sonja Sekula; for women: MC **D** MC, Dorothy Berea, Shirley Broughton, Mili Churchill, Eleanor Goff, Sara Hamill, Judith Martin **FP** Hunter Playhouse, New York NY 14 December 1947

1948
DREAM
Solo **M** John Cage **C** MC **FP** Stephens College, Columbia MO 8 May 1948;

Hunter Playhouse, New York NY 15 January 1950

THE RUSE OF MEDUSA
A lyric comedy in one act by Erik Satie, translated from the French by M. C. Richards **M** Erik Satie Directed by Helen Livingston and Arthur Penn. Dances by MC **S** Willem and Elaine de Kooning **C** Mary Outten Properties by Albert Lanier, Bruce Johns, Buckminster Fuller, Ray Johnson, Forrest Wright, Ruth Asawa, Raymond Spillenger **Cast** Baron Medusa, a very rich rentier: Buckminster Fuller; Polycarp, his servant: Isaac Rosenfeld;

Astolfo, affianced to Frisette: William Shrauger; Frisette, Medusa's daughter: Elaine de Kooning; Jonas, a costly mechanical monkey: MC; Page: Alvin Charles Few **FP** Black Mountain College NC 14 August 1948
See 1948 below, *The Monkey Dances*

A DIVERSION
M John Cage (*Suite for Toy Piano*) **C** for MC: himself; for women: Mary Outten **D** Sara Hamill, Louise Lippold, MC **FP** Black Mountain College NC 20 August 1948
NP solo version, with the subtitle "short suite" **FP** North Shore County Day

287

MC at Sullivan Street Studio, ca. 1953. Photograph: Saul Leiter.

Theatre, Winnetka IL 3 February 1949
NP quartet version **D** Dorothy Berea, Mili Churchill, Anneliese Widman, MC **FP** Hunter Playhouse, New York NY 15 January 1950

ORESTES

Solo **M** (sometimes performed in silence) John Cage **C** MC **FP** Black Mountain College NC 20 August 1948

[THE] MONKEY DANCES

Solo in seven parts: "Quadrille," "Valse," "Pas vite," "Mazurka," "Un peu vif," "Polka," "Quadrille" **M** Erik Satie (from *Le Piège de Méduse*) **C** Mary Outten; tail by Richard Lippold, hat by MC **FP** Black Mountain College NC 20 August 1948; City Center, New York NY 18 December 1949

1949
EFFUSIONS AVANT L'HEURE

M John Cage (*A Valentine out of Season*) **C** practice clothes **D** Tanaquil

LeClercq, Betty Nichols, MC **FP** Jean Hélion's studio, Paris 10 June 1949, and again at the Théâtre du Vieux Colombier, Paris 11 July 1949
NP under the title *Games* **D** Tanaquil LeClercq, Pat McBride, MC **FP** Hunter Playhouse, New York NY 15 January 1950
NP MCDC under the title *Trio* **D** Jo Anne Melsher, Marianne Preger, Remy Charlip **FP** Theater de Lys, New York NY 30 December 1953

AMORES

M John Cage (*Amores I* and *IV*, 1943) **C** practice clothes **D** Tanaquil LeClercq, MC **FP** Jean Hélion's studio, Paris 10 June 1949, and again at the Théâtre du Vieux Colombier, Paris 11 July 1949; Hunter Playhouse, New York NY 15 January 1950
ST MCDC **D** Carolyn Brown, MC **FP** Theater de Lys, New York NY 30 December 1953

DUET

M ? **C** Léonor Fini **D** Betty Nichols, Milorad Miskovitch **FP** at a garden fête, Paris, summer 1949

TWO STEP

Solo **M** Erik Satie (*La Diva de "l'Empire," intermezzo américain*, 1900) **C** MC **FP** New York City Dance Theater, City Center, New York NY 18 December 1949

1950
POOL OF DARKNESS

M Ben Weber (ballet, opus 26) **C** MC **D** Dorothy Berea, Mili Churchill, Anneliese Widman, MC **FP** Hunter Playhouse, New York NY 15 January 1950

BEFORE DAWN

Solo **M** (in silence) **C** MC **FP** Hunter Playhouse, New York NY 15 January 1950

WALTZ

M Erik Satie (*Je te veux*) **D** Martha Jane Adams, Doskye Barnes, Blanche Duffy, Evelyn Ellis, Evelyn Landry, Mary Elizabeth Norckauer, Suzanne Phebus, Betty Reed, Mark Allen Bergeron, Ellis Jordan, Wilson Manuel, Dick Wakefield **FP** Louisiana State University Dance Group, Baton Rouge LA 27 June 1950

See 1950, *Waltz*

RAG-TIME PARADE

M Erik Satie (from the ballet *Parade*, 1917) **C** from thrift shops **D** Doskye Barnes, Blanche Duffy, Evelyn Landry, Suzanne Phebus, Wilson Manuel, Mark Allen Bergeron **FP** Louisiana State University Dance Group, Baton Rouge LA 27 June 1950
NP MC and Company **D** Sudie Bond, Marianne Preger, Rachel Rosenthal, Julie Walter, François Canton, Remy Charlip **FP** Cooper Union, New York NY 24 November 1950

ST MCDC **D** Carolyn Brown, Anita Dencks, Viola Farber, Jo Anne Melsher, Remy Charlip, Paul Taylor **FP** Black Mountain College NC 22 August 1953; Theater de Lys, New York NY 30 December 1953

WALTZ
Solo **M** Erik Satie (*Je te veux*) **FP** Cooper Union, New York NY 24 November 1950

1951
SIXTEEN DANCES FOR SOLOIST AND COMPANY OF THREE
In sixteen parts: solo, trio, solo, duet, solo, quartet, solo, quartet, solo, duet, solo, trio, solo, quartet, duet, quartet **M** John Cage **C** and properties: Eleanor de Vito, John Cage, Remy Charlip, MC; coat a gift from Antoinette Larrabee and Constance Smith; mask by Remy Charlip after a sketch by John Heliker **D** MC, Dorothy Berea, Mili Churchill, Anneliese Widman **FP** Bennett Junior College, Millbrook NY 17 January 1951; Hunter Playhouse, New York NY 21 January 1951
NP solo suite from the above: Nos 3, 5, 9, 11, and 16 **FP** University of Washington, Seattle WA 12 April 1951

MC also performed no. 9 separately, and a suite of eight numbers from the complete work was performed by MC, Dorothy Berea, Joan Skinner, and Anneliese Widman at the Brooklyn Museum, Brooklyn NY 14 November 1951
ST American Dance **D** MC, Natanya Neumann, Joan Skinner, Anneliese Widman **FP** Alvin Theatre, New York NY 18 April 1953

VARIATION
Solo **M** Morton Feldman **C** MC **FP** University of Washington, Seattle WA 12 April 1951; Theater de Lys, New York NY 1 January 1954

BOY WHO WANTED TO BE A BIRD
Solo **M** (in silence) **FP** Martha's Vineyard MA summer 1951

1952
SUITE BY CHANCE
In four movements **M** Christian Wolff (For Magnetic Tape) **C** Remy Charlip **D** MC, Sudie Bond, Jo Anne Melsher, Marianne Preger, Remy Charlip **FP** (preview): Dancers Studio, New York NY winter 1952
NP Merce Cunningham and Company

D MC, Carolyn Brown, Jo Anne Melsher, Natanya Neumann, Marianne Preger, Joan Skinner (Preger's name appears in the program but she was in fact ill and unable to perform.) **FP** University of Illinois, Urbana IL 24 March 1953; Brooklyn Institute of Arts and Sciences, Brooklyn NY 15 April 1953
NP MCDC, first two movements only **D** MC, Carolyn Brown, Viola Farber, Jo Anne Melsher, Remy Charlip **FP** Black Mountain College NC 22 August 1953
NP MCDC, complete work **D** MC, Carolyn Brown, Anita Dencks, Viola Farber, Jo Anne Melsher, Marianne Preger, Remy Charlip **FP** Theater de Lys, New York NY 29 December 1953

SUITE OF SIX SHORT DANCES
Solo **M** recorder pieces, arranged by W. P. Jennerjahn **FP** Black Mountain College NC, spring 1952

Excerpts from SYMPHONIE POUR UN HOMME SEUL
In two parts **M** Pierre Schaeffer, with the collaboration of Pierre Henry (*Eroica, Apostrophe,* and *Strette* from *Symphonie pour un homme seul* **C** street clothes **D** part I: solo; part II: MC, Natanya Neumann, Joan Skinner, Anneliese Widman, Joanne Finkelor, Jo Anne Melsher, Marianne Preger, Greta Rosenzweig, Remy Charlip, Ben Garber, Donald McKayle **FP** Festival of the Creative Arts, Brandeis University, Waltham MA 14 June 1952
NP MCDC under the title *Collage* **D** part I: MC; part II: Carolyn Brown, Anita Dencks, Viola Farber, Marianne Preger, Remy Charlip, Paul Taylor **FP** Theater de Lys, New York NY 30 December 1953
NP MCDC part I only, solo **FP** Marine's Memorial Theatre, San Francisco CA 15 November 1955
ST University of Illinois Dance Group **FP** University of Illinois, Urbana IL 4 March 1959
NP MC and Carolyn Brown concert; solo under the title *Collage I* (essentially a new solo) **FP** University of Pittsburgh, Pittsburgh PA 21 May 1958
NP MCDC solo under the title *Collage* (a reworking of the above) **FP** University of Rochester, Rochester NY 23 February 1963; Hunter Playhouse, New York NY 12 February 1965

At the performance at the Sixteenth American Dance Festival, Connecticut College, New London CT 16 August 1963, and thereafter, the solo was

given under the title *Collage III.*
See 1955, *The Young Disciple*

LES NOCES
"A Choral Ballet in four scenes" **M and text** Igor Stravinsky **S C** Howard Bay **D** The Bride: Natanya Neumann; The Groom: MC; The Parents: Joan Skinner, Ronne Aul, Anneliese Widman, Donald McKayle; The Guests: Phyllis Backer, Helaine Berley, Adelaide Case, Jo Anne Melsher, Marianne Preger, Naima Wallenrod, Remy Charlip, Ben Garber **FP** Festival of the Creative Arts, Brandeis University, Waltham MA 14 June 1952

BRIGADOON
Musical play in three (originally two) acts. Book and lyrics by Alan Jay Lerner **M** Frederick Loewe Staged by Batchelor Owen **Ch** MC **S** Barrie Greenbie **C** Ruth Young **D** Harry Beaton: MC; Meg Brockie: Jo Anne Melsher; Jean MacLaren: Louise Hobson **FP** Burnsville School of the Arts, Parkway Playhouse, Burnsville NC 15 August 1952

[Theater Piece]
Performed by John Cage, Nicola Cernovich, MC, Charles Olson, Robert Rauschenberg, M. C. Richards, David Tudor **FP** Black Mountain College NC [16 August?] 1952

1953
SOLO SUITE IN SPACE AND TIME
Solo in five parts: "At Random," "Stillness," "Repetition," "Excursion," "For the Air" **M** John Cage (*Music for Piano 1–20*) **C** MC **FP** Louisiana State University, Baton Rouge LA 23 June 1953; MCDC, Theater de Lys, New York NY 30 December 1953
See 1956, *Suite for Five in Space and Time*

DEMONSTRATION PIECE
In four movements **M** (in silence) **D** Barbara Brown, Dorcas Brown, Bobbie Chachere, Alida Dureau, Katie Planche Freidrichs, Sybill Gaines, Sonya LeBlanc **FP** Louisiana State University Dance Group, Baton Rouge LA 23 June 1953

EPILOGUE
M Erik Satie **D** Barbara Brown, Dorcas Brown, Bobbie Chachere, Alida Dureau, Katie Planche Freidrichs, Sybill Gaines, Sonya LeBlanc **FP** Louisiana State University Dance Group, Baton Rouge LA 23 June 1953

BANJO
M Louis Moreau Gottschalk (*Le Banjo,* opus 15, 1855) **C** Remy Charlip **D** MC, Carolyn Brown, Viola Farber, Jo Anne Melsher, Remy Charlip, Paul Taylor **FP** MCDC, Black Mountain College NC 21 August 1953; Theater de Lys, New York NY 29 December 1953
See 1957, *Picnic Polka*

DIME A DANCE
M "The Whole World," a program of nineteenth-century piano music selected by David Tudor. "The Run": Moritz Moszkowski, *The Juggleress, Phantasiestuck,* Opus 52 No. 4. "The Fall": *Arabian National Hymn,* [Baptist]. "The Glide": Lund Skabo, *Prelude.* "The Waltz": Louis Moreau Gottschalk, *Radieuse, Grande valse de concert,* Opus 72. "The Tango": Alois Haba, *Tango.* "The Five-Four": György Kosa, *Schüchterne Sehnsucht* [Timid Yearning]. "The Polka": Ludwig Stasny, *Kutschke-Polka,* Opus 155. "The Tarantella": Génari Karganov, *Tarentelle,* Opus 4. "The Swing": Claude Debussy, *Rêverie.* "The Lunge": Louis Moreau Gottschalk, *Souvenir de Porto Rico* [*Marche des Gibaros*], Opus 31. "The Insect": Charles V. Alkan, *Gros temps,* from *Les Mois,* Opus 74. "The Jump-Turn": Charles Breton, *Springtime of Youth, Gavotte.* "The Eclectic" (*Der Eklektiker*): Ludwig van Beethoven, *Bagatelle,* Opus 126 No 4 **C** Remy Charlip **D** MC, Ethel Brodsky, Carolyn Brown, Anita Dencks, Viola Farber, Jo Anne Melsher, Deborah Moscowitz, Remy Charlip, Timothy La Farge, Paul Taylor **FP** MCDC, Black Mountain College NC 21 August 1953
NP MCDC **D** MC, Carolyn Brown, Anita Dencks, Viola Farber, Jo Anne Melsher, Marianne Preger, Remy Charlip, Paul Taylor **FP** Theater de Lys, New York NY 31 December 1953

In 1971, MC began to include "The Run" from *Dime a Dance* in Event performances. In 1972 he taught Chris Komar a solo ("Oriental Dance") originally composed for *Dime a Dance* but never used, which Komar performed, also in Events. This was again danced by Jared Phillips in an Event at the Joyce Theater, New York NY 17 September 1994, and thereafter.

SEPTET
M Erik Satie (*Trois morceaux en forme de poire,* 1903) **C** Remy Charlip **D** MC, Carolyn Brown, Anita Dencks, Viola

Farber, Jo Anne Melsher, Remy Charlip, Paul Taylor (Marianne Preger was to dance in the first performance, but was unable to; her part was divided between Anita Dencks and Viola Farber.) (There are normally six people in the dance; the title refers to the fact that there are seven sections.) **FP** MCDC, Black Mountain College NC 22 August 1953

NP MCDC **D** MC, Carolyn Brown, Marianne Preger, Jo Anne Melsher, Remy Charlip, Paul Taylor **FP** Theater de Lys, New York NY 29 December 1953

ST MCDC **D** Robert Swinston, Kristy Santimyer, Karen Radford, Carol Teitelbaum, Chris Komar, Dennis O'Connor **FP** City Center Theater, New York NY 6 March 1987

ST Rambert Dance Company **R** Chris Komar **FP** Theatre Royal, Glasgow, Scotland 20 November 1987

ST Pacific Northwest Ballet **R** Chris Komar **FP** Seattle Center Opera House, Seattle WA 15 November 1989

ST Repertory Dance Theatre **R** Chris Komar **FP** Capitol Theatre, Salt Lake City UT 8 March 1991

ST White Oak Dance Project **R** Chris Komar, Robert Swinston, MC, Carolyn Brown **FP** Broward Center for the Performing Arts, Fort Lauderdale FL 25 March 1996

See 1970, *Objects*

UNTITLED SOLO
(called Solo at first performance)
Solo **M** Christian Wolff (*For Piano I*) **C** MC **FP** MCDC, Black Mountain College NC 22 August 1953; Theater de Lys, New York NY 31 December 1953

FRAGMENTS
In three parts, the second in silence **M** Pierre Boulez (*Étude à un son* and *Étude II*) **C** Remy Charlip **D** MC, Carolyn Brown, Anita Dencks, Jo Anne Melsher, Marianne Preger, Remy Charlip, Paul Taylor **FP** MCDC, Theater de Lys, New York NY 30 December 1953

1954
MINUTIAE
M John Cage (*Music for Piano 1–20*) **S** Robert Rauschenberg **C** Remy Charlip **D** MC, Carolyn Brown, Anita Dencks, Viola Farber, Jo Anne Melsher, Marianne Preger, Remy Charlip **FP** MCDC, Brooklyn Academy of Music, Brooklyn NY 8 December 1954

NP MCDC **D** MC, Carolyn Brown,

Anita Dencks, Viola Farber, Marianne Preger, Remy Charlip **FP** Bard College, Annandale-on-Hudson NY 24 May 1955 (where Jo Anne Melsher's part was distributed among the other women)

1955
SPRINGWEATHER AND PEOPLE
M Earle Brown (*Indices*) **C** Remy Charlip, with the collaboration of Robert Rauschenberg, Ray Johnson, and Vera Williams **D** MC, Carolyn Brown, Anita Dencks, Viola Farber, Marianne Preger, Remy Charlip **FP** MCDC, Bard College, Annandale-on-Hudson NY 24 May 1955; Henry Street Playhouse, New York NY 27 May 1955

NP MCDC **M** Earle Brown (*Indices*) in orchestral version **C** Robert Rauschenberg **D** MC, Carolyn Brown, Viola Farber, Marianne Simon (formerly Preger), Cynthia Stone, Remy Charlip **FP** Brooklyn Academy of Music, New York NY 30 November 1957

NP duets excerpted from the complete work under the title *Suite from Springweather and People* **D** MC, Carolyn Brown **FP** University of Pittsburgh, Pittsburgh PA 21 May 1958

THE YOUNG DISCIPLE
"A martyrology in three acts," by Paul Goodman. Directed and designed by Julian Beck **Ch** MC **M** Pierre Schaeffer with the collaboration of Pierre Henry (*Symphonie pour un homme seul*), and Ned Rorem (for the song "The Midnight Sun") Cast: A Man: Henry Proach; A Woman: Margery Hargrove; The Young Disciple: Hooper Dunbar; Caspar: William Vines; Melchior: Walter Mullen; Balthasar: Shirley Stoliar; A Tolerant Man: Ace King; A Child: Sharon Stock; A Boy: Mark William; An Old Crone: Judith Malina; Our Master: Philip Smith; An Old Woman, Ernestine: Katherine Lurker; An Old Woman, Jessie: Jean Barr **FP** The Living Theatre, New York NY 12 October 1955

1956
GALAXY
"A quartet of solos" **M** Earle Brown (*Four Systems*) **C** Remy Charlip **D** Carolyn Brown, Viola Farber, Marianne Preger, Remy Charlip **FP** MCDC, University of Notre Dame, South Bend IN 18 May 1956; Brooklyn Academy of Music, Brooklyn NY 12 January 1957

NP MCDC, trio version subtitled "a trio of solos" **D** Carolyn Brown, Viola

Farber, Marianne Simon **FP** Ball State Teachers College, Muncie IN 1 July 1958

NP MC and Carolyn Brown; Carolyn Brown's solo only, under the title *Nebulosa* **FP** Kungl Teatern, Stockholm, Sweden 5 October 1958

LAVISH ESCAPADE
Solo **M** Christian Wolff (*For Piano II*) **C** MC **FP** MCDC, University of Notre Dame, South Bend IN 18 May 1956; Brooklyn Academy of Music, Brooklyn NY 12 January 1957

SUITE FOR FIVE
IN SPACE AND TIME
In eight parts: solo: "At Random"; trio: "Transition"; solo: "Stillness"; duet: "Extended Moment"; solo: "Repetition"; solo: "Excursion"; quintet: "Meetings"; solo: "For the Air" **M** John Cage (from *Music for Piano*) **C** Robert Rauschenberg **D** MC, Carolyn Brown, Viola Farber, Marianne Preger, Remy Charlip **FP** MCDC, University of Notre Dame, South Bend IN 18 May 1956

This piece was made by adding the trio, duet, and quintet to an earlier solo of MC's, *Solo Suite in Space and Time* (1953).

NP MCDC, under the title *Suite for Five*. In six parts: solo: "At Random"; trio: "Transition"; solo: "Stillness"; duet: "Extended Moment"; solo: "Excursion"; quintet: "Meetings" **D** as above **FP** Cornell College, Mount Vernon IO 11 October 1956; Brooklyn Academy of Music, Brooklyn NY 12 January 1957

NP MC and Carolyn Brown; duet version under the title *Suite for Two* **D** solo, "At Random": MC; solo, "A Meander": Carolyn Brown; solo, "Stillness": MC; duet, "Extended Moment": Carolyn Brown, MC **FP** University of Pittsburgh, Pittsburgh PA 21 May 1958

NP MCDC In seven parts: solo: "At Random"; solo: "A Meander"; trio: "Transition"; solo: "Stillness"; duet: "Extended Moment"; solo: "Excursion"; quintet: "Meetings" **D** as for first performance **FP** Ball State Teachers College, Muncie IN 1 July 1958; Hunter Playhouse, New York NY 14 February 1965

Trio and Quintet included in Events; MC's solos included in early Events

The solo "Stillness" was revived in an Event at the Joyce Theater, New York NY 30 November 1985, danced by Rob

Remley, and again in an Event at the Joyce on 16 September 1994, danced by Thomas Caley.

NOCTURNES
In five parts, "from dusk to the witching hour" **M** Erik Satie (*Nocturnes* for piano) **S** **C** Robert Rauschenberg **D** MC, Carolyn Brown, Viola Farber, Marianne Preger, Remy Charlip, Bruce King **FP** MCDC, Jacob's Pillow, Lee MA 11 July 1956; Brooklyn Academy of Music, Brooklyn NY 12 January 1957

1957
LABYRINTHIAN DANCES
"area without exit" In four parts **M** Josef Matthias Hauer (*Zwolftonspiel Mai 55, Juli 52, Juli 56,* and *Labyrinthischer Tanz*) **S** **C** Robert Rauschenberg **D** MC, Carolyn Brown, Viola Farber, Marianne Simon, Remy Charlip, Bruce King **FP** MCDC, Brooklyn Academy of Music, Brooklyn NY 30 November 1957

CHANGELING
Solo **M** Christian Wolff (*Suite*) **C** Robert Rauschenberg **FP** MCDC, Brooklyn Academy of Music, Brooklyn NY 30 November 1957

PICNIC POLKA
M Louis Moreau Gottschalk (*Ses Yeux, Polka de concert*, Opus 66 **C** Remy Charlip **D** MC, Carolyn Brown, Viola Farber, Marianne Simon, Remy Charlip, Bruce King **FP** MCDC, Brooklyn Academy of Music, Brooklyn NY 30 November 1957

A companion piece to *Banjo*, 1953, with which it was always performed

1958
ANTIC MEET
In nine parts: "opener," "room for two," "mockgame," "sports and diversions"; #1, "sports and diversions"; #2, "social," "bacchus and cohorts," "sports and diversions"; #3, "a single," "exodus." **M** John Cage (*Concert for piano and orchestra*, or, sometimes, *Solo for Piano with Fontana Mix*, or *WBAI*) **S** **C** Robert Rauschenberg **D and properties** MC, Carolyn Brown, Viola Farber, Cynthia Stone, Marilyn Wood, Remy Charlip **FP** MCDC, Eleventh American Dance Festival, Connecticut College, New London CT 14 August 1958; Phoenix Theatre, New York NY 16 February 1960

NP MC and Carolyn Brown; MC's solo

"a single" only, under the title *Ett Nummer* **M** John Cage (*Variations*) **FP** Kungl Teatern, Stockholm, Sweden 5 October 1958

Some sections (e.g. "room for two") included in early Events

SUMMERSPACE
"a lyric dance" **M** Morton Feldman (*Ixion*) **S C** Robert Rauschenberg **D** MC, Carolyn Brown, Viola Farber, Cynthia Stone, Marilyn Wood, Remy Charlip **FP** MCDC, Eleventh American Dance Festival, Connecticut College, New London CT 17 August 1958; Phoenix Theatre, New York NY 16 February 1960
NP New York City Ballet; revised for classic ballet **D** Anthony Blum, Kay Mazzo, Patricia Neary, Sara Leland, Carol Sumner, Deni Lamont **FP** New York State Theater, New York NY 14 April 1966
ST Cullbergbaletten, under the Swedish title *Sommarrymd* **FP** Stadsteatern, Stockholm, Sweden 22 October 1967
ST The Boston Ballet **FP** Music Hall, Boston MA 7 November 1974
ST Théâtre du Silence **FP** Salle des Sports, La Rochelle, France 29 October 1976; Beacon Theatre, New York NY 21 March 1978

Danced as part of early Events

NATTVANDRARE
M Bo Nilsson (*Rörelser, Slagfigurer, Kvantiteter*) **C** Nicola Cernovich **D** MC, Carolyn Brown **FP** MC and Carolyn Brown, Kungl Teatern, Stockholm, Sweden 5 October 1958
NP MCDC, under the title *Night Wandering* **M** titles given as *Bewegungen, Quantitaten, and Schlagfiguren* **C** Robert Rauschenberg **D** MC, Carolyn Brown **FP** Thirteenth American Dance Festival, Connecticut College, New London CT 18 August 1960; Hunter Playhouse, New York NY 12 February 1965
ST 5 x 2 Plus **FP** University of Alaska, Anchorage AK 3 September 1977; American Place Theatre, New York NY 26 April 1978

Jasper Johns, *Numbers*, 1964, Sculp-metal on canvas, 110 x 85", commissioned for the lobby of the New York State Theater, Lincoln Center. Johns had MC step in the upper right-hand corner of the painting, so that "Merce would get his foot in the door" of the new theater.

1959

FROM THE POEMS OF WHITE STONE
M Chou Wen-Chung, with poems by Chiang Kuei (c. 1155–c. 1221 A.D.) **C** Robert Rauschenberg **D** MC, Carolyn Brown, Viola Farber, Judith Dunn, Marilyn Wood, Remy Charlip **FP** MCDC, University of Illinois, Urbana IL 14 March 1959

GAMBIT FOR DANCERS AND ORCHESTRA
In six parts: prelude, interlude, postlude, prelude, interlude, postlude **M** Ben Johnston **C** and projection: Robert Rauschenberg **D** MC, Carolyn Brown, Viola Farber, Judith Dunn, Marilyn Wood, Remy Charlip **FP** MCDC, University of Illinois, Urbana IL 14 March 1959

THE CAVE AT MACHPELAH
Play in three acts by Paul Goodman. Directed and designed by Julian Beck Dances by MC **M** Ned Rorem Cast: Hagar: Dina Paisner; Ishmael: Ira Lewis; Isaac (as a child): Harris Weiss; Abraham: Philip Huston; Sarah: Judith Malina; Menassah: Frank Maguire; Kiriath: Emy Boselli; An Angel of the Lord: Louis McKenzie; Ephron: Joseph Chaikin; Eleazar: Jamil Zakkai; Isaac (as a boy): Thomas Victor; A Ram: Jerome Raphel; Isaac (as a man): George Miller; Rebekah: Judith Malina. Sons of Ishmael: Jetur: Murray Paskin; Mishma: Jerome Raphel; Tema: Daniel Lutsky; Hadad: Garry Goodrow; Kedema: Henry Proach **FP** The Living Theatre, New York NY 11 June 1959

Robert Rauschenberg, *Story*, 1964, mixed media, left panel 95⅛ x 47½″, right panel 105 x 47½″.

RUNE

M Christian Wolff (*Music for MC*; sometimes performed to *For Pianist* with *Duo II for Pianists*) **C** Robert Rauschenberg **D** MC, Carolyn Brown, Viola Farber, Marilyn Wood, Judith Dunn, Remy Charlip **FP** MCDC, Twelfth American Dance Festival, Connecticut College, New London CT 14 August 1959; Phoenix Theatre, New York NY 16 February 1960
NP MCDC **C** Mark Lancaster **D** Chris Komar, Louise Burns, Susan Emery, Lise Friedman, Catherine Kerr, Neil Greenberg **FP** Théâtre de Basel, Basel, Switzerland 18 October 1982; City Center Theater, New York NY 22 March 1983
NP MCDC **S** Mark Lancaster

C Mark Lancaster with Suzanne Gallo **D** Frédéric Gafner, Kimberly Bartosik, China Laudisio, Banu Ogan, Jeannie Steele, Glen Rumsey **FP** City Center Theater, New York NY 9 March 1995

Some sections included in Events

1960
THEATRE PIECE

M John Cage **D** MC, Carolyn Brown **FP** Composers' Showcase, Circle in the Square, New York NY 7 March 1960

THE COOK'S QUADRILLE

A show for children by Juliette Waung, Steve Paxton, Julia Hurd, and Bernice Mendelsohn. Duet **Ch** MC **M** MC (tape) **D** Juliette Waung, Steve Paxton

FP The Living Theatre, New York NY 3 June 1960

CRISES

M Conlon Nancarrow (*Rhythm Studies #1, #2, #4, #5, #6* for player piano. At a performance at Northern Illinois University, DeKalb IL 11 February 1961, and thereafter, the music was listed as *Rhythm Studies # 1, 2, 4, 7, and 6*) **C** Robert Rauschenberg **D** MC, Carolyn Brown, Viola Farber, Marilyn Wood, Judith Dunn **FP** MCDC, Thirteenth American Dance Festival, Connecticut College, New London CT 19 August 1960; Hunter Playhouse, New York NY 12 February 1965

HANDS BIRDS

Solo **M** Earle Brown ("*December 1952*," from *Folio*) **C** Robert Rauschenberg **D** Carolyn Brown **FP** MC and Carolyn Brown, Venice Biennale, XXIII Festival Internazionale di Musica Contemporanea, Teatro la Fenice, Venice 24 September 1960

The title is a poem by M. C. Richards; the dance's original title was *Diana the Huntress*

WAKA

Solo **M** Toshi Ichiyanagi (*Music for Piano 2*) **C** Robert Rauschenberg (from *From the Poems of White Stone*) **D** Carolyn Brown **FP** MC and Carolyn Brown, Venice Biennale, XXIII Festival Internazionale di Musica Contemporanea, Teatro la Fenice, Venice 24 September 1960

MUSIC WALK WITH DANCERS

M John Cage (*Music Walk*) **D** MC, Carolyn Brown **FP** MC and Carolyn Brown, Venice Biennale, XXIII Festival Internazionale di Musica Contemporanea, Teatro la Fenice, Venice 24 September 1960

1961
SUITE DE DANSES

Dance for television. Director: Jean Mercure **M** Serge Garrant **C** Jasper Johns **D** MC, Carolyn Brown, Judith Dunn, Marilyn Wood. MCDC, filmed for Société Radio-Canada, Sérénade Estivale, Montreal, Canada 12 June 1961

ÆON

M John Cage (*Atlas Eclipticalis* and the electronic version of *Winter Music*) **C and objects** Robert Rauschenberg **D** MC, Carolyn Brown, Viola Farber, Judith Dunn, Marilyn Wood, Shareen Blair, Valda Setterfield, Remy Charlip, Steve Paxton **FP** MCDC, Montréal Festival, La Comédie Canadienne, Montréal, Canada 5 August 1961; Fourteenth American Dance Festival, Connecticut College, New London CT 17 August 1961

The title was originally announced (in the American Dance Festival flyer) as *Combines*.
NP MCDC **M** John Cage (*Winter Music* alone) **D** MC, Carolyn Brown, Judith Dunn, Viola Farber, Marilyn Wood, Steve Paxton **FP** East High School, Denver CO 9 February 1962; Philharmonic Hall, New York NY 13 August 1963

The number of dancers was flexible: the original cast consisted of six women and three men; the third performance, on tour in Colorado in February 1962, had a cast of six, four women and two men; at the beginning of 1963 a fifth woman and a third man were added, but on occasion during that year the cast was again reduced to six. During the 1964 world tour, the cast was enlarged to five or six women and four men (one more than the original cast). *Æon* was not performed as a repertory work after the conclusion of that tour, but sections were used in Events.

1962
THE CONSTRUCTION OF BOSTON

A collaboration by Niki de Saint-Phalle, Robert Rauschenberg, Jean Tinguely, and Kenneth Koch (text). Directed by MC. Cast: Irving Blum, MacIntyre Dixon, Elmarie Dooley, Richard Libertini, Öyvind Fählstrom, Viola Farber, Steve Paxton, Maxine Groffsky, Henry Geldzahler, Jean Tinguely, Niki de Saint-Phalle, Robert Rauschenberg, Frank Stella, Billy Klüver **FP** Maidman Theatre, New York NY 4 May 1962

1963
FIELD DANCES

M John Cage (At a performance at the Phoenix Theatre, London 10 August 1964, and sometimes thereafter, the music was identified as *Variations IV*.) **C** Robert Rauschenberg **D** MC, Carolyn Brown, Viola Farber, Shareen Blair. **FP** MCDC, University of California, Los Angeles CA 17 July 1963; Hunter Playhouse, New York NY 12 February 1965

NP MCDC **M** (in silence) **C** black leotards and tights **D** Carolyn Brown, Barbara Lloyd, Sandra Neels, Valda Setterfield, Albert Reid, Peter Saul, Gus Solomons, Jr. **FP** Saville Theatre, London 3 December 1966; Brooklyn Academy of Music, New York NY 1 April 1967

NP MCDC **M** John Cage (see note above) **C** Remy Charlip (from *Minutiae*) **D** Carolyn Brown, Barbara Lloyd, Sandra Neels, Yseult Riopelle, Valda Setterfield, Albert Reid, Peter Saul, Gus Solomons, Jr. **FP** Twentieth American Dance Festival, Connecticut College, New London CT 6 August 1967 **ST** University Dance Company, Ohio State University **R** Margaret Jenkins, Peter Saul **FP** Regional American College Dance Festival, Heinz Hall for the Performing Arts, Pittsburgh PA 12 March 1973 **ST** State University of New York at Buffalo **R** Valda Setterfield **FP** Albright-Knox Gallery, Buffalo, New York NY 19 May 1973

Included in Events; danced in repertory in conjunction with *Open Session* or *Collage III* (see *Excerpts from Symphonie pour un homme seul*, 1952) and *Cross Currents* (see 1964)

STORY

M Toshi Ichiyanagi (Variously identified as *Kaiki, Music for Piano* (electronic version), and *Sapporo*) **S C** Robert Rauschenberg **D** MC, Carolyn Brown, Viola Farber, Shareen Blair, Barbara Lloyd, William Davis, Steve Paxton. **FP** MCDC, University of California, Los Angeles CA 24 July 1963

Included in early Events; "Objects" trio revived in 1985 for Events; other excerpts revived for Events at the Joyce Theater, New York NY 13 September 1994

1964
OPEN SESSION

Solo **M** (in silence) **C** MC **FP** MCDC, Wadsworth Atheneum, Hartford CT 19 March 1964

Sometimes performed in conjunction with *Field Dances* (1963)

PAIRED

M John Cage (*Duet for Cymbal*) **C** Robert Rauschenberg **D** MC, Viola Farber **FP** MCDC, Wadsworth Atheneum, Hartford CT 21 March 1964; Hunter Playhouse, New York NY 14 February 1965

WINTERBRANCH

M La Monte Young (*2 sounds (April 1960)*) **C and object**: Robert Rauschenberg **D** MC, Carolyn Brown, Viola Farber, Barbara Lloyd, William Davis, Steve Paxton **FP** MCDC, Wadsworth Atheneum, Hartford CT 21 March 1964; New York State Theater, New York NY 4 March 1965

Performed in part or in its entirety in Events

ST The Boston Ballet **FP** Music Hall, Boston MA 7 November 1974

MUSEUM EVENT #1

M John Cage (*Atlas Eclipticalis*) **C and properties**: Robert Rauschenberg **D** MC, Carolyn Brown, Viola Farber, Shareen Blair, Deborah Hay, Barbara

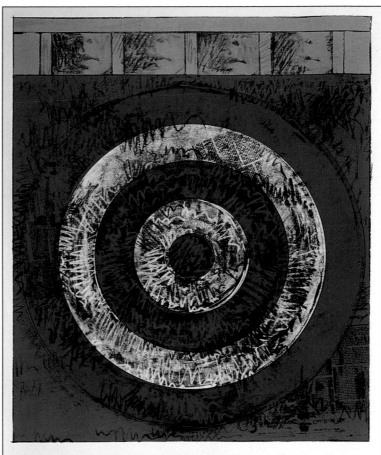

Jasper Johns, "Target" poster, 1968. This was Jasper Johns's first silk screen print.

Lloyd, Sandra Neels, William Davis, Steve Paxton, Albert Reid **FP** MCDC, Museum des 20. Jahrhunderts, Vienna, Austria 24 June 1964

This was the first Event performance by Merce Cunningham Dance Company; subsequent Events are not listed in this chronology.

CROSS CURRENTS

M Conlon Nancarrow, arranged by John Cage (a collage of the *Rhythm Studies for player piano*) **C** MC **D** MC, Carolyn Brown, Viola Farber **FP** MCDC, Sadler's Wells Theatre, London 31 July 1964

NP MCDC **M** John Cage (*Variations IV*) **D** as above **FP** Mangaldas Town Hall, Ahmedabad, Gujarat, India 21 October 1964; Skidmore College, Saratoga Springs NY 10 February 1965

Included in Events and Lecture-Demonstrations

ST US Terpsichore **R** Chris Komar **FP** Brandeis High School, New York NY 3 October 1980 **ST** Werkcentrum Dans **R** Chris Komar **FP** Schouwburg, Rotterdam 19 September 1984

1965
VARIATIONS V

M John Cage (*Variations V*) Film: Stan VanDerBeek. Distortion of video images: Nam June Paik **C** street and practice clothes **D** MC, Carolyn Brown, Barbara Lloyd, Sandra Neels, Albert Reid, Peter Saul, Gus Solomons, Jr. **FP** MCDC, French-American Festival, Philharmonic Hall, New York NY 23 July 1965

Film version made in Hamburg, July 1966; produced by Studio Hamburg; directed by Arne Arnbom

Frank Stella, poster for the Merce Cunningham Dance Company's first Latin American tour, summer 1968.

HOW TO PASS, KICK, FALL AND RUN

M John Cage (stories from *Silence, A Year from Monday*, and elsewhere) **D** MC, Carolyn Brown, Barbara Lloyd, Sandra Neels, Valda Setterfield, Albert Reid, Peter Saul, Gus Solomons, Jr. **FP** MCDC, Harper Theatre, Chicago IL 24 November 1965; Juilliard Concert Hall, New York NY 27 March 1966 (excerpts only, under the title *Composition X*); Hunter Playhouse, New York NY 9 December 1966

Excerpts used in Events

1966
PLACE

M Gordon Mumma (*Mesa*) **S C** Beverly Emmons **D** MC, Carolyn Brown, Barbara Lloyd, Sandra Neels, Valda Setterfield, Albert Reid, Peter Saul, Gus Solomons, Jr. **FP** MCDC, Fondation Maeght, Saint-Paul de Vence, France 6 August 1966; Hunter Playhouse, New York NY 9 December 1966

1967
SCRAMBLE

M Toshi Ichiyanagi (*Activities for Orchestra*) **S C** Frank Stella **D** MC, Carolyn Brown, Barbara Lloyd, Sandra Neels, Yseult Riopelle, Valda Setterfield, Albert Reid, Gus Solomons, Jr. **FP** MCDC, Ravinia Festival, Chicago IL 25 July 1967; Brooklyn Academy of Music, Brooklyn NY 2 December 1967

Excerpts performed in Events

Two performances of the Event version of *Scramble* were given in a repertory program in Germany in 1988. **M** Takehisa Kosugi, Michael Pugliese, David Tudor **C** William Anastasi and Dove Bradshaw (Duisburg), Mark Lancaster (Cologne) **D** Helen Barrow, Kimberly Bartosik, Emma Diamond, Victoria Finlayson, Chris Komar, David Kulick, Patricia Lent, Larissa McGoldrick, Dennis O'Connor, Kristy Santimyer, Robert Swinston, Carol Teitelbaum, Robert Wood **FP** Theater der Stadt Duisburg, 1 July 1988, and Opernhaus, Cologne 3 July 1988 **ST** Accademia Nazionale di Danza **R** Susana Hayman-Chaffey **FP** Teatro Olimpico, Rome, Italy 4 July 1995

1968
RAINFOREST

M David Tudor (*Rainforest*) **S** Andy Warhol (*Silver Clouds*) **C** Jasper Johns (uncredited) **D** MC, Carolyn Brown, Barbara Lloyd, Sandra Neels, Albert Reid, Gus Solomons, Jr. **FP** MCDC, 2nd Buffalo Festival of the Arts Today, State University College at Buffalo, New York NY 9 March 1968; Brooklyn Academy of Music, Brooklyn NY 15 May 1968

WALKAROUND TIME

M David Behrman ("...*for nearly an hour...*") **S** after Marcel Duchamp's *Large Glass*, supervised by Jasper Johns **C** Jasper Johns (uncredited) **D** MC, Carolyn Brown, Barbara Lloyd, Sandra Neels, Valda Setterfield, Meg Harper, Albert Reid, Gus Solomons, Jr., Jeff Slayton **FP** MCDC, 2nd Buffalo Festival of the Arts Today, State University College at Buffalo, New York NY 10 March 1968; Brooklyn Academy of Music, Brooklyn NY 22 May 1968

Excerpts included in an Event at Philadelphia Museum of Art, 16 October 1987, with Jasper Johns's decor, and thereafter in other Events

ASSEMBLAGE

A film for television. Directed by Richard Moore **M** John Cage, David Tudor, Gordon Mumma **D** MC, Carolyn Brown, Sandra Neels, Valda Setterfield, Meg Harper, Susana Hayman-Chaffey, Jeff Slayton, Chase Robinson, Mel Wong **FP** MCDC, KQED-TV, San Francisco CA 14 October–3 November 1968

Original working title: *Ghirardelli Square*

1969
CANFIELD

M Pauline Oliveros (*In Memoriam: NIKOLA TESLA, Cosmic Engineer*) **S** Robert Morris **C** Jasper Johns (uncredited) **D** MC, Carolyn Brown, Sandra Neels, Valda Setterfield, Meg Harper, Susana Hayman-Chaffey, Jeff Slayton, Chase Robinson, Mel Wong **FP** MCDC, Nazareth College, Rochester NY 4 March 1969 (without decor); Brooklyn Academy of Music, Brooklyn NY 15 April 1969 (without music)

Performed in part and in its entirety in Events

1970
TREAD

M Christian Wolff (*For 1, 2 or 3 People*) **S** Bruce Nauman **C** MC **D** MC, Carolyn Brown, Sandra Neels, Valda Setterfield, Meg Harper, Susana Hayman-Chaffey, Jeff Slayton, Chase Robinson, Mel Wong, Douglas Dunn **FP** MCDC, Brooklyn Academy of Music, Brooklyn NY 5 January 1970

SECOND HAND

In three parts **M** John Cage (*Cheap Imitation*) **C** Jasper Johns **D** part I (a reconstruction of *Idyllic Song*, 1945) MC; part II MC, Carolyn Brown; part III MC, Carolyn Brown, Sandra Neels, Valda Setterfield, Meg Harper, Susana Hayman-Chaffey, Jeff Slayton, Chase Robinson, Mel Wong, Douglas Dunn **FP** MCDC, Brooklyn Academy of Music, Brooklyn NY 8 January 1970

SIGNALS

M David Tudor, Gordon Mumma, John Cage (*First Week of June*) (These were the musicians and the title of the music at the first performance; at subsequent performances the title changed according to the date, and the piece was composed and performed by the musicians who were with the company at the time.) **C** MC **D** "Solos for 1, 2 or 3": Susana Hayman-Chaffey, MC, Mel Wong; "Duet for 2": Susana Hayman-Chaffey, Mel Wong; "Trio for 3 or 4": Valda Setterfield, MC, Mel Wong, Douglas Dunn; "Sextet for 5 or 6": Louise Burns, Susana Hayman-Chaffey, Valda Setterfield, MC, Douglas Dunn, Mel Wong **FP** MCDC, Théâtre de France, Paris 5 June 1970; Brooklyn Academy of Music, Brooklyn NY 4 November 1970

ST Ohio Ballet **R** MC, Chris Komar **FP** University of Akron OH 20 February 1981

NP White Oak Dance Project **R** Chris Komar, Robert Swinston, Meg Harper **M** David Tudor, Takehisa Kosugi, John Adams, D'Arcy Philip Gray **C** Brice Marden **D** Nancy Colahan, Rob Besserer, Mikhail Baryshnikov, John Gardner, Ruthlyn V. Salomons, Kate Johnson **FP** New York State Theater, New York NY 1 March 1994

Performed in part or in its entirety in Events

OBJECTS

M Alvin Lucier (*Vespers*) **S** Neil Jenney **D** MC, Carolyn Brown, Sandra Neels, Meg Harper, Susana Hayman-Chaffey, Louise Burns, Chase Robinson, Ulysses Dove, Douglas Dunn **FP** MCDC, Brooklyn Academy of Music, Brooklyn NY 10 November 1970

Excerpt (game of jacks) used in Events

1971
LOOPS

Event for soloist **M** Gordon Mumma (*Biophysical and ambient signals from FM telemetry*) Performed in front of Jasper Johns's *Map* (Based on Buckminster Fuller's Dymaxion Air Ocean World). Slides: Charles Atlas **FP** The Museum of Modern Art, New York NY 3 December 1971

NP under the title *Loops and Additions* **FP** Composers' Showcase, Whitney Museum of American Art, New York NY 18 May 1973

Performed in Events and in repertory in combination with *Changing Steps* (1973) and/or *Exercise Piece I & II* (1978)

1972
LANDROVER

In four parts **M** John Cage, Gordon Mumma, David Tudor (*52/3*; the title refers to the piece's duration, and may vary when only some parts of the dance are given) **C** Jasper Johns **D** Carolyn Brown, MC, Ulysses Dove, Douglas Dunn, Meg Harper, Nanette Hassall, Susana Hayman-Chaffey, Chris Komar, Sandra Neels, Chase Robinson, Valda Setterfield **FP** MCDC, Brooklyn Academy of Music, Brooklyn NY 1 February 1972

NP MCDC **M** John Cage, Martin Kalve, David Tudor **D** Karole Armitage, Louise Burns, Ellen Cornfield, Catherine Kerr, Chris Komar, Robert Kovich, Joseph Lennon (in MC's role), Susan Emery, Lisa Fox, Lise Friedman, Alan Good **FP** City Center Theater, New York NY 27 February 1980

Excerpts performed in Events

TV RERUN

M Gordon Mumma (*Telepos*) **S C** Jasper Johns **D** MC, Carolyn Brown, Sandra Neels, Valda Setterfield, Meg Harper, Susana Hayman-Chaffey, Nanette Hassall, Douglas Dunn, Ulysses Dove, Chris Komar **FP** MCDC, Brooklyn Academy of Music, Brooklyn NY 2 February 1972

Excerpts performed in Events

Merce Cunningham Studio, 498 Third Avenue, 1970. Left to right: Valda Setterfield, MC, Mel Wong, Chase Robinson, Susana Hayman-Chaffey. Photograph: Jack Mitchell.

Chess game, Cadaqués, Spain, 1960s. Left to right: Teeny Duchamp, John Cage, and MC. Photograph: James Klosty.

FP Théâtre Municipal, Roanne 19 January 1988

Excerpts performed in Events by MCDC

1974
WESTBETH

A work for video. Directed by Charles Atlas and MC **M** John Cage **C** Mark Lancaster, from a design by Jasper Johns (for *Un Jour ou deux*, 1973) **D** Karen Attix, Ellen Cornfield, Meg Harper, Catherine Kerr, Chris Komar, Robert Kovich, Brynar Mehl, Charles Moulton, Julie Roess-Smith, Valda Setterfield, George Titus. MCDC videotaped at Merce Cunningham Studio, Westbeth, New York NY, fall 1974; first public showing following a live performance of the dance, Merce Cunningham Studio, Westbeth, New York NY 14 February 1975, at which Susana Hayman-Chaffey performed in the place of George Titus

Performed in Events

1975
EXERCISE PIECE

C Mark Lancaster **D** Karen Attix, Ellen Cornfield, Meg Harper, Catherine Kerr, Chris Komar, Robert Kovich, Charles Moulton, Julie Roess-Smith, Valda Setterfield **FP** MCDC, Merce Cunningham Studio, Westbeth, New York NY 14 February 1975

See *Exercise Piece* I and II (a and b) (1978)

REBUS

M David Behrman (*Voice with Melody-Driven Electronics*) **S C** Mark Lancaster **D** Karen Attix, Ellen Cornfield, MC, Meg Harper, Susana Hayman-Chaffey, Catherine Kerr, Chris Komar, Robert Kovich, Brynar Mehl, Charles Moulton, Julie Roess-Smith **FP** MCDC, Music Hall, Detroit MI 7 March 1975; Minskoff Theater, New York NY 18 January 1977

SOUNDDANCE

M David Tudor (*Toneburst*) **S C** Mark Lancaster **D** Ellen Cornfield, MC, Meg Harper, Susana Hayman-Chaffey, Catherine Kerr, Chris Komar, Robert Kovich, Brynar Mehl, Charles Moulton, Julie Roess-Smith **FP** MCDC, Music Hall, Detroit MI 8 March 1975; Minskoff Theater, New York NY 19 January 1977

NP MCDC **R** Chris Komar, Meg Harper **M** David Tudor (*Untitled 1975/1994*) **S C** (new) Mark Lancaster

---

BORST PARK

M Christian Wolff (*Burdocks*) **C** The Company **D** MC, Ulysses Dove, Meg Harper, Nanette Hassall, Chris Komar, Sandra Neels **FP** MCDC, Brooklyn Academy of Music, Brooklyn NY 8 February 1972

1973
CHANGING STEPS

M David Behrman, John Cage, Gordon Mumma, David Tudor **C** Charles Atlas **D** Douglas Dunn, Meg Harper, Susana Hayman-Chaffey, Chris Komar, Robert Kovich, Barbara Lias, Brynar Mehl, Sandra Neels, Valda Setterfield, Julie Roess-Smith **FP** MCDC, as part of Event #65, Brooklyn Academy of Music, Brooklyn NY 22 March 1973 **NP** MCDC, combined with excerpts from *Loops* (1971) under the title *Changing Steps/Loops* **M** John Cage (*Cartridge Music*) **D** Karen Attix, Ellen Cornfield, MC, Meg Harper, Susana Hayman-Chaffey, Catherine Kerr, Chris Komar, Robert Kovich, Brynar Mehl, Charles Moulton, Julie Roess-Smith **FP** Music Hall, Detroit MI 7 March 1975 Thereafter performed in repertory in conjunction with *Loops* and *Exercise Piece* I or II (a and b).

Performed in part or in its entirety in Events; in an Event performance at the Centre Georges Pompidou, Paris

24 October 1979, performed by MCDC with Théâtre du Silence

Video version directed by Elliot Caplan and MC **M** John Cage (*Cartridge Music*) **C** Mark Lancaster, Suzanne Gallo **D** Helen Barrow, Kimberly Bartosik, Emma Diamond, Victoria Finlayson, Alan Good, Chris Komar, David Kulick, Patricia Lent, Larissa McGoldrick, Dennis O'Connor, Kristy Santimyer, Robert Swinston, Carol Teitelbaum, Robert Wood. Videotaped at Sundance Institute, Provo UT, and Sunrise Studios, Orem UT, October 1988; first public screening at Anthology Film Archives, New York NY 15 May 1989
ST Théâtre du Silence **FP** Théâtre de la Ville, Paris 17 April 1979
ST Purchase Dance Corps **FP** State University of New York, Purchase NY 2 April 1987
ST Urepco (University Repertory Dance Company) **FP** Arena Health Club, Target Center, Minneapolis MN 20 February 1993 (preview); University of Minnesota, Minneapolis MN 15 April 1993
ST North Carolina School of the Arts, School of Dance **FP** Stevens Center, Winston-Salem NC 13 May 1993
ST Ohio State University Dance Company **FP** Sullivant Theatre, Columbus OH 23 February 1995

UN JOUR OU DEUX

M John Cage (*Etcetera*) **S C** Jasper Johns, assisted by Mark Lancaster **D** Françoise Ambrière, Claude Ariel, Michèle Baude, Michel Berges, Anny Carbonnel, Josyane Consoli, Alain Debrus, Michaël Denard, Marie-Claude Dubus, Philippe Gerbet, Jean-Paul Gravier, Jean Guizerix, Colette Hauleux, Wladimir Huot, Danielle Joly, Charles Jude, Jeanine Julien, Gérard Lignon, Francis Malovik, Thierry Mongne, Wilfride Piollet, Chantal Quarrez, Laure Renaudel, Jessica Sordoillet, Pascal Vernier, Pascal Vincent **FP** Ballet de l'Opéra de Paris, Salle Garnier, Paris 6 November 1973
NP Ballet de l'Opéra; revised and shortened version **R** MC and Chris Komar **D** Olivier Ageorges, Sophie Boulineau, David Bouvier, Florence Branca, Rodrigue Calderon, Annie Carbonnel, Isabelle Cividino, Pierre Darde, Laurence Debia, Patrick Félix, Philippe Gerbet, Alexandra Gonin, Olivia Grandville, Jean Guizerix, Muriel Hallé, Laurent Hilaire, Bruno Lehaut, Carole Maison, Francis Malovik, Marie-Claude Maniglier, Christian Mesnier, Myriam Nacéri, Wilfride Piollet, Laurent Quéval, Eric Quillère, Kim Ta **FP** Salle Garnier, Paris 31 January 1986
NP excerpts under the title *Suite* **D** Wilfride Piollet, Jean Guizerix

D (in order of appearance) Robert Swinston, Jeannie Steele, Frédéric Gafner, Thomas Caley, Jean Freebury, Jenifer Weaver, Michael Cole, Glen Rumsey, Kimberly Bartosik, Emma Diamond **FP** City Center Theater, New York NY 15 March 1994

SOLO

Solo **M** John Cage (*Child of Tree*) **C** Sonja Sekula (from *Dromenon*, 1947) **FP** MCDC, Music Hall, Detroit MI 8 March 1975; Minskoff Theater, New York NY 18 January 1977

The music's title is from *Finnegans Wake*.

BLUE STUDIO: FIVE SEGMENTS

Solo Videotape by MC and Charles Atlas. WNET/TV Lab, October 1975

1976
TORSE

In three parts **M** Maryanne Amacher ((Remainder. 18.] R[]D[=An afterimage.
(Also used as a classifier of seeds).*
*Hollis Frampton, A STIPULATION OF TERMS FOR MATERNAL HOPI) **C** Mark Lancaster **D** Karen Attix, Ellen Cornfield, Morgan Ensminger, Meg Harper, Susana Hayman-Chaffey, Catherine Kerr, Chris Komar, Robert Kovich, Charles Moulton, Julie Roess-Smith **FP** MCDC, McCarter Theatre, Princeton NJ 15 January 1976 (part I only; in subsequent performances the parts were performed in alternation); Minskoff Theater, New York NY 19 January 1977
NP MCDC Film version directed by Charles Atlas **D** Karole Armitage, Louise Burns, Ellen Cornfield, Morgan Ensminger, Lisa Fox, Meg Harper, Chris Komar, Robert Kovich, Julie Roess-Smith, Jim Self. Filmed in September 1977 at the University of Washington, Seattle WA; first public screening, New York Public Library for the Performing Arts, Lincoln Center, New York NY 13 April 1978

Excerpts performed in Events; the complete work was performed as Event #3, Dance Umbrella, Camera Mart/Stage One, New York NY 4 October 1979

SQUAREGAME

M Takehisa Kosugi (*S.E. Wave/E.W. Song*) **S C** Mark Lancaster **D** Karole Armitage, Karen Attix, Ellen Cornfield, MC, Morgan Ensminger, Meg Harper, Susana Hayman-Chaffey, Catherine Kerr, Chris Komar, Robert Kovich, Raymond Kurshals, Charles Moulton, Julie Roess-Smith **FP** MCDC, Festival Theatre, Adelaide, Australia 24 March 1976; Minskoff Theater, New York NY 19 January 1977
NP MCDC. Videotape version under the title *Squaregame Video*. Directed by Charles Atlas **D** Karole Armitage, Karen Attix, Ellen Cornfield, MC, Morgan Ensminger, Meg Harper, Susana Hayman-Chaffey, Catherine Kerr, Chris Komar, Robert Kovich, Raymond Kurshals, Julie Roess-Smith. Merce Cunningham Studio, Westbeth, New York NY May 1976

Performed in part or in its entirety in Events

VIDEO TRIANGLE

M David Tudor (*Rainforest*) **C** Mark Lancaster **D** Ellen Cornfield, MC, Meg Harper, Catherine Kerr, Chris Komar, Robert Kovich. Taped with MCDC as part of Event for Television, WNET "Dance in America" series, directed by Merrill Brockway, in Nashville TN November 1976

1977
TRAVELOGUE

M John Cage (*Telephones and Birds*). **S C** Robert Rauschenberg (*Tantric Geography*) **D** Karole Armitage, Ellen Cornfield, MC, Morgan Ensminger, Meg Harper, Chris Komar, Robert Kovich, Julie Roess-Smith **FP** MCDC, Minskoff Theater, New York NY 18 January 1977

INLETS

M John Cage (*Inlets*) **S C** Morris Graves, realized by Suzanne Joelson **D** Karole Armitage, Ellen Cornfield, MC, Lisa Fox, Chris Komar, Robert Kovich **FP** MCDC, University of Washington, Seattle WA 10 September 1977; City Center Theater, New York NY 26 September 1978

See *Inlets 2* (1983)

FRACTIONS I

A work for video. Directed by Charles Atlas and MC **M** Jon Gibson (*Equal Distribution*) **S C** Mark Lancaster **D** Karole Armitage, Louise Burns, Graham Conley, Ellen Cornfield, Meg Eginton, Lisa Fox, Chris Komar, Robert Kovich. MCDC videotaped at Merce Cunningham Studio, Westbeth, New York NY November–December 1977, edited in another version under the title *Fractions II* (with Lisa Fox in the solo danced by Karole Armitage in *Fractions I*)
NP MCDC. Stage version under the title *Fractions* New **S C** Mark Lancaster **D** Karole Armitage, Louise Burns, Ellen Cornfield, Meg Eginton, Lisa Fox, Chris Komar, Robert Kovich, Jim Self **FP** Boston English High School, Boston MA 26 February 1978; City Center Theater, New York NY 3 October 1978 (first performance with decor).
NP Repertory Understudy Group of the Cunningham Dance Foundation (RUG) (excerpts only) **R** Chris Komar and Robert Swinston **C** Mark Lancaster (from Events) **D** Erin Bahn, Thomas Caley, Corrine Hodges, Florence Leonard, Jared Phillips, Graham Smith, Cheryl Therrien, Rachel Whiting **FP** Emergency Fund for Student Dancers Summer Dance Benefit, Merce Cunningham Studio, New York NY 11 August 1993

Excerpts performed in Events

1978
EXERCISE PIECE I

M Meredith Monk **C** Suzanne Joelson **D** Meg Eginton, Susan Emery, Lise Friedman, Rob Remley **FP** MCDC, as part of Event #215, Roundabout Theatre, New York NY 25 March 1978
NP MCDC, as part of *Changing Steps et cetera* **M** John Cage (*Cartridge Music*) **C** Mark Lancaster **D** Meg Eginton, Susan Emery, Lise Friedman, Rob Remley **FP** City Center Theater, New York NY 30 September 1978

EXERCISE PIECE II

in two parts **M** John Cage (*Cartridge Music*) **C** Mark Lancaster **D** (a) Karole Armitage, Louise Burns, Ellen Cornfield, Chris Komar, Robert Kovich, Lisa Fox, Jim Self (b) Meg Eginton, Susan Emery, Lise Friedman, Alan Good, Catherine Kerr, Joseph Lennon, Rob Remley **FP** MCDC, as part of *Changing Steps et cetera*, Royal Alexandra Theatre, Toronto, Ontario 18 August 1978

EXCHANGE

M David Tudor (*Weatherings (Nethograph #1)*; subsequent performances numbered consecutively, #2, #3, etc; beginning with the performance at Artpark, Lewiston NY on 3 August 1979, the title was given simply as *Weatherings*) **S C** Jasper Johns **D** Karole Armitage, Louise Burns, Ellen Cornfield, MC, Meg Eginton, Susan Emery, Lisa Fox, Lise Friedman, Alan Good, Catherine Kerr, Chris Komar, Robert Kovich, Joseph Lennon, Rob Remley, Jim Self **FP** MCDC, City Center Theater, New York NY 27 September 1978

Filmed by Charles Atlas, in 1978; film stock unedited
NP MCDC (Choreography somewhat revised) **D** Helen Barrow, Kimberly Bartosik, Michael Cole, Emma Diamond, Victoria Finlayson, Alan Good (in MC's role), Chris Komar, David Kulick, Patricia Lent, Larissa McGoldrick, Randall Sanderson, Robert Swinston, Carol Teitelbaum, Jenifer Weaver, Robert Wood **FP** City Center Theater, New York NY 12 March 1991

TANGO

Solo **M** John Cage (*Letter to Erik Satie* with *Sound Anonymously Received*) **S C** Mark Lancaster **FP** MCDC, City Center Theater, New York NY 5 October 1978

1979
LOCALE

Filmdance. Directed by Charles Atlas and MC **M** Takehisa Kosugi (*Interspersion*) **C** Charles Atlas **D** Karole Armitage, Louise Burns, Ellen Cornfield, Meg Eginton, Susan Emery, Lisa Fox, Lise Friedman, Alan Good, Catherine Kerr, Chris Komar, Robert Kovich, Joseph Lennon, Rob Remley, Jim Self. Filmed at Merce Cunningham Studio, Westbeth, New York NY January–February 1979; first public screening, City Center Theater, New York NY 24 February 1980
NP MCDC, stage version New **C** Charles Atlas **D** as above **FP** Théâtre de la Ville, Paris 9 October 1979; City Center Theater, New York NY 19 February 1980

Performed in part or in its entirety in Events

ROADRUNNERS

M Yasunao Tone (*Geography and Music*) **C** Mark Lancaster **D** Karole Armitage, Louise Burns, Ellen Cornfield, MC, Meg Eginton, Susan Emery, Lisa Fox, Lise Friedman, Alan Good, Catherine Kerr, Chris Komar, Robert Kovich, Joseph Lennon, Rob Remley, Jim Self **FP** MCDC, American Dance Festival, Duke University, Durham NC 19 July 1979; City Center Theater, New York NY 20 February 1980

1980
EXERCISE PIECE III

M John Cage (*Cartridge Music*) **C** Mark Lancaster **D** Meg Eginton, Lise Friedman, Catherine Kerr, Neil Greenberg, Joseph Lennon **FP** MCDC, City Center Theater, New York NY 23 February 1980, as part of *Changing Steps et cetera*

DUETS

M Peadar and Mel Mercier (Percussion; arranged by John Cage and John Fullemann. Beginning with a performance at the Woodstock Playhouse, Woodstock NY 13 June 1980, the music was listed as John Cage: *Improvisation III*, with Peadar and Mel Mercier named as percussion players) **C** Mark Lancaster **D** Susan Emery, Rob Remley, Karole Armitage, Alan Good, Catherine Kerr, MC, Meg Eginton, Chris Komar, Lise Friedman, Joseph Lennon, Louise Burns, Robert Kovich **FP** MCDC, City Center Theater, New York NY 26 February 1980

NP American Ballet Theatre **R** MC, assisted by Chris Komar New **C** Mark Lancaster **D** Elaine Kudo, Gregory Osborne, Lisa de Ribere, Kevin McKenzie, Amy Rose, Ross Stretton, Cheryl Yeager, Johan Renvall, Susan Jaffe, Ronald Perry, Christine Spizzo, Robert La Fosse **FP** Metropolitan Opera House, New York NY 18 May 1982

FIELDING SIXES

M John Cage (*Improvisation IV*); musicians: Paddy Glackin and Matt Molloy **S C** Monika Fullemann **D** Karole Armitage, Louise Burns, Ellen Cornfield, Meg Eginton, Susan Emery, Lise Friedman, Alan Good, Neil Greenberg, Catherine Kerr, Chris Komar, Robert Kovich, Joseph Lennon, Rob Remley **FP** MCDC, Sadler's Wells Theatre, London, England 30 June 1980; City Center Theater, New York NY 19 March 1981

NP Ballet Rambert **R** Chris Komar **S C** Mark Lancaster **D** Catherine Becque, Lucy Bethune, Mary Evelyn, Paul Melis, Bruce Michelson, Albert van Nierop, Robert North, Michael Popper, Cathrine Price, Quinny Sacks, Diane Walker, Elizabeth Wright **FP** Royal Northern College of Music, Manchester, England 11 February 1983; Sadler's Wells Theatre, London, England 11 March 1983

NP MCDC **S C** William Anastasi **D** Helen Barrow, Victoria Finlayson, Alan Good, Neil Greenberg, Catherine Kerr, Chris Komar, Patricia Lent, Karen Radford, Rob Remley, Kevin Schroder, Robert Swinston, Megan Walker, Susan

Quinn Young **FP** City Center Theater, New York NY 13 March 1986

1981
CHANNELS/INSERTS

Filmdance. Directed by Charles Atlas and MC **M** David Tudor (*Phonemes*) **C** Charles Atlas **D** Karole Armitage, Louise Burns, Ellen Cornfield, Susan Emery, Lise Friedman, Alan Good, Neil Greenberg, Catherine Kerr, Chris Komar, Judy Lazaroff, Joseph Lennon, Rob Remley, Robert Swinston, Megan Walker. Filmed at Merce Cunningham Studio, Westbeth, New York NY January 1981; first public screening, Carnegie Hall Cinema, New York NY 21 March 1982

NP MCDC, stage version **C** Charles Atlas **D** as above **FP** City Center Theater, New York NY 24 March 1981

NP MCDC New **C** Charles Atlas **D** Helen Barrow, Kimberly Bartosik, Michael Cole, Emma Diamond, Victoria Finlayson, Frédéric Gafner, Alan Good, David Kulick, Patricia Lent, Larissa McGoldrick, Randall Sanderson, Robert Swinston, Carol Teitelbaum, Jenifer Weaver **FP** City Center Theater, New York NY 19 March 1992

ST Dayton Contemporary Dance Company **R** Chris Komar **C** Suzanne Gallo **FP** Victoria Theatre, Dayton OH 2 February 1996

Excerpts performed in Events

10'S WITH SHOES

M Martin Kalve (*All Happy Workers Babies & Dogs*) **S C** Mark Lancaster **D** Karole Armitage, Louise Burns, Ellen Cornfield, Alan Good, Neil Greenberg, Chris Komar, Joseph Lennon **FP** MCDC, City Center Theater, New York NY 17 March 1981

Performed in Events

GALLOPADE

In six parts: "Street Fair," "50 Looks with Poses," "The Bed-Ridden Hop and Chess Game," "L'Amour and the Bounce Dance," "Gallop." **M** Takehisa Kosugi (*Cycles*) **C** Mark Lancaster **D** MC, Susan Emery, Lise Friedman, Catherine Kerr, Judy Lazaroff, Rob Remley, Robert Swinston, Megan Walker **FP** MCDC, Théâtre de Beaulieu, Lausanne, France 3 June 1981 (preview without decor); Sadler's Wells Theatre, London 10 June 1981; City Center Theater, New York NY 20 March 1982

"The Bed-Ridden Hop" was first

given in a Studio Event at the Merce Cunningham Studio, Westbeth, New York NY 4 October 1980.

1982
TRAILS

M John Cage (*Instances of Silence*) **S C** Mark Lancaster **D** Louise Burns, Ellen Cornfield, Lise Friedman, Alan Good, Neil Greenberg, Catherine Kerr, Chris Komar, Joseph Lennon, Robert Swinston, Megan Walker **FP** MCDC, City Center Theater, New York NY 16 March 1982

Excerpts performed in Events

NUMBERS

In three parts: part I: Accumulation (solo [Neil Greenberg] joined by two others to become a trio, joined by another to become a quartet, joined by the others to become a septet); part II: group dance; part III: first section in reverse order, subtracting instead of adding **D** Louise Burns, Ellen Cornfield, Neil Greenberg, Susan Emery, Judy Lazaroff, Rob Remley, Susan Quinn Young **FP** MCDC, City Center Theater, New York NY 18 March 1982, as part of Event #1 (performed previously as a work in progress)

Used only in Events

QUARTET

M David Tudor (*Sextet for Seven*) **C** Mark Lancaster **D** Helen Barrow, MC, Susan Emery, Judy Lazaroff, Rob Remley **FP** MCDC, Grand Casino de Génève, Geneva 16 October 1982 (preview in practice costumes); Théâtre des Champs-Elysées, Paris 27 October 1982; City Center Theater, New York NY 16 March 1983

1983
COAST ZONE

Filmdance. Directed by Charles Atlas and MC **M** Larry Austin (*Beachcombers*) **C** Mark Lancaster and Charles Atlas **D** Helen Barrow, Louise Burns, Susan Emery, Lise Friedman, Alan Good, Neil Greenberg, Catherine Kerr, Judy Lazaroff, Joseph Lennon, Rob Remley, Robert Swinston, Susan Quinn Young. MCDC filmed at Synod House of Cathedral of St. John the Divine, New York NY January 1983; first public screenings, Dean Junior College, Franklin MA 7 April 1984; Merce Cunningham Studio, Westbeth, New York NY 16 April 1984

NP MCDC, stage version **D** Helen

Barrow, Louise Burns, Lise Friedman, Alan Good, Neil Greenberg, Catherine Kerr, Judy Lazaroff, Joseph Lennon, Rob Remley, Robert Swinston, Megan Walker, Susan Quinn Young **FP** City Center Theater, New York NY 18 March 1983

Excerpts performed in Events

INLETS 2

M John Cage (*Inlets*) **C** Mark Lancaster **D** Helen Barrow, Susan Emery, Karen Radford, Alan Good, Chris Komar, Joseph Lennon, Megan Walker **FP** MCDC, Festival de Lille, Le Colisée, Roubaix 26 October 1983; City Center Theater, New York NY 8 March 1984

NP Les Etoiles et le Ballet de l'Opéra/Le GRCOP; another variation **R** MC, Chris Komar **C** Mark Lancaster **D** Katia Grey, Florence Claudet, Fabienne Ozanne, Florence Lambert, Serge Daubrac, Jean-Christophe Paré, Bruno Lehaut **FP** Opéra-Comique/Salle Favart, Paris 3 December 1983; French Institute, New York NY 19 April 1988

ST Concert Dance Company of Boston **R** Chris Komar **FP** Agassiz House Dance Studio, Radcliffe Yard, Cambridge MA 13 April 1986 (preview); Emanu-El Y, New York NY 21 March 1987; Strand Theater, Boston MA 10 April 1987

ST Sharir Dance Company **R** Chris Komar **FP** Paramount Theatre, Austin TX 11 March 1988

ST De Rotterdamse Dansgroep **R** Catherine Kerr **FP** Schouwburg, Rotterdam, The Netherlands 9 February 1991

ST Charleroi/Danses **R** Catherine Kerr **FP** Centre Chorégraphique de la Communauté Française de Belgique, Charleroi, Belgium 13 December 1991

ST Maggio Danza **R** Catherine Kerr **FP** Piccolo Teatro del Comunale, Florence, Italy 6 December 1994

A variation on *Inlets* (1977)

ROARATORIO

"An Irish circus on *Finnegans Wake*" **M** John Cage (1979) Text: John Cage, drawn from *Finnegans Wake* by James Joyce **C** Mark Lancaster **D** Helen Barrow, Louise Burns, MC, Susan Emery, Lise Friedman, Alan Good, Neil Greenberg, Catherine Kerr, Chris Komar, Judy Lazaroff (whose role was later divided among other dancers), Joseph Lennon, Karen Radford, Rob Remley, Robert Swinston, Megan Walker, Susan Quinn

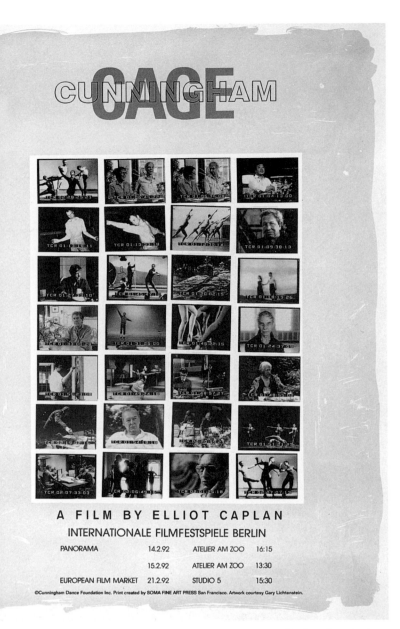

A FILM BY ELLIOT CAPLAN
INTERNATIONALE FILMFESTSPIELE BERLIN

PANORAMA	14.2.92	ATELIER AM ZOO	16:15
	15.2.92	ATELIER AM ZOO	13:30
EUROPEAN FILM MARKET	21.2.92	STUDIO 5	15:30

©Cunningham Dance Foundation Inc. Print created by SOMA FINE ART PRESS San Francisco. Artwork courtesy Gary Lichtenstein.

Gary Lichtenstein's poster for *Cage/Cunningham*, 1991, a film by Elliot Caplan.

Young **FP** MCDC, Festival de Lille, Le Colisée, Roubaix 26 October 1983; Brooklyn Academy of Music, Brooklyn NY 7 October 1986

Excerpts performed in Events

1984
PICTURES
M David Behrman (*Interspecies Smalltalk*) **S C** Mark Lancaster **D** Helen Barrow, Louise Burns, MC, Lise Friedman, Alan Good, Neil Greenberg, Catherine Kerr, Chris Komar, Joseph Lennon, Patricia Lent, Karen Radford, Rob Remley, Robert Swinston, Megan Walker, Susan Quinn Young **FP** MCDC, City Center Theater, New York NY 6 March 1984

DOUBLES
M Takehisa Kosugi (*Spacings*) **S C** Mark Lancaster **D** Louise Burns, Lise Friedman, Alan Good, Neil Greenberg, Rob Remley, Megan Walker, Susan Quinn Young **FP** MCDC, American Dance Festival, Duke University, Durham NC 28 June 1984; City Center Theater, New York NY 6 March 1985
ST Rambert Dance Company **R** Chris Komar **FP** Birmingham Repertory Theatre, Birmingham, UK 30 January 1990

PHRASES
M David Tudor (*Fragments*) **S** William Anastasi **C** Dove Bradshaw **D** Helen Barrow, Louise Burns, MC, Victoria Finlayson, Alan Good, Neil Greenberg, Catherine Kerr, Chris Komar, Joseph

Lennon, Patricia Lent, Karen Radford, Rob Remley, Robert Swinston, Megan Walker, Susan Quinn Young **FP** MCDC, Théâtre Municipal d'Angers, France 7 December 1984; City Center Theater, New York NY 5 March 1985

1985
DELI COMMEDIA
Videodance. Directed by Elliot Caplan. **M** Pat Richter (*I Can't Go On to the Next Thing Until I Find Out about You*) **C** Dove Bradshaw **D** Brenda Daniels, Frey Faust, Kristy Santimyer, Carol Teitelbaum, Bill Young. Produced by Cunningham Dance Foundation. Taped at Merce Cunningham Studio, Westbeth, New York NY January 1985

Excerpts performed in Events

NATIVE GREEN
M John King (*Gliss in Sighs*) **S C** William Anastasi **D** Helen Barrow, Alan Good, Chris Komar, Patricia Lent, Robert Swinston, Megan Walker **FP** MCDC, City Center Theater, New York NY 12 March 1985

ARCADE
M John Cage (*Études Boreales I–IV*) **S C** Dove Bradshaw **D** Dede Barfield, Theodore Brunson, Lisa Collins, William DeGregory, Elizabeth Farrell, Ramon Flowers, Jeffrey Gribler, Laurie LeBlanc, Mary LeGere, Veronica Lynn, Kelly McManus, Edward Myers, Robin Preiss **FP** Pennsylvania Ballet, Academy of Music, Philadelphia PA 10 September 1985 (preview), 11 September 1985
NP MCDC **D** Helen Barrow, Victoria Finlayson, Alan Good, Neil Greenberg, Catherine Kerr, Patricia Lent, Karen Radford, Rob Remley, Kristy Santimyer, Kevin Schroder, Robert Swinston, Megan Walker, Susan Quinn Young **FP** University of Pennsylvania, Philadelphia PA 14 November 1985; City Center Theater, New York NY 11 March 1986

1986
GRANGE EVE
M Takehisa Kosugi (*Assemblage*) **S C** William Anastasi **D** Helen Barrow, MC, Victoria Finlayson, Alan Good, Catherine Kerr, Chris Komar, Patricia Lent, Karen Radford, Rob Remley, Kristy Santimyer, Kevin Schroder, Robert Swinston, Megan Walker, Susan Quinn Young **FP** MCDC, City Center Theater, New York NY 18 March 1986

Excerpt ("cane dance") performed in Events

POINTS IN SPACE
Videodance. Directed by Elliot Caplan and MC **M** John Cage (*Voiceless Essay*) **S** William Anastasi **C** Dove Bradshaw **D** Helen Barrow, MC, Victoria Finlayson, Alan Good, Catherine Kerr, Chris Komar, David Kulick, Patricia Lent, Karen Radford, Rob Remley, Kristy Santimyer, Kevin Schroder, Robert Swinston, Megan Walker, Susan Quinn Young. MCDC videotaped at BBC TV Centre, London, England May 1986; first public screening, Herbst Theatre, San Francisco CA 21 November 1986; first broadcast, BBC2, England 18 July 1987
NP MCDC, stage version (MC's, Schroder's, and Walker's roles omitted) **D** Helen Barrow, Victoria Finlayson, Alan Good, Catherine Kerr, Chris Komar, David Kulick, Patricia Lent, Karen Radford, Rob Remley, Kristy Santimyer, Robert Swinston, Susan Quinn Young **FP** City Center Theater, New York NY 10 March 1987
ST Ballet de l'Opéra de Paris, **R** Chris Komar, Catherine Kerr **FP** Opéra de Paris Garnier, Paris 6 June 1990

Excerpts performed in Events

1987
FABRICATIONS
M Emanuel Dimas de Melo Pimenta (*Short Waves*) **S C** Dove Bradshaw **D** Helen Barrow, MC, Victoria Finlayson, Alan Good, Catherine Kerr, Chris Komar, David Kulick, Patricia Lent, Dennis O'Connor, Karen Radford, Rob Remley, Kristy Santimyer, Robert Swinston, Carol Teitelbaum, Susan Quinn Young **FP** MCDC, Northrop Auditorium, Minneapolis MN 21 February 1987; City Center Theater, New York NY 3 March 1987

Excerpts performed in Events

SHARDS
M David Tudor (*Webwork*) **S C** William Anastasi **D** Helen Barrow, Victoria Finlayson, Alan Good, Catherine Kerr, David Kulick, Patricia Lent, Rob Remley, Susan Quinn Young **FP** MCDC, City Center Theater, New York NY 4 March 1987

CAROUSAL
M Takehisa Kosugi (*Rhapsody*) **S C** Dove Bradshaw **D** Helen Barrow, Victoria Finlayson, Alan Good, Cather-

MC at Ace Gallery, Los Angeles, 1991. Photograph: Betty Freeman.

ine Kerr, Chris Komar, David Kulick, Patricia Lent, Larissa McGoldrick, Dennis O'Connor, Karen Radford, Rob Remley, Kristy Santimyer, Robert Swinston **FP** MCDC, Jacob's Pillow, Lee MA 18 August 1987; Joyce Theater, New York NY 2 March 1988

1988
ELEVEN
M Robert Ashley (*Problems in the Flying Saucer*) **C** William Anastasi **D** Helen Barrow, Victoria Finlayson, Alan Good, Chris Komar, David Kulick, Patricia Lent, Larissa McGoldrick, Dennis O'Connor, Kristy Santimyer, Robert Swinston, Carol Teitelbaum **FP** MCDC, Joyce Theater, New York NY 9 March 1988

Excerpts performed in Events

FIVE STONE
M John Cage, David Tudor (*Five Stone*) **S C** Mark Lancaster **D** Helen Barrow, MC, Victoria Finlayson, Alan Good, Chris Komar, David Kulick, Patricia Lent, Larissa McGoldrick, Dennis O'Connor, Kristy Santimyer, Robert Swinston, Carol Teitelbaum, Robert Wood **FP** MCDC, Freie Wolksbühne Berlin, Berlin, Germany 16 June 1988
See *Five Stone Wind* below

FIVE STONE WIND
M John Cage, Takehisa Kosugi, David Tudor (*Five Stone Wind*) **S C** Mark Lancaster **D** Helen Barrow, Kimberly Bartosik, MC, Emma Diamond, Victoria Finlayson, Alan Good, Chris Komar, David Kulick, Patricia Lent, Larissa McGoldrick, Dennis O'Connor, Kristy

Santimyer, Robert Swinston, Carol Teitelbaum, Robert Wood **FP** MCDC, First New York International Festival of the Arts, The Plaza, World Financial Center, New York NY 9 July 1988 (preview without decor and with only partial costuming); Festival d'Avignon, Cour d'honneur du Palais des Papes, Avignon 30 July 1988 (without decor); Maison de la Culture, Grenoble 22 November 1988 (first performance with full decor); City Center Theater, New York NY 28 February 1989

1989
CARGO X
M Takehisa Kosugi (*Spectra*) **C** Dove Bradshaw **D** Kimberly Bartosik, Emma Diamond, David Kulick, Larissa McGoldrick, Dennis O'Connor, Kristy

Santimyer, Robert Wood **FP** MCDC, University of Texas, Austin TX 27 January 1989; City Center Theater, New York NY 1 March 1989

FIELD AND FIGURES
M Ivan Tcherepnin (*The Creative Act—Electronically Varied Heterothonies on a Text by Marcel Duchamp*) **S C** Kristin Jones and Andrew Ginzel **D** Helen Barrow, Kimberly Bartosik, Emma Diamond, Victoria Finlayson, Alan Good, Chris Komar, David Kulick, Patricia Lent, Larissa McGoldrick, Dennis O'Connor, Kristy Santimyer, Robert Swinston, Carol Teitelbaum, Robert Wood **FP** MCDC, Northrop Auditorium, Minneapolis MN 17 February 1989; City Center Theater, New York NY 7 March 1989

Jasper Johns, *Ocean*, 1996, lithograph, 27⅞ x 36¾″.

INVENTIONS

M John Cage (*Sculptures Musicales*) **S C** Carl Kielblock **D** Helen Barrow, Kimberly Bartosik, Michael Cole, Emma Diamond, Victoria Finlayson, Alan Good, Chris Komar, David Kulick, Patricia Lent, Larissa McGoldrick, Dennis O'Connor, Kristy Santimyer, Robert Swinston, Carol Teitelbaum, Robert Wood **FP** MCDC, Théâtre Antique, Arles 23 July 1989 (preview without decor; performed in costumes by Mark Lancaster); University of California, Berkeley CA 23 September 1989; City Center Theater, New York NY 14 March 1990

AUGUST PACE

M Michael Pugliese (*Peace Talks*) **S C** Afrika (Sergei Bugaev) **D** Victoria Finlayson, Robert Swinston, Emma Diamond, Dennis O'Connor, Carol Teitelbaum, David Kulick, Kimberly Bartosik, Chris Komar, Helen Barrow, Robert Wood, Larissa McGoldrick, Michael Cole, Patricia Lent, Alan Good, Jenifer Weaver **FP** MCDC, University of California, Berkeley CA 22 September 1989; City Center Theater, New York NY 13 March 1990
NP Ballet de l'Opéra de Paris, duets nos. 5 and 7 only **R** MC, Helen Barrow, Robert Wood, Patricia Lent, and Alan Good **D** Wilfride Piollet and Jean Guizerix **FP** Opéra de Paris Garnier, Paris, "Carte blanche à Jean Guizerix," 23 October 1990

Excerpts performed in Events

1990
POLARITY

M David Tudor (*Virtual Focus*) **S** William Anastasi, from drawings by MC **C** William Anastasi **L** Carl Kielblock **D** Helen Barrow, Victoria Finlayson, Alan Good, Chris Komar, Patricia Lent, Robert Swinston, Carol Teitelbaum **FP** MCDC, City Center Theater, New York NY 20 March 1990

From time to time MC has choreographed material intended for performance only in Events (see, for example, *Numbers*, 1982). Some of this material consists of transitions too brief to identify, but other sequences are longer and have remained in the body of material available for Events. There were three such sequences in 1990:

WALKING DANCE

D Emma Diamond, Randall Sanderson **FP** MCDC, Teatro Pérez Galdós, Las Palmas, Canarias, June 1990, as part of one of four Events Canarias

WALKAROUND TIME FALLS

D MCDC + RUG **FP** MCDC, Damrosch Park, Lincoln Center, New York NY 18 August 1990, as part of an Event for Lincoln Center Out-of-Doors

FOUR LIFTS

D Helen Barrow, Michael Cole, Alan Good, David Kulick, Patricia Lent, Larissa McGoldrick, Jenifer Weaver, Robert Wood **FP** MCDC, Théâtre National Populaire, Villeurbanne, France 17 September 1990, as part of Event 1, 4ème Biennale de la Danse, Lyon

1991
NEIGHBORS

M Takehisa Kosugi (*Streams*) **S C** Mark Lancaster **D** Victoria Finlayson, Alan Good, David Kulick, Patricia Lent, Larissa McGoldrick, Robert Swinston **FP** MCDC, City Center Theater, New York NY 13 March 1991

TRACKERS

M Emanuel Dimas de Melo Pimenta (*Gravitational Sounds*) **S C** Dove Bradshaw **D** Helen Barrow, Kimberly Bartosik, Michael Cole, MC, Emma Diamond, Chris Komar, Emily Navar, Randall Sanderson, Carol Teitelbaum, Jenifer Weaver, Robert Wood **FP** MCDC, City Center Theater, New York NY 20 March 1991

Excerpts performed in Events

Robert Rauschenberg, *Immerse*, 1994, acrylic on primed linen canvas, 121½ x 436″. This painting was made for use as a backdrop in the Merce Cunningham Dance

BEACH BIRDS

M John Cage (*FOUR³*) **C L** Marsha Skinner **D** Helen Barrow, Kimberly Bartosik, Michael Cole, Victoria Finlayson, Alan Good, David Kulick, Larissa McGoldrick, Randall Sanderson, Robert Swinston, Carol Teitelbaum, Jenifer Weaver **FP** MCDC, Theater 11, Zürich, Switzerland 20 June 1991; City Center Theater, New York NY 17 March 1992

NP MCDC, film version under the title *Beach Birds For Camera*. Choreography slightly revised, with three additional dancers. Directed by Elliot Caplan. Design: Elliot Caplan, Tim Nelson, Matthew Williams, Marsha Skinner **D** Helen Barrow, Kimberly Bartosik, Michael Cole, Emma Diamond, Victoria Finlayson, Frédéric Gafner, Alan Good, David Kulick, Patricia Lent, Larissa McGoldrick, Randall Sanderson, Robert Swinston, Carol Teitelbaum, Jenifer Weaver. Filmed at Kaufman Astoria Studios and Industria Superstudio, New York NY December 1991

LOOSESTRIFE

M Michael Pugliese (*Mixed Signals*) **S C** Carl Kielblock **D** Helen Barrow, Kimberly Bartosik, Michael Cole, MC, Emma Diamond, Victoria Finlayson, Frédéric Gafner, Alan Good, Chris Komar, David Kulick, Patricia Lent, Larissa McGoldrick, Randall Sanderson, Robert Swinston, Carol Teitelbaum, Jenifer Weaver **FP** MCDC, Théâtre de la Ville, Paris 10 September 1991; City Center Theater, New York NY 18 March 1992

1992
CHANGE OF ADDRESS

M Walter Zimmermann (*Self-Forgetting*; words from Meister Eckhart) **S C** Marsha Skinner **D** Helen Barrow, Kimberly Bartosik, Michael Cole, Emma Diamond, Victoria Finlayson, Frédéric Gafner, Alan Good, Chris Komar, David Kulick, Patricia Lent, Larissa McGoldrick, Randall Sanderson, Robert Swinston, Carol Teitelbaum, Jenifer Weaver **FP** MCDC, University of Texas, Austin TX 31 January 1992; City Center Theater, New York NY 24 March 1992

TOUCHBASE

M Michael Pugliese (*Icebreeze*) **S C** Mark Lancaster **D** Shelley Baker, Steven Brett, Amanda Britton, Alexandra Dyer, Paul Old, Sarah Warsop, Glenn Wilkinson **FP** Rambert Dance Company, Royalty Theatre, London, England 20 June 1992

NP MCDC **D** Michael Cole, Emma Diamond, Jean Freebury, David Kulick, Patricia Lent, Robert Swinston, Carol Teitelbaum **FP** City Center Theater, New York NY 10 March 1993

ENTER

M David Tudor (*Neural Network Plus*) **S C** Marsha Skinner; backdrop and costume photography from a video still by Elliot Caplan. Rideau de scène: John Cage (*Where R=Ryoanji R/2–March 1990*) **D** Helen Barrow, Kimberly Bartosik, Michael Cole, MC, Emma Diamond, Jean Freebury, Frédéric Gafner, Alan Good, Chris Komar, David Kulick, Patricia Lent, Larissa McGoldrick, Randall Sanderson, Robert Swinston, Carol Teitelbaum, Jenifer Weaver **FP** MCDC, Opéra de Paris Garnier, Paris 17 November 1992; City Center Theater, New York NY 9 March 1993

1993
DOUBLETOSS

M Takehisa Kosugi (*Transfigurations*) **S L** MC, with Aaron Copp **C** MC, with Suzanne Gallo **D** Helen Barrow, Kimberly Bartosik, Michael Cole, Emma Diamond, Jean Freebury, Frédéric Gafner, Alan Good, Chris Komar, David Kulick, Patricia Lent, Larissa McGoldrick, Robert Swinston, Carol Teitelbaum, Jenifer Weaver **FP** MCDC, Northrop Auditorium, Minneapolis MN 26 February 1993; City Center Theater, New York NY 16 March 1993

1993
CRWDSPCR

M John King (*"blues 99"*) **S C** Mark Lancaster **D** Kimberly Bartosik, Michael Cole, Emma Diamond, Jean Freebury, Frédéric Gafner, Alan Good, Chris Komar, Patricia Lent, Glen Rumsey, Jeannie Steele, Robert Swinston, Carol Teitelbaum, Jenifer Weaver **FP** MCDC, American Dance Festival, Duke University, Durham NC 15 July 1993; City Center Theater, New York NY 8 March 1994

1994
BREAKERS

M John Driscoll (*CyberMesa*) **S C** Mary Jean Kenton **D** Kimberly Bartosik, Thomas Caley, Michael Cole, Emma Diamond, Jean Freebury, Frédéric

Company's Event performances.

Gafner, China Laudisio, Banu Ogan, Jared Phillips, Glen Rumsey, Jeannie Steele, Robert Swinston, Cheryl Therrien, Jenifer Weaver **FP** MCDC, City Center Theater, New York NY 9 March 1994

NP Boston Ballet **R** Chris Komar, Robert Swinston **D** Donatella Accardi, Devon Carney, Melinda DeChiazza, Lawrence Edelson, Branden Faulls, Natasha Fielding, Sarah Foster, Emily Gresh, Ayuka Hirota, Karla Kovatch, Joseph Sterrett, Susanna Vennerbeck, Olivier Wecxsteen, Yuri Yanowsky **FP** Kennedy Center, Washington DC 22 March 1994; Wang Center for the Performing Arts, Boston MA 2 March 1995

OCEAN
Conception: John Cage and MC **M** Andrew Culver (*Ocean 1–95*), David Tudor (*Soundings: Ocean Diary*) **S C** Marsha Skinner **D** Kimberly Bartosik, Thomas Caley, Michael Cole, Emma Diamond, Jean Freebury, Frédéric Gafner, China Laudisio, Matthew Mohr, Banu Ogan, Jared Phillips, Glen Rumsey, Jeannie Steele, Robert Swinston, Cheryl Therrien, Jenifer Weaver **FP** MCDC, kunstenFESTIVALdes-

Arts, Cirque Royal, Brussels 18 May 1994; Lincoln Center Festival '96, New York NY 30 July 1996

4'33"
Ch The Company **M** John Cage (*4'33"*) **C** street clothes **L** Aaron Copp **D** Kimberly Bartosik, Lisa Boudreau, Thomas Caley, Michael Cole, MC, Emma Diamond, Jean Freebury, Frédéric Gafner, China Laudisio, Matthew Mohr, Banu Ogan, Jared Phillips, Glen Rumsey, Jeannie Steele, Robert Swinston, Cheryl Therrien, Jenifer Weaver **FP** MCDC, Central Park SummerStage, New York NY 15 July 1994
Performed in Events

1995
THE SLOUCH
Event material **D** The Company **FP** MCDC, in a MinEvent at City Center Theater, New York NY 7 March 1995

GROUND LEVEL OVERLAY
M Stuart Dempster (*Underground Overlays*) **S** Leonardo Drew **C** Suzanne Gallo **L** Aaron Copp **D** Kimberly Bartosik, Lisa Boudreau, Thomas Caley, Michael Cole, Jean Freebury, Frédéric Gafner, China Laudisio, Matthew

Mohr, Banu Ogan, Jared Phillips, Glen Rumsey, Jeannie Steele, Robert Swinston, Cheryl Therrien, Jenifer Weaver **FP** MCDC, City Center Theater, New York NY 8 March 1995

WINDOWS
M Emanuel Dimas de Melo Pimenta (*Microcosmos*) **S** after an etching by John Cage (*Global Village 1–36, 1989*) **C** Suzanne Gallo **L** Aaron Copp **D** Kimberly Bartosik, Lisa Boudreau, Thomas

MC, untitled drawing, ca. 1996.

Caley, Michael Cole, Jean Freebury, Frédéric Gafner, China Laudisio, Matthew Mohr, Banu Ogan, Jared Phillips, Glen Rumsey, Robert Swinston, Cheryl Therrien, Jenifer Weaver **FP** MCDC, Montpellier Danse 95, Opéra Berlioz, Le Corum, Montpellier, France 23 June 1995

1996
TUNE IN/SPIN OUT
M John Cage (*FOUR⁶*) **C** Suzanne Gallo and MC **L** Kelly Atallah **D** Kimberly Bartosik, Lisa Boudreau, Thomas Caley, Michael Cole, Jean Freebury, Frédéric Gafner, China Laudisio, Matthew Mohr, Banu Ogan, Jared Phillips, Jeannie Steele, Robert Swinston, Cheryl Therrien, Jenifer Weaver **FP** MCDC, University of Texas, Austin TX 31 January 1996

An earlier, incomplete version of *Rondo*, see below; excerpts given in Events as a work-in-progress

INSTALLATIONS
M Trimpin **S** video installation by Elliot Caplan **L** Elliot Caplan, with Kelly Atallah **C** Elliot Caplan and Suzanne Gallo **D** Kimberly Bartosik, Lisa Boudreau, Thomas Caley, Michael Cole, Jean Freebury, Frédéric Gafner, China Laudisio, Matthew Mohr, Banu Ogan, Jared Phillips, Glen Rumsey, Jeannie Steele, Robert Swinston, Cheryl Therrien **FP** MCDC, Meany Theater, University of Washington, Seattle WA 2 May 1996

RONDO
In two parts: part I consists of eight short dances (two solos, a duet, a trio, a quartet, a quintet, a sextet, and a septet), whose order and distribution change at each performance; part II is an ensemble, in the course of which there are three duets **M** John Cage (*FOUR⁶*) **C** Suzanne Gallo and MC **L** Kelly Atallah **D** Kimberly Bartosik, Lisa Boudreau, Thomas Caley, Michael Cole, Jean Freebury, Frédéric Gafner, China Laudisio, Matthew Mohr, Banu Ogan, Jared Phillips, Glen Rumsey, Jeannie Steele, Derry Swan, Robert Swinston, Cheryl Therrien **FP** MCDC, Ludwigsburger Schlossfestspiele, Theater im Forum, Ludwigsburg, Germany 2 June 1996; American Dance Festival, Duke University, Durham NC 20 June 1996

Ground Level Overlay, 1995. Left to right: Jeannie Steele
and Thomas Caley. Photograph: Beatriz Schiller.

Selected Bibliography

BOOKS AND JOURNALS

Adam, Judy, ed. *Dancers on a Plane: Cage Cunningham Johns*. New York: Alfred A. Knopf; London: Thames & Hudson; in association with Anthony d'Offay Gallery, 1990. Essays by Susan Sontag, Richard Francis, Mark Rosenthal, Anne Seymour, David Sylvester, and David Vaughan.

Cage, John. *Silence: Lectures and Writings*. Middletown CT: Wesleyan University Press, 1961.

———. *Catalogue of Compositions*, ed. Robert Dunn. New York: Edition Peters, 1962.

———. *A Year from Monday: New Lectures and Writings*. Middletown CT: Wesleyan University Press, 1967.

———. *M: Writings '67–'72*. Middletown CT: Wesleyan University Press, 1972.

———. *Empty Words: Writings '73–'78*. Middletown CT: Wesleyan University Press, 1980.

———. *For the Birds: In Conversation with Daniel Charles*. Boston and London: Marion Boyars, 1981.

———. *Themes and Variations*. Tarrytown NY: Station Hill Press, 1982.

———. *X: Writings '79–'82*. Middletown CT: Wesleyan University Press, 1983.

———. *Roaratorio*, ed. Klaus Schöning. Königstein: Athenäum, 1985.

———. *I–VI: Charles Eliot Norton Lectures*. Cambridge MA: Harvard University Press, 1990.

———. *Composition in Retrospect*. Cambridge MA: Exact Change, 1993.

———. *John Cage: Writer: Previously Uncollected Pieces*, selected and introduced by Richard Kostelanetz. New York: Limelight Editions, 1993.

Cage, John, and Joan Retallack. *Musicage: Cage Muses on Words Art Music*. Middletown CT: Wesleyan University Press, 1996.

Cohen, Selma Jeanne, ed. *Time to Walk in Space. Dance Perspectives* 34 (summer 1968). Essays by John Cage, Clive Barnes, Edwin Denby, Jill Johnston, Arlene Croce, Carolyn

Brown, David Vaughan, and Merce Cunningham.

Cunningham, Merce. "The Function of a Technique for Dance." In *The Dance Has Many Faces*, edited by Walter Sorrell. New York and Cleveland: World Publishing Company, 1951. Reprinted in *Contact Quarterly* (spring–summer 1982).

———. *Changes: Notes on Choreography*, ed. Frances Starr. New York: Something Else Press, 1968.

———. "Choreography and the Dance." In *The Creative Experience*, edited by Stanley Rosner and Lawrence E. Abt. New York: Grossman, 1970. Reprinted in *The Dance Anthology*, edited by Cobbett Steinberg. New York: New American Library, 1980.

———. *The Dancer and the Dance: Conversations with Jacqueline Lesschaeve*, rev. ed. New York and London: Marion Boyars, (paperback) 1991.

Duberman, Martin. *Black Mountain: An Exploration in Community*. New York: E. P. Dutton, 1972; (paperback) New York: Anchor Press/Doubleday, 1973.

Feldman, Elyn. "*Banjo*—Cunningham's Lost 'American' Piece." In *Dance: Selected Current Research*, edited by Lynette Y. Overby and James H. Humphrey. New York: AMS Press, 1989.

Fetterman, William. *John Cage's Theatre Pieces*. Amsterdam: Harwood Academic Publishers/G+B Arts International, 1996.

Foster, Susan Leigh. *Reading Dancing: Bodies and Subjects in Contemporary American Dance*. Berkeley: University of California Press, 1986.

de Gubernatis, Raphael. *Cunningham*. Arles and Paris: Editions Bernard Coutaz, 1990.

Harris, Dale. "Merce Cunningham." In *Contemporary Dance*, edited by Anne Livet. New York: Abbeville Press, 1978.

Harris, Mary Emma. *The Arts at Black Mountain*. Cambridge MA: MIT Press, 1987.

Jowitt, Deborah. *Dance Beat: Selected Views and Reviews, 1967–1976*. New York: Marcel Dekker, 1977.

———. *The Dance in Mind*. Boston: David R. Godine, 1985.

———. *Time and the Dancing Image*. New York: William Morrow, 1988.

Kirby, Michael. *Happenings*. New York: E. P. Dutton, 1965.

Klosty, James, ed. *Merce Cunningham*, 2d ed. New York: Proscenium Publishers, 1987. Photographs, introduction, foreword to the second edition, and an interview with Merce Cunningham by James Klosty. Essays by Carolyn Brown, Viola Farber, Yvonne Rainer, Douglas Dunn, Paul Taylor, Richard Nelson, Lewis L. Lloyd, John Cage, Gordon Mumma, Earle Brown, Pauline Oliveros, Christian Wolff, Robert Rauschenberg, Jasper Johns, Lincoln Kirstein, and Edwin Denby.

Kostelanetz, Richard, ed. *John Cage: Documentary Monographs in Modern Art: An Anthology*, 2d ed. New York: Da Capo, 1991.

———. *Conversing with Cage*. New York: Limelight Editions, 1988.

———, ed. *Merce Cunningham: Dancing in Space and Time: Essays 1944–1992*. Pennington NJ: a cappella books, 1992.

———, ed. *Writings about John Cage*. Ann Arbor: University of Michigan Press, 1993.

Kriegsman, Sali Ann. *Modern Dance in America: The Bennington Years*. Boston: G. K. Hall, 1981.

Lartigue, Pierre, ed. *Merce Cunningham/John Cage. L'Avant-Scène/Ballet/Danse* 10 (September–November 1982).

Livet, Anne, ed. *Contemporary Dance*. New York: Abbeville Press, 1978.

Mazo, Joseph. *Prime Movers: The Makers of Modern Dance in America*. New York: William Morrow, 1977.

McDonagh, Donald. *The Rise and Fall and Rise of Modern Dance*, rev. ed. Pennington NJ: a cappella books, 1990.

———. *The Complete Guide to Modern Dance*. New York: Doubleday, 1976.

Robertson, Allen, and Donald Hutera. *The Dance Handbook*. Boston: G. K. Hall & Co., 1990. Introduction by Merce Cunningham.

Sarabhai, Mrinalini. *Creations*. New York and Ahmedabad, India: Mapin, 1986. Foreword by Merce Cunning-

ham and introduction by Buckminster Fuller.

Siegel, Marcia B. *At the Vanishing Point*. New York: Saturday Review Press, 1972.

———. *Watching the Dance Go By*. Boston: Houghton Mifflin, 1977.

———. *The Shapes of Change: Images of American Dance*. Boston: Houghton Mifflin, 1979.

———. *The Tail of the Dragon: New Dance, 1976–1982*. Durham and London: Duke University Press, 1991.

Tomkins, Calvin. *The Bride and the Bachelors: Five Masters of the Avant-Garde: Duchamp, Tinguely, Cage, Rauschenberg, Cunningham*. New York: Viking Compass Books, 1968; (paperback) New York: Penguin Books, 1976.

———. *Off the Wall: Robert Rauschenberg and the Art World of Our Time*. New York: Doubleday, 1980.

———. *Duchamp*. New York: Henry Holt, 1996.

Vaughan, David. "From Diaghilev to Cunningham: Contemporary Artists Work with Dance." In *Das Ballett und die Künste*. Cologne: Ballett-Bühnen-Verlag, 1981.

———. " 'Then I Thought About Marcel': Merce Cunningham's *Walkaround Time*." In *Art and Dance: Images of the Modern Dialogue, 1890–1980*. Boston: Institute of Contemporary Arts, 1982. Catalogue of an exhibition at the Institute of Contemporary Arts.

———, ed. *Merce Cunningham: Creative Elements. Choreography and Dance* 4, part 2 (1997). Essays by Joan Acocella, Marilyn Vaughan Drown, Nelson Rivera, John Holzaepfel, Gordon Mumma, William Fetterman, Thecla Schiphorst, and Elliot Caplan.

Volta, Ornella. *Satie et la danse. Avec un témoignage de David Vaughan*. Paris: Editions Plume, 1992.

ARTICLES

Banes, Sally, and Noël Carroll. "Cunningham and Duchamp." *Ballet Review* 11, no. 2 (summer 1983): 73–79.

Becker, Nancy F. "Filming Cunningham Dance: A Conversation with Charles Atlas." *Dance Theatre Journal* 1, no. 1 (spring 1983): 22–24.

Brown, Carolyn. "McLuhan and the Dance." Ballet Review 1, no. 4 (1966): 13+.

———. "On Chance." Ballet Review 2, no. 2 (1968): 7.

Charlip, Remy. "Composing by Chance." Dance Magazine (January 1954): 17–19.

[Croce, Arlene]. "An Interview with Merce Cunningham." Ballet Review 1, no. 4 (1966): 3+.

Cunningham, Merce. "Space, Time and Dance." trans/formation 1, no. 3 (1952). Reprinted in Modern Culture and the Arts, edited by James B. Hall and Barry Ulanov. New York: McGraw-Hill, 1967.

———. "The Impermanent Art." Arts 7, no. 3 (1955). Reprinted in Esthetics Contemporary, edited by Richard Kostelanetz. Buffalo NY: Prometheus Books, 1978, rev. ed. 1989.

———. "Summerspace Story." Dance Magazine (June 1966): 52–54.

———. "Diary of a Cunningham Dance." New York Times, 15 March 1981.

———. "A Collaborative Process Between Music and Dance." TriQuarterly 54 (spring 1982). Reprinted in A John Cage Reader, edited by Peter Gena and Jonathan Brent. New York: C. F. Peters, 1982.

———. "Story: Tale of a Dance and a Tour." Dance Ink 6, no. 1 (spring 1995); no. 2 (summer 1995); no. 3 (fall 1995).

Greskovic, Robert. "Merce Cunningham as Sculptor." Ballet Review 11, no. 4 (winter 1984): 88–95.

Grossman, Peter Z. "Talking with Merce Cunningham about Video." Dance Scope 13, no. 2–3 (Winter–Spring, 1979): 56–58.

Jordan, Stephanie. "Freedom from Music: Cunningham, Cage and Collaborators." Contact 20 (autumn 1979).

Kraft, Susan. "Remembering Chris Komar." Contact Quarterly 22, no. 1 (winter/spring 1997): 38–41.

Lorber, Richard. "Experiments in Videodance." Dance Scope 12, no. 1 (fall/winter 1977/78): 7–16.

Macaulay, Alastair. "On the Clouds: The Merce Cunningham Season." Dancing Times (July 1985): 856–858.

———. "The Merce Experience." The New Yorker, 4 April 1988, pp. 92–96.

———. "Anno Domini: The Merce Cunningham Season." Dancing Times (January 1990): 348–351.

———. "Happy Hooligan." The New Yorker, 27 April 1992, pp. 90–93.

Mackrell, Judith. "Cunningham at Sadler's Wells (With a Footnote on the plight of the Uncritical Reviewer)." Dance Theatre Journal 3, no. 3, Autumn 1985, pp. 32–33.

Poster, William S. "Something New, Simple and Fundamental." Ballet Review 1, no. 4 (1966): 6.

Potter, Michelle. " 'A License to Do Anything': Robert Rauschenberg and the Merce Cunningham Dance Company." Dance Chronicle 16, no. 1 (1993): 1–43.

Roth, Moira. "The Aesthetic of Indifference." Artforum (November 1977).

Sayers, Lesley-Anne. "Telling the Dancer from the Dance." Dance Now 1, no. 4 (winter 1992–93): 16–19, 21.

Vaughan, David. "Locale: The Collaboration of Merce Cunningham and Charles Atlas." Millenium Film Journal 10/11 (fall/winter 1981–82): 18–22.

———. "Channels/Inserts: Cunningham and Atlas (Continued)." Millenium Film Journal 12 (fall/winter 1982–83): 126–130.

———. "Cunningham, Cage and Joyce: 'this longawaited messiagh of roaratorios.' " Choreography and Dance 1, part 4 (1992): 79–89.

———, moderator. "The Forming of an Aesthetic: Merce Cunningham and John Cage." Transcript of a discussion with Earle Brown, Remy Charlip, and Marianne Preger-Simon; Dance Critics Association conference, 16 June 1984. Ballet Review 13, no. 3 (fall 1985): 23–40.

———, moderator. "Cunningham and His Dancers." Transcript of a discussion with Carolyn Brown, Douglas Dunn, Viola Farber, Steve Paxton, Marianne Preger-Simon, Valda Setterfield, and Gus Solomons; "Merce Cunningham and the New Dance: The Modernist Dance Impulse," State University of New York Festival, 7 March 1987. Ballet Review 15, no. 3 (fall 1987): 19–40.

MC's hand positions for Valda Setterfield in Second Hand, 1970.

Windows, 1995. Left to right: Jean Freebury, Banu Ogan, Jared Phillips, Lisa Boudreau, Cheryl Therrien, and Glen Rumsey. Photograph: Marc Ginot.

INDEX

Illustrations in **bold**

Pages 308–313: MC in the early stages of creating a dance to be incorporated into a multimedia film, installation, and computer project titled *Hand-drawn Spaces*. Working at the motion capture studio at Biodivision, San Francisco, in April 1997, in collaboration with Paul Kaiser and Shelley Eshkar of Riverbed Media, MC choreographs on screen using "Biped," a computer program designed especially for him by Michael Girard and Susan Amkraut of Unreal Pictures. Reflective spheres are attached to dancers Jeannie Steele and Jared Phillips to track their form and movement with optical sensors. The data is stored in the computer, where MC can refine it, manipulate it, and develop a choreography. Photographs: Shelley Eshkar.

Rondo, 1996. Left to right: Kimberly Bartosik, Jared Phillips, Thomas Caley, Lisa Boudreau, Banu Ogan, Frédéric Gafner, Jeannie Steele, Cheryl Therrien, Michael Cole, Derry Swan, and Glen Rumsey. Photograph: Bruce R. Foley.

7 FOR MERCE ON HIS 77TH

There once was a dancer named Merce
Who loved, simply loved, to rehearse
And dance all the sections
In different directions,
And then do them all in reverse.

He knew a composer named Cage
Who declined to write notes on a page
But told the musicians
To take their positions
And breathe rhythmically on the stage.

Their work was a brilliant advance
Of randomness in modern dance,
Which many folks guessed
Was genius, and the rest
Left quietly when given the chance.

The work of these tireless men
Was based on the study of Zen,
And *Finnegans Wake*
And a week at the lake
Where they fished for striped bass
        now and then.

Into their computer, they'd feed
Random data the program would read
And produce a new work,
Until one day some jerk
Programmed it to print *Les Sylphides.*

Merce had no cherce but say, "Yes,"
And the piece was a shining success,
With Mischa, Mark Morris,
A Norwegian men's chorus,
And me in the title role, Les.

I must say, the part was not hard:
It was minimalist avant-garde.
I came out and bowed
And waved to the crowd,
And went home and worked in my yard.

—Written and spoken by Garrison Keillor
   at the Brooklyn Academy of Music,
   19 May 1997, at a benefit for the
   Merce Cunningham Dance Foundation.

Robert Rauschenberg, *Trophy I*, 1959. Combine painting. 65½ x 40½".

Unless otherwise noted, all photographs and artworks are courtesy of, and copyright by, the artists and/or The Merce Cunningham Dance Foundation Archives: p. 2 copyright © JoAnn Baker; pp. 24–26 copyright © The Estate of Barbara Morgan, New York; p. 28 copyright © The Estate of Barbara Morgan, New York; p. 31 copyright © The Estate of Barbara Morgan, New York; p. 40 copyright © Dance Collection, NYPL for the Performing Arts, Astor, Lenox and Tilden Foundations; p. 41 copyright © Dance Collection, NYPL for the Performing Arts, Astor, Lenox and Tilden Foundations; p. 44 top copyright © The Estate of Fred Fehl, New York; p. 44 center and bottom copyright © 1948 Clemens Kalisher; p. 45 copyright © 1948 Clemens Kalisher; p. 51 copyright © Werner Bischof/Magnum Photos, Inc., New York; pp. 54–55 copyright © John Linquist Collection, Harvard Theatre Collection, Houghton Library; p. 70 Robert Rauschenberg/Licensed by VAGA, New York, NY; p. 71 courtesy Margarete Roeder Gallery, New York; pp. 74–75 copyright © The Estate of Arnold Eagle, New York; p. 75 insets top and bottom copyright © John Linquist Collection, Harvard Theatre Collection, Houghton Library; p. 79 copyright © The Estate of Arnold Eagle, New York; pp. 80–81 copyright © Robert Rauschenberg/Licensed by VAGA, New York, NY; pp. 86–87 courtesy Margarete Roeder Gallery, New York; p. 90 copyright © Philip Dyer/The Estate of Hans Wild; p. 92 left copyright © John Linquist Collection, Harvard Theatre Collection, Houghton Library; p. 96 copyright © Curtis Publishing Company; p. 98 copyright © Robert Rauschenberg/Licensed by VAGA, New York, NY; p. 99 copyright © 1978 The Imogen Cunningham Trust; p. 102 copyright © 1957 Vytas Valaitis/Newsweek, Inc. All rights reserved. Reprinted by permission; p. 116 copyright © Fred McDarrah; p. 126 copyright © Robert Rauschenberg/Licensed by VAGA, New York, NY; p. 128 copyright © Robert Rauschenberg/Licensed by VAGA, New York, NY; p. 138 copyright © Max Waldman Archives Box 5094, Westport., CT 06881; p. 147 top copyright © Herve Gloaguen/Agence Rapho; p. 152 left copyright © Fred W. McDarrah; p. 153 copyright © Herve Gloaguen/Agence Rapho; p. 157 copyright © Herve Gloaguen/Agence Rapho; p. 158 right copyright ©

Herve Gloaguen/Agence Rapho; p. 176 copyright © Jasper Johns/Licensed by VAGA, New York, NY; p. 189 right copyright © Jasper Johns/Licensed by VAGA, New York, NY; p. 192 copyright © The Andy Warhol Foundation for the Visual Arts/ARS, New York; p. 194 courtesy the collection of Adam and Carolyn Barker-Mill, London, copyright © Estate of David Tudor; p. 199 below copyright © Robert Rauschenberg/Licensed by VAGA, New York, NY; pp. 200–201 copyright © 1977 Lois Greenfield; p. 204 photograph of Mark Lancaster's costume swatches by Art Becofsky; p. 209 bottom right copyright © 1979 Lois Greenfield; p. 216 copyright © 1981 Lois Greenfield; p. 218 copyright © 1982 Lois Greenfield; p. 222 copyright © Agence de Presse Bernard; p. 226 copyright © 1984 JoAnn Baker; p. 230 top and bottom copyright © Robert Hill/British Broadcasting Company; p. 236 copyright © 1987 Jonathan Atkin, NYC; p. 249 copyright © Jasper Johns/Licensed by VAGA, New York, NY; p. 258 copyright © 1991 by Henmar Press, Inc., 373 Park Avenue South, New York, 10016; p. 291 copyright © Jasper Johns/Licensed by VAGA, New York, NY; p. 292 copyright © Robert Rauschenberg/Licensed by VAGA, New York, NY; p. 293 copyright © Jasper Johns/Licensed by VAGA, New York, NY; p. 301 copyright © Jasper Johns/Licensed by VAGA, New York, NY; pp. 302–303 copyright © Robert Rauschenberg/Licensed by VAGA, New York, NY; p. 319 courtesy Kunsthaus Zurich, copyright © Robert Rauschenberg/Licensed by VAGA, New York, NY.

Library of Congress Catalog Card Number: 97-70518

Hardcover ISBN: 0-89381-624-8

Paperback ISBN: 0-89381-767-8

Designed by Wendy Byrne

Printed and bound by Mariogros Industrie Grafiche s.p.a., Italy.

Separations by Sele Offset, Torino, s.r.l., Italy

The Staff at Aperture for
Merce Cunningham: Fifty Years is:
Michael E. Hoffman, *Executive Director*
Melissa Harris, *Editor*
Stevan A. Baron, *Production Director*
Ivan Vartanian, *Assistant Editor*
David Frankel, *Copy Editor*
Helen Marra, *Production Manager*
Maura Shea, *Editorial Assistant*
Nell Elizabeth Farrell, *Editorial Work-Scholar*

• • •

Our gratitude to Tommaso Zanzotto who has provided a generous contribution towards underwriting the cost of translating the English language text for the foreign editions of *Merce Cunningham: Fifty Years*.

Aperture Foundation publishes a periodical, books, and portfolios of fine photography to communicate with serious photographers and creative people everywhere. A complete catalog is available upon request. Address:
20 East 23rd Street,
New York, N Y 10010.
Phone: (212) 598-4205.
Fax: (212) 598-4015.

Aperture Foundation books are distributed internationally through:

Canada:
General Publishing,
30 Lesmill Road,
Don Mills, Ontario, M3B 2T6.
Fax: (416) 445-5991.

United Kingdom:
Robert Hale, Ltd.,
Clerkenwell House,
45-47 Clerkenwell Green,
London EC1R OHT.
Fax: 171-490-4958.

Continental Europe:
Nilsson & Lamm, BV,
Pampuslaan 212-214,
P.O. Box 195,
1382 JS Weesp, Netherlands.
Fax: 31-294-415054.

For international magazine subscription orders for the periodical *Aperture*, contact Aperture International Subscription Service, P.O. Box 14, Harold Hill, Romford, RM3 8EQ, England. Fax: 1-708-372-046. One year: £30.00. Price subject to change.

To subscribe to the periodical *Aperture* in the U.S.A. write
Aperture,
P.O. Box 3000, Denville, NJ 07834.
Tel: 1-800-783-4903.
One year: $44.00.

For a video catalog or to order videos from the Cunningham Dance Foundation Video Collection contact Anna Brown, Cunningham Dance Foundation, Media Department,
55 Bethune Street, New York, NY 10014.
Tel: (212) 255-8240 ext. 26.
E-mail anna@merce.org.

First edition
10 9 8 7 6 5 4 3 2 1